A Brief History of Australia

A BRIEF HISTORY OF AUSTRALIA

BARBARA A. WEST

WITH FRANCES T. MURPHY

Facts On File
An imprint of Infobase Publishing

A Brief History of Australia

Facts On File, Inc.
An imprint of Infobase Publishing
132 West 31st Street
New York NY 10001

Library of Congress Cataloging-in-Publication Data
West, Barbara A., 1967–
  A brief history of Australia / Barbara A. West with Frances T. Murphy.
    p. cm.
  Includes bibliographical references and index.
  ISBN 978-0-8160-7885-1 (acid-free paper) 1. Australia—History. I. Murphy, Frances T.
II. Title.
  DU108.W47 2010
  994—dc22   2009031925

Facts On File books are available at special discounts when purchased in bulk quantities for businesses, associations, institutions, or sales promotions. Please call our Special Sales Department in New York at (212) 967-8800 or (800) 322-8755.

You can find Facts On File on the World Wide Web at http://www.factsonfile.com

Text design by Joan M. McEvoy
Maps by Jeremy Eagle
Composition by Hermitage Publishing Services
Cover printed by Art Print, Taylor, Pa.
Book printed and bound by Maple-Vail Book Manufacturing Group, York, Pa.
Date printed: June, 2010
Printed in the United States of America

10 9 8 7 6 5 4 3 2 1

This book is printed on acid-free paper.

CONTENTS

LIST OF ILLUSTRATIONS

LIST OF MAPS

ACKNOWLEDGMENTS

We would like to thank Michael Leigh and the Sidney Myer Asia Centre at the University of Melbourne for their generous support for Barbara West as an honorary fellow, which allowed us to use all the library and database resources of the university. Without these, this book could not have been written. We also thank the National Library of Australia, State Library of Victoria, State Library of South Australia, and National Archives of Australia for their generous permission to reprint photo images from their collections.

Thank you to Claudia Schaab for offering us the opportunity to explore Australian history to this depth and guiding the manuscript through the publication process quickly and painlessly. Thank you also to Bronwyn Collie for her careful and considered editing.

We dedicate this book to our mothers, Kathleen West-Hennahane and Bett Murphy.

INTRODUCTION

Australia is a mass of contradictions. The oldest land on Earth was one of the last to be found by European sailors during the Age of Exploration. Members of the oldest continuously surviving culture on Earth became citizens of the country in which they live only in 1967. The sixth-largest country in the world by landmass in 2006 had only a million more people than the U.S. state of New York and just over half the population of the U.S. state of California; it is the 53d largest in the world by population. Despite its relatively low population, about 22 million in 2009, and very low population density, about 7.5 people per square mile (2.8 people per sq. km), Australia is sometimes said to be overpopulated relative to the amount of water and fertile soil available for human use.

In trying to understand these and a host of other contradictory and unfamiliar aspects of the country, both academic and popular authors writing about Australia often try to pin down the entire place in a single catchphrase. The historian Geoffrey Blainey, before his reputation was sullied by claims of racism in the late 1980s and 1990s, was one of the country's most respected writers on the nature of Australian identity. He located the key to understanding the place and its people in *The Tyranny of Distance* (1966), that is, both Australia's distance from Europe and North America and the great distances one has to travel within the country to move between cities. Other attempts at locating Australia's identity in a catchphrase title include *The Working Man's Paradise* (Lane 1948), *The Lucky Country* (Horne 1971), *A Secret Country* (Pilger 1992), and *In a Sunburned Country* (Bryson 2000). While all of these capture some essence of the place, none of them works entirely. Australia is all of these things, and more.

This brief history of Australia begins with a chapter that places it in context, exploring the land and its people in broad brushstrokes. This is followed by a chapter on precontact Aboriginal culture based on the work of archaeologists and other prehistorians, as well as ethnographers who have spoken at length with contemporary Aboriginal peoples about their histories. The remainder of the book takes a largely chronological look at Australian history since the first documented sighting of the landmass by a European in the 17th century. From William Janszoon through Quentin Bryce, colonialism through gay rights, Australia's political, economic, and social trends are explored in greater or lesser detail, depending on available resources and the interests of nonspecialist readers. In conjunction with the suggested reading list, three appendixes, a chronology, and extensive bibliography, *A Brief History of Australia* provides a comprehensive introduction to the country and its people.

1

DIVERSITY—
LAND AND PEOPLE

To have any basic understanding of Australia's history, events in time and place must be put into their proper context. This chapter provides a brief overview of the land upon which generations of Australians have made their mark and some of the most important demographic features of today's population.

Land

Australia is the world's sixth-largest country by territory, more than 2.9 million square miles (7.6 million sq. km) in size. In addition to the mainland and island-state of Tasmania, about 155 miles (250 km) apart at their closest points, Australia controls 8,222 other islands, from the well-known tourist destinations of Kangaroo Island and Fraser Island to the uninhabited Nepean Island, just off the coast of the more famous Norfolk Island, site of one of Australia's most brutal penal colonies. Similar in size to the continental United States, Australia measures about 2,300 miles (3,700 km) from Cape York in far north tropical Queensland to South East Cape in Tasmania, and 2,485 miles (4,000 km) from Byron Bay, New South Wales, to Steep Point, Western Australia. The total length of Australia's coastline is 37,118 miles (59,736 km), about 60 percent of which is the mainland and 40 percent islands. Since 1936, Australia has also held a large amount of the Antarctic territory but without the possibility of sovereignty with the implementation of the Antarctic Treaty of 1959.

Politically, Australia is divided into six states, New South Wales, Queensland, South Australia, Tasmania, Victoria, and Western Australia, and two territories similar to Washington, D.C., in the United States: the Australian Capital Territory (ACT) and the Northern Territory, both

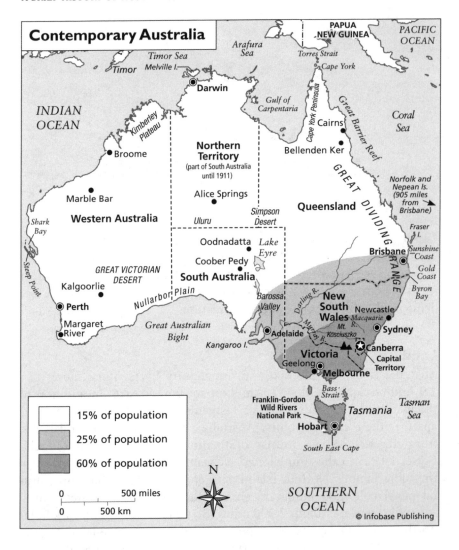

Contemporary Australia

PAPUA NEW GUINEA

PACIFIC OCEAN

Arafura Sea

Torres Strait

Timor Sea

Cape York

Timor

Melville I.

Darwin

INDIAN OCEAN

Gulf of Carpentaria

Cape York Peninsula

Cairns

Great Barrier Reef

Coral Sea

Kimberley Plateau

Broome

Northern Territory
(part of South Australia until 1911)

Bellenden Ker

GREAT

Marble Bar

Western Australia

Alice Springs

Uluru

Simpson Desert

Queensland

Norfolk and Nepean Is. (905 miles from Brisbane)

Shark Bay

Oodnadatta

Lake Eyre

Coober Pedy

South Australia

DIVIDING RANGE

Fraser I.

Brisbane Sunshine Coast

Gold Coast

Byron Bay

Steep Point

GREAT VICTORIAN DESERT

Kalgoorlie

Nullarbor Plain

Barossa Valley

Darling R.

New South Wales Newcastle

Macquarie

Perth

Great Australian Bight

Kangaroo I.

Adelaide

Murray R.

Mt. Kosciuszko

Sydney

Margaret River

Victoria

Canberra

Capital Territory

Geelong

Melbourne

Bass Strait

Tasman Sea

Franklin-Gordon Wild Rivers National Park

Tasmania

Hobart

South East Cape

15% of population

25% of population

60% of population

0   500 miles
0   500 km

N

SOUTHERN OCEAN

© Infobase Publishing

administered by the Commonwealth government from Canberra in the ACT. The island-continent is also divided into three time zones: eastern, central, and western.

Within these various natural and political boundaries, Australia encompasses a wide variety of landscapes and forms; even within states and territories, deserts and rain forests exist within fairly close proximity of each other. The average rainfall for the country as a whole differs from year to year but ranges from just 6.5 inches (165 mm) to slightly more than 11.8 inches (300 mm) per year. Across all years, the driest region in the country is Lake Eyre in South Australia with just five inches (125 mm) per year, while the wettest is at Bellenden Ker, Queensland, with more than 157 inches (4,000 mm) of rain per year (Geoscience Australia 2008a).

This vast variation, however, masks the fact that the continent is dominated far more by its lack of water than by the few areas with an abundance of this resource; Australia is the second driest continent on Earth after Antarctica. About 35 percent of the Australian continent can be classified as desert because of lack of rainfall, while a further 35 percent receives less than 20 inches (500 mm) of rain per year and is thus classified as arid or semiarid. The largest desert is the Great Victoria Desert in South Australia and Western Australia, at 134,653 square miles (348,750 sq. km), or about 4.5 percent of the Australian mainland (Geoscience Australia 2008b). An interesting feature of Australian deserts is that they do not resemble the Sahara or high deserts of California and Nevada. Because of the great antiquity of Australian deserts, plants have had time to adapt to the arid conditions and thus in most places where rabbits, camels, or cattle have not overgrazed the land, they are covered with grasses, shrubs, and even trees.

While the desert regions in Australia have been expanding for hundreds if not thousands of years, especially in the western plateau and

The age of the Australian desert means that a plethora of plants have adapted to the dry conditions; newer deserts, such as the Sahara, have far less plant life. (Robyn Mackenzie/ Shutterstock)

central lowlands, the area covered by rain forest has been shrinking precipitously. According to the Australian Rainforest Foundation, since the start of the 18th century the continent has lost at least three quarters of its tropical rain forest and nearly as much of its subtropical forest to the logging industry. As a result, today rain forest makes up just 0.5 percent of Australia's mainland. Many of the remaining 16,216 square miles (4.2 million ha) are located in state and national park reserves and thus are protected; however, in some areas, logging continues to threaten their existence.

Australia is also currently experiencing severe degradation of some of its most important river systems. The country's largest system, the Murray-Darling, which covers about 386,102 square miles (1 million sq. km) in South Australia, Victoria, New South Wales, the ACT, and Queensland, is experiencing such stress that areas near its mouth in South Australia are under immediate threat of permanent degradation due to high acidity and salinity. The Macquarie River system in New South Wales is under similar stress, as are many others in southern and central Australia, resulting in vociferous debate between environmentalists and irrigators over the amount of water that can be taken from these rivers each year.

In the early 1980s another of Australia's river systems, the Franklin-Gordon in the island state of Tasmania, was the site of the fiercest environmental battle the country has yet seen. From 1979, when the Hydro-Electric Commission (HEC) named the Franklin-Gordon as an appropriate place for a dam project, through the summer of 1982–83, when the Franklin River blockade saw more than 1,200 people arrested for civil disobedience in the region, the entire country focused on the battle between the state government and HEC on one side and the federal government and environmentalists on the other. Eventually, in July 1983 a narrow, one-vote victory in Australia's highest court put a permanent stop to the dam project. The region was then able to move forward as the Western Tasmanian Wilderness National Parks World Heritage Area, having been accepted as a heritage site by the United Nations Educational, Scientific, and Cultural Organization (UNESCO) in December 1982, saving one of the country's last wild river systems (Wild Rivers 2008).

As is the case with its wet and dry areas, Australia is also a land of contrasts in elevation, though it contains no mountains equivalent in size to the Rockies, Alps, or Andes. The Great Dividing Range, which runs from Australia's top end in the Cape York Peninsula all the way south to the Grampians in Victoria, with an eastern spur that reemerges from Bass Strait to form the highlands of Tasmania, never rises to even half the height of Mont Blanc, Europe's highest peak. Nonetheless, from its highest point at 7,310 feet (2,228 m) at Mount Kosciuszko in New South Wales to the lowest, at Lake Eyre in South Australia, at 49 feet (15 m) below sea level, Australia encompasses significant plateaus, highlands, and lowlands. If Australia's offshore islands are counted in this statistic, there is even greater variation as Mawson's Peak, located on Heard Island near Antarctica, is taller than Kosciuszko, at 9,006 feet (2,745 m) (Australian Bureau of Statistics 2008, "Geography"). At the low end, Lake Eyre is a massive salt sink with 3,741 square miles (9,690 sq. km) of surface area and draining about one sixth of the mainland in a catchment area of 440,156 square miles (1,140,000 sq. km). Despite receiving water from such rivers as the Diamantina, Warburton, Macumba, and Cooper's Creek, Lake Eyre is often totally dry and has filled to capacity only three times in more than 150 years, the last in 1984 (Geoscience Australia 2009, "Largest Waterbodies").

In conjunction with these extremes in elevation, Australia exhibits great variation in average temperatures. The extremes range from 123.6°F (50.7°C) at Oodnadatta, South Australia, in 1960 to -9.4°F (-23°C) at Charlotte Pass, in Kosciuszko National Park, New South Wales, in 1994. The hottest place in the country is Marble Bar, Western Australia, with an annual mean temperature of over 99.5°F (37.5°C), while Collinsvale, Tasmania, a suburb of Hobart, is the coldest place with annual mean temperature of just 45.5°F (7.5°C) (Geoscience Australia 2010, "Climatic Extremes").

While most of these figures set Australia apart from other countries in the world, perhaps the most dramatic of all concerns the relative age of the land upon which its people have made their home. In contrast with much of North America's landscape, which dates from the last ice age about 20,000 years ago, most of Australia's geographic features were formed millions of years ago and have not been significantly altered by glaciation for about 290 million years (Australian Bureau of Statistics 2008, "Geography of Australia"). Virtually the only relatively new feature of Australia is its coastline, which came into being about 12,000 years ago, when rising sea levels at the end of the last ice age separated Tasmania, the Torres Strait Islands, New Guinea, and thousands of other, smaller islands from the mainland. At the other end of the spectrum, some sands in Western Australia have been found to be 4.25 billion years old (Geoscience Australia 2007), almost a billion years older than the first bacterial life that emerged in the world's oceans. Since that time long ago, the Australian landmass has moved around the Earth

THE PLATYPUS

The European scientific community in the 19th and early 20th centuries was very interested in Australia because of its vast array of unique plants and animals. A prime example is the platypus, one of only two monotremes in the world today; the other, the echidna, lives only in Australia and neighboring New Guinea.

The first mention of the platypus in English documents occurred in 1799, when the governor of New South Wales, John Hunter, sent a preserved skin back to England. Hunter was fascinated by the combination of body parts, which seem to have been assembled from other animals. Indeed, much of the scientific community in Britain at the time was suspicious that the sample was a hoax, a combination of mammalian, reptilian, and avian features stitched together after death.

But the platypus was no hoax. Rather, it is an animal that, like mammals, is covered in fur. At first it was thought that it lacked nipples or mammary glands, until its primitive mammary glands were discovered in 1824. Additionally, platypuses have a bill and webbed feet like a duck's; the males of the species also have a poisonous spur on their back feet. The most anomalous feature of the platypus is that the female lacks any kind of uterus and instead has oviducts that release eggs directly into the cloaca, a segment of the excretory tract; males urinate through their cloaca but have a penis that excretes semen.

While the mystery of platypus reproduction was solved in the late 19th century, it was another 100 years before all of the creature's capabilities became known. In 1985 a German physiologist, Henning

and has been attached to all the other landmasses in two supercontinents, Rodinia and Pangaea, and to South America, Africa, Antarctica, and India in Gondwana.

Despite the millions of years during which Australia was connected to other landmasses, in the past 50 million years or so the continent has been adrift in the ocean, completely separated from any other land formation. As a result of this long separation, more than 80 percent of Australia's mammals, reptiles, frogs, and flowering plants are unique to the continent, along with half of its bird life and most of its freshwater fish (About Australia: Flora and Fauna 2008). Among the most famous of this animal life are the world's only two monotremes, or egg-laying

Platypuses are very difficult to photograph, as they are nocturnal and very shy. (Susan Flashman/Shutterstock)

Scheich, discovered that platypuses use electrolocation both for finding the large amount of food they need each day (equivalent to about half their body weight) and for avoiding obstacles in the murky waters they inhabit. Then in May 2008 the mapping of the platypus genome revealed the animal's final mystery: Just as its outward appearance seems, the platypus is a mixture of mammalian, reptilian, and avian features and branched off from other mammals about 166 million years ago.

mammals, the platypus and echidna; a variety of marsupials or pouched mammals, including kangaroos, koalas, and wombats; deadly funnel-web spiders; and frilled neck lizards. Another Australian animal icon, the dingo, is actually a fairly recent import from Asia, having arrived from there between 6,000 and 15,000 years ago (Australian Fauna 2007).

In addition to its unique animal life, Australia is the source of a vast amount of mineral wealth, including 50 percent of the world's titanium, 40 percent of its bauxite, 33 percent of its diamonds, 22 percent of its uranium, 20 percent of its zinc-lead, 12.5 percent of its iron ore, and 95 percent of its opal. Australia is also among the world's leading sources of copper, nickel, silver, and gold (Geoscience Australia

2009a, "Minerals Factsheets"). As a result of this wealth, while the U.S. economy struggled with debt and recession in the early years of the 21st century, Australia was on an economic boom, with sales of primary resources to India and China leading the way until about the middle of 2009. In fact, in early 2010 Australia was the only G-20 country that had not experienced recession as a result of the global economic downturn.

People

The population of Australia at 6:33 P.M. on January 22, 2010, was estimated by the Australian Bureau of Statistics to be 22,124,694 (Australian Bureau of Statistics 2009, "Population Clock"). This number is based on a formula that one birth occurs in Australia every one minute, 55 seconds; one death occurs every three minutes, 57 seconds; and the net gain from migration is one person every two minutes, 38 seconds. The total population increase is one person every one minute, 33 seconds (Australian Bureau of Statistics 2009, "Population Clock"). For a landmass approximately the size of the continental United States, a population of just over 22 million people would seem to be low, and the population density is one of the lowest in the world, at about 7.5 people per square mile (2.6 people per sq. km). But according to some of the world's leading scientists, Australia is already overcrowded, and substantially so! Jared Diamond cites an estimate that Australian soil and water resources are enough to support a population of only about eight million (2005, 398).

Although throughout the 20th century the most significant cause of this population growth was natural increase, making up "67% of the population growth between 1901 and 1994" (Australian Bureau of Statistics 2006), immigration has in many years been a far more important factor. For example, in 2006–07 the net increase from migration was 155,600 people, representing 56 percent of the overall population increase in that year (Australian Bureau of Statistics 2007, "Migration"). This feature of Australian society is nothing new. In such boom years as those that followed the gold rush of 1851 and the postwar "populate or perish" years starting in 1945, migration provided many thousands more Australians than did natural increase. During World War I, World War II, and the depression in the 1930s, however, immigration nearly ceased.

The United Kingdom has been the most consistent source of Australian migrants over the past 200 years. Even during the peak of postwar migration, when displaced persons from Europe flocked to Australia by the tens of thousands, the United Kingdom provided the largest number of migrants. As late as 2006, 23 percent of the country's overseas-born population hailed from there (Australian Bureau of Statistics 2007, "Migration").

Because of this overwhelming majority in the early days, the popular image of Australia is of a largely homogeneous Anglo population prior to the start of European migration in the late 1940s; however, this image is not entirely accurate. The country's Aboriginal people have always constituted a small percentage of the population. In addition, even in the days of the First Fleet in 1788, immigration to Australia was never entirely English or even British. The First Fleet carried people of English and Scottish nationality but also Germans, Norwegians, and both black and white Americans to Australia's shores. Irish convicts arrived in 1791, and that country has continued to be an important source of immigrants, so much so that the dominant population in Australia is usually referred to as Anglo-Celtic rather than simply Anglo or English. Significant numbers of Chinese, Japanese, and Malays from Indonesia resided in the Northern Territory long before there was any large-scale European immigration to that region; in 1888 the Chinese population of the Northern Territory was seven times larger than the white one (Thompson 1994, 37). The gold rushes of the 1850s also drew people from all over the world to Australia's shores, as did the scores of inland expeditions in the decades that followed. Although small in number, Australia was also home to a population of Muslims from Afghanistan, Pakistan, and India starting in the 1860s; the country's first mosque was built in Renmark, South Australia, in 1861 and the second in that state's capital, Adelaide, in 1889 (Islamic College).

Since the influx of European migrants after 1945 and the dismantling of the white Australia policy in the final quarter of the 20th century, Australia has become increasingly diverse. In 2006 the next largest migrant populations after the British and New Zealanders were Italians, Chinese, Vietnamese, Filipinos, Greeks, South Africans, Germans, and Malaysians (Australian Bureau of Statistics 2008, "Country of Birth"). Although smaller in number than the Italian or Chinese populations, Australia's Greeks are so numerous that Melbourne is the world's third-largest Greek city after Athens and Thessaloniki (City of Melbourne 2004). Furthermore, in the past decade increasing numbers of Africans from Sudan, Somalia, and Ethiopia have made their homes in some of Australia's largest cities and some selected provincial towns such as Warrnambool and Shepparton in the state of Victoria.

Australia's large migrant population, where 24 percent of the current population was born overseas and another 26 percent had at least one parent born overseas, means that at least 200 languages and dialects are spoken in the country's 8.1 million households. While English is the national language, 16 percent of the population speaks another language at home, with Italian, Greek, Arabic, Cantonese, Mandarin, and Vietnamese the most common (Australian Bureau of Statistics 2008, "Country of Birth").

This great diversity of people lends great religious diversity to the country as well, with 6 percent of the population adhering to a wide variety of non-Christian faiths, including Islam, Buddhism, and Judaism, and another 31 percent professing no faith at all. Of the Christian faiths, the largest percentage are Roman Catholic, at 26 percent; followed by Anglican, 19 percent; and others such as Greek and Russian Orthodox, Uniting, and Baptist, 19 percent (Australian Bureau of Statistics 2006, "Religious Affiliation").

Since the landing of the First Fleet in 1788, Australia has been a predominantly urban society. As the food historian Michael Symons notes, "this is the only continent which has not supported an agrarian society" (1982, 10); Aboriginal hunting and gathering quickly gave way to processed and preserved imports. Rather than small, family-run farms on which a majority of people lived and worked, from the beginning white Australia supported a small number of large, industrial-scale sheep and cattle stations while the majority of people lived in and around the continent's coastal cities and towns. Today about 88 percent of the Australian population lives in urban areas, with 64 percent living in the capital cities alone, which is double the rate of the United States (Clancy 2009). For the historian Geoffrey Blainey, this strong centralization is the result of Australia's "tyranny of distance": The vast distances and high cost of transport within the country have made decentralized settlements unviable from the earliest days of white settlement (1966). In addition, the arid nature of most of the continent and the extreme heat and humidity in the far north have made large-scale settlement in these regions next to impossible. As a result, 85 percent of the continent's population lives in what Blainey calls the Boomerang Coast, a stretch of land from Adelaide in the south through Brisbane in the north and including Melbourne, Sydney, Hobart, and Canberra (Nicholson 1998, 52–53). Altogether, this territory makes up less than a quarter of the country's landmass.

In addition to their centralized settlement pattern, Australians enjoy one of the highest qualities of life on Earth; in 2009 Australia ranked second on the United Nations's Human Development Index (HDI) behind Norway (United Nations Development Program [UNDP]). Rather than looking strictly at gross domestic product (GDP) or other economic factors, the HDI combines income purchasing power (purchasing power parity, or PPP), life expectancy, and educational attainment (United Nations Development Program 2008, 7). Australia ranks just 22nd in the world on the income measurement, at U.S.$34,923 per person, but first in educational attainment and fifth in life expectancy, at 81.4 years (UNDP). In comparison, the United States is 13th on the HDI overall: ninth in purchasing power, 21st in educational attainment, and 26th in life expectancy at 79.1 years (UNDP 2). Additionally, the *Economist* magazine ranks Melbourne, Australia's second-largest city, as the world's second most livable city after Vancouver, Canada, while Perth, Adelaide, and Sydney, the capitals of Western Australia, South Australia, and New South Wales, respectively, also make the top 10 at fourth, seventh, and ninth (Economist Intelligence Unit 2008).

Despite the relative livability of Australia, the country's population does not share equally in the benefits of good health and well-being, high educational attainment, or income distribution, setting it apart from the other countries with very high HDI rankings. For example, in terms of income inequality, Australia resembles the United States, at 13th on the HDI, far more than it does Norway. In Australia the lowest 10 percent of income earners make just 45 percent of the national median, while the highest 10 percent make 195 percent of the median; the comparable figures for the United States are 38 percent and 214 percent, and for Norway 55 percent and 157 percent (Smeeding 2002, 6). In other words, Norway's richest and poorest people are more like each other in terms of purchasing power than those in Australia or the United States.

While poverty, lack of education, and poor health care can be found in small pockets throughout the Australian population, on average the least-well-off group are the approximately 2 percent who identify as Aboriginal or Torres Strait Islander, who together make up the country's Indigenous people. As a result of harsh and discriminatory laws that have impeded self-determination for more than 200 years, this population in 2001 had a life expectancy that on average was 18 years less than that of other Australians, a household income rate only 62 percent that of non-Indigenous Australians, an unemployment rate more than three times the national average, and much lower educational attainments (Australian Human Rights Commission 2006). Another repercussion of generations of repression and this vast inequality is that

Indigenous people, while constituting a tiny proportion of the general population in Australia, made up 22 percent of the prison population in 2005; some 6 percent of the Indigenous male population between 25 and 29 were imprisoned, compared to only 0.6 percent of men that age overall (Australian Human Rights Commission 2006). While some efforts have been made at both the federal and the state/territory levels to deal with this inequality, far more needs to be done to right the wrongs of the past 220 years.

Like its land and people, Australia's history is one of diversity and great contrasts. On the one hand, Australia is home to the oldest surviving culture on Earth, where for between 45,000 and 60,000 years countless thousands of generations lived and died but left relatively few markers behind through which we can understand their long history. On the other hand, Australia's non-Indigenous population can be dated back only as far as 1788, 168 years after the landing of the *Mayflower* pilgrims in the United States and 224 years after French Huguenots landed in Florida. In the approximately 220 years between 1788 and the present, non-Indigenous Australians have transformed their culture and territory so thoroughly that very little of the original remains. It is with this process of transformation that this book is primarily concerned.

2

ABORIGINAL HISTORY
(60,000 BP–1605 C.E.)

Aboriginal history from 60,000 years ago until Australia was first sighted by Europeans in 1606 is as complex and varied as the history of any other group of people on Earth. Saying that today's population of Aboriginal Australians are members of the oldest surviving culture in the world by many tens of thousands of years is not synonymous with saying that their culture has not changed during this very long period of time, or even that it had not changed prior to the arrival of Europeans in the early 17th century. Tremendous ecological changes, from the rise of global sea levels that separated Tasmania, New Guinea, and Australia's mainland, to the loss of the continent's megafauna, certainly contributed to great changes in people's social and material lives. Other changes in social structures, social systems, languages, and technological know-how are also sure to have taken place over the course of this span of 60,000 years. Migration, warfare, floods, drought, animal and plant extinctions, overseas trade, and a vast array of other factors were also at play in the lives of the millions of individuals who lived and died on the continent before the arrival of the Dutch.

Despite this certain diversity and change, the historical record for these populations remains fairly sparse for a number of reasons. First, at no point in their precolonial history did Australia's Aboriginal populations develop writing, and so they left no record of events. Second, ecological change has placed the earliest archaeological sites on the continent under water. Third, our science is not yet able to verify with 100 percent reliability the dates of organic materials from as far back as the earliest migrations. Finally, vastly different views of the nature of existence between Aboriginal and other peoples mean that Aboriginal oral histories have often been misunderstood when told to outsiders.

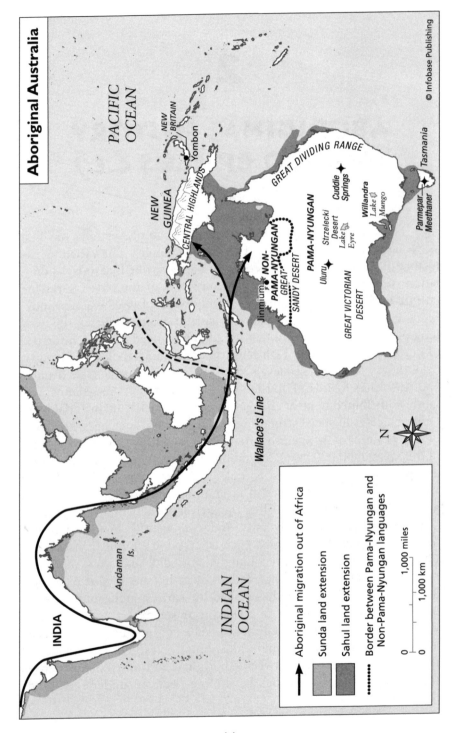

Aboriginal Australia

© Infobase Publishing

PACIFIC OCEAN

INDIAN OCEAN

INDIA

Andaman Is.

Wallace's Line

NEW GUINEA

NEW BRITAIN

Yombon

CENTRAL HIGHLANDS

GREAT DIVIDING RANGE

GREAT SANDY DESERT

Jinmium

NON-PAMA-NYUNGAN

PAMA-NYUNGAN

Uluru

GREAT VICTORIAN DESERT

Strzelecki Desert

Lake Eyre

Cuddie Springs

Willandra

Lake Mungo

Parmepar Meethaner

Tasmania

N

Aboriginal migration out of Africa

Sunda land extension

Sahul land extension

Border between Pama-Nyungan and Non-Pama-Nyungan languages

0   1,000 miles
0   1,000 km

As a result of this confluence of factors, most Aboriginal history has to be patched together from a very incomplete archaeological record, linguistic evidence from our contemporary knowledge of Aboriginal languages, genetic comparisons between contemporary peoples who may have descended from common ancestors, oral histories and other stories gathered at the time of the first interactions between Aboriginal and non-Aboriginal peoples, and ethnographic information gathered over the past 400 years of interaction. Of course, a certain degree of conjecture based on these various sources of information is also inherent in this kind of salvage history writing but will be kept here to only the most viable hypotheses based on the hard evidence currently available.

Ancient Prehistory: 60,000–22,000 BP

Since the arrival of the first Aboriginal people about 60,000 years ago, the Australian continent has undergone tremendous change. When they arrived, present-day Australia, Tasmania, the Torres Strait Islands, and the island of New Guinea were all connected. These lands formed the continent of Sahul, a landmass approximately the size of contemporary Europe west of the Ural Mountains. The continent contained a large number of unique plant and animal species due to its long period of isolation (about 38 million years) from other landmasses, including an estimated 13 species of so-called megafauna. These were very large versions of contemporary kangaroos, wombats, and other marsupials; many other species of megafauna had died out prior to the continent's inhabitation by humans. The climate was generally cooler and drier than the region is today, with periglacial and even glacial regions in the Highlands of New Guinea and the Dividing Ranges of southeastern Australia. Nonetheless, Sahul 60,000 years ago encompassed the same wide variety of ecological niches as today's separate landmasses. Tropical forests covered the northern lowlands, while temperate forests existed in the south and highlands of the north. The center of the continent contained both deserts and savannahs, as it does today. Some pollen studies appear to show that even the continent's dry center contained some forest land, but this hypothesis has not been accepted by all archaeologists or other scientists working in this area.

Even though there is no absolute certainty about the direction from which the ancient migrating population arrived on Sahul, the most viable hypothesis is that after spending thousands of years leaving Africa, passing through the Middle East and India, and heading south through mainland Southeast Asia, which was then much larger than today, a small group of migrants sailed across about 35 miles of open sea to land somewhere in Sahul's far north, or contemporary New Guinea. Other hypotheses, such as migration direct from India or even the in situ evolution of humanity in Sahul, have been disproven in recent decades with the development of mitochondrial deoxyribonucleic acid (mtDNA) analysis.

Like the migration route, the period of initial migration is also a highly contested feature of Aboriginal Australian history that involves archaeologists, physical anthropologists, geneticists, linguists, botanists, and a host of other scientists. Most Aboriginal people themselves find this debate irrelevant or even insulting, for it discounts their own origin myths, which are timeless. Nonetheless, until the 1960s, most scientists believed the original period of migration was as recent as about 10,000–12,000 years ago, or about the same time as the colonization of the Americas from northern Asia. With the development of advanced carbon 14 dating techniques, this date was pushed out toward 40,000 years before the present (BP) by the middle of the 1980s. And with the development of thermoluminescence dating in the 1990s, 60,000 years BP has become a common estimate. Genetic testing of mitochondrial DNA, which looks at female lineages of certain genes and determines age through the evaluation of gene mutations, has also provided dates of around 60,000 years BP for the initial peopling of the continent.

Nonetheless, contradictory evidence from other disciplines has compelled scientists to continue exploring this intriguing subject. For example, pollen studies that show an increase in the existence of fire on the continent, which may indicate human use of fire to clear territory and make hunting easier, have indicated that it is remotely possible that humans were using fire in Australia as far back as 185,000 years ago. The use of TL on materials found in Jinmium, Western Australia, has likewise produced a date as far back as 176,000 years, though this has since been forcefully rebutted by others. On the other side of the debate, archaeologists have found very few sites in Sahul that can be verified as having existed more than 40,000 years ago. In their review of all the evidence that had been retested using thermoluminescence and other techniques, O'Connell and Allen (2004) conclude that even with these new technologies, 45,000 BP is the earliest date for which we can be certain of human inhabitation of Sahul. Nevertheless, because their conclusions do not take genetic evidence into account, many consider this a conservative date.

C14 AND
LUMINESCENCE DATING

Radiocarbon dating refers to the process of measuring the amount of the radioisotope carbon 14, or C14 (carbon atoms with eight neutrons rather than the usual six) in an organism after it dies. All living things sustain an amount of C14 in balance with the amount present in the atmosphere. This amount remains constant in the organism until the moment of death, at which time the C14 begins to decay at a half-life rate of 5,730 years. C14 has approximately 10 half-lives, or 57,000 years, the furthest back radiocarbon dating can go. The dating process compares the amount of C14 in the atmosphere to that remaining in the organism, thus providing its time of death. Organisms suitable for such dating are animal or human bone, charcoal, peat, marine shell, and antlers or parts thereof.

In the 1960s scientists working on the problem of dating non-carbon-bearing samples developed several methods of luminescence dating, the most common of these being thermoluminescence, or TL. This method can date inorganic material containing crystalline minerals that when either heated, as with pottery, or exposed to sunlight, as with sediments, accumulate radiation. Subsequent reheating of the material at temperatures of 842°F (450°C) or greater releases this energy in the form of light, the thermoluminescence. This creates a blank slate or "time-zero" for the material to accumulate new energy over time. The amount of light released in the heating process is correlated with the amount of radiation stored within the material. Measurement of this light provides the date of last firing or exposure to sunlight. While thermoluminescence has an age range that is often far greater than that of C14 dating, it is used in conjunction with a variety of other methods of dating and biological processes for greater accuracy.

Another problem with our understanding of the initial peopling of Sahul is whether one migrant population settled and spread slowly to all corners of the continent, from the Highlands of New Guinea to the southern tip of Tasmania, or whether there was a continual flow of migrants over many thousands of years. Discrepancies in the archaeological record, such as the fact that the oldest archaeological sites have been found in Australia's southeastern states of New South Wales and Tasmania rather than northern regions, and the odd division of Australian languages into two groupings, Pama-Nyungan and non-Pama-Nyungan, have convinced many scholars over the years that Australia was populated by several waves of people from India as well as Southeast Asia. In addition, simulation studies, which use computer modeling in the creation of hypotheses, have posited that there have to have been multiple migratory groups to Sahul to prevent incest and sex imbalances.

What these simulation studies do not tell us, however, is whether or not these multiple migrations took place over several years, decades, centuries, or even millennia. As a result of recent studies, physical anthropologists and geneticists working in the area of mtDNA believe they have answered this long-standing question in favor of the shortest possible time lag between migrations. Their data show with relative certainty that Australia, New Guinea, and all of Melanesia were populated by a single group of migrants who left Africa 70,000 years ago at the earliest and populated their current home about 58,000 years ago, plus or minus 8,000 years (Hudjashova et al. 2007). This same evidence also points to a long period of relative isolation after this initial migration, whereby even prior to the submergence of the land bridge linking Australia and New Guinea, the populations of these two regions remained largely separate. The only exception to this trend evidenced by the genetic material tested so far is an influx of New Guineans into northern Australia about 30,000 years ago.

The history of this population remains fairly vague after they began settling Sahul. We do not know whether communities fought wars against each other or were so spread out on the vast continent as to be able to live peaceably. We do not know how soon their proto-Australian language or languages began dividing into the vast number of Australian and Papuan languages evident by the time of European contact in the 17th century. We do not know whether the Dreaming stories and their accompanying rituals, which make up the backbone of Aboriginal religion even today, were imported with them, were developed during the period of migration, or were begun after settlement on the continent. The list of unanswered and probably unanswerable questions about this most ancient of populations is very long.

Nevertheless, on the basis of the somewhat sparse archaeological record of about 100 sites identified to be older than 22,000 years, the period of the last glacial maximal (LGM) and a period of dramatic change on the continent, we do have a very good idea about a few aspects of life on prehistoric Sahul. Archaeologists working at sites as far removed as Lake Mungo's Willandra area in western New South Wales, Parmepar Meethaner in Tasmania, and Yombon on New Britain, New Guinea,

Midden of mollusk shells and crustaceans near Weipa, on the northwest coast of the Cape York Peninsula, Queensland (National Archives of Australia: A1200, L26732)

have found remains dating from before 22,000 BP. While some aspects of these ancient populations' tool kits and subsistence regimes were similar, others differed. For example, people in all three regions lived on a food collectors' diet consisting largely of fish, shellfish, and small mammals. Of course local fruits, roots, greens, mushrooms, and other gathered foods would also have made up a substantial portion of their diet, as attested by the evidence provided by contemporary food collectors. But none of these foods left behind remains that could survive in middens, prehistoric garbage dumps the way that shells and bones could, and so their exact importance can only be surmised today. Other material finds include grinding stones for processing seeds and grains; tools made from flaked chert (a sedimentary rock), which often had been carried relatively long distances; and even a few tools prepared from animal bones, mostly those of kangaroos and large wallabies. In the north heavy stone axes have been found in the most ancient middens, while in the south this kind of tool emerged only in the past few thousand years (Hiscock 2008, 110).

In addition to information about the content of the earliest Aboriginal people's diet and tool kits, middens are important sources of information about ancient social structures. The small size of the pre-LGM middens found in Australia, Tasmania, and New Guinea indicates that the people who created them must have migrated often, from daily to seasonally, depending on locale and season. This kind of migration pattern is generally indicative of very low populations and population densities; relative equality between all adults, where the only distinctions are age and sex; no craft specialization or division of labor aside from those based on age and sex; no formal political or leadership roles; no concept of private property; a highly varied diet; and minimal risk of starvation.

Cultural anthropologists refer to societies organized in this manner as *bands,* social units made up of groups of related people who live together, move together, and, when necessitated by food shortages or conflict, split up and create two new bands or move in with other kinsfolk to expand preexisting bands. This inherent mobility, which facilitates access to foods as they ripen or become available and ability to harvest them in a sustainable manner, also limits people in band societies to minimal portable possessions, usually just carrying bags, weapons, and possibly some light tools or ritual objects. Everything else, from heavy stone tools to clothing, is made from local resources in each new residence. Housing would have been in either caves or lean-tos made anew in each location.

Some of the features associated with band societies, such as having a highly varied diet and minimal risk of starvation, may seem contradictory to the modern image of premodern life as "solitary, poor, nasty, brutish, and short," as Thomas Hobbes put it in 1651. And we cannot be certain that life in pre-LGM Sahul was similar to the life of food collectors who lived in bands in the 20th century, where on average only about four hours per day were required to make, gather, and hunt all the necessities of life. Nonetheless, there is no evidence that this ancient Sahul population differed significantly from these more contemporary band societies. The Australian environment probably provided significant protein and vegetable matter in the form of seafoods, fish, mammals, grubs, roots, and fruit. The very low populations and population densities probably allowed each group to move as needed to seek out sources of food and water. Unlike most agricultural societies, which are at great risk of famine because most calories are consumed from just one grain, such as corn, rice, or wheat, or from a single starch such as sago, potatoes, or cassava, food collectors have access to a wide array of foods. There is very little risk inherent in food collecting because when there is a shortage of one food, a variety of others is usually available, and there is always the possibility for migration to new, more resource-rich areas.

In general, then, we can conclude that life in pre-LGM Sahul was of a very small scale. Small groups of related individuals moved with relative frequency to find food, shelter, and water. While all adults likely had a say in a move, the words of elders and men were probably taken more seriously than those of younger people or women. This is merely conjecture, but evidence of other food collecting band societies, including Aboriginal Australians at the time of European contact, suggests that men's freedom from pregnancy and breast-feeding probably gave them greater mobility, knowledge of further distances, and thus a greater say in a band's movements. Aside from these differences based on age and gender, these societies would have exhibited no class or caste distinctions and all members of the band would have had access to food and other things as needed.

Prehistory: 22,000 BP–1605 C.E.

Sahul's climate changed dramatically during the period of the last glacial maximal, between 22,000 BP and 17,000 BP. Average temperatures were quite a bit lower than previously, and dry winds made those temperatures feel even colder. Evaporation rates were higher than either today or in the previous period, and rainfall is estimated to have been about half of what it is today (Hiscock 2008, 58). This period was exceptionally difficult for humans in Sahul due to loss of food sources through extinctions, lack of water, and the cold. As a result of these changes, many pre-LGM settlements show no activity at all during this period; some of these sites are at Lake Eyre and the Strzelecki and Great

Sandy deserts (Hiscock 2008, 60). These sites were probably so dry that even underground and other previously reliable water sources dried up and thus could not support life; another theory is that the areas around these sites became so dry that it was impossible for large groups to carry enough water with them to migrate into them.

Another feature of Sahul during the LGM was the final extinction of a large group of animals referred to as megafauna, including 10-foot-tall kangaroos and diprotodontids, which looked most like contemporary rhinoceroses but were marsupials rather than placental mammals. The cause of this extinction remains a contentious issue today with some scientists, such as Tim Flannery (1994, 2004), claiming a direct link between this mass extinction and the Aboriginal population's hunting or land-use schemes, and others favoring a direct link between climate change and extinction. Stan Florek (2003) of the Australian Museum in Sydney is a proponent of the latter theory, who argues that temperature changes without any significant rise in moisture levels contributed to the drying out of the continent's inland lakes and thus the death of the animals that relied on their water. Peter Hiscock (2008, 72–75) likewise draws on evidence from a variety of archaeologists, especially Judith Field's work at Cuddie Springs, to argue for climate change as the source of not only LGM extinctions but also those of many other large marsupials between 200,000 BP and the LGM. Along with Hiscock, the present author cannot rule out that humans may have assisted in the extinction of some animals through either hunting or disrupting their natural habitats, but it seems clear that the earliest Aboriginal populations did not kill off Sahul's megafauna.

After the end of the last glacial maximal about 17,000 years ago, conditions in Sahul began to change. These changes were not rapid by contemporary standards but over the course of thousands of years did force the human population on Sahul to make many significant adaptations. The most important cause of these changes was the rise in global sea levels, which over the course of 10,000 years eventually separated the Australian mainland from Tasmania and New Guinea. In addition to the loss of territory, climate change affected the continent in ways that are still not understood. Warmer conditions and an increase in carbon dioxide (CO_2) in the atmosphere may have set the stage for more plant life. Greater rainfall may have opened up certain desert locations that had been abandoned during the LGM, while warmer temperatures may have caused this additional moisture to evaporate as soon as it fell.

While domestication of animals and plants was largely impossible in the Australian context because of a lack of suitable native species

22

(Diamond 1999), post-LGM archaeological sites indicate other, significant changes in both social and material life for humans on the continent. Socially, the decrease in available territory caused by inundation contributed to higher population densities. This fundamental change, however, does not seem to have brought about any categorical change in social structure. Post-LGM Aboriginal societies remained bands, organized around the dual principles of kinship and residence and exhibiting all of the relative equality of their pre-LGM ancestors. Even in New Guinea, where population pressures about 9,000 years ago contributed to the domestication of plants and the development of a horticultural subsistence base, extensive redistribution systems eliminated differences in wealth almost as soon as they emerged and no formal leadership roles developed prior to the colonial era. The same was certainly true in Australia, where horticulture could not develop, making it impossible to accumulate large food surpluses.

The combination of higher population densities and climate change also caused many material changes to post-LGM Aboriginal life, especially the need for more intensive utilization of resources in each locality. For example, many of the chert tools and fragments found in pre-LGM and LGM era middens had been carried far from their original sources. For many archaeologists, this indicates greater mobility at that time due to the requirements of hunting and gathering in the cold, dry climate. This mobility also points to the ability of each band to roam far and wide without encroaching on the territory of other bands. In some post-LGM sites, most chert remains are found quite close to their source and thus indicate longer residence in each place and reduced mobility due to an increase in overall population (O'Connell and Allen 2004). However, these conclusions have been challenged by findings that some large stone tools, such as axes, were discovered farther from their original sites during the pre- and post-LGM periods than during that period, when dryness and cold may have prevented some migratory routes and camping sites from being used. Many post-LGM sites also indicate that trade relations increased in that period and thus gave each band access to a somewhat wider array of goods without their being forced to migrate.

Another important material change in the post-LGM context was the widespread creation of art and body decorations. Very few pre-LGM sites indicate the presence of red or yellow ochre or any other artistic media. All of the rock art for which Aboriginal Australians are famous, such as X-ray art of animals and dot paintings showing song lines and the footsteps of the ancestors, was created in the post-LGM

X-ray painting and dot painting are the two best-known forms of traditional Aboriginal art. This example comes from the Kakadu region of the Northern Territory. (Neale/Shutterstock)

period. Whether this material change is indicative of greater complexity in Aboriginal religious and ritual life at this time or another result of higher population densities and reduced mobility may never be known. A further possibility is that all pre-LGM rock art was destroyed by inundation or simply eroded over time. The fact that there are two possible examples of pre-LGM rock art in the Cape York Peninsula area of northern Australia in the form of ochre smudges on rock overhangs may provide evidence for this theory.

After the LGM, Aboriginal people also began to make more widespread changes to their natural environment than they had prior to and during the LGM. The use of fire is one land management strategy that may have been practiced prior to the LGM but nonetheless became very widespread after it, as seen at a large number of post-LGM archaeological sites. As do contemporary Aboriginal people, these ancient ancestors may have used fire to locate and isolate animals for easier hunting as well as to promote the growth of vegetation, which would also have attracted animals. In addition to the use of fire to control plant growth, there is evidence that both plants and small animals were carried from place to place to encourage their growth in new habitats. Lack of suitable candidates for domestication, such as those that could have provided enough food effectively to replace hunting and gathering, however, meant that domestication of these plants never occurred. Indeed, even in the postcolonial context, the only native Australian plant to have been domesticated for widespread human consumption is the macadamia nut, and no native animal has been domesticated (Diamond 1999).

As have other aspects of the most ancient Aboriginal history, this hypothesis concerning greater control of the natural environment in the post-LGM period has been challenged. For example, some prehistorians have used evidence of heavily used stone axes in a few pre-LGM sites, combined with pollen studies indicating greater forest cover in central Australia prior to 60,000 BP, to argue that the first migrants to the country cut down large swaths of forest in that region. The argument is that the resulting lack of trees contributed to desertification, indicating very intensive interactions between pre-LGM populations and their environment (Groube 1989, Miller, Mangan, Pollard, Thompson, Felzer, and Magee 2005). This remains a contentious hypothesis that requires far more evidence than is currently available.

In addition to exerting their control over the land through the use of fire and over certain animals and plants, the post-LGM Aboriginal population in some locales dug channels and weirs for trapping fish and eels. These land management practices indicate not only a deep knowledge of the local environment but also, contrary to what the early British settlers thought, a strong commitment to particular parcels of land. While Aboriginal people did not have large food surpluses because of a lack of domesticable plants and animals that would have allowed them to build permanent towns and cities, they did not simply live in a state of nature. Each community owned the rights to use parcels of land and their resources and managed those parcels with complex strategies of burning, planting, animal transfers, and animal management.

Culture

As is the case with so many features of precontact life there is contemporary debate about whether the conceptual and structural aspects of Aboriginal cultural life evident to Europeans in the 19th century were continuations from the past or relatively new adaptations to the colonial world. For example, Peter Hiscock believes that the complex Aboriginal kinship systems evident to Europeans at the end of the 19th century were the result of dramatic population loss from smallpox in 1789 rather than a continuation of precontact structures, while others, such as Ian Keen and Josephine Flood, disagree (Molloy 2008).

Kinship

While many aspects of Aboriginal life changed dramatically with the arrival of Europeans and the devastation of communities through disease and genocide, the evidence both from Australia and from band societies more generally is that although specific details of each kin structure may have changed, the centrality of kinship did not. The foundation of Aboriginal culture and society in the period before European contact had to have been kinship. All laws, residential patterns, taboos, and other aspects of communal life were dictated by kinship principles. Individual relationships, from food sharing requirements and other etiquette rules to potential marriage partners, were also dictated largely by kinship, in association with residency, which itself was largely directed by kinship. In the contemporary world this code remains very important, even for the majority of Aboriginal Australians who live in urban areas.

Rather than blood ties, the most important aspect of Aboriginal kinship systems is classification. In U.S.-American kinship there is a degree of classification, such as all children of your parents' siblings are classified as cousins. This pattern is quite different from other kinship systems, in which the children of your mother's siblings are called something different from the children of your father's siblings; some systems are even more complex in that mother's and father's older siblings' children are called something different from their younger siblings' children. Aboriginal classification included not only cousins but everyone in the band or even tribe. For example, a father, his brothers, and his male lineal cousins are all called father; a mother, her sisters, and her female lineal cousins are all called mother. This does not mean that Aboriginal people did not know who their actual mother and father were, but that rights and responsibilities extended far beyond the nuclear family.

Classificatory kinship systems create very large webs of ties between individuals that cut across not only time but space. If two strangers of the same tribe meet, they immediately figure out how they are connected, as cousins, mother and child, father and child, grandparent and child, or whatever, so they are able to use the appropriate kinship term to refer to each other and to obey all the other taboos associated with kinship. One of the most interesting aspects of these kinship rules for many outsiders is the pattern of avoidance relationships many Aboriginal people are required to follow. The most common of these is the in-law avoidance relationship, in which men and women are not permitted to be alone in the room with their spouse's parents, are not permitted to speak to them directly, and must never engage in joking or other lighthearted activity with them. While not all Aboriginal groups had these kinds of avoidance relationships between categories of relatives, many did and still do to this day.

Although Aboriginal Australians had one of the simplest tool kits of all the colonized peoples in the world, they may also have had some of the most complex structures to manage their webs of kinship. In many tribes each individual was a member of a family, lineage, clan, tribe, subsection, section, and moiety. Individuals had to manage different kinds of relationships with each person based on these categories, including joking and avoidance requirements, exogamy and endogamy rules, and obligations of social and economic reciprocity.

Religion

Dreaming stories form the basis of Australian Aboriginal religion. They provide explanations for how and why the world is the way it is, which usually relate to the actions of ancestors who created the world. The world depicted in these stories is much more complex than that of most Westerners, for whom the natural and supernatural, past and present, sacred and profane are separate. For Aboriginal Australians, these planes of existence are intertwined. Ancient ancestors created the world and everything in it, including rocks, lakes, animals, humans, the wind, and rain, but are also active in the present. Their past actions cannot be separated from present actions, especially in ritual, which remakes the world each time it is undertaken. The song lines or footprints of these ancient ancestors continue to cross the Australian continent and carry information back and forth from one community to another. Sacred spaces along these lines coexist with everyday or profane spaces, often materialized in rocks, rivers, and other geological features. Because of this continual sacred presence and the association in English with sleeping, many Aboriginal people prefer not to use the term *Dreaming* to refer to their religious beliefs but instead rely on the term used in their own language. Anthropologists sometimes use "the everywhen" to refer to the context of Dreaming stories in order to indicate their timelessness (Bourke, Bourke, and Edwards 1998, 79).

As is the case with specific kinship structures, Aboriginal religion is another area of indigenous culture in which 19th-century concepts and ideas may not represent beliefs and practices that are as ancient as the Aboriginal population in Australia as a whole. As mentioned, there is little evidence for the rock art that depicts Dreaming stories in Australia prior to the post-LGM period. The archaeologist Bruno David takes this argument even further, claiming that modern Dreaming did not emerge until between 3500 and 1400 BP (2002, 209). He reminds us that "modern Dreaming stories cannot be used as evidence for the Dreaming's great antiquity, despite the possibility that a story's contents may represent traces of particular historical events passed down in folk memory" (2002, 91). That said, there is solid archaeological evidence that Dreaming has been the basis of Aboriginal Australian religion for several thousand years, affecting both belief and practice through the present.

Another feature of Aboriginal religion is the sacred or totemic nature of certain plants, animals, geographic features, and other aspects of nature, including the Moon. Each clan not only is represented by its totem but is said to embody and be descended from it. For example, members of the kangaroo clan are believed to have had the same ancestor as contemporary kangaroos; the same is true of the spinifex clan, witchety grub clan, and so on. As a result, these animals and plants are sacred to their particular groups, who must not hunt or eat them or use them for other profane purposes.

As do other religions, Aboriginal religion has a body of myth contained in its creation stories, rules and prohibitions to follow, and a series of rituals that bring the myths to life. Religious rituals, regardless of the tradition in which they originate, are about regularly enacting the sacred moments of the believers' history. For example, Christians partake in communion to reenact the last supper, when the apostles gave life to Jesus despite the sacrifice of his body on Earth. Aboriginal rituals likewise reenact the most important moments in the lives of their sacred ancestors as a way of connecting past and present. Rituals also provide moments for younger Aboriginal people to learn from their elders the words to songs, the moves to dances, the beat to songs, and the power of the ancestors in the past and present world.

Language

A third feature of Aboriginal culture that is evident today and indicative of great changes over the tens of thousands of years of Aboriginal residence in Australia is the clustering of all Aboriginal languages into two large groups, Pama-Nyungan and non-Pama-Nyungan, which is sometimes also called Arafuran (Clendon 2006). The former family

THE MACASSANS ON MAREGE

Prior to European settlement, Australia's northern Aboriginal people on the Kimberley and Arnhem coasts had regular contact with fishermen from the Indonesian archipelago, who called the Australian continent Marege. Starting in about the 1720s the Macassans, from the city of Makassar in southern Sulawesi, made annual visits southward with the December monsoonal winds in search of trepang, or sea slug, a Chinese delicacy also known as sea cucumber or *bêche-de-mer*. The trepang industry increased dramatically between 1770 and 1780, coinciding with China's expanding economic power in the 18th century. By the 1820s demand was so high that trepang was Indonesia's largest export to China.

Unlike the British, the Macassans did not try to colonize the land or people of Marege. Their main motivation was to supply the lucrative Chinese markets with an important resource, the trepang. This goal meant building long-term, meaningful relationships with the people who could help them meet their goal. For the Yolngu and other Aboriginal peoples in the region, this was a partnership of predictable seasonal interactions with people who recognized their status as owners of the land and who, importantly, departed with the northern monsoonal winds.

Despite their lack of colonial intentions, the arrival of the Macassans resulted in significant changes to the indigenous societies of the continent's north coast, particularly to the Yolngu of eastern Arnhem Land. The introduction of dugout canoes led to the shift of hunting from land to sea, where dugong and turtles flourished. It was also the Macassans who were unwittingly responsible for several outbreaks of smallpox between the 1780s and 1870s that devastated Australia's Aboriginal populations generally. Occasional localized violence between the two groups, often over access to women, broke out and, according to the anthropologist Ian McIntosh (2006), led to the almost complete annihilation of clans at Dholtji (Cape Wilberforce) through violence and introduced disease.

includes the languages spoken in nine-tenths of the country's geographic territory, from the rain forests of Queensland to the temperate regions of Western Australia and Victoria, including most of the arid center of the country. The latter category, however, contains 90 percent of the continent's precolonial language diversity in just 10 percent of its territory (see map on page 14). Many theories have been put forward to explain both the prevalence of Pama-Nyungan throughout the continent, despite its relatively young age, estimated at about 5,000 years (O'Grady and Hale 2004, 91), and the great diversity of the non-Pama-Nyungan languages. Some of these theories include the separation of these two groups in antiquity and subsequent differentiation over time; others posit that an incoming migratory group introduced dingoes, new stone tool technology, and Pama-Nyungan languages several thousand years ago (Mulvaney and Kamminga 1999, 73–74). It is more likely, according to O'Grady and Hale, that a single population spread their language across nine tenths of the continent as a result of an unknown internal factor. Some hypotheses concerning this spread include innovations in intellectual property such as songlines, kinship structures, and art styles; developments in material culture; or natural causes (O'Grady and Hale 2004, 92).

As is evident from these few select cultural features and historical trends, even prior to the colonial period in Australia the continent housed a dynamic, diverse population that over many millennia had continually adapted to climate and social change. The Aboriginal Australians living in the far north of the country had also adapted to a trading regime, with fishermen and traders visiting their territory from the islands of contemporary Indonesia. Although the exact date of their first landing in Australia is unknown, the early 15th century is posited as the most probable time when fishermen from the north first arrived in large numbers. Macassan hunters of trepang began to interact with Aboriginal Australians two centuries later. The Chinese may also have landed in the far north, although it is possible that the Ming dynasty statue found near Darwin was carried by Macassans rather than Chinese sailors themselves.

3

EUROPEAN EXPLORATION
AND EARLY SETTLEMENT
(1606–1850)

The European "discovery" of Australia and the entire South Pacific region was part of the much larger process of European exploration and colonization throughout the world that began with Bartolomeu Diaz's Portuguese expedition to the Cape of Good Hope at the southern tip of Africa in the 1480s and continues today in French New Caledonia and elsewhere. The earliest explorers were the Portuguese and Spanish, who were driven by the twin motivations of "God and gold" to seek new routes to the East and to expand the boundaries of the known world.

Despite the importance of Spain and Portugal in the Age of Exploration, there is only circumstantial evidence that explorers from those countries sailed as far south as Australia during this period. The one exception to this is Portuguese sailor Luis Váez de Torres, who sailed from Peru under the Spanish flag with Pedro Fernández de Quiros, European discoverer of the Solomon Islands. On their 1606 expedition Torres's ship became separated from the others and wound up sailing through the strait between Australia and New Guinea only a short time after Janszoon's historic landing on Cape York (Kenny 1995). There is little doubt that Torres saw the mainland, but he seems to have mistaken it for yet another island and failed to go ashore or report to the Spanish the existence of the legendary southern continent. Nonetheless, his charts did later end up in the library of Captain James Cook, who persisted in his long and difficult journey through the Great Barrier Reef in the hope that the information was accurate and that he could sail to the west between Australia and New Guinea. Today the strait explored by Torres bears his name in honor of his early achievement.

New Holland and New South Wales, 17th–19th Centuries

New Guinea

PACIFIC OCEAN

Arafura Sea

Torres Strait

Port Essington—
Melville I.

Possession I.—
Wenlock R.

Cape York

INDIAN OCEAN

Bonaparte Archipelago

Pennefather R.

Gulf of Carpentaria

CAPE YORK PENINSULA

Great Barrier Reef

Coral Sea

Karrakatta Bay

Monte Bello Is.

New Holland
(1606–1829)

1786

New South Wales

Shark Bay   Hutt R.

Lake Eyre

Murchison R.

Lake Torrens

Mt. Hopeless

Darling R.

Geraldton

Dirk Hartog I.

Abrolhos Is.   Swan R.

Esperance

Great Australian Bight

Nuyts Archipelago

Liverpool Plains

Port Jackson

Cape Naturaliste   Albany   Archipelago of the Recherche

Murray R.

Botany Bay

N

0   500 miles
0   500 km

© Infobase Publishing

Van Diemen's Land (Tasmania)

Point Hicks

Bass Strait

Tasman Sea

The Dutch Explorers

In 1606 the Dutch sailor Willem Janszoon (sometimes abbreviated to *Jansz*) became the first European to document the existence of Australia. Between that first sighting and 1756, 19 Dutch ships were sent to Australia during the course of eight separate expeditions and a further 23 ships approached the continent while maneuvering to or from the Dutch colonies in the Indonesian archipelago (Sheehan 2008).

These expeditions were part of the larger mercantile and military exploits of the Verenigde Oost-Indische Compagnie, or United (Dutch) East India Company (VOC). The background for this exploration was geopolitical in nature. The 80 years' war between Protestant Holland and Roman Catholic Spain and Portugal meant that the Dutch lost access to the exotic spices sold in the markets at Lisbon. Their answer to this problem was to seek their own path to the spice islands, resulting in their 1595 mission around the Cape of Good Hope and the eventual establishment of the very successful Dutch colony in what is today Indonesia.

One of the ships on that first mission in 1595 was the *Duyfken*, or "Little Dove," which was to make history just seven years later as the first fully documented European ship to call in on the Australian continent, probably at the Pennefather River on the west coast of the Cape York Peninsula. The *Duyfken* on this fateful trip was captained by Willem Janszoon. His mission, when he set sail under a VOC flag from Bantam in West Java, was to find out whether great wealth in gold was actually to be found in New Guinea, as persistent rumors maintained (Kenny 1995). Besides gold he would also have been seeking other salable commodities, from spices to fur.

Although neither Janszoon nor other VOC sailors found much to recommend the Australian continent, which they called New Holland, they soon charted a significant amount of the coastline: 11,713 miles (18,850 km), or 52.5 percent of the continent, from as far south as Nuyts Archipelago on the Great Australian Bight, along the western and northern coasts to western Cape York. In 1642 they also claimed Tasmania, which they called Van Diemen's Land in honor of the VOC governor-general who had commissioned Abel Tasman's expedition. The landing party placed the flag of the prince of Orange on the shore but saw no indigenous Tasmanians. Tasman was vague about the borders of his country's new colony, but for nearly two centuries the prior Dutch exploration of west Australia, still called New Holland, was respected by the other European powers, which turned their attention to the relatively unexplored east coast.

Although Tasman failed to make contact with the Aboriginal people, certainly other Dutch explorers did have interactions with them, of both a positive and a negative nature. Reports vary, but it can be stated with relative certainty that at least one Dutchman was killed when Janszoon's crew went ashore at the Wenlock River on the Cape York Peninsula. Jan Carstenszoon, who landed on Australia's west coast in 1623, even offered financial incentives to his crew for the capture of Aboriginal people, and a number of them were taken back to Dutch headquarters in Batavia (Jakarta) and Ambon, where their trail disappears. In 1629 the Dutch ship *Batavia* was wrecked off the west coast and two of the survivors were banished to the mainland for mutiny. The two were provided with food, guns, and a number of trade goods such as mirrors and beads and told to "learn what they could about the country" as the first recorded European inhabitants of Australia/New Holland (Kenny 1995, 26). They were never seen by Europeans again but must have interacted in some way with the local population.

The English Explorers

Although Captain James Cook is the most famous of the English sailors to have landed in Australia, he was not the first. Cook's 1770 voyage was preceded by that of the British ship the *Triall*, or *Tryell*, which in 1622 was wrecked on rocks that were probably to the north of the Monte Bello Islands, Western Australia. A number of survivors made it to Batavia (Jakarta) and described their harrowing experience, although their directions failed to turn up the rocks that caused the wreck, or the ship itself. In 1681 the *London* also approached New Holland's west coast, but there is no evidence it landed near where the captain was able to draw the Abrolhos Islands, the location where the *Batavia* mutineers had held their rebellion in 1629.

Almost 100 years prior to Cook, in 1688, the Englishman William Dampier, often described as a reluctant pirate or buccaneer but also acknowledged as a knowledgeable naturalist (Wood 1969, Kenny 1995), was sailing with a group of pirates who had snatched the *Cygnet* and left its captain behind on a stopover in the Pacific. After visiting Southeast Asia, the pirates needed to avoid both Dutch and English ships and thus sailed to the east of the Philippines, south into Indonesia, and finally to Timor, where they turned south and landed in Australia (Wood 1969, 220).

In 1699 after the publication of a best seller based on his first journey, Dampier set sail again for the South Pacific, this time with the backing and legitimacy of the English Admiralty and Royal Society. Scientific exploration was the raison d'être of his mission, but what exactly he was expected to achieve was left vague: "He was told to discover 'such things' as might tend to the good of the nation and not to annoy the King's subjects or allies" (Kenny 1995, 23).

His new ship, the *Roebuck*, sailed for New Holland at the start of 1699 and landed at Shark Bay, near Dirk Hartog Island, in July. He sailed north for about 994 miles (1,600 km) over the next five weeks, exploring all along the way. The results of this journey did not add significantly to what was known about the world at the time, as remained the case until 1770 when Cook finally made his way to the east coast of Australia, but did provide important descriptions of the continent's unfamiliar plant and animal life, as well as judgmental descriptions of Aboriginal life (see Wood 1969, 221). Upon his return to Britain, Dampier penned his second best seller, *A Voyage to New Holland,* in which he described not only his Australian adventures but also time spent in New Guinea, Timor, and Brazil.

For 71 years between William Dampier's second journey to New Holland and James Cook's historic landing on the east coast, European activity in New Holland was extremely limited. Even the Dutch sent only two expeditions, in 1705 and 1756, which resulted in almost no new information about the imposing southern continent. After their final expedition, under Lt. Jean Etienne Gonzal, the VOC gave up on their large find in the South Pacific and left it to the Aboriginal people and occasional shipwreck victims.

This changed in 1768, when the British, following their victory over France and Spain in the Seven Years' War in 1763, began thinking about expanding their colonial holdings and their scientific knowledge in the Pacific. James Cook's first journey to New Holland in 1770 was motivated by these twin ambitions. His publicly stated task, given by the Royal Society, was to be in Tahiti on June 3, 1769, to observe the transit of Venus across the Sun, which previous British teams had failed to do during the transit of 1761.

The Royal Society, anxious to ensure its second attempt did not fail, approached the king and government with a request for £4,000 and a ship to send a scientific expedition to the South Seas for the express purpose of observing the transit. When the king agreed to the sum, the navy provided Lieutenant James Cook, who had had significant experience in North America, to command the ship HMB *Endeavour* and co-observe the transit with Charles Green, a Royal Society astronomer. The expedition was to observe the transit, chart new territory, gather as many specimens from the natural world as possible, and provide drawings, journals, and maps upon their return. As such the *Endeavour* carried a number of the best English scientific minds of the time, including Joseph Banks, an Oxford-trained botanist and later Cook's good friend. Cook was also secretly directed by his superior officers to search the South Seas for sites that might yield financial gain, specifically in New Zealand, which had been "discovered" by Abel Tasman in 1642.

The expedition, by most accounts, was a success. As a result of the scientific explorations of Banks, Daniel Solander, and the others, about 1,400 new plant species and 1,000 animals were taken back to London. The one fairly significant failure on the scientific front, however, was

JAMES COOK

James Cook's international military experience with the British Royal Navy began in 1758, when he sailed on the *Pembroke* and participated in the capture of Quebec, Canada. For several years Cook remained on the northeast coast of North America, surveying Nova Scotia and Newfoundland on the *Northumberland* and wintering in Halifax. His time in the Americas was interrupted in 1762 when he returned to England to marry Elizabeth Bates, 14 years his junior, but this brief period did not hinder the rise of Cook's fortunes in the navy. In 1763 he took command of his first ship, the *Grenville,* a 69-ton schooner armed with 12 guns, which he sailed back to England each fall, returning to North America in the spring.

During his years on the Atlantic, Cook became widely known for his charts and scientific observations as well as his acquaintance with the governor of Newfoundland and Labrador, Sir Hugh Palliser, who later rose to the rank of admiral. Cook's observations of a solar eclipse in Newfoundland in 1766, which assisted in the establishment of the island's longitude, were the basis of his next promotion, from master to lieutenant and expedition leader in 1770 on the 368-ton barque *Endeavour.* The stated purpose of this journey was to observe the transit of Venus from Tahiti, but Cook also had secret orders to chart as much territory as he could, stake claims for England where possible, and gather such scientific data as were available to him and his team. As a result of this journey, both Australia and New Zealand were claimed for England and the stage was set for the later colonization of both locations.

In 1772 Cook sailed again for the southern Pacific but failed to return to Australia. In 1776 Cook sailed on his third journey as expedition commander, this time in search of the mythical Northwest Passage connecting the Atlantic and Pacific Oceans. He began by revisiting New Zealand and Tahiti; stopping off in Tonga; naming the Sandwich Islands (Hawaii) after his friend John Montague, earl of Sandwich; and then sailing north into the Bering Sea. Thwarted by ice in his effort to sail eastward, Cook returned to the Sandwich Islands in November 1778 and was killed at Kealakekua Bay on Valentine's Day, 1779.

the observation of the transit of Venus: Cook and Green's observations differed by 42 seconds (Phillips 2008).

Despite the failure of the expedition's stated mission, when Cook, Banks, and the others returned in 1771, they received a warm welcome in London due to their other accomplishments, scientific and other-

A replica of Captain James Cook's ship HMB Endeavour, during his first voyage to Australia. Cook's home harbor of Whitby, Yorkshire, England. (George Green/Shutterstock)

wise. In political terms, certainly the most important was the claiming for England of New Zealand in 1769 and New South Wales in 1770. In New Zealand this event happened at Mercury Bay and in Australia at Possession Island, off the Cape York Peninsula, which Cook also named. Cook had actually landed on the eastern Australian coast four times, starting with Botany Bay, before he took possession of the land for King George III in August. In addition to New South Wales, Cook provided the newly "discovered" continent with many other place-names. The first was Point Hicks on the northern Victorian coast, named for the *Endeavour's* first lieutenant, Zachary Hicks, the first to see this outcropping of land.

In addition to the vast number of scientific specimens and amount of knowledge they gathered, Cook and his crew provided the backdrop for Britain's later colonization of its new possession. It was actually the ship's head botanist, Banks, who in 1779 suggested to the Pitt government in London that Botany Bay might be a suitable place to deposit criminals who had been sentenced to transportation. The American colonies had been used for that purpose for many decades; about 50,000 people were sent there between 1650 and 1775 (Morgan and Rushton 2004). For a few years after the American Revolution stopped this practice, convicted felons in England served their sentences in the hulls of prison ships, until transportation began anew in 1788, commencing a whole new chapter in Australian history.

Before this initial settlement, however, in 1772 Cook and Captain Tobias Furneaux sailed again for the southern ocean to continue English exploration of the new continent. Although Cook never returned to Australian waters, Furneaux, in the HMS *Adventure,* used the opportunity to survey Van Diemen's Land. While he explored much of the region, he was badly mistaken in his report to Cook that Van Diemen's Land was connected to the New South Wales mainland. Cook had no reason to doubt his second in command and thus never returned to the region to investigate it for himself.

The last important English explorer of Australia's unknown coastlines was Matthew Flinders. Together with his childhood friend Dr. George Bass and William Martin, Flinders began in 1795 by exploring the intricate coastline around Port Jackson in their tiny, six-foot boat, the *Tom Thumb.* Their expertise led the second governor of the new colony, John Hunter, to provide them with a real ship in which to clarify the status of Van Diemen's Land as an island or peninsula. The three explorers returned to Port Jackson in 1798 having circumnavigated the island and thus were able to confirm its separation from the mainland. After journeying to England to gain support for his plan to circumnavigate Terra Australis, in 1801–02 Flinders was the first to chart the entire southern coast of the continent, from Cape Leeuwin in the far southwest, across the Bight, into Port Phillip Bay in Victoria, and north to Port Jackson. In July 1802 Flinders began his 11-month journey around the continent, which he called Australia, thus proving to all that New Holland and New South Wales were the same landmass. Unfortunately, after completing this journey, Flinders never returned to Australia again. On his way back to England he was held prisoner in Mauritius from December 1803 through June 1810 because of the Napoleonic Wars between Britain and France and died at the age of 40 after completing his massive work, *A Voyage to Terra Australis,* published just one day before his death in July 1814 (Cooper 1966).

The French Explorers

The first of the large number of French explorers who landed in New Holland during the 17th–19th centuries was probably Abraham Duquesne-Guitton, who in 1687 was blown off course on his way to Siam, or Thailand, and saw land he believed to be Eendrecht Land in

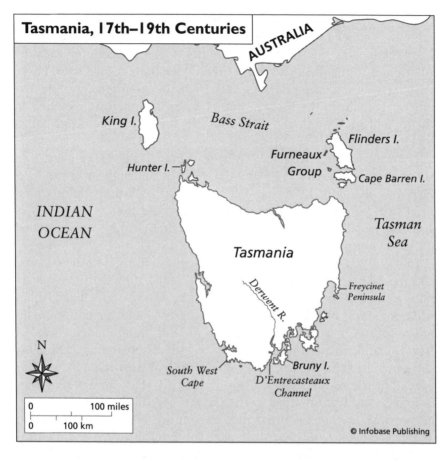

Tasmania, 17th–19th Centuries

AUSTRALIA

King I.

Bass Strait

Hunter I.

Furneaux Group

Flinders I.

Cape Barren I.

INDIAN OCEAN

Tasmania

Tasman Sea

Derwent R.

Freycinet Peninsula

N

South West Cape

Bruny I.

D'Entrecasteaux Channel

0   100 miles
0   100 km

© Infobase Publishing

what is today Western Australia. In the same year, Duquesne-Guitton's nephew, Nicolas Gedeon de Voutron, is also believed to have visited New Holland and even landed at the site of the Swan River, contemporary Perth, which he recommended to his government as a suitable location for a new colony (Tull 2000).

Despite the promise of the new continent, French exploration in the South Pacific did not expand until 1766, when Louis-Antoine de Bougainville undertook an around-the-world journey that included the Great Barrier Reef off Australia's east coast. In 1772 de Bougainville was followed to Australia by François de Saint-Alouarn, who not only explored the west coast of New Holland but landed at Dirk Hartog Island and claimed that land for France. He left behind statements of proclamation and several coins in bottles buried on the island. France never followed up on the claim, however, and the bottles were not found until 1998 (Shark Bay World Heritage Area 2007).

The year 1772 also carried the first French ship into Australia's eastern waters, when Marc-Joseph Marion Dufresne landed in Van Diemen's Land. Dufresne's sailors also had the first violent encounter with the Aboriginal Tasmanians after early friendly relations turned sour. In the ensuing volley of stones and spears from the Aboriginal people and musket balls from the French, one of Dufresne's men was speared in the leg and an Aboriginal man lost his life, the first of thousands killed by European guns.

Dufresne was followed in 1788 by Jean-François de La Pérouse, who spent about six weeks in Botany Bay just days after most of the First Fleet had abandoned the site. A few members of Arthur Phillip's First Fleet had, however, remained at Botany Bay, and the two rival parties spent six amiable weeks together while the French ships reprovisioned for their continuing exploration (Marchant 1967).

In 1792, under Antoine-Raymond-Joseph de Bruni d'Entrecasteaux, and in 1802 under Nicolas Baudin, the French turned their explorations south to Van Diemen's Land. The latter mission, which had begun with two ships, Nicolas Baudin in *Le Géographe* and Captain Hamelin in *Le Naturaliste,* spent several months in 1801 along the west coast of New Holland, charting territory, gathering plant and animal specimens, and generally fulfilling the intellectual nature of their mission, as symbolized by the names of their ships. Eventually Hamelin was sent back to France and Baudin sailed in the *Casuarina* with Louis de Freycinet, his previous mission's cartographer, to continue his work in the region of Van Diemen's Land. For their part, the English feared the political motives of Baudin's 1802 mission and quickly sent their own ship to plant the Union Jack, almost literally, under Baudin's nose on King Island (Marchant and Reynolds 1966).

While these 19th-century expeditions from France were largely scientific in nature, the French dream of a colonial empire did not die with the Revolution in 1789–99, and in 1822 Louis-Isidore Duperrey, who had sailed with Freycinet, set off on his own mission of exploration. He called in at Sydney in 1824 but never arrived at the Swan River site he was to scope out for possible colonization. His mission did push the English, however, to lay claim to the western half of the continent, as they did on Christmas Day, 1826. The Dutch had made a prior claim to that territory, but their long neglect and failure to leave any lasting settlement left it open to the British. Another Frenchman, Hyacinthe de Bougainville, son of Louis-Antoine de Bougainville, was also sent on a political mission to New South Wales when he was directed to spy on the Sydney colony during his time there in mid-1825.

The last significant French expedition to New South Wales was in 1838, when Dumont d'Urville rejected Port Essington, near contemporary Darwin, as a possible site for a colony because of the climate, flies, mosquitoes, and ants (Dyer 2005, 17). As a result of these French expeditions to the South Pacific numerous places, especially around Tasmania, today bear French names: the Freycinet Peninsula, Bruny Island, d'Entrecasteaux Channel, Cape Naturaliste, Bonaparte Archipelago, and Archipelago of the Recherche.

Initial English Settlement, 1788–1799

The motivation behind the British settlement of Australia is often described as the establishment of a penal colony, to replace Britain's loss of the American colonies in 1776. Certainly, many of the first Britons to reside in Australia were prisoners who had been transported to the new colony at Port Jackson for theft, prostitution, and other crimes. Nevertheless, to give primacy to this motivation is to ignore British leaders' geopolitical impulse at that time to prevent their European rivals from expanding their own empires.

After Britain's loss in the American War of Independence in 1781, during which France, Spain, and the other European powers had sided with the Americans as a way of weakening their British enemy, the British government under William Pitt, the younger, needed to secure Britain's influence in Asia and the Pacific region. Certainly part of the motivation for sending Cook to claim land in the South Pacific that the Dutch had previously rejected was to prevent the French from claiming it first. One of the clearest signs that this was the impetus behind the sailing of the First Fleet to Australia in 1788 was that the governor of the new colony, Arthur Phillip, had risen to prominence in Britain as an international spy in France and South America (Clarke 2003, 44, 47).

The First Fleet, under Phillip, sailed from England in May 1787, after a drunken night of revelry of the ships' sailors and officers, with 443 sailors, 759 convicts (191 of whom were women), 13 children of convicts, 160 marines, 51 officers, 27 wives, 19 children of free parents, and nine staff members for Governor Phillip (Clarke 2003, 49). Interestingly, among the convicts were not only people of English and Scottish nationality but also Germans, Norwegians, and both black and white Americans (Molony 2005, 33). The 11-ship contingent took just over eight months to arrive at Botany Bay on January 19–20, 1788, only to be bitterly disappointed at what they found. Instead of the green fields and forests described by Cook and Banks, the First Fleet arrived in the middle of summer, when heat and lack of rain made the entire landscape appear dry as dust and as infertile as the desert. Most distressing was the lack of freshwater. In less than a week, Phillip was forced to transfer his small colony to the slightly more promising region of Port Jackson, contemporary Sydney. On the second day of this short move, January 26, British flags and musket fire announced the establishment of Britain's newest colony. January 26 continues to be celebrated throughout much of the country as Australia Day, except in many Aboriginal communities, where the day is marked as Invasion Day or Survival Day to denote the beginning of the disease, violence, and invasive government policies that destroyed life as they knew it.

The early years of the colony at Port Jackson were very difficult for everybody involved. The Aboriginal population, which was vastly larger than Cook and Banks had reported, began dying of introduced diseases almost immediately. The worst epidemic was smallpox, which killed an estimated 50 percent of the population in a matter of months in 1789. Despite its emergence in New South Wales at the time of settlement, the source of this epidemic was actually contact between trepangers from the Indonesian archipelago and Aboriginal people in Arnhem Land rather than the First Fleet (Hiscock 2008, 13). The convicts and soldiers of the settlement also suffered, from lack of food, clothing, and shelter and from violence at the hands of the Aboriginal people; even Governor Phillip suffered a fairly serious wound to the side from an Aboriginal spear in a formalized retaliation for some wrong (Perkins 2008, episode 1).

The worst problem faced by the colonists during the first several years of settlement was lack of food. Following the First Fleet, which lost one of its supply ships off Norfolk Island, the British sent a provision ship to provide extra food and support. Unfortunately, after loading with supplies at the Cape of Good Hope, the ship, HMS *Guardian,* crashed into an iceberg and was destroyed trying to return to the cape. As a result, the Second Fleet pulled into Port Jackson in June 1790 with its human cargo of 733 convicts and many hundreds of others akin to those who sailed with the First Fleet, before any additional supplies arrived to support the burgeoning colony.

Producing food in the harsh climate around Sydney was almost as great a challenge as the lack of imported supplies. The First and Second Fleets arrived on Australia's shores with very few agricultural implements; the first plow arrived only in 1796, eight years into the life of the colony (Clarke 2003, 52). The hoes, shovels, and axes with which the convicts tried to break the dry, dusty earth and fell the heavy eucalyptus trees were woefully inadequate to the task. Seeds carried from the Dutch colony at the Cape of Good Hope were so barren that the new colonists began to believe the Dutch had purposefully sold them shoddy goods. As a result, rationing and protecting limited food stores became a top priority for Phillip throughout his four-year tenure as the colony's governor. It was even possible to be sentenced to hang for stealing food in these first, crucial years, though one of the first to be convicted of this crime was pardoned on condition that he become the colony's hangman. His first act was to hang his accomplice (Clarke 2003, 54).

Once the fundamental problem of food was solved, just prior to Phillip's departure in 1792, the New South Wales colony had to establish basic social and economic structures in a land where about 80 percent of adults were technically prisoners and thus outside the normal functioning of society. One of the most important things that all governments in the colony did was to encourage marriages among all the single people in residence, convicts or otherwise. Female convicts who received an offer of marriage were usually freed in order to take up that offer, and, after 1816, male convicts could apply to have their wives and families transported to New South Wales at no cost. If the husband was not eligible for his ticket of leave, parole, or freedom, he was "given" to his wife to serve out the end of his sentence (Hirst 2005, 109). These marriages, the authorities believed, would improve both the morality and the industriousness of the colony's population.

Despite the emphasis on morality, one institution that had only nominal support from the colonial structure was the church. The First Fleet sailed with a chaplain, the Reverend Richard Johnson, who was "a product of the evangelical revival in England" (Clark 1995, 13), but neither Governor Phillip nor his officer corps had any real belief in the Protestant mission. Unlike the early settlements in the Pacific established by Spain, Portugal, and France, England's Australian colony was little interested in saving souls. Ecclesiastical leaders from both the Anglican and, after 1791, the Roman Catholic traditions were welcomed in the colony, but only for the purpose of maintaining order among the convicts, if possible. References to God do not occur in any of the documents related to the founding of the colony, either those produced in England before sailing or those produced in the colony after settlement (Molony 2005, 32–33). For a large number of convicts as well, the religious hierarchy in the colony was seen as merely an extension of the British class structure that kept them poor and indentured, and most saw the priests and vicars as merely "civil servants in cassocks" (Clark 1995, 13).

Although the First Fleet is recorded to have had passengers from a variety of nationalities, the dominant majority were English, who were at least nominally Protestant. This changed in 1791, when Port Jackson received its first boatload of Irish Catholic convicts, the first of more than 26,500 convicts sent directly from Ireland to New South Wales between 1791 and 1853. While some members of this group were thieves and other common felons, a large number were actual or reputed revolutionaries who had participated in various uprisings against the British. These differences in religion and loyalty to Britain between Irish and English convicts caused considerable conflict in the colony. The major problems from the point of view of the colonial leadership in the early years, as the judge advocate David Collins wrote in his journal, were the supposed ignorance and folly of Irish convicts, who believed they could escape and walk to China, or that the French were going to arrive to liberate them, or even that Ireland had finally overthrown the British and the Irish were thus no longer bound to the terms of their sentences (O'Farrell 2000, 22–23). Rather than seeing these fantasies as the result of generations of struggle for freedom by the Irish, the British considered them further signs of Irish stupidity and superstition.

A second important structural commitment made by the colonial government was to provide land grants to officers and convict labor to work that land in order to promote self-sufficiency in food and other products. Free settlers who arrived in New South Wales were also eligible for land and convict labor. As part of this deal, Francis Grose, Phillip's replacement prior to the arrival of the second governor, allowed convicts to be paid in rum, which motivated many of them far more than had other goods (Clark 1995, 20). As a result of their control of labor through their control of rum, the New South Wales Corps gained the nickname the Rum Corps; their later rebellion against Governor Bligh is called the Rum Rebellion for the same reason (Clarke 2003, 59).

A third issue that had to be worked out for the smooth functioning of the new colony was the relationship between the settlers and the Aboriginal people. According to both his orders and, seemingly, his disposition, Governor Phillip was more humane than subsequent colonial governors. His intention, according to Manning Clark, was "to open an intercourse with the natives, and to cultivate their affections, enjoining all his subjects to live in amity and kindness with them" (1995, 12). Phillip was so taken with the civilization and striking behavior of the Indigenous people that he gave the place-name *Manly* to their home by the cove. At the same time, the two Aboriginal men with whom Phillip had any kind of relationship, Bennelong and Arabanoo, were both kidnapped by white soldiers and presented to him to serve as potential translators and intermediaries between their people and the governor. Arabanoo quickly succumbed to smallpox and died while being held captive, but Bennelong survived the epidemic and went on to learn English and even travel back to England with Phillip when he returned home in 1792. Upon his return to Australia, Bennelong found adjusting to the conditions of his life very

Portrait of Bennelong, circa 1795 (ink on card) by Lt. George Austin Woods (19th century) (Dixson Galleries/State Library of New South Wales/The Bridgeman Art Library)

difficult. While living in Sydney he was often drunk and finally he rejected white society entirely and returned to his own people and former way of life. When he died in 1813, his rejection of the white world was deemed by the *Sydney Gazette* to be the result of his being "naturally barbarous and ferocious . . . a thorough savage" (Perkins 2008, episode 1).

Whether or not Phillip himself sought friendly relations with the Aboriginal people is a matter for debate, but certainly not all of the governor's charges were concerned about maintaining "amity and kindness." Among convicts and officers, stealing Indigenous implements, canoes, and other objects became a sport. In conjunction with this theft, the realization that the settlements at Port Jackson and later Rose Hill (Parramatta) and elsewhere were going to be permanent moved a significant number of Aboriginal people to oppose them with force. From 1790 until 1802 Pemulwuy led a band of fighters from the Bidjigal tribe in the Eora Resistance, which frequently attacked settlements along the Hawkesbury River and the Port Jackson area more generally (Clarke 2003, 56; Australian Museum 2004). One of the people attacked by the fighters was Phillip's personal gamekeeper, McIntyre, who had probably killed a number of Aboriginal people as part of his role as a hunter.

At this provocation, in 1790 Phillip sent a punitive expedition against the Aboriginal people, the first of many over the next century and a half (Australian Museum 2004). While Pemulwuy escaped capture for a dozen years, in 1802 he was killed and his head removed from his body, preserved in spirits, and sent to Joseph Banks in England for research purposes (Molony 2005, 36). For three years after his death, Pemulwuy's son, Tedbury, continued the Eora fight against the white settlers, until he too was killed in battle (Newbury 1999, 13).

A final problem that emerged in these early days of the colony and continued for more than 100 years was that of bushrangers; Murray Johnson estimates that about 2,000 of these characters roamed the Australian countryside between 1790 and the 1920s (2007, 31). While a few of these individuals, such as Ned Kelly and Jack Donohue (of "Wild Colonial Boy" fame), have become famous for the Robin Hood–like mythology that emerged around them, many were simply thieves who preferred cattle rustling to working. During difficult economic times, bushranging was also the only choice for some individuals; the same was true for escaped convicts. The first bushranger in Australia was John "Black" Caesar, whose nickname was derived from his race as either a West Indian or a "native of Madagascar" (Johnson 2007, 32). Caesar was a convict who escaped from Port Jackson numerous times between 1790 and 1796. While on his many leaves from his captors he generally lived by stealing from settlers' and the government's gardens, an act that could not go unpunished. He was captured in 1796, having been mortally wounded, earning the bounty hunters a reward of five gallons of rum.

Colonial Expansion: 1800–1831

After the relative success of Britain's New South Wales colony at Port Jackson, as well as a second one established at the same time on Norfolk Island, in the first few years of the 19th century other settlements were begun. The same combination of geopolitical motivation, especially preventing the French from settling the region, and the need to settle convicts was also at play in these years. The first of the 19th-century settlements was established at Port Phillip in 1803 with Captain David Collins in charge of a small contingent of convicts and officers. The first settlement outside New South Wales, on the Derwent River in southeast Van Diemen's Land, was soon set up in light of Baudin's explorations of the region; the following year it absorbed Collins's small group as well and Collins himself took over as commander of the southern settlement, which he called Hobart Town. A second settlement in Van Diemen's Land, at Port Dalrymple, contemporary Launceston, in the north, was likewise established at this time (Clark 1995, 26–27).

The early years of the 19th century were also characterized by a distinct change in the attitudes and official policy of the colony toward the Indigenous people. Aboriginal people had been described by Cook and Banks using the concepts of Jean-Jacques Rousseau, who defined all tribal peoples as "noble savages." Governor Phillip had inherited this tradition and tried to uphold it to some extent. By 1800, however, the vast differences between the two people's ways of life led to more significant misunderstandings and violence between them. The British looked upon the food collectors, with their limited tool kits and very short working days, as lazy, indolent, and stupid for not wanting to participate in the white world. The Aboriginal people were equally horrified at some aspects of the colonial world, such as their land settlements but also the corporal punishment of white men caught stealing from an Aboriginal camp (Clark 1995, 31). While Phillip had ordered one or two military maneuvers against the Aboriginal people around Port Jackson, by 1806 these were regular occurrences in the countryside around all the colonial areas in New South Wales and Van Diemen's Land. In the towns as well, Aboriginal people, some of whom had succumbed to the plentiful supply of rum, were harassed and driven from view. The "noble savage" had been replaced in the minds of most whites with a racially inferior brute who had to be controlled or eliminated for the good of the colony (Clark 1995, 32).

As a result of these differing ways of life and Europeans' notion of racial superiority, there are dozens if not hundreds of examples of violence between settlers and Aboriginal people, with the violence going both ways. There are examples of white men and women who were ambushed and killed by Aboriginal groups and plenty of sheep, cattle, and other objects were stolen. Nevertheless, the relative positions of the Aboriginal and settler communities at the time were that one possessed spears, the other guns; one was dying by the thousands of introduced diseases to which the other had relative immunity; and one had occupied the land for tens of thousands of years, while the other had invaded and annexed land without compensation to the other. Because of these factors, a greater degree of blame for the violence must be laid at the feet of the colonizers than the Aboriginal fighters who were defending their people and way of life.

For example, in the 1820s in the Bathurst region of New South Wales, the murder of seven to nine white men led eventually to the slaughter of at least a third of the Wiradjuri people in the region. In the first three years of the decade, the white population of Bathurst had exploded from 114 to 1,267 as large landowners brought more convicts and laborers in to work with their sheep and cattle. This gave the white community far greater contact and strife with the local Aboriginal people, the Wiradjuri; the resulting violence is sometimes called the Bathurst war or the 1824 war. One of the leading characters in this drama was a Wiradjuri leader named Windradyne, or Saturday as he is often called. In late 1823 Windradyne was captured trying to free a number of his own people who were being held by the white authorities. After a severe beating and a month-long imprisonment, Windradyne was released and returned to his people, among whom he continued the struggle against white settlements. By early 1824 the war had taken a turn for the worse with the murder of seven stockmen by Aboriginal warriors and at least 100 Aboriginal women and children at the hands of white vigilantes. At that time Governor Brisbane declared martial law, authorizing the murder of Aboriginal people on sight. This act did little to quell the violence in the region and eventually led to the deaths of about 1,000 Wiradjuri people before Windradyne sought peace with his enemies. Nonetheless, Windradyne's ability to lead his warriors about 100 miles (160 km) from Bathurst to Parramatta on December 28, 1824, without being detected by the hundreds of white soldiers in the region, is sometimes credited with ending Governor Brisbane's administration (Mackenzie 2004).

For all the violence between Aboriginal and white people, hundreds if not thousands of Aboriginal people lost their lives to both vigilante and authorized gunmen. Nonetheless, almost no white murderers were ever brought to account. The only exception occurred in 1838. After the Myall Creek massacre of 28 Wirrayaraay women, children, and elderly men by white stockmen, the owner of the station on which it happened, Henry Dangar, reported the incident to the authorities as murder. The initial trial saw the acquittal of the 11 stockmen charged with the offense, but at a second trial on a different charge, seven stock-men were convicted and hanged. Although both the *Australian* and *Sydney Morning Herald* newspapers expressed outrage at this outcome, reflecting the dominant tone of the period, there were a few voices who cheered the fact that justice had been brought to bear (Markham 2000). It never happened again in this manner, but Myall Creek has come to represent a moment in colonial history that today could contribute to reconciliation between Aboriginal and white Australians; toward that end, "the Myall Creek Massacre and Memorial Site was added to the

National Heritage List on 7 June 2008" (Myall Creek massacre recognized 2008).

Along with this change in attitude toward Aboriginal people, which generated increasing violence in the first half of the 19th century, another important transformation was the expansion of the country's merino sheep population. At the center of this change were John and Elizabeth Macarthur. The Macarthurs and their eldest child had arrived in the New South Wales colony with the Second Fleet in 1790, John as a member of the New South Wales Corps with his family as free settlers, and soon established their farm on the Parramatta River not far from the Port Jackson colony. The farm was successful, but John was a strong-willed character and in 1801 was shipped back to England to face a court-martial and jail term for having dueled with a superior officer in the New South Wales Corps, or Rum Corps. During his absence Elizabeth managed the family farm and grew its burgeoning herd of merinos from 1,000 to 4,000 head. John returned, triumphant, in 1805 with orders from the secretary of state, Earl Camden, for 10,000 acres (4,047 ha) of land and 30 convicts to work it (Clarke 2003, 66). The Macarthur family fortunes, however, did not progress entirely smoothly from this period. In 1808 members of the Rum Corps committed mutiny against the governor of the colony, William Bligh, because he failed to respect and maintain the established power structures of the colony, including Macarthur's economic might. In reaction the British government returned the entire corps to England, and their leader, Major Johnston, was arrested. Macarthur, despite having retired from the officer corps, returned to England with Johnston to serve as a witness at his court-martial. At the trial in 1811 Johnston was found guilty and dismissed in disgrace from his position; Macarthur was denied the right to return to New South Wales until 1817, leaving Elizabeth in charge of the farm, shipping, and other economic interests the family had developed.

Following Macarthur's lead, numerous other free settlers, freed convicts, and former military officers joined Australia's wool rush of the first half of the 19th century. Squatters took their herds beyond the established 19 counties around Sydney and set up vast sheep runs between Port Jackson and Port Phillip. Even with a three-year depression in the early 1840s, by 1850 Australian wool made up 50.5 percent of all the wool imported by Britain, up from just 6.6 percent in 1831 (Dye and LaCroix 2000, 19).

The years of John Macarthur's absence from New South Wales largely coincide with the so-called age of Macquarie in the colony, named for

ELIZABETH VEALE MACARTHUR

Elizabeth Veale and John Macarthur married in 1788 and quickly had their first son, Edward. Just one year into their marriage, John was sent to Port Jackson as part of the New South Wales Corps and his family accompanied him, arriving in June 1790. Life was difficult for Elizabeth after the family's arrival at Port Jackson. Her second son, James, died in infancy and establishing a home suitable for a family with an educated and comfortable background initially proved difficult in the new colony. Nevertheless, less than four years after their arrival on Australian soil their small farm at Parramatta was doing very well. Their sons, Edward, William, and James, who had been named after his dead brother, all received a primary education in the colony and then further education back in England, while their daughters, Elizabeth, Mary, and Emmeline, all remained in New South Wales and married into the highest level of colonial society.

Through her busy child-rearing years and the eight years during which her husband, John, was exiled in England, Elizabeth continued to be an important presence in the colony. Her home was considered the most refined and stable of all those established in the early colonial years thanks to her kindness to servants and valuing of education. The family's businesses also thrived under her watchful eye.

Although Elizabeth's family was very successful, her latter years were not always happy ones. Not long after her husband returned from exile in 1817, he began to spend more and more time away from his family. He suffered from what was called melancholia, probably a form of depression, and experienced bouts of rage when he believed Elizabeth had been unfaithful to him. Despite his moods, Elizabeth remained loyal to her husband and fought to keep the family together until his death in 1834. For the remaining 16 years of her life, she continued to write letters to her friends and relations in England and to enjoy watching her children's successes, particularly those of William and James, both of whom followed in their parents' footsteps and took up sheepherding.

the governor who had been sent to repair the damage caused by the Rum Rebellion against Bligh. Macquarie was a complex character, who, on the one hand, believed in the superiority of British and Protestant institutions (Clark 1995, 36). On the other hand, Macquarie gave orders to cease the "molestation" of the country's Aboriginal people and advocated granting land and power to deserving former convicts. For his latter, pro-emancipist views, as well as his sobriety and evangelical religion, Macquarie continually struggled against the power of the colony's wealthy civilians and military leaders, who were absolutely opposed to granting rights and privileges to former convicts. He also eliminated the use of rum as the primary currency in the colony, greatly benefiting the majority but angering those who controlled the trade in that beverage.

During his 11 years in office Macquarie saw the colony expand and develop economically: Its population rose from 11,590 to 38,778, a 20-fold increase; Sydney developed into a proper city; and the continent's interior was further explored (Clarke 2003, 71). But for all the good Macquarie did, for which he is often known today as "the father of Australia," he was dismissed in disgrace in 1821. He had angered the wealthy by promoting the economic power of emancipated convicts. He had frustrated the British colonial office by his inability to cut back expenditures, in part caused by the influx of 19,000 new convicts between 1814 and 1821; another factor in the cost of running the colony in these years was a string of bad luck with weather, flooding, and caterpillars. To keep people busy and the economy working, Macquarie responded by creating public works projects. Dozens of new towns, hundreds of buildings, and more than 300 miles (480 km) of roads to connect all of these new structures to each other and to the capital in Sydney were built by out-of-work convicts. A report written by John Thomas Bigge outlined Macquarie's activities from the point of view of the disgruntled wealthy elite, who wanted Macquarie replaced. This was done in late 1821, when Sir Thomas Brisbane arrived in the colony as the sixth governor of New South Wales. Macquarie sailed to London in February 1822 and died just two and a half years later, dejected that his efforts to raise the poor and emancipated convicts in the colony had been thwarted.

After Macquarie's departure, the class structure of New South Wales was no longer that of a penitentiary but of a full-fledged colony. In 1823 the British Parliament signed the papers granting New South Wales full colonial status, and Van Diemen's Land was legally separated from the mainland colony (Clark 1995, 52). Governors Brisbane and Darling, who between them led the New South Wales colony through 1831, were ordered to roll back the policies of previous governors with regard to rewarding freed convicts with land and laborers. Instead, land grants were made available only to those with at least £250 available to them for improvements and investment. This meant that native-born white Australians and freed convicts were usually excluded, while free immigrants began to swell the numbers of the local elite.

This is not to say, however, that the emancipists, former convicts, and native-born white Australians accepted the concept of their inferiority to the "exclusives," the term for those wealthy few who had entered the colony as free migrants. Many still believed that the land of Australia belonged to them as its natural inheritors and that they deserved a "fair go" because of their race (Clarke 2003, 81); Aboriginal Australians and other nonwhites were not seen to be deserving of this privilege. Their voice became public in 1824, when William Charles Wentworth, who had been born en route to Australia in 1790, and Dr. Robert Wardell began publishing their emancipist newspaper, the *Australian*. In many ways, these two created the white Australian identity; before 1824 the term *Australian* had been used to refer only to Aboriginal people. By 1830, thanks to Wentworth and Wardell, it was used predominantly to refer to native-born whites.

In the same period, when battles of words between emancipists and exclusives dominated New South Wales politics, in Van Diemen's Land Governor George Arthur was fighting a war of attrition against the Indigenous population. The Black War against Aboriginal Tasmanians, which began about 1825, included a period of martial law after 1828, during which it was legal to shoot any Aboriginal person seen in or around white settlements. In 1830 this policy was expanded with the creation of the Black Line. This entailed arming every white man in the colony, including convicts, about 2,200 people in total; lining them up across northern Tasmania; and attempting to push the Aboriginal people south, where they would be isolated in controllable locations. This effort failed when only two people were captured, but between 1830 and 1834 the island's remaining Aboriginal population was rounded up on Arthur's orders and removed to Flinders Island (Macintyre 2004, 65); the few survivors returned to a small reservation in southern Van Diemen's Land in 1847.

The last inhabitant of this reserve, Trugannini, died in 1876, giving rise to the myth that the Tasmanian people died out entirely. Far from their dying out, the 2001 Australian census found that nearly 16,000 people identify themselves as Aboriginal Tasmanian. Many of these are the descendants of Aboriginal Tasmanian women who fled from Arthur's soldiers and other efforts to round them up and European sealers who lived on Tasmania's many offshore islands (Perkins 2008, episode 2). While their Aboriginal languages have all but disappeared, many other aspects of their societies and culture survive to the present day.

The other important event in this period was the founding in 1829 of Australia's first free colony at Swan River, contemporary Perth, in Western Australia. The motivation behind this settlement, as was the case on the east coast, was preventing the French from settling in the region. Likewise, the Swan River colony awarded large grants of land to those who claimed to have the capital to work it. The major difference between the colonies was the fact that Swan River took no convicts; however, this does not mean that it was worked by free laborers. Instead of convicts, the new colony was worked by indentured laborers imported from Britain, whose time and effort were as controlled by legal contracts as those of convicts.

The Last Colonial Push, 1831–1850

Unlike the British settlements at Port Jackson, Swan River, and Van Diemen's Land, which had been motivated at least in part by a desire to prevent the French from colonizing Australia, the new colonies of Victoria and South Australia were entirely domestically driven. Victoria, or Port Phillip as it was called at the time, was eventually carved out of the larger New South Wales colony after colonial officials were pushed by the actions of a few investors from Van Diemen's Land.

John Batman arrived at Port Phillip in 1835 as the representative of the Port Phillip Bay Association, which hoped to settle the mainland region just across Bass Strait from Van Diemen's Land. The association expected to import thousands of cattle to the relatively lush lands of Port Phillip, which had been explored in 1824 by Hamilton Hume when he walked the 560 miles (900 km) from Port Jackson to Port Phillip. Batman provides the only known example of land negotiations and a treaty between colonizers and Aboriginal people in Australia. He purchased about 100,000 acres of land around Port Phillip at the cost of "20 pairs of blankets, 30 knives, 12 tomahawks, 10 looking glasses, 12 pairs of scissors, 50 handkerchiefs, 12 red shirts, 4 flannel jackets, 4 suits, and 50 pounds of flour" (Clark 1995, 85). With this bargain of a purchase, Batman created panic in the minds of colonial officials in Sydney and London alike; the transaction was seen to throw all previous British land acquisitions into doubt and thus could not be considered legal by the New South Wales governor or the London offices.

Nonetheless, in 1836, just one year after Batman's claims along the Yarra River were rejected by these officials, settlers began to move into the new region, forcing the colonial office to recognize the new colony under Superintendent William Lonsdale. The main city was laid out in 1839 by Robert Hoddle and named *Melbourne,* after Britain's prime minister at the time, Viscount Melbourne. Until 1850 the region was subordinate to the colonial headquarters in Sydney, but in that year Charles LaTrobe, who had been superintendent since 1839, became the first lieutenant governor of the new colony of Victoria (Clarke 2003, 107–108).

While Port Phillip, as part of New South Wales, accepted convict labor until 1840, South Australia was formed as Australia's only convict-free colony in 1836. Rather than settling the new land through land grants and convict labor, in South Australia land was to be sold at artificially established prices, high enough to prevent the poor and freed convicts from buying it. The proceeds from these sales would then be used to fund the transportation of willing laborers to work the new territories (Clarke 2002, 38–39). This project was jointly enacted by the British government and a joint-stock company, the South Australian Company (SAC), which controlled the sale of land and the funds raised.

From the beginning, this was an awkward marriage of two very different systems with two very different personalities at their head. John Hindmarsh, the first governor appointed from London, and James Hurtle Fisher, the first commissioner appointed by the SAC, fought incessantly (Clarke 2002, 47). At the same time, the vast majority of the land that was sold off to investors continued to sit unused, valuable only as a commodity to be bought and sold on the free market. In the first four years of existence, South Australia produced only 443 acres (180 ha) of productive farmland and laborers sat idle, living off supplies provided by the colony's sponsors in Britain (Clarke 2002, 47).

Fortunately, after this difficult start, conditions improved in South Australia under George Gawler, who replaced both Hindmarsh and Fisher in 1838. Rather than relying on a market-driven land policy, Gawler invested heavily in infrastructure for the colony, using both government and corporate funds to pay some of the 10,400 new laborers who arrived between 1838 and 1840 to build the city of Adelaide, among other projects. In the process he overspent his meager £12,000 budget by more than a quarter of a million pounds and was recalled in 1841 to London, where he found his reputation in tatters (Hetherington 1966). Nonetheless, Gawler had saved the colony from ruin and even set the stage for colonial prosperity. Cattle, sheep, gardening, and wine became the lifeblood of the new colony with a population that differed significantly from that of the other Australian colonies. Lacking an image of the degenerate convict, South Australia presented a more civilized front to the world, with its combination of free English settlers and German Lutherans, who had been driven from their homeland by religious persecution (Welsh 2004, 145).

In conjunction with the creation of new settlements, there was also at this time a push inland as white settlements grew and expanded along the coast. In the 1830s Edward Eyre, who had arrived from England in 1833, started moving sheep overland across vast distances. After several overland trips to Adelaide and one mostly by sea to the Swan River in the west, Eyre set off in 1840 on the journey that made him famous. On June 18 Eyre, six other white men, two Aboriginal men, 13 horses, 40 sheep, and provisions for the group for three months departed from Adelaide in search of grazing pastures, water, and other resources for the benefit of pastoral Australia. Central Australia, however, contained no territory suitable for a pastoral paradise, and Eyre struggled almost from the very beginning. Pushing northward he was stopped by such barriers as Mount Hopeless and Lake Torrens, a tributary of Lake Eyre. Thwarted in his northward exploration, Eyre sent much of his party home and with just one white companion, a trusted Aboriginal companion named Wylie, and two other Aboriginal scouts turned his sights to the west, where his luck was not much better. The scouts murdered Eyre's white companion and stole most of the group's provisions, leaving Eyre and Wylie to push westward alone. They made it to the coast near contemporary Esperance, Western Australia, where a French ship welcomed them aboard and replenished their stores, and finally to Albany, Western Australia. Although he had relatively little to show for his inland exploration, Eyre was awarded the founder's gold medal of the Royal Geographic Society in 1847. He later served as one of the government's most knowledgeable protectors of Aboriginal people from 1841 to 1844 (Dutton 1966).

Following in Eyre's footsteps, his acquaintance Charles Sturt (the two had met in 1837) also longed to be the first explorer to discover the vast inland sea that most people still believed existed in the center of the continent. Sturt had spent his early years in Australia exploring in the north, charting its rivers inland and even "discovering" and "naming" the Darling and Murray Rivers. These, in fact, were to be his most celebrated accomplishments for his 1844 expedition, which began by following the course of the Murray-Darling northward, led him into the Simpson Desert, where he finally had to acknowledge that his quest for an inland sea was doomed to failure (Gibbney 1967).

In addition to the creation of new settlements and the exploration of new territory, another important trend between 1831 and 1850 was the influx of free laborers who migrated to Australia, both with and without assistance from the British government. In part this infusion of free individuals and families came about with the cessation of transportation to New South Wales in 1840. In the early years of the 19th century, the British had created an image of Botany Bay and all of Britain's settlements in Australia as "hell upon earth" (White 1981, 16) in order to deter potential criminals from their crimes. As a result of the propaganda, criminals sentenced to transportation often cried at the thought of exile, while members of British polite society feared even accidentally rubbing shoulders with those who had worked as jailers and other officials in the colony (White 1981, 16–20). Stories of rampant drunkenness, debauchery, sodomy, and even cannibalism among convicts and soldiers alike circulated throughout Britain as cheap novels created for commercial success became the source of ethnographic "facts" about the colony. Although this image outlasted the actual policy of transportation, with its elimination the possibility of great wealth began to outstrip the myth of hell on earth and greater numbers of free investors and laborers began arriving. Migration started to expand in this decade and exploded in the next, as a result not only of the diminishment of Botany Bay's negative image but of the discovery of gold.

Conclusion

Between 1606 and 1850 Australia went from being a legend among European seafarers to one of the most prosperous regions of the British Empire. The colony's rocky start, when food shortages, Aboriginal resistance, and unfamiliar ecology made even survival difficult, was overcome, and, with the help of sheep and cattle, prosperity began to be the norm rather than the exception. There were difficult moments along the way, even after the vast grazing lands beyond Sydney's Blue Mountains were opened. For example, the depression of 1840 produced a sharp decrease in the value of land and stock. But even with this downturn, 1840 is often cited as a key year in the development of the Australian financial system: The colony's non-Aboriginal economy outpaced the Aboriginal one in terms of gross domestic product (GDP) for the first time, and market economy principles surpassed those of colonial dependency (Butlin 1994). According to Butlin, by 1848 the combined Aboriginal and non-Aboriginal GDP had finally surpassed the Aboriginal GDP of 1788, and wealth in wool, cattle, and other primary industries had established a firm base for the burgeoning urban economy. By 1850 Australia was host to more than 500 industrial companies, about half of which operated in the new cities of Sydney and Melbourne; the other half were flour mills that by necessity were located closer to the source of their raw material (Molony 2005, 119). Together the extraction of resources and their processing provided a firm economic base upon which was built a wealthy provincial society after the discovery of gold in New South Wales and Victoria just one year into the second half of the 19th century.

4

GOLD RUSH AND GOVERNMENTS (1851–1890)

From the earliest days of the 19th century, small amounts of gold had been found throughout the New South Wales colony. Convict builders of the Great Western Road, which stretched over the Blue Mountains and Bathurst Plains, found small flakes of gold as early as 1815, while similar finds occurred in other areas of New South Wales in the 1820s and 1830s (Johnson 2007, 24). While the new colony could certainly have used the revenue from this valuable mineral, most colonial leaders sought to keep the news under wraps. The administrators' problem was that New South Wales was a penal colony at this time, and thus its image was supposed to be one of deprivation in order to deter potential criminals in Britain from committing crimes. News of easily obtainable wealth in the colony would not have served the jailers well, and thus it was suppressed for many decades.

Gold in New South Wales

By midcentury, however, with the initial cessation of punitive transportation to New South Wales in 1840 and fear of population decline in response to the California gold rush of 1849, gold took center stage in Australia, with the bureaucrats' blessings. The first person to hit pay dirt was Edward Hargraves, an English-born Australian who had traveled to California to try his hand at prospecting in 1849–50. While there he recognized that California's goldfields resembled the terrain of New South Wales. In January 1851 Hargraves returned to Sydney and set off with John Lister to find gold. Their first good luck was at Lewis Ponds Creek, where they found five specks of the precious metal; they were soon joined by William, James, and Henry Tom, and their finds at

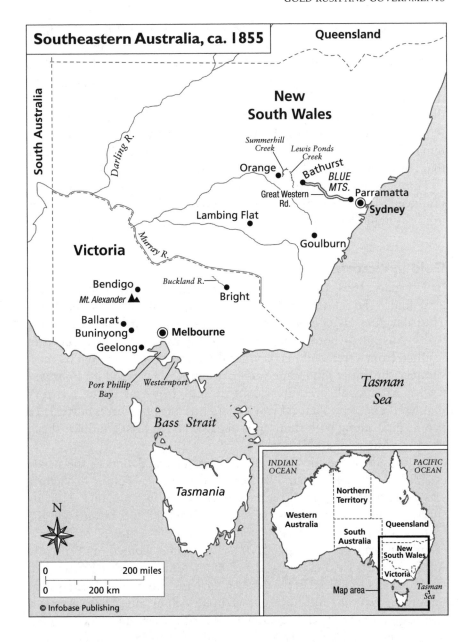

Southeastern Australia, ca. 1855

Queensland

New South Wales

South Australia

Darling R.

Summerhill Creek

Lewis Ponds Creek

Orange

Bathurst

BLUE MTS.

Great Western Rd.

Parramatta

Sydney

Lambing Flat

Murray R.

Goulburn

Victoria

Bendigo

Mt. Alexander ▲▲

Buckland R.

Bright

Ballarat

Buninyong

Geelong

Melbourne

Port Phillip Bay

Westernport

Tasman Sea

Bass Strait

Tasmania

N

0   200 miles
0   200 km

© Infobase Publishing

INDIAN OCEAN

PACIFIC OCEAN

Northern Territory

Western Australia

South Australia

Queensland

New South Wales

Victoria

Map area

Tasman Sea

Summerhill Creek near Bathurst encouraged Hargraves to publicize the news far and wide.

Rather than obtaining gold wealth itself, Hargraves's motive seems to have been a desire to claim the £10,000 governmental reward for having found gold in the colony. In subsequent years, while Hargraves was leading the comfortable life of a successful explorer, his team members fought bitterly for recognition of their part in the initial finds at Lewis Ponds and Summerhill Creeks. Their tenacity was rewarded in 1853 with a £1,000 reward each and then in 1890 with full recognition by the legislative assembly that "Messrs Tom and Lister were undoubtedly the first discoverers of gold obtained in Australia in payable quantity" (cited in Mitchell 1972, 347). In the end, however, Hargraves's story remains the founding myth of Australia's gold rush, and it is his name that has been associated ever since with the initial finds of 1851.

Throughout the decade of the 1850s New South Wales's goldfields produced about 140 tons of the precious metal and attracted diggers from throughout the world.

Gold in Victoria

In February 1851 just a month after Hargraves and Lister's initial gold finds, the south coast of Port Phillip suffered from the Black Thursday fires, which burned from Westernport in the east to the South Australian border in the west (Molony 2005, 121). The fires resulted from a tremendous drought the previous year, so that by mid-summer the entire landscape was parched. A north wind on February 6 whipped a small fire out of control until a quarter of the territory that would become Victoria just six months later had been burned; 12 people died, along with thousands of cattle and at least a million sheep (Romsey Australia 2008).

As a result of the fires, as well as a loss of population to the newly established goldfields around Bathurst, when the new colony of Victoria was proclaimed on July 1, the new government was anxious about its survival. The new legislative assembly offered a £200 reward for the first significant amount of gold found within 200 miles of Melbourne (Commonwealth of Australia 2007). The gambit worked, and in early August Thomas Hiscock, a blacksmith from Buninyong, discovered gold. His find was announced in the *Geelong Advertiser* on August 12, and soon Buninyong was the third-busiest town in the colony, after Melbourne and Geelong (Buninyong and District Historical Society, Inc. 2005). Soon news of even greater finds was reported from nearby Ballarat, which at the time was nothing more than a sheep station, and by November the world's richest goldfield had been opened on and around Mount Alexander in what is today Castlemaine (Molony 2005, 122).

Within days of the publication of Hiscock's find in Buninyong, the Victorian government had changed its attitude toward gold prospectors.

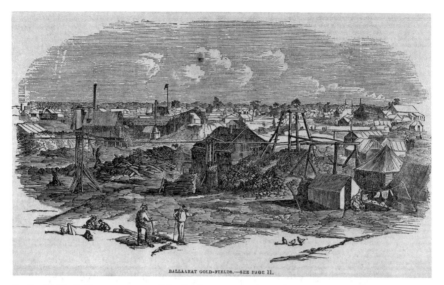

BALLAARAT GOLD-FIELDS.—SEE PAGE 11.

In the 1860s Ballarat was one of the busiest cities in Australia, owing to its goldfields.
(Picture Collections, State Library of Victoria)

From offering a financial reward for the discovery of gold, the government under Lieutenant Governor LaTrobe began staking a claim to all the gold found in the colony. British law at the time stated clearly that mineral rights were retained by the Crown rather than private landowners or individual diggers. Rather than claiming all Victorian gold for itself, however, the legislative assembly began charging prospectors and diggers a licensing fee of 30 shillings (one pound, 10 shillings) per month. Many prospectors took great umbrage with this fee, which had to be paid prior to commencing any search for gold, and on August 25, 1851, the first protests against the fee erupted in Buninyong on the very day the policy was announced there (Buninyong and District Historical Society, Inc. 2005).

During the 1850s miners and independent diggers took more than 1,000 tons of gold out of the ground in Victoria; when that was combined with that removed from New South Wales, Australian gold constituted 40 percent of the world's production for the decade (Molony 2005, 122). As a result of this tremendous boom, the population of Victoria exploded, from a mere 80,000 people in 1851 to more than half a million in 1861 (Clarke 2003, 116); the total population of Australia hit 1 million in 1861. The initial gold finds in New South Wales and Victoria also led prospectors to search the rest of the Australian continent. In 1859 gold was found in Canoona, Queensland; in 1867 in

Gympie, Queensland; in 1873 in Palmer River, Queensland; in 1872–73 in the Northern Territory; in 1885 in the Kimberley district of Western Australia; and in the 1890s the continent's last gold rushes occurred at Kalgoorlie and Coolgardie, both in Western Australia (Johnson 2007, 25). Today gold mining continues at various sites in Australia, especially in Western Australia and South Australia, making the country the third-largest extractor of this metal in the world (Geoscience Australia 2008).

Social and Economic Changes

Although Australian society had undergone significant changes in each decade from 1788 onward, the first decade of the gold rush produced some of the most long-lasting and significant changes. The first to be felt at the local level was large-scale population movement away from cities and agrarian towns to the goldfields. This affected every aspect of life in the Australian colonies, from law and order to food production. By the end of 1851, Melbourne was down to just two police constables, the rest having quit their jobs to prospect for gold in central Victoria (Johnson 2007, 25). Wheat production in Victoria plummeted almost 75 percent in the first two years of that colony's gold rush, from 30,023 acres (12,150 ha) in 1851 to 8,006 acres (3,240 ha) in 1853 (Cowie). Sheep and cattle were left untended as well, sparking fear of mass starvation throughout the colonies. As a result of these shortages, the price of food skyrocketed and even the simplest fare of bread, cabbage, potatoes, and eggs could cost a day's wages or more (Symons 1982, 60).

About six months after the initial exodus from Australia's towns and cities into the goldfields, the colonies began to experience a massive influx of migrants seeking instant mineral wealth. Britons, many of whom had forsaken the possibility of wealth in California because of the reputation of its goldfields for lawlessness, flocked to Australia, with its well-established British laws and customs. British and Irish miners were also joined by young, educated, and largely middle-class men from France, Germany, Italy, and the Americas, as well as others from throughout the world.

While all miners suffered the difficult conditions of payment of licenses and standing in pits that rapidly filled with water and occasionally collapsed, killing the miners inside, two groups stand out as having had the worst experiences: Chinese and Aboriginal people. The former, who first arrived in Victoria in about 1855, numbered 24,062 by 1861 (Clark 1995, 140). They arrived in large teams of 600 to 700

Fear and distrust of the Chinese were rampant in Australia from the early 1850s until well into the 20th century. Popular images of the time did nothing to educate the public as to the true conditions under which these men lived and worked. (Rare Printed Collections, State Library of Victoria)

men, mostly as indentured laborers, who searched for scattered remains of gold in abandoned mine shafts and other locations that had been vacated by European miners. Most had little to show for their hard work because their contracts stipulated that they turn over the preponderance of their earnings to the headmen who had sponsored their voyages. Despite these factors, white miners reacted with fear to the presence of this culturally and racially distinct group (Johnson 2007, 26). As a result, the legislative councils of both Victoria and New South Wales passed laws restricting Chinese entry to the colonies and limiting the movement of those already there. Nevertheless, the pull of gold was so great that Chinese miners began landing in South Australia and walking hundreds of miles to Victoria's goldfields, often in single-file lines of up to 700 men (Clark 1995, 141–142). Fearful of loss of their jobs and reduction of their wages, white miners occasionally took the law into their own hands, for example, in 1857 at the Buckland River in Victoria and in 1861 at Lambing Flat in New South Wales. Nearly 1,000 people participated in the storm of violence in 1861, when even European women and their children suffered if they were found to be associated in any way with Chinese miners. The all-white, all-male juries that heard the cases in Goulburn formally acquitted every plaintiff on the charges of rioting, while the more serious and accurate charges of murder and rape were never taken to court (Clark 1995, 142).

The displacement of the Aboriginal populations of central Victoria and New South Wales that had begun in the late 18th and early 19th centuries was completed in the 1850s by the large influx of whites, Chinese, and other miners. A few Aboriginal communities attempted to maintain their small-scale food-collecting way of life, but for the most part those who remained in these regions became an impoverished lower class. Some Aboriginal men worked doing odd jobs in and around the goldfields and towns or traded fish, game, or handmade tools and artwork, while some Aboriginal women were pulled into prostitution or begging. A few Aboriginal men took up positions as shepherds or stockmen to replace the white laborers who left to dig for gold, but even these positions were tenuous; when the white men returned, having been largely unsuccessful in their diggings, Aboriginal men were immediately turned out. Some men and women suffered from alcohol abuse, and most children were at least partially malnourished. Introduced European diseases, from influenza to syphilis, further eroded the viability of Aboriginal communities, and the murder of Aboriginal people was not an uncommon occurrence in the goldfields. The few Aboriginal families and individuals who escaped the ravages of these features of colonial life struggled to survive on the margins of the white world. Just as other diggers were, they were required to purchase licenses to engage in mining, and the argument that the land and thus its resources belonged to them failed to hold sway with the goldfields commissioners (Clark and Cahir 2001).

Starting in about 1855, coincidentally the same year as the first Chinese arrived in southeastern Australian goldfields, once readily accessible alluvial gold became more difficult to find. From this period forward, the real money was made by companies with the capital to invest in machinery rather than by individual diggers. Miners who remained in the fields mostly sold their labor to these large companies and perhaps did a bit of digging and panning on the side. As a result of this shift, many of those who had left their urban and agrarian jobs throughout Australia went back to them.

Merchants and others who catered to the nouveau riche were particularly fortunate, and many grew wealthy by importing foodstuffs such as Irish butter, English ham, and American ice and "champagne" (Symons 1982, 60–61). But laborers, too, benefited from the influx of wealth in Australian society, and many were able to buy homes and luxuries that only the richest in European society could afford. In 1859

Henry Kingsley wrote in his novel *The Recollections of Geoffry Hamlyn* that the Australian condition was a "working-man's paradise" (cited in Symons 1982, 62), and just a year later Australians were the wealthiest people per capita in the world (Harcourt 2008), with per capita income 50 percent higher than in the United States and 100 percent higher than in Britain (Molony 2005, 136–137).

Political Changes

The many social and economic changes wrought on Australian society in the 1850s had both immediate and long-term political ramifications. The most immediate occurred in December 1852, when the British authorities decided to end all convict transportation to Australia's east coast. This decision was made partly in response to pressure brought to bear by free settlers and Australian-born leaders who wanted to see their country prosper as a real colony rather than the final resting place of Britain's criminal class. The other factor in the decision, however, was gold. With thousands of middle-class migrants paying for their passage to the gold fields of New South Wales and Victoria, it made little sense to spend governmental funds to ship criminals to a place where they could potentially become millionaires at the end of their sentences (Clark 1995, 131). The last convict ship, the *St. Vincent,* arrived in Van Diemen's Land in early 1853, and in late winter that year, on August 10, a festival was held to celebrate the closure of this phase of the island's history.

While the end of transportation had been a central political issue in both Australia and Britain for several decades prior to Hargraves's find near Bathurst, some of the other ramifications of his discovery were the direct result of either the gold itself or the activities it engendered. One of the most widely cited examples is the Eureka Stockade and miners' revolt in Ballarat in late 1854.

From almost the first week that gold was discovered in Victoria the colonial government had been charging miners a 30-shilling fee for a miner's license. For miners who struck it rich in Ballarat or Bendigo this was easily affordable; however, many miners considered it unfair to charge them for the license prior to their finding any gold. They also thought that they were unfairly paying to maintain a colonial government that they had had no say in choosing. The final indignity was from the commissioners on the goldfields, who had the right to request that a miner show his license at any time. Starting in 1852, when they were allowed to keep half the fees they collected from illegal miners, these commissioners took their jobs very seriously and began using harassment and violence to check licenses (LaCroix 1992, 208).

As a result of these outrages, as well as the poverty many miners suffered when surface or alluvial gold disappeared from the fields by 1853, there were occasional demonstrations and publications rallying against the license fee scheme and the lack of representative government (Public Record Office 2003). The most important of these stemmed from the Ballarat Reform League, whose 1854 charter was a statement of democratic ideals that challenged the colonial status quo on every level. Instead of working with the miners to resolve their issues, the goldfields commissioner, Robert Rede, increased the pressure on them, leading to a riot on October 30.

This riot was probably the last straw in a series of events that were building toward the eventual denouement of the Eureka Stockade, Australia's only armed rebellion against the British. On the evening of the 30th the miners met on Bakery Hill and raised the flag of the Southern Cross, which, with its blue background and white cross and stars, represents the most obvious constellation in the Southern Hemisphere. Using the flag as their sacred object, the miner Peter Lalor led hundreds of others in swearing an oath of allegiance: "We swear by the Southern Cross to stand truly by each other and fight to defend our rights and liberties" (Eureka Centre 2008). The flag was later moved to the Eureka diggings, and, on December 1, a large wooden stockade was erected around about an acre of land to protect the flag and men.

At dawn Sunday, December 3, 1854, Commissioner Rede and the numerous soldiers in his command finally put an end to the miners' protest. The battle was over almost before it even began. Only about 150 miners were stationed behind the walls of the stockade, and most of them had abandoned their watch posts in favor of a night's sleep. On the government's side, no such relaxation was permitted. By 3:30 A.M. a contingent of about 276 soldiers and police had encircled most of the stockade, but it was not until 4:45 A.M. that a sentry within the stockade noticed the soldiers less than 300 yards away and fired a warning shot. Lalor reacted immediately to the warning by standing on a stump to warn his troops to wait until the soldiers were closer before firing; by placing himself in such a position, he received several gunshot wounds and had to have his arm amputated after the event. Many other leaders were not even present for the brief, 15- to 20-minute skirmish. Nonetheless, the battle was not without its dramatic moments. For example, the Canadian miner Captain Ross died defending the Southern Cross flag, thus allowing Constable John King to haul it down and carry it away. At least 23 other miners also died on that day, and dozens of others were wounded by the superiorly armed soldiers, of whom five or six perished and 12 were wounded (Goodman 1994).

By 7:00 A.M. the same day, the police and soldiers had arrested 120 diggers, torn down the stockade, and cleaned up the remains of the battle. Most of these 120 men were later released without charge, but 13 were charged with high treason and tried in Melbourne in January (Public Record Office 2003, Goodman 1994). The first man tried on these charges was John Joseph, an African American, while all the other Americans arrested as part of the revolt had previously been released on petitions by the U.S. consul in Melbourne. Not a single miner, including Joseph, was convicted, and many of the rebellion's leaders later held important positions in the colony. Peter Lalor, who evaded capture on the day because of his injuries, went on to become the speaker of the legislative assembly of Victoria.

The ramifications of the Eureka Stockade, as this event has become known, have been a source of debate among both historians and political scientists ever since. At the time it led to significant changes in the goldfields, including the replacement of license fees with a one-pound "miner's right" fee, which allowed a miner to vote, and a 3 percent export duty (LaCroix 1992, 214). The Gold Fields Act of 1855 also created miners' courts, with nine elected members to settle disputes and set claim sizes (LaCroix 1992, 215).

Over the long run, however, the consequences of the Eureka Stockade have been more difficult to pinpoint. For example, the historian Manning Clark saw in the events the birth of Australian nationalism and democracy, while others have been more circumspect in their analysis. David Goodman believes that the most the events achieved was a slight transformation in public opinion against colonial government (Goodman 1994). Without a doubt, however, the Eureka Stockade was an important moment in Australian history.

Governments

One of the most significant changes to the Australian colonies in the 1850s was the provision for self-rule that the British Parliament had conceded to all but Western Australia by 1859. The process actually began as early as 1842, when New South Wales gained the right to self-rule through a legislative council. In 1850 this was expanded with the Australian Colonies Act, which not only separated Port Phillip from New South Wales but also created legislative councils for Victoria, Van

Diemen's Land, and South Australia when it took effect in July 1851. After much consideration and political maneuvering both in Britain and in the colonies, an electoral formula was agreed upon: Ten members, or one third, of each council would be appointed by the governor of each colony while 20 members would be elected, with priority given to large landowners.

The next phase in the gradual establishment of self-rule was at the end of 1852, when the colonial office in London invited the four legislative councils to begin penning constitutions, continuing the almost inevitable march toward independence. The vociferous discussions that this invitation engendered led to the hardening of two radically different views of the kind of society Australians wanted to see in their newly emerging country. Conservatives wanted the new constitutions to reflect the interests of large landowners, while liberals favored a more democratic system.

While at first conservatives were able to dictate the form of government to be established in each colony, this period lasted for only a couple of years. Between 1856 and 1858 New South Wales and Victoria had given all men the vote for the lower house and had lifted the property ownership requirement for serving on that body; by 1861 the same had occurred in South Australia and Tasmania, as Van Diemen's Land was called after 1855. When Queensland was created in 1859 from the northern regions of New South Wales, that colony adopted the same amended constitution as New South Wales. While women and Aboriginal people still had many years to wait for the franchise, the democratic process had begun to break down the British class system inherited by the colonies.

Governing the Land and Its People

While the period 1850–59 was a decade of establishing governments in the five free Australian colonies, the 1860s was a decade in which liberals used those governments to transform the societies in which they lived. Manning Clark calls the period from 1861 through 1883 "the Age of the Bourgeoisie" (1995, 151), while Frank Clarke refers to it as "the Long Boom" (2003, 121). The expansion of wealth produced by the gold rush of the previous period led to a desire for greater political involvement among previously unrepresented groups, such as merchants and laborers. As a result, the squatters or exclusives, who had dominated all aspects of Australian colonial life until the 1850s, began having to listen to and even act upon the wishes of others. One of the first wishes of the newly emerging classes of influential people was opening up access to the millions of acres of land that had previously been tied up by pastoral squatters. In 1861 a liberal government in New South Wales dominated by Premier Charles Cowper, John Robertson, and Henry Parkes passed two land acts, the Alienation Act and the Occupation Act, which finally allowed for the purchase of Crown lands. The price was set at one pound per acre, with 20 percent due at the time of sale and the rest within three years. The idea was originally despised by the conservative landowners who dominated the upper chamber of parliament but did eventually pass and thus served as a model for Victoria's Duffy Act in 1862 and later Queensland's Selection Act in 1868 and South Australia's Strangways Act in 1869.

Despite the intention of providing access to land, the judgment of history on these acts has largely been negative (Davidson 1981). Most "selectors," the term coined in 1868 to refer to people who purchased the 80- to 640-acre (32- to 260-ha) parcels of land (Johnson 2007, 45), remained miserably poor as they struggled with infertile soil, inconsistent rainfall, and plots that were too small to provide an adequate living under these conditions. Victoria and New South Wales experienced a rapid rise in bushranging in these decades as the sons of marginal farmers found other ways of occupying themselves when family plots failed or simply could not be divided among a group of brothers. The most famous of these selector-era bushrangers was Edward "Ned" Kelly (Clarke 2003, 128). Henry Lawson, one of Australia's best-known writers, was also a selector's son but instead of taking to a life of crime, the young Lawson moved to the city and began eulogizing the rural way of life in his poems and short stories.

Perhaps because of differences in the implementation of their land acts, or differences in climate and ecology, selectors in South Australia

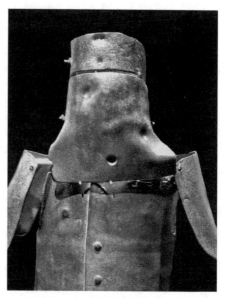

Ned Kelly's armor from the firefight at Glenrowan in June 1880 (Neale Cousland/ Shutterstock)

NED KELLY

Ned Kelly was born in 1855, the first of eight children of an emancipist who had been transported to Van Diemen's Land in 1841, and his native-born wife. Upon his father's death in 1866, Ned left school and took up bushranging, interspersed with legitimate work in the timber industry and assisting his stepfather, George King, in horse theft.

Despite this early criminal activity, the real turning point in Ned's life occurred in 1878, when a corrupt policeman went to the Kelly/King residence to arrest Ned's younger brother for horse theft and then claimed that Ned shot at him; the truth of this claim has never been determined. As a result, both Ned and his brother went into hiding, along with their friends Joe Byrne and Steve Hart: the Kelly gang was born. The foursome killed two policemen, one in self-defense, the other during a shoot-out between the two groups. The Kelly gang went on to capture a sheep station and rob several banks, netting them more than £4,000.

The Kelly gang could not run from law indefinitely, and the end finally occurred on June 28, 1880. They had been planning a train robbery in the town of Glenrowan, Victoria, and had captured about 60 people in the town's hotel bar in preparation for their heist. They foolishly allowed the town's schoolteacher to leave the hotel, and he warned the train crew of their plans. Instead of holding up the train, the Kelly gang met a band of policemen in the early dawn of June 28, and even their homemade body armor could not save them. Ned was the only gang member to be captured alive, though he had been shot in the legs where his armor could not protect him. Joe Byrne was killed in the shoot-out, while Dan Kelly and Steve Hart are reported to have committed suicide. Ned was later tried and sentenced to hang in the Melbourne jail, which occurred on November 11, 1880.

generally did not suffer the great failure rates of those in Victoria and New South Wales. They still worked extraordinarily hard to make their wheat and other farms viable, but many were able to survive as farmers on their plots. As a result, farmers in South Australia opened up about 2 million acres (809,371 ha) of land through the selection process and by the end of the 1860s were producing half of all Australian wheat (Clarke 2003, 129).

In Queensland, too, selectors did not suffer to the same degree as those in Victoria and New South Wales. However, the real agricultural story in Queensland from the 1860s was the development of plantation farming of cotton and sugarcane. Both of these were viable crops in the tropical and semitropical north, along with cattle, but it was sugarcane that was the real growth industry after 1864. In that year Queensland's parliament passed the Sugar and Coffee Regulations, which released land for plantation agriculture; the result was that by 1881 the colony was producing more than 19,000 tons (17,236,510 kg) of processed sugar (Irvine 2004, 3).

In addition to extra land, this industry could develop only by using very cheap labor. In this case, the labor was provided by indentured servants introduced from the neighboring Melanesian islands of New Guinea, Vanuatu, the Solomon Islands, and elsewhere; they were referred to as *Kanakas* in the original documents. During a 40-year period beginning in 1863, more than 62,000 indentured Melanesians worked in Queensland (Mortensen 2000, Irvine 2004).

While a small number of Melanesians had previously been imported to Queensland, the era of "blackbirding" began in earnest in 1863. In that year Henry Ross Lewin, working under Captain Robert Towns, the owner of a large cotton plantation on the Logan River (Mortensen 2000), began importing Melanesian laborers. Prior to 1880 indentured Melanesians worked in many different capacities in Queensland, including tending sheep and cattle, fishing, pearl shell diving and processing, domestic service, cotton, and sugarcane. Starting in 1880, however, a change in Queensland law restricted Kanakas to "tropical and semi-tropical agriculture" and thus kept them largely tied to sugar plantations (Mortensen 2000).

The nature of this labor exchange has been of great interest since the period in which it began. At the time many people and organizations, including the Anti-Slavery Society, the Royal Navy, even Queen Victoria herself, considered the practice to be inhumane or outright slavery (Mortensen 2000). Not surprisingly, planters and merchants argued against the slavery claim (Mortensen 2000), and this point of view was largely upheld in Australian courts at the time. Henry Ross Lewin's name has frequently been linked to the illegal practices of impersonating missionaries to lure islanders onto European ships or just outright kidnapping men and women from their villages (Mortensen 2000). At the same time, at least a quarter of the indentured laborers in the 1890s had already served at least one three-year term in Queensland and were returning for another (University of Sydney), and the 1992 *Call for Recognition* compiled by the Australian Human Rights and Equal Opportunity Commission claims that only between one quarter and one third of Queensland's indentured laborers "were 'in varying degrees illegal'" (cited in Irvine 2004, 4).

Despite the evidence that the Queensland plantation system was not as evil as that in the American South in its use of black laborers, it can be seen as both a cause and an effect of one of the worst aspects of Australian society, then and now: racism. Melanesian laborers were imported into Australia for two reasons, both of which had racism at their core. First, it was believed that whites could not work in the tropical heat but blacks would be unaffected by it, and the cost of white labor would have been financially unviable in labor-intensive sugarcane production. Second, having cheap black laborers in Australia contributed to the further development of "racism in the workers' movement, which was based on fear of cheap competition" (Molony 2005, 159–160). While some of those calling for an end to the practice of black indentured labor did so for humanitarian reasons, many were motivated by a racist desire for a "white Australia," and it was this interest that eventually ended the practice entirely in the early 20th century. This was achieved by the new Commonwealth government in 1901 through the Pacific Island Labourers Act, which ended the importation of Melanesian and Polynesian laborers after 1904 and allowed for the deportation of any who were still in Australia at the end of 1906, with almost no exceptions (Pacific Island Labourers Act 1901). After 31,301 of their friends and relatives died doing plantation work (Thompson 1994, 40) the last islanders were deported, some against their will, to make way for a "white Australia."

Education Policy

Despite the centrality of land and agricultural issues in the latter half of the 19th century, most Australians in this period were actually city dwellers. More than 65 percent of all Australians lived in cities and towns by the 1890s (Clarke 2003, 144), with "Marvelous Melbourne" the largest of all (Clarke 2003, 146–147). One of the most important priorities for many of these city dwellers was the development of an educational system to raise the status of their colonial sons and daughters.

Education had always had a role in the Australian colonies, even if primarily as a form of class-based social control (Snow 1991). The children of the colonial elite had been attending private religious schools in the cities and towns almost since the earliest days of the New South

Wales colony. Many of these children, especially the boys, then moved back to England to continue their education. At the same time, the children of the poorest families and single parents were often put into the orphan schools developed for girls in 1795 on Norfolk Island and 1801 in Sydney and for boys in 1818 in Sydney (Snow 1991, 257). Upon the arrival of Governor Macquarie in 1810 the Protestant educational system grew both in Sydney and in its immediate environs (Clark 1995, 37). This growth was further expanded in 1830, when the archdeacon of New South Wales recommended the formation of high schools "in which scholars would be given 'a liberal education,'" thus elevating elite boys and men above their "convict servants" (Clark 1995, 101).

Throughout this early period education in Australia largely meant religious education provided by priests and ministers, nuns and brothers. In the 1840s the liberal governors Bourke and Gipps both tried to break the grip of religious institutions on the schools in New South Wales, but in that colony, as well as in Van Diemen's Land, the liberals failed and education for many remained a purview of religious institutions (Clark 1995, 102–103). At the same time, each colony also funded a number of secular schools, thus draining their coffers twice to achieve the same, minimal results. In the first half of the 19th century only South Australia, with its relative lack of Roman Catholics and Anglicans, managed to create and maintain an entirely secular education system (Clark 1995, 103).

The political and economic changes produced in Australia by the gold rush transformed this educational setting. By the mid-1850s both New South Wales and Victoria had taken the step of creating secular, liberal universities, Sydney in 1850 and Melbourne in 1853 (Molony 2005, 133–134). In 1872 Victoria introduced the first Education Act in the colonies, which provided for free, secular, compulsory schooling for all children and ended state funding of religious schools; by 1875 this had resulted in the construction of 600 new schools (Government of Victoria 2008). By 1895 all the other colonies had followed suit (Clark 1995).

One group that did not approve of this policy were the Irish Catholics, many of whom thought that their taxes were being wasted on schools that were inappropriate for their children. In reaction, in the 1870s and 1880s they poured local and international resources into building Catholic schools and staffing them with priests, nuns, and brothers, mainly from Ireland (O'Farrell 2000, 108). Two competing results have stemmed from this development. On the one hand, Frank Clarke sees in the construction of these schools a physical and organizational structure for the continuation of Irish separatism until "well into the twentieth century" (2003, 144). On the other, Patrick O'Farrell believes that the vast resources poured into community development and the construction of imposing edifices contributed to a much greater integration of the Catholic community within itself and with the non-Catholic world (2000, 110), despite "their defiant profession of separate identity" (2000, 111). Building schools, as well as hospitals and churches, required "the goodwill, cooperation and trust of non-Catholics" in councils, banks, building companies, and other companies and organizations throughout the colonies (2000, 110).

One of the continuing legacies of this period of educational reform is that throughout Australia three kinds of schools developed alongside each other: Protestant schools with their largely bourgeois and squatter elite populations, Catholic schools with their largely Irish working-class populations, and state schools that catered to the Protestant working class, dissenters, atheists, and the poorest of the poor (Clark 1995, 172–173). While the population of students attending these different schools has changed over the past 130 years, the debate about what kind of educational system will work best for Australia has not ceased. In fact, in the second half of the 20th century the Australian government and its state counterparts reinstated the policy of funding religious schools, and the debate over public funding continues almost as briskly today as it did in 1870 (Gawenda 2008).

Further Exploration

Among the programs that the newly wealthy colonies funded in the 1860s–80s was exploration of the interior of their vast, dry continent. One of the most daring of these expeditions was that of Robert O'Hara Burke, usually known as the Burke and Wills Expedition but originally as the Victorian Exploring Expedition. After several years of fund-raising and planning, in late August 1860, Burke, William Wills, 17 other men, 24 camels, and 20 tons (18,144 kilograms) of supplies set off from Melbourne to walk to the north coast of the Gulf of Carpentaria (Phoenix 2008).

Despite the years of planning, the expedition was almost certainly doomed from the outset. Choosing Burke as leader was a compromise among several factions of the Exploration Committee, all of whom had supported people with greater experience. Burke had never been outside the settled areas of Australia, had no surveying experience, and was essentially a soldier, though even his war experience was extremely

CAMELS AND THEIR HANDLERS

Between 1840 and the 1930s about 20,000 camels were imported to Australia to assist in the exploration of the continent's dry inland regions. The first expedition to use a camel was the Horrocks Expedition of 1846, which used a single camel to carry supplies around Lake Torrens in South Australia. The first large-scale shipment of camels arrived in Australia in 1860 to accompany Burke and Wills on their ill-fated journey from Melbourne to the Gulf of Carpentaria; they were followed by thousands of others. In the 1930s these camels were replaced by trains, trucks, and other forms of transportation and about 20,000 domesticated animals were released into the wild. That population has multiplied to between half a million and a million head today, the world's largest wild camel population.

In addition to camels, about 2,000 "Afghan" cameleers entered Australia at this time. Many of these young men, who were from India, Pakistan, and Afghanistan, went home at the end of their three-year contracts. Others, however, decided to stay on, because they had done well in business or had married locally. As a result, Muslim communities developed in all Australian cities at the time, with mosques, markets, and other organizations springing up to support them. A number of "Afghans" in Australia in the late 19th and early 20th centuries were not cameleers at all but herbalists, religious leaders, and merchants who had immigrated to support the burgeoning Muslim communities. Unlike the camels, however, which today can be seen from the road on any journey into the central Australian outback, this population has remained fairly invisible. Individuals either migrated or integrated so fully into the surrounding society that their legacy was not widely known until Australian historians began writing about them in the 1980s.

limited (Phoenix 2008). But he did not offend the sensibilities or politics of any of the committee members and thus received the nod two months before the voyage was to begin.

The expedition continued to be haunted by bad decisions. On the day before its departure two men were dismissed for drunkenness and as the entourage gathered at the starting point in Melbourne's Royal Park, a third was dismissed for the same reason; three replacements were pulled from the crowd of about 15,000 people who were present to see them off (Phoenix 2008). That first day, three of the expedition's

Although the mission was deadly for both men, the Burke and Wills Australian Exploring Expedition made both household names in Australia. (Pictures Collection, State Library of Victoria)

wagons broke down and, after traveling just four miles, the entire group settled in for the night in Moonee Ponds, today an inner suburb of Melbourne (Phoenix 2008).

In addition to Burke's incompetence and erratic behavior, such as hiring and firing personnel on a daily basis, the expedition was hampered by bad weather. Rain and cold in Victoria hindered the wagons' movement and stymied the camels, which were accustomed to desert terrain (Phoenix 2008). Conditions did not improve much after crossing the Murray River into New South Wales. Burke fired several men and reduced the wages of others to save money, abandoned all of the expedition's scientific instruments as too heavy, and forced the two scientists on the journey to work as laborers (Phoenix 2008). George Landells, the man in charge of the camels and their "Afghan" cameleers, quit in disgust and was replaced by John King, who could speak the "Afghans'" language but had no experience with camels.

At Cooper's Creek Burke made the fateful decision to split his party, leaving behind four of his men and their supplies while he, Wills, King, and Charley Gray set off for their final destination. Rather than leaving the group at Cooper's Creek with a written order, Burke directed them to wait for three months and after that to turn around, assuming the others had perished or turned east toward the settled regions of

Queensland; as they were pulling out, Wills contradicted Burke's order and told the remainder to wait for four months (Phoenix 2008). Finally, after two months of difficult travel since leaving their provisions behind at Cooper's Creek, Burke, Wills, and Billy the horse arrived as far north as the expedition was to go. They never saw a beach front or open ocean, but wading through tidal mangrove swamps they certainly knew they had reached the north coast. And then it was time to turn around.

The return trip to Cooper's Creek was even more wretched than the outbound journey. The rainy season made travel almost impossible in some places, mosquitoes bit the men incessantly, food was scarce, illness took the life of Charley Gray and incapacitated the others, and most of the camels and Billy had to be killed to feed the three survivors (Phoenix 2008). On April 21, 1861, they finally arrived back at the depot at Cooper's Creek, four months and five days after departing, only to find that the other half of the expedition had departed that very morning. Rather than following the Cooper's Creek contingent toward Menindee, where other members of the expedition had been left behind, Burke led his exhausted and ill companions along the creek itself toward Mount Hopeless.

In the end, seven members of the expedition died, including both Burke and Wills, and very little was accomplished, with the exception of their being the first whites to cross the continent from south to north. But in the 19th century, being the first white explorer to cross the continent was no inconsequential act, even if all scientific specimens and observations had to be sacrificed in the process. The South Australian explorer John Stuart had twice failed in his attempt to cross south to north prior to Burke and Wills's accomplishment and only reached the north coast at what is today Darwin in 1862.

In addition to those of Stuart and Burke and Wills, numerous other geographic and scientific explorations of inner Australia took place during this period of economic success. Although less well known than those of these other men, Ernest Favenc's name should be added to the list of intrepid explorers of the north in the latter half of the 19th century. In 1878 Favenc led a five-man party to find a route suitable for a railway line from outback Queensland to Darwin. The group traveled overland for seven months before reaching Darwin. Favenc led a second journey in 1881–82 that tried to reach the Gulf of Carpentaria but was thwarted by bad weather and rough conditions. Finally, in 1883 he succeeded in this mission by following the Macarthur River and thus discovered "the only practical road to the gulf" (Gibbney 1972, 160).

Governing Aboriginal People in Australia

Accompanying Favenc on this successful gulf trip was one of the few female explorers to have ventured beyond settled Australia in the 19th century, Emily Caroline Creaghe. Emily, or Caroline as she is often called, kept a diary of her journey, which is one of the best sources of information on black–white relations in the far north at the time. The situation depicted is grim. For example, her entry for February 8, 1883, states that Jack Watson, owner of a large cattle property, "has 40 pairs of black ears nailed round the walls, collected during raiding parties after the loss of many cattle speared by the blacks" (European Network 2008). On February 20 she wrote of their hosts, "They brought a new black in with them. She cannot speak a word of English. Mr. Shadforth put a rope round her neck and dragged her along on foot, he was riding. This seems to be the usual method" (European Network 2008). And the next day, following up on the treatment of this woman, "The new gin whom they call Bella is chained up to a tree a few yards from the house. She is not to be loosed until they think she is tamed" (European Network 2008).

Queensland had a variety of government bodies and individual positions to oversee the Aboriginal population, such as the Royal Commission of 1876, which was to "improve[e] the conditions of the Aborigines in Queensland . . . [and] 'report from time to time to the Government'" (Queensland Government). Unfortunately, neither this board nor the individuals appointed as protectors after 1897 were willing or able to provide any real independence or even protection to the colony's Aboriginal community.

The newly opened lands of far north Queensland were not the only territory in which the Aboriginal people suffered at the hands of the white colonizers in the second half of the 19th century. In New South Wales, South Australia, and Victoria colonization continued to cause misery for the Indigenous population. While the primary concept underlying most white contact with Aboriginal people in the late 18th and early 19th centuries had been elimination, in the latter years of the 19th century this turned to "containment and control" (Thinee and Bradford 1998, 20). The most important structures for these activities were the colonies' Aborigines protection boards, protectors of Aborigines, and the more than 200 church missions and government reserves upon which Aboriginal peoples were "contained."

The first institutions and positions of this sort had actually been established much earlier in the century. Governor Macquarie had established an Aboriginal children's home in Parramatta in 1814 and in 1815 a reserve at George's Head for the last members of the Broken Bay Aboriginal community (New South Wales Aboriginal Land Council 2007). In 1824 an Aboriginal mission was established by a Congregational missionary, the Reverend L. E. Threlkeld, at Lake Macquarie, north of Sydney (Gunson 1967, 528). In 1842 this was followed by a provision of the New South Wales Land Act that required the inclusion "in every pastoral lease [of] a reservation preserving a wide range of native title rights" (Aboriginal Law Bulletin), although this was rarely if ever done with the thought of providing a livelihood or economic independence for the Aboriginal people. In Van Diemen's Land George Augustus Robinson served as a Protector of Aborigines from 1829 until the position was abolished in 1849, but as did that of many others who served in this position in the Australian colonies, his work proved far more detrimental to the Aboriginal people than if he had not been there "protecting" them at all. Robinson was instrumental in rounding up the surviving Aboriginal people after Arthur Phillip's Black War and housing them on Flinders Island, where a large proportion died (Perkins 2008, episode 2).

After the failure of Robinson to protect the Aboriginal people supposedly in his care, his position was eliminated, but the paternalistic concept of protecting this population from the onslaught of white colonists did not die. In 1860 the nine-year-old colony of Victoria appointed its own Board of Protection with the stated mission of protecting the few surviving Aboriginal people living there. Its job was to oversee the various government reserves and church missions that were established for housing and educating, or, more aptly, containing and civilizing, Victoria's Aboriginal population. Altogether 34 missions and reserves were established on Victorian territory.

The tragic history of this period in Victorian history can be seen in the story of the reserve at Coranderrk in a hilly region 45 miles (72 km) east of Melbourne. Coranderrk was established under the leadership of Wonga, who took the first name *Simon*, and Barak, who took the name *William*, leaders of the Wurundjeri clan (Perkins 2008, episode 3). In 1859 Wonga, under the influence of John Green, a Scottish minister who arrived each Sunday to preach to the Wurundjeri people, turned to the Victorian parliament for a land grant. He envisioned a place where his people could "plant corn and potatoes and work like white men" and thus accommodate themselves to the new world in which they lived (Perkins 2008, episode 3). Unfortunately, the parliamentarians ignored his request for years, until the Aboriginal leader finally took matters into his own hands in 1863. Just as the whites had for more

The community leader William Barak stands in the middle of about 40 of his fellow residents at Coranderrk. (Pictures Collection, State Library of Victoria)

than 30 years in Victoria, the Wurundjeri settled on unclaimed Crown land, built houses, and began farming (Perkins 2008, episode 3).

With the settlement of Coranderrk a fait accompli, the Board of Protection supported the establishment of the reserve, but with the provisos that it was the board and not the Wurundjeri themselves who would control the purse strings, and residents of the reserve had to become Christian. These decisions were just two of many over the course of the subsequent 60 years in which the board's paternalistic attitude toward Aboriginal people was more important to its members than actual support for Coranderrk. Another example includes forcing the Wurundjeri and other clans that moved onto the successful reserve to grow hops instead of other crops in 1872 and then, instead of paying the Aboriginal farmers for their crop, merely providing rations to the community. This economic structure served to keep community members dependent on the board for their livelihood, and thus to keep them poor. Perhaps the most damaging government decision, however, was an act in 1886 that made it illegal for "half-caste" people under the age of 34 to reside on state reserves (Perkins 2008, episode 3). The act resulted in the separation of parents from their children and caused a rapid decrease in the community's population so that by

1924 Coranderrk was closed and its small remaining population moved to another reserve, Lake Tyers, much farther away from Melbourne (Coranderrk Mission History 2004).

New South Wales also had a Protector of Aborigines from 1881 forward and an Aborigines Protection Board from 1883. Their jobs, as in Victoria, were "to 'educate,' care [for] and 'protect' Aboriginal peoples" (Thinee and Bradford 1998, 11) by overseeing the seven church missions and 134 government reserves that were established or continuing operations in New South Wales after 1881 (Thinee and Bradford 1998, 340–341). The people who occupied these positions, however, saw it as their primary duty "to control the lives of those [9,000 or so] Aboriginal people" who lived in the colony (Thinee and Bradford 1998, 11, 20). In South Australia there had been an early Protector of Aborigines from 1839 to 1856, but the protector himself, Matthew Moorhouse, had failed so utterly—even participating in a massacre of Aboriginal people in 1841—that the position was abolished until 1881 (Human Rights and Equal Opportunity Commission [HREOC] 2007). At that time all remaining government reserves were transferred to church missions, but very little changed for Aboriginal people themselves, who continued to be treated, at best, as children and, at worst, as animals.

The Outback

While the southern and eastern Australian colonies were working through the growing pains of relative independence in the latter half of the 19th century, Western Australia and the Northern Territory were still coming into their own. The former had officially become a penal colony only in 1850, to bolster its tiny white population of fewer than 6,000 (Welsh 2004, 139); the last shipload arrived in 1868. This difference from the eastern colonies also meant that local governance structures were slower to develop in the west, with the first elected representative council sitting in 1870 and first self-governing parliament in 1890 (Welsh 2004, 251, 253). A final difference from the eastern colonies related to the Aboriginal population, which was both much larger and more independent than elsewhere in this period. The British government retained control over the reserves and missions until 1897, and thus "some Aborigines [sic] enjoyed better conditions than those elsewhere" (Welsh 2004, 271) since local farmers were less successful in their pursuit of Aboriginal land.

The Northern Territory at that time was only marginally more connected to the other Australian colonies than Western Australia, largely because of geographic proximity. It was only in 1863 that the territory came into being as an entity when South Australia formally took control from New South Wales. Prior to this period this vast territory, 520,902 square miles (1,349,129 sq. km), which is almost twice as large as Texas, was only nominally held by New South Wales and governed from far-away Sydney. More important at that time than the Australians or British were Macassan trepangers from the Indonesian archipelago who had been arriving each year since the mid-18th century to catch and prepare trepang, or sea slugs, for sale on the Chinese market. In the first half of the 19th century, British attempts at controlling this lucrative trade failed miserably. Three white settlements in the far north, Fort Dundas on Melville Island (1824–28), Fort Wellington on Raffles Bay (1827–29), and Fort Victoria at Port Essington (1838–49), all failed as a result of the hot, humid climate and disease (Australian Heritage Database 2002).

Finally in 1863, when South Australia took control of the territory, the colonial government began to make some headway in the region by pouring millions of pounds into exploring and developing it. The greatest success story of this period was the completion of the Overland Telegraph in 1872. The electric telegraph had been invented in the 1830s and then perfected in the 1840s, when Samuel Morse sent his first message. Australia built its first line about a decade later, in 1853, when Melbourne and Williamstown were connected by an American who had managed the New York and Buffalo Telegraph Company (Taylor 1980, 17).

South Australians became interested in the new technology almost immediately. The government appointed an Englishman, Charles Todd, its first superintendent of telegraphs in 1854. He installed his first line, from Adelaide to Port Adelaide, in February 1856 and then worked with the Victorian superintendent to connect Adelaide and Melbourne in July 1858. At the same time, Queensland was also developing its telegraphic capacities with a view to connecting the continent to the rest of the world.

For the next decade, Todd worked as an astronomer in South Australia to fulfill the second part of his commitment to the government, while others laid the groundwork that eventually led to his overland success in 1872. Francis Gisborne arrived from England with a proposal to connect Moreton Bay, Queensland, to Batavia (Jakarta) via an undersea cable (Taylor 1980, 26–27). The first overland expeditions also succeeded in this decade, with Burke and Wills and John McDouall Stuart completing the journey in the early 1860s. Another event that set the stage for Todd to begin was the completion of a telegraph line that crossed the United States from New York to San Francisco, a distance of nearly 3,000 miles (about 4,800 km), proving that overland routes were viable (Taylor 1980, 35). The last problem that had to be cleared up was where to land an undersea cable in Australia. Gisborne's company favored Queensland, as did the English firm Telegraph Construction and Maintenance Company. But a subsidiary of the latter company, the British-Australian Telegraph Company, formed in January 1870, favored Port Darwin, which gave Todd and the South Australian government the chance to lobby for the ultimate connection to run overland to Port Augusta and Adelaide rather than to Queensland. By offering to fund the overland project with government funds and to have it completed by January 1, 1872, South Australia won the contract in June 1870 (Taylor 1980, 37–40).

With no time to spare, Todd began the extraordinary task of completing a project many times larger than anything he had ever undertaken, across territory that had been crossed by white men only twice, and with a budget that had essentially been pulled from the air. The first task was to send John Ross and a team of surveyors and explorers to scout the route and determine the availability of water, timber for telegraph poles, and other resources (see Giles 1995); they left on July 8. While they explored, Todd made plans from Adelaide and gathered tenders for the northern and southern sections of the line; his government team was to build the middle third. At this point, much of Adelaide's small business community was involved with the preparations, building wagons, carving 30,000 insulator pins for the line, and supplying clothing, animals, and food; the all-important line itself was ordered from England (Taylor 1980, 50).

For just under two years, teams of men, horses, and bullocks labored in some of the world's most difficult terrain to complete Todd's dream of connecting Australia and England via telegraph. They were thwarted by searing heat and lack of water in one season and tremendous floods in the next, but through it all the 36,000 poles kept going in and the line kept extending. After the landing of the overseas cable from Java to Darwin in October 1871, the southern section, from Port Augusta to the Treuer River, was the first to be completed, in January 1872. Over the next six months work continued overland, and by June 20 the citizens of Adelaide were receiving their first transcontinental telegraphs, although a short gap had to be bridged manually (Taylor 1980, 184). This gap was finally closed and problems with both the undersea cable and termite damage to the poles were solved so that on November 15, 1872, the governor of South Australia could declare a public holiday

Frequent repairs to the line were made by operators resident in the many telegraph stations located all across central Australia. Bob Carew is working on this line in 1921. (Image courtesy of the State Library of South Australia, SLSA: PRG1365/1/133)

to celebrate the achievement (Flinders Ranges Research 2008). Todd's dream had become a reality.

Despite this geographic and technological connection between the Northern Territory and the rest of the Australian colonies, there were significant differences between them. The most important was the fact that the Northern Territory was not (and still is not) entirely self-governing. Unlike in Queensland and Victoria, which became independent colonies upon breaking away from New South Wales, governance of the Northern Territory was simply transferred from Sydney to Adelaide. In 1911 South Australia transferred responsibility for the territory to the new Commonwealth government, which held it until a degree of self-government was permitted in 1978. Since that time, the territory has had a legislative assembly and chief minister who have similar powers to those of their counterparts in the six Australian states. Nevertheless, important differences remain because the federal government "retains the power to make laws for the Northern Territory, and can override laws of the Northern Territory Legislative Assembly" (Northern Land Council 2003).

Another important difference between the Northern Territory and eastern and southern colonies was demographic. Even with the opening of telegraph stations throughout the territory, the white population did not begin to rival that of either the large Aboriginal population of about 50,000 (Thompson 1994, 53) or the significant Chinese one. In 1888 the Northern Territory had a white population of just 1,000 and a Chinese one seven times larger (Thompson 1994, 37). White fears of Chinese supremacy in the territory, however, meant that after 1888 "vessels from China were quarantined and Chinese residents were restricted to a radius of twenty miles around Darwin"; in addition, "the South Australian government . . . placed a poll tax on Chinese entering the Northern Territory" (Thompson 1994, 37). Just two years later, the Chinese population was down to 4,000, while the white population had remained about the same, at 1,000 (Thompson 1994, 37). While the loss of 3,000 people must have had a great effect on the Chinese community, the decrease in number and proportion did not seriously affect the strong economic position of the Chinese in the territory. By 1890 Palmerston (present-day Darwin) had 39 Chinese businesses including laundries, cafes, shoemakers, tailors, and brothels (Thompson 1994, 52). The Chinese also provided the vast majority of fresh food in the territory, from fish to vegetables; worked on the Palmerston railway with Japanese and Indian colleagues; and maintained a thriving community that has survived into the present (Thompson 1994, 52–53).

Today the demographics of the Northern Territory are still very different from those of the rest of the country, with extremely low population density, relatively high numbers of Aboriginal people, and relatively high ownership of the land by Aboriginal communities. The Northern Territory houses about 1 percent of all Australians, with about 221,000 people on about one sixth of the country's territory; this works out to be about 2.36 people per square mile (one person per .79 km^2).

About 29 percent of this population, or about 60,000 people, are of Aboriginal or Torres Strait Islander descent, while the national average is less than 2.5 percent. This 29 percent of the population owns almost half of all land in the territory, while the national average is about 14 percent (Northern Land Council 2003). Some of this land, such as that around Uluru (Ayer's Rock), Kata Tjuta (the Olgas), and Karlu Karlu (Devil's Marbles), has been leased back to the federal government for tourism purposes, but much of it remains in at least nominal control of Aboriginal cooperatives and corporations.

Conclusion

Most of the 19th century was very good for Australia's few white residents. Wealth and population expanded exponentially with wool and then gold feeding the colonial coffers and luring ever larger numbers of settlers from Britain, Ireland, Europe, and even the Americas to take advantage of the new frontier. This was largely an urban population that settled in Melbourne, Adelaide, Sydney, Brisbane, and Perth to make money as merchants for the expanding primary products industries and in the service industries that they supported. This mainly urban population, however, was not entirely separated from the land, and the dream of exploring "the bush" or even owning a small plot of farmland was still very strong. Henry Lawson and many others wrote about the rural experience, while the entire population followed with interest the activities of bushrangers like Ned Kelly. Thousands of families left the cities and settled areas as "selectors" who struggled to survive on small, dry plots of land with little possibility of long-term success.

These difficulties paled in comparison, however, to those experienced by Australia's Aboriginal population during this century. At the start of the 19th century the territory that became Victoria still housed tens of thousands of seminomadic Aboriginal people, who maintained their strict marriage laws and social taboos. By midcentury their number had been reduced to about 2,000 people, and by the end of the century the few surviving communities were housed on government reserves and Christian missions and lived in constant fear of intervention by the Aboriginal Protection Board. The situation in the other colonies was very similar, and even the large numbers of Aboriginal people in the Northern Territory were beginning to fall under mission and government control.

This era of white prosperity in Australian history could not continue forever, and by 1893 much of urban and rural life in Australia had been transformed by debt, drought, and economic depression.

5

FEDERATION AND
IDENTITY FORMATION
(1890–1919)

The 19th century began for the small non-Aboriginal population in Australia as a period of tremendous growth and optimism. Trade and primary production had begun to solve the food problems suffered at the end of the 18th century, and increasing numbers of both convicts and free settlers were expanding the population to a sustainable level. As the century progressed, non-Aboriginal Australia's fortunes grew exponentially. The transportation of convicts ended, leaving a settlement of free colonizers set on achieving prosperity and stability. By the early 1880s gold mining and wool and wheat production had exploded, leaving Australia's colonizers among the richest people in the world, with the exception of those unlucky families who had staked their money and luck on rural selections in Victoria and New South Wales.

The 1890s

Starting in 1888, the dream of continual economic growth in Australia was in peril. Worldwide prices in both wool and wheat had decreased during the decade, affecting primary producers throughout the continent (Clarke 2003, 150). In Victoria land speculation led to a slump in prices that affected not only the marginal selector population in rural areas but also the inhabitants of what had previously been "Marvelous Melbourne." This regional problem became an issue for all the Australian colonies in 1890 with a crash in markets worldwide, starting in Argentina and spreading to Australia through the collapse of financial institutions in Britain (Clark 1995, 185). While bank failures in Britain were not as common as they were during the 1930s depression, the withdrawal of capital from Australian enterprises hit the colonies hard. Multiple bank failures, reduced prices, high unemployment rates, and land devaluation were some of the major causes and effects of the deteriorating Australian economic climate of the time.

Making matters more difficult, Australia's already dry conditions worsened during the 1890s. A combination of drought and a plague of rabbits threatened rural recovery for much longer than even in Argentina, where the crisis had begun (McLean 2005). In Queensland the introduction of the cattle tick, possibly from India, reduced the cattle population by about 43 percent and further exacerbated the problems caused by these other macroeconomic factors (Molony 2005, 181). Government policies dictated by laissez-faire ideologies during these years also tended to exacerbate rather than diminish the problems generated overseas. The number of public works projects was reduced rather than increased, and, especially in Victoria, banks were left to fail, taking consumer savings and confidence with them (Clarke 2003, 153–155).

Although 1890 through 1894 were very difficult years in eastern Australia, the rest of the continent did not suffer to the same extent. In 1890 Western Australia had finally joined New South Wales, Victoria, Tasmania, Queensland, and South Australia as a self-governing colony, only to be blessed two years later with gold rushes in the outback towns of Coolgardie and Kalgoorlie. These events drained population from the more established eastern colonies and helped to ease some of the effects of depression and unemployment there; 50,000 people departed Melbourne and another 50,000 left regional Victoria in the first half of the 1890s (Molony 2005, 175). While Melbourne remains a large, cosmopolitan city today, it has never recovered the position it held from the mid-1850s through the early 1890s as the world's most prosperous and expensive city. Today it is not even Australia's largest city, trailing behind Sydney by several hundred thousand people.

Another long-term ramification of the depression of the 1890s is the development of Labor Party politics. Labor unions first emerged in Australia in 1840 when Sydney's Australian Society of Compositors was organized (Clarke 2003, 157). This action was followed by a burgeoning of other associations, including the first women's union in the colonies in 1882, formed by Victoria's dress makers (Molony 2005, 172). By 1860 Melbourne's Trades Hall Council had emerged to assist all the working people's associations in that city, followed by Sydney's in 1871 (Clarke 2003, 158).

During Australia's boom years from the 1850s through the 1880s, these unions seemed to represent their members' interests with significant success; workers and owners worked together to manage the years of prosperity to the benefit of both groups. Of course, many people were left out of this pact, including Aboriginal people, Chinese and other nonwhite workers, as well as many women (Thompson 1994, 40–41). In fact, the one major source of conflict between labor unions and owners in this period was over the migration of Chinese and other nonwhite laborers; owners wanted cheaper labor regardless of skin color, while workers preferred to maintain de facto white Australia policies. With the exception of Melanesian Kanakas in Queensland and Asian laborers in the Northern Territory, workers' associations largely won these battles, underpinning the power they held in the colonies.

As later events were to illustrate, however, the workers' power was almost entirely an illusion. This fact was brought home to all in the labor strikes that accompanied the economic downturn of the 1890s. The most severe of these widespread strikes lasted for about four months in late 1890 and included action by the Maritime Officers' Association, Queensland's shearers, and the many others who walked out in support of these two groups. Various other unions, such as coal miners in 1893 and 1896 and shearers in 1891 and 1894, also tried to use strikes to improve workers' conditions and rates of pay. Unfortunately for them, all the colonial governments supported the owners against the unions in these strikes and used the police and military to protect nonunion, or "scab," laborers as well as private company property (Clarke 2003, 158–159). In the end, the almost endless supply of workers thanks to the high unemployment rates caused by the depression meant that unions had nothing to use as a bargaining chip and the power they had seemingly accumulated during the boom years evaporated.

Having had the illusion of power taken away from them, as well as the knowledge that strikes could produce almost none of their aims except under limited circumstances, Australia's laborers began to emphasize political organization. Prior to this turn of events, the most important ideological difference that marked Australian politics was between those who supported free trade and those who supported protective tariffs; no organized party or body was looking after workers' interests at the governmental level. After 1893 many unions put their efforts toward this end and very rapidly Labor Parties throughout the colonies were participating in elections (Duckworth 1892, 440); by 1899 Queensland was home to the first Labor Party government in the world (Clarke 2003, 162–163). Between 1894 and 1900 Labor Parties throughout the colonies made impressive gains in the areas of workers' wages, conditions, safety, and hours, as well as land and income taxes that benefited the working class (Clarke 2003, 163). The legacy of a strong Labor Party movement continues to be alive and well in Australia today, where a federal Labor government was elected in a landslide vote in November 2007.

Federation
Introduction
Another long-term effect of the depression and strikes of the 1890s was a push for federation, from both the unions, who feared the effects of another depression, and employers, who feared further strike action (Clark 1995, 189). On both sides, greater centralization of power through the creation of an Australian commonwealth was felt to be preferable to the continued separation of the six Australian colonies.

The six Australian colonies at the end of the 19th century were still very separate and considered themselves economic rivals. This rivalry was evident at midcentury during the New South Wales and Victorian gold rushes, as well as a decade later with the scramble for ownership of the telegraph line that would connect Australia to the rest of the world. One of the most important symbolic features of the colonies' separation was the use of different gauge rail lines in each of the five mainland colonies, requiring passengers from Sydney to Melbourne to get off and change trains at the border and those from Sydney to Adelaide to do so twice. This situation was only rectified in 1995 when Brisbane, Sydney, Melbourne, Adelaide, and Perth were finally connected by standard-gauge rails (National Railway Museum 2001).

Despite these rivalries and the lack of cooperation, however, the seeds had been sown for federation. Each of the colonies had developed the same kind of parliamentary and judicial systems, which allowed for the federation of these systems with relative ease. Likewise, an early push for a "white" Australia had been seen in each colony, whether this meant excluding Chinese and other non-European migrants or effectively banning Aboriginal people from colonial public life. The colonies had also established similar land acts and educational policies. Just one year into the new century these seeds were harvested; Australia's first Commonwealth parliament convened and the long process of constructing a national identity began in earnest.

The Process
While a number of visitors to Australia as early as the 1820s had either spoken or written about an eventual federation of the separate colonies,

and several committees had been convened in the 1850s and in 1883 to look into the possibility, seemingly intractable differences seemed to stand in the way. The chief problem was that leaders in Victoria favored tariffs and other protectionist actions, while those in New South Wales desired a greater degree of openness to free trade. This difference stemmed largely from New South Wales's greater size, as a result of which the colonial government gained much of its revenue from land sales, while Victoria's small size meant that taxes and tariffs provided most of its revenue.

The real breakthrough on federation after decades of false starts and local objections occurred in 1887, when Henry Parkes became the premier of New South Wales for the fourth time. Parkes had been convinced of the need for federation and in October 1889 announced his intention to set aside the colonies' differences on trade and tariffs in order to make it happen (Welsh 2004, 287). Parkes's explanation for this was that not one of the six colonies had the ability to defend itself against outside aggression and that federation was the only answer to this problem.

Despite Parkes's intentions, federation was still 12 years in the making, interrupted not only by the depression of the early 1890s, but also by the political and semantic wrangling among the colonies' representatives. Many conventions and meetings were held, including the Australasian Federation Conference in Melbourne in March 1890, the First National Australasian Convention in March 1891, the Victorian and New South Wales Federation Leagues Conference in 1893, and the colonial premiers' meeting in 1895. This last meeting called for each colony to elect delegates to participate in the writing of a new constitution (Welsh 2004, 300). Prior to this time, however, a draft constitution had already been written by the delegates to the 1891 convention and edited by the Queensland premier, Samuel Griffith (Welsh 2004, 291); the content of the second constitution of 1897–98 resembled Griffith's to a great extent. Both borrowed heavily from similar documents written in Canada, Switzerland, and, especially, the United States.

The next stage in the process required that each of the colonies hold a referendum to provide the new commonwealth with the legitimacy of public opinion. The first referendum was held in 1898 and failed to attract even 50 percent of eligible voters. This meant that in New South Wales the required threshold of 80,000 votes in favor of the proposal was not reached, 71,412 for and 65,954 against (Welsh 2004, 325). Therefore, the whole referendum went down and had to be repeated the following year. In 1899 the second referendum passed in Victoria, New

South Wales, South Australia, Tasmania, and Queensland. In Victoria the yes votes were 93 percent of the 163,783 votes cast, or 152,653 in favor, and the other colonies had similar rates.

THE AUSTRALIAN CONSTITUTION

The drafting of Australia's current constitution took place at a series of meetings between 1897 and 1898 called the National Australasian Convention, or sometimes simply the Federation Convention. The first one took place in Adelaide, South Australia, in May 1897 and included 50 popularly elected delegates from South Australia, New South Wales, Victoria, Tasmania, and Western Australia; Queensland did not send delegates. The election for these delegates in South Australia saw the first Australian female voters as well as the first female candidate, Catherine Helen Spence, who was not successful. The second two sessions of the Federation Convention, held in Sydney in September 1897 and Melbourne in the first three months of 1898, included a Queensland delegation and produced a constitution with four "essential characteristics": federation under the British Crown, a democratic bicameral legislative system, an independent judiciary, and an inherent difficulty in amending or dissolving it.

Catherine Helen Spence was the first woman in Australia to stand in an election. She lost her bid to represent South Australia at the Federation Convention in 1897–98. (Image courtesy of the State Library of South Australia SLSA:B36575)

For inspiration and models, the drafters looked to existing federal constitutions, those of the United States, Switzerland, Canada, and the German federation of 1871, with that of the United States playing the

At the time, the premier of Western Australia, John Forrest, feared the loss of revenue to his region from its large gold reserves and refused to hold a referendum at all. He was moved to do so in 1900, however,

most important role. Basically, as in the United States, the Australian constitution dictates that any area of rights and responsibilities not specifically granted to the Commonwealth is assumed to be the purview of the individual states and territories. An important difference, however, is that the British monarch remains the head of state in Australia, with the governor-general serving as his or her representative.

Australia also shares with the United States a bicameral legislative branch of government but, unlike the United States, does not have a separation of powers between the executive branch of government and the legislative. This is the result of Australia's parliamentary system, which was borrowed from Britain, whereby the head of government or prime minister is the leader of the party or coalition of parties with the majority vote in the lower house of parliament. The ministers who serve in the prime minister's cabinet are also all from either the House of Representatives or the Senate.

The third branch of Australia's government is the judiciary, or legal branch. The one significant change on the American system argued for by members of the Judiciary Committee of the Federation Convention was that the Australian High Court was to be able to hear all appeals from the state supreme courts, not just cases related to questions of constitutionality. As in the United States, federal judges are chosen by the government, including the seven High Court judges. In addition to the High Court, Australia's constitution provides for a series of federal courts, located in each state and territory; these are the Federal Magistrates Court, which is a lower branch of the federal system and set up only in 1999, and Family Court, which deals with divorce, custody, and child welfare.

The framers of Australia's constitution made dissolving it impossible without changing the entire system of government and made even amending it very difficult. The difficulty in changing the constitution is reflected in the 35 attempts that have failed, compared with just eight successes. The first such amendment was passed in 1906 and concerned the simple fact of when senators' terms would begin, while the most recent was the passage of three separate amendments in 1977 concerned with the retirement of judges, filling of empty Senate seats, and holding of referendums.

when the leaders of the goldfields regions threatened to secede from the colony and join the commonwealth on their own. As a result, when a referendum was finally held in the west, it passed easily and Western Australia joined the other five colonies.

Having been approved throughout the Australian colonies, the next step toward federation was to gain the authorization of the colonies' masters in London. The Australians sent a delegation of eight men to England, including those who would become the first and second prime ministers of Australia, Edmund Barton and Alfred Deakin, to accompany the act to the imperial capital. They were confronted with some opposition based on the desire for an independent judiciary and were forced into a compromise whereby some court cases could be appealed from the Australian High Court to the monarch's privy council in London (Hunt 1968, 97). But with that slight change, in May 1900 Joseph Chamberlain, the British secretary of state for the colonies, presented the Commonwealth of Australia Constitution Act to the House of Commons, and in July Queen Victoria signed the act into law; the date of enactment was set for January 1, 1901. Australia as a country thus entered the world on that day as something of a hybrid, combining independence on many issues with dependence on the British Empire for others.

National Identity Formation

With the creation of a federal Australian government in 1901, the next project that needed to be undertaken was to create a set of national characteristics with which the new Australian citizens could identify. The creation of an imagined national community of Australians (Anderson 1983) that would not only attract migrants but also contribute to patriotism and loyalty to the new state required both legal policies and cultural forms that would be easily identifiable as uniquely Australian.

This was, and in some ways remains, a difficult project in Australia, for the new country lacked some of the most important features that nationalists in other countries had traditionally used to build national sentiment. The European countries, where modern nationalism was born, had ancient histories, unique languages, and long-standing attachments to certain territories to connect their mass populations to the idea of a common national identity. Nationalists in the United States could draw on both the mythological settlement of the country by seekers of religious freedom and the bloody revolution against

Britain in their creation of a national identity. But while the American model was useful for Australian politicians in drawing up a constitution for their country, this nationalist model was less than inspiring down under. Australian nationalists were loath to draw on the idea of a nation founded by prisoners and their equally unsavory masters and, politically, remained connected to the British through their common head of state. As a result, for the most part the nationalist project in Australia involved creating local symbols to which the population could attach their loyalty and generating at least symbolic separation between what it meant to be an Australian and what it meant to be British.

Legislation

In the construction of national identity, all nations must delineate boundaries: Who can be considered a member of the nation, and who is an outsider? One of the first actions by the new federal government on taking power in 1901 was to enact the legal standard for becoming a member of the Australian community. The restrictions this entailed provide a clear view of what the government and the electorate who chose it saw as the basis of Australian identity. The most important standard in the early 20th century was whiteness, meaning fair-skinned people of northern European descent. Even darker-skinned Italians and other southern Europeans were generally excluded because they were seen as only "partly white" and certainly not of the same race as those whose ancestors had immigrated from Britain (Andreoni 2003).

In focusing on race as an important marker of national identity, Australian politicians in the early 20th century were drawing on about a century of experience in the colonies of racializing, or using race as a category with which to marginalize, exclude, or even hunt down certain peoples. When it came to migrants, the first large-scale movement in this direction occurred in the 1850s when Victoria, New South Wales, and South Australia all enacted policies to exclude Chinese miners. Arguably, however, the first racial policies in the colonies were those of the early governors who allowed the extermination of Aboriginal people. With regard to this population, the Constitution of 1901 expressly stated that Aboriginal people were not to be counted in either state or federal censuses and thus defined them as outside the nation entirely; full citizenship rights were awarded to this population only with a change in the Constitution in 1967 (Cameron 2000).

In addition to the Commonwealth's exclusion of Aboriginal people from the national body politic, by 1911 all of the states and territories of Australia, with the exception of Tasmania, had likewise legislated Aboriginal people out of the general community. Tasmania did not bother because most whites in the state mistakenly believed that the last Aboriginal person there had died in the 1870s. In the remaining states and territories, Aboriginal protection boards were created or restored in the first decade of the century not to provide protection but to oversee and control all aspects of Aboriginal life (Welsh 2004, 487). Aboriginal protectors, who were often policemen, controlled the wages of the few Aboriginal workers who were actually paid cash for their labor and even decided the composition of Aboriginal households and compounds. Protectors, under the guise of providing education, Christianity, or a trade, could remove any Aboriginal child under the age of 18 from a family and place him or her into a government- or church-sponsored reserve or mission. For the most part, it was so-called half-caste children, or those with at least one white relative in their family tree, who experienced this kind of trauma, but the practice was not exclusive to them. The policy, which remained in effect until the early 1970s, resulted in what is today called the Stolen Generations, children who were taken from their parents and sent to live either in a large white institution or, less commonly, with a white family, often never to find their own families again.

It is only today, nearly 40 years after the last Aboriginal children were taken from their families, that white Australians are starting to come to terms with the legacy of this destructive, genocidal policy. Since the mid-1990s several mainstream Australian films, such as *Rabbit Proof Fence* and *Australia,* have depicted the reality of life for the mothers and children who successfully and, more commonly, unsuccessfully protected themselves from the long arms of Aboriginal protectors. In 2008 the Australian government also finally acknowledged its role in the destruction of thousands of families when Prime Minister Kevin Rudd issued a formal apology to the Stolen Generations.

White Australia policies did not deal only with the country's Aboriginal people. With regard to migrants, three separate bills passed just before Christmas 1901 together created the legal basis for the centrality of whiteness in Australian identity, or what is sometimes called the White Australia policy: the Pacific Islander Labourers Act, Section 15 of the Post and Telegraph Act, and the Immigration Restriction Act (National Archives of Australia 2005). The first of these acts limited the ability of Melanesians working in Queensland's sugar industry to remain in the country after federation. Section 15 of the Post and Telegraph Act required that all ships carrying Australian post employ only white workers. This was believed necessary because the Commonwealth did not want to subsidize nonwhite labor. The third of the acts, the Immigration Restriction Act, set the standard for becoming an Australian through migration. The requirements for this were being white, sane, healthy, able-bodied, and able to pass a dictation test (National Communications Branch 2007). The act also specifically mentioned criminals, prostitutes, and contract laborers as those who should be excluded from becoming Australians. Contract laborers were mentioned specifically to prohibit the migration of former or current indentured Melanesians who had been working in Queensland, just in case a small number of them slipped through any cracks in the Pacific Islander Labourers Act.

While all three acts "aimed at excluding all non-European migrants" (National Archives 2005), the most effective device in this regard was the dictation test. Rather than stating explicitly that Australia would welcome only whites, which would have irritated both Britain and its ally Japan, the dictation test emerged as an equally restrictive legal requirement. Previously, similar methods had been tested and found to exclude nonwhites in Tasmania, New South Wales, and Western Australia, as well as in the Natal district of South Africa. The 1901 Commonwealth version of the act stated that Australia could "exclude any person who 'when asked to do so by an officer fails to write out a dictation and sign in the presence of the officer, a passage of 50 words in length in a European language directed by the officer'" (National Archives 2005). Rather than stating that the required language be English, which would have allowed African Americans and well-educated Japanese migrants to enter the country, the Commonwealth allowed immigration officers to choose any European language they thought would exclude an undesirable migrant. In the first few of the 57 years in which this policy was in place a small number of people actually passed and were grudgingly allowed entry to the country, 46 of 805 in 1902–03 and six of 554 in the 1904–09 period; nobody between 1909 and 1958, when the requirement was dropped, passed the dictation test (National Archives 2005).

The identification of a white Australia extended beyond the creation of legislation within that country to the international sphere. As one of the allied nations in World War I, Australia was allowed to send a small delegation to the Paris peace treaty conference at Versailles in 1919; it included Prime Minister William Morris "Billy" Hughes. Although Australia was to play a generally small role in the conference, one lasting effect of its delegation's presence was the rejection of the concept of racial equality in the preamble to the League of Nations charter. This measure was introduced twice by Japan and both times was defeated in its entirety, largely at the behest of Hughes (Lake and Reynolds 2008). He was concerned that acceptance of racial equality at the international level would threaten the legitimacy of the carefully legislated White Australia policy and thus made a "pestiferous varmint" of himself throughout the proceedings, according to the U.S. president, Woodrow Wilson (Manela 2007, 182).

A second feature of Australian identity codified by law in this early period concerned the centrality of labor in the new country. Despite the restriction on migrants holding labor contracts, the most foundational document of the early Australian nation, the 1901 Constitution, provided for the relatively fair treatment of laborers. Section 51 (xxxv) of the Australian Constitution, known commonly as the "labour power" section, "provides that the federal Parliament may enact laws with respect to the prevention and settlement of interstate industrial disputes by conciliation and arbitration. Thus [the] Constitution guarantee[s] working women and men that their wages would be determined by machinery which was independent of government, of capital and of labour" (Isaac and MacIntyre 2004). Using the powers granted to it in the Constitution, in 1904 the Parliament established a labor court, the Commonwealth Court of Conciliation and Arbitration, which required unions and employers to seek conciliation on their differences and, if that failed, to abide by the Labour Court's decision (Isaac and MacIntyre 2004). Then in 1907 this Labour Court, under Justice Henry Higgins, handed down a decision that was used for generations to point to the relative equality between labor and employer in Australia. Higgins stated in his decision that "the rate of wages must no longer depend on the 'usual, unequal contest' between the employer, who could afford to wait and to choose, and the labourer, who must at all costs win bread" (Thompson 1994, 165–166). The minimum wage was thus established in Australia with a "standard of 'fair and reasonable' . . . as 'the normal needs of an average employee regarded as a human being in a civilised country'" (Thompson 1994, 166).

The identification of Australia as a "working man's paradise" was not new to the Commonwealth. From the 1850s workers in the Australian colonies had a much higher standard of living than their counterparts in most of the rest of the world, and their unions seemed to represent them with great success. For example, the eight-hour workday was instituted in Melbourne in 1856 (Thompson 1994, 156). With the depression and strikes of the 1890s labor's power shifted from unions to the political sphere but was nonetheless stronger than in many other nations, winning "shorter working days, a minimum wage and compulsory arbitration, as well as anti-sweating laws and laws governing factory conditions" (Thompson 1994, 157) in the early 20th century. Although he meant it ironically, the title of William Lane's socialist novel *The Workingman's Paradise* (1892) actually gave language to the identification many Australians had with their new country.

While the identification with a workingman's paradise was felt by many Australians in the early 20th century, the reality was not always so positive. To begin, union representation was limited to full-time employees in only certain jobs and workplaces. Most women did not have such representation; nor did Chinese, Aboriginal, or other nonwhite workers, part-time or casual workers, or many men in smaller companies and businesses (Thompson 1994, 157). Indeed, as many historians have argued, there was a connection in many Australians' minds at the time between a white Australia and an Australia that was fair and equal for laborers. Providing fairness and equality among white men was believed to require that others be excluded. This was seen first in the goldfields of the 1850s, when Chinese miners were abused and driven off for fear that they would drive down salaries (Thompson 1994, 172). It was also seen with Aboriginal Australians; after the 1890 strikes, only whites were allowed to work as sheep shearers or underground miners, two of the highest-paid wage positions in the country at the time (Thompson 1994, 173). Women, too, were excluded from the workingman's paradise and generally earned far less than the minimum wage established for men with comparable skills; male teachers in early 20th-century Tasmania made about £220 per year, while women made £120 (cited in Thompson 1994, 178).

Despite the difficulties women faced in establishing their equality in economic terms, Australia became a world leader in 1902 when the Commonwealth government granted women the right to vote in federal elections. Prior to this, South Australia and Western Australia, in 1894 and 1898, respectively, had given women the right to vote in colonial elections. As a point of comparison, the first country in the world to give women the right to vote was New Zealand, in 1893; the United States only gave women the vote in 1920 and Britain in 1928, though in 1918 women over 30 had received the vote in Britain. Despite this legislation, however, women in Australia were not immediately able to take up the political opportunities granted by suffrage; women did not enter either the Senate or House of Representatives until 1943 (Welsh 2004, 349). In this instance, legislation did not lead to a change in national identity toward greater political equality at that time. Nonetheless,

VIDA JANE MARY GOLDSTEIN

South Australia and Western Australia granted suffrage to women prior to federation, and in 1902 the Commonwealth and New South Wales followed suit. Tasmania did the same in 1903 and Queensland in 1905, but Victorian women had to fight until 1908 for the vote. One of the most important figures in that fight was Vida Goldstein, who began her political activity in 1891, when she and her mother helped gather many of the 30,000 signatures on the Women's Suffrage Petition, or Monster Petition, in favor of the vote for Victorian women.

By 1899 Goldstein had become the undisputed leader of the women's suffrage movement in Australia. She became a full-time organizer of the United Council for Women's Suffrage in 1900 and from that year until 1905 wrote and edited much of the content in the feminist publication *Women's Sphere* (Crooks 2008). She also served as president of the Women's Political Association from 1903 until 1919, when she went overseas. In 1902 Goldstein traveled to the United States in order to represent Australia at the International Womanhood Suffrage Conference; while there she testified before the U.S. Congress and met and spoke with President Theodore Roosevelt. During her time in the United States, the Australian Commonwealth government granted women the right to vote and stand for federal elections and President Roosevelt wanted to meet "the only woman in the US with a right to vote" (Victorian Women's Trust 2008: 12).

When the vote was finally won by Victorian women in 1908, Goldstein did not give up her political activism. By 1903 she was already a veteran of national electoral politics, having run for a Senate seat in that year and lost; in 1910 she tried again for a Senate seat, then in 1913 and 1914 for federal House seats, before running again for the last time for a Senate seat in 1917. Despite her losses in electoral politics, Goldstein remained one of Australia's foremost political activists almost to the time of her death from cancer in 1949 (Brownfoot 1983).

Source: Crooks, Mary. *Foreword to Woman Suffrage in Australia,* by Vida Goldstein, 1908. Reprint (Melbourne: Victorian Women's Trust, 2008), 1–2; Victorian Women's Trust. *Annual Report,* 2006–07 (Melbourne, Vic.: Victorian Women's Trust: 2008); Brownfoot, Janice N. "Goldstein, Vida Jane Mary (1869–1949)." In *Australian Dictionary of Biography.* Vol. 9. (Melbourne: Melbourne University Press, 1983).

in 2007 Australia elected its first female deputy prime minister, Julia Gillard, and in 2009 had a significantly higher percentage of women in both the Senate (29 percent) and House of Representatives (25.3 percent) than did the United States, with 16 percent and 17.5 percent, respectively. Australia's figures were also higher than those in Britain, where in 2008 just 20 percent of both the House of Commons and House of Lords were female.

Images

Although the seeds of a specifically Australian identity may have been sown by such early emancipists as William Wentworth and Lachlan Macquarie, true political nationalism is considered to have emerged in the 1880s (Alomes 2003, 575). While this political nationalism is clear in the Constitution, federation, and legislation, it is also evident in the poetry and visual art of the period.

One of the clearest signs that poetry served a significant role in the creation of Australian national identity is the number of important politicians who took the time to write verse dedicated to the country and its land, animals, and people. This trend began much earlier than the 1880s—William Wentworth published several volumes of verse early in the 19th century—and included the early work of many of the key figures of the federation movement. For example, prior to taking political office, Henry Parkes had poems printed in three important publications, including the *Sydney Morning Herald*. In 1842 Parkes had his first book of poems, *Stolen Moments,* produced by the Sydney publisher Samuel Augustus Tegg; a second volume, *Fragmentary Thoughts,* appeared in 1889 just after Parkes set the stage for bridging the colonies' differences on tariffs and working toward federation. Less well known, Alfred Deakin likewise wrote poetry, as well as drama and other literary forms, prior to stepping into the role of elder Victorian statesman and then Australian prime minister.

According to the Australian historian John Hirst, the best poem written about the federation of the continent's colonies was produced in 1877, long before the political process caught up with the poets' "sacred cause" (2005, 198). The work, "The Dominion of Australia: A Forecast," was written by James Brunton Stephens when he worked as the headmaster of a school in Brisbane, Queensland (Hirst 2005, 199). Politicians in the late 1880s also valued Stephens's work; Parkes cited it at Tenterfield when he opened the door to federation there (Hirst 2005, 199). Alfred Deakin's early foray into verse likewise contributed to his use of other authors' poems to highlight and emphasize points he made in his speeches. In 1898 he turned to William Gay's sonnet "Federation" to conclude his entreaty to the voters of Victoria to approve the referendum on federation (Hirst 2005, 200–201); Deakin, Henry Parkes, and Edmund Barton also gave their written endorsements to Gay's work when it was first published.

In addition to the speeches and events that contributed to the eventual federation, the ceremony itself on January 1, 1901, inspired a great outpouring of verse. That day "and for the days before and after, the newspapers gave over a large part of their space to poetry," including works by Brunton Stephens and George Essex Evans, who won a New South Wales government prize for the best poem "celebrating the inauguration of the Commonwealth" (Hirst 2005, 203). Essex Evans's winning entry in the New South Wales contest for best federation poem drew upon classic imagery, such as that in these lines:

> Free-born of Nations, Virgin white,
>   Not won by blood nor ringed with steel,
> Thy throne is on a loftier height,
>   Deep-rooted in the Commonweal! (cited in Hirst 2005, 203)

Despite the importance of these "true, new poet[s] of the 1890s" (Hirst 2005, 2–4) today very few Australians have even heard of William Gay or George Essex Evans. Their classical images of freedom's fires and white virgins failed to arouse any long-standing association with Australia or Australian identity and thus quickly disappeared from the public imagination.

This does not mean, however, that poetry itself was rejected by the Australian public: far from it. Indeed, even today two of Australia's best-known literary figures on both the domestic and international stage are the poets Henry Lawson and Andrew Barton "Banjo" Paterson. Both men wrote about rural or "bush" Australian life and the landscape in which it took place. Despite this similarity, the two often disagreed and their literary feud, which took place mainly in the pages of the *Bulletin* in the 1890s, attracted further public interest to the work of both men. While the Australia that both authors wrote about was often far removed from the experience of urban Australians, their depictions of rural life, whether through Paterson's romanticism or Lawson's melancholy, struck a cord with the reading public. Among numerous other literary works, Paterson gave to Australia both "Waltzing Matilda," which has become the "unofficial national anthem," and *The Man from Snowy River,* which tells the story of an underestimated stockman who outdoes all his older, bigger rivals to catch an escaped horse worth a great deal of money; it has been made into several films and television series and speaks volumes of the Australian penchant for giving the underdog a chance.

While Australian authors turned to the subject of Australian identity fairly early in the 19th century, and this trend hit a crescendo at federation, Australian visual artists were slower to take up the task of representing the new country in their work. Prior to the 1880s, most artists who took their craft seriously left the colonies and traveled to continental Europe or England to study under the recognized masters and to paint traditional European subjects. The most significant Australian national works of the 19th century emerged only in the 1880s from painters from the Heidelberg school, such as Tom Roberts, Arthur Streeton, and Frederick McCubbin, who all worked outside Melbourne. They "captured Australian light, the changing colours of the bush" (Alomes 2003, 575). They produced scenes recognizable to the Australian public and began to see themselves and their work as part of the grand project of creating a national identity.

Despite the efforts of 19th- and early 20th-century Australian writers and painters, the push for a unique artistic culture to represent the new nation did not last very long (Alomes 2003, 582). The fundamental problem was the difference between rural Australia, where very few people actually lived or worked, and urban Australia, which resembled the English world to such a degree that many English visitors at the start of the 20th century commented on its similarities with home (Alomes 2003, 582). Most of the writers and painters whose works have remained important in Australia turned their hands to rural themes, as the cited examples show. While these have since become classics because they are uniquely Australian, at the time most did little to awaken a national consciousness in a population that had minimal experience with the bush. Indeed, the centrality of these rural images led many early 20th-century urban Australians to think of themselves as less Australian than their rural counterparts and thus as somehow inferior to the bushman or bushwoman, farmer, or drover while "authentic" Australian urban identity remained somewhat problematic.

A second problem in the creation of an Australian national consciousness and identity was the lack of national independence. Although federation in 1901 joined the six colonies and provided for a Commonwealth government, the head of state remained the British monarch. Australia remained very much a segment of the larger British Empire with its far-flung economic and geographic interests, a condition that resulted in a "'schizoid love-hate' for Britain" (Souter 1976, 21–22). As a result, some of the most important moments in the cre-

One of the rural Australian scenes depicted by the Heidelberg School painter Tom Roberts in his 1894 painting The Golden Fleece *(The Bridgeman Art Library)*

ation of Australian identity were the times when Australians could see themselves in contrast to their English cousins. In the early 20th century, the most vivid of these moments occurred during times of war and the more friendly sporting battles that took place between Australia and England every season on the cricket pitch and rugby field.

War

While a small number of Australian soldiers fought along with their British allies in New Zealand in 1863–65 and an even smaller number participated in the British war in Sudan in 1885, they did not do so as Australians but rather as Victorians, South Australians, New South Welshmen, and so forth. The first time Australians joined a British war as Australians was in the Boer War of 1899–1902. The first contingents to participate did so as Victorians, New South Welshmen, Queenslanders, and so on, but in 1901 the new Commonwealth government sent an army to fight alongside the British to secure their colonial hold on South Africa. Altogether, between December 1899 and May 1902, 16,175 Australians served on the battlefields of South Africa, where 518 of them died of wounds or fever and a further 882 were wounded; six Australian "bushmen," as they were known, were honored with the Victoria Cross, the highest honor in the British army (Molony 2005, 179).

At the start of the Boer War in South Africa, most Australian combatants and even the Australian public at home supported the war wholeheartedly as their way of contributing to the strength of the British Empire (Penny 1967, 107–108). However, the experience also provided some Australians with an opportunity to see themselves as members of a nation separate from Britain and its empire. This tendency strengthened toward the end of the war when increasing casualties, the "'scorched earth' tactics" (Welsh 2004, 331) of the British war machine, and hardship tilted support away from the war. In a period when Australian nationalism was floundering over the issues of independence and the rural-urban divide, the war, which had previously provided a way for the Australian colonies and, after 1901, the brand new federation to "prove" their Britishness, began to serve the nationalists' cause. In this context, Lt. Harry "Breaker" Morant emerged as a powerful national symbol.

The actual events surrounding the adoption of Morant and his colleagues as symbols of the new Australian nation were hardly patriotic. Morant and his fellow soldiers in the Bushveldt Carbineers, Peter Handcock, George Witton, Robert Lenehan, and the only non-Australian, Harry Picton, were all charged with the murders of a number of Boer prisoners of war. In addition, Handcock was charged with the murder of a missionary of German descent who had probably seen the murders of the others; Morant was charged with "instigating and commanding that killing" (Henry 2001). At their court-martial all of the men claimed that they had been ordered to kill the prisoners for having committed atrocities against the British and having donned British uniforms to mislead their enemy (Boer War 2008). Certainly, some Boer guerrillas had done both of these things during the course of the war, and there is evidence that the British and their imperial

Lt. Harry "Breaker" Morant in his Bushveldt Carbineer uniform, 1900 (Pictures Collection, State Library of Victoria)

allies killed them for it, usually without recourse. In this case, however, the presence of a German witness resulted in much greater exposure for the case and the need for a public investigation, trial, and conviction (Henry 2001). On a larger scale, some commentators have argued that Morant and Handcock, the only two to have received the death penalty, were made scapegoats for the uncivilized way the British waged war against the Boers in general. This included the creation of concentration camps for women and children and the deaths from cholera and hunger of tens of thousands of Boer civilians.

Since the early 20th century, Morant and his colleagues have been used by Australian nationalists as powerful symbols of Australian victimhood at British hands and thus Australian distinctiveness from the mother country (Henry 2001). George Witton's release from prison shows the interest that tens of thousands of Australians took in the case. While Morant and Handcock were sentenced to be executed by firing squad in Pretoria, South Africa, in February 1902, their fellow Carbineer George Witton was sentenced to jail for life. He was transported to England to serve his sentence but was released after only two years, in 1904, after 80,000 Australians signed a petition to King Edward VII; the Australian government also pressured the British authorities for Witton's release (Thornton 2008). Upon his release, Witton wrote his own account of events in South Africa; his 1907 book *Scapegoats of the Empire* depicts the Carbineers as expedient sacrifices for the British government. In 1980 this image of Morant, in particular, as an Australian victim of British war policy was revived by the Australian filmmaker and nationalist Bruce Beresford in his movie *Breaker Morant,* in which many of the actual events of the case were distorted to justify the idea of a republican Australia free at last of British control (Henry 2001). In late 2009 the issue emerged again when two senior Australian military officers presented petitions to the Australian Parliament and Queen Elizabeth II to pardon Morant because, they claim, the court case against them contained 10 different grounds for a mistrial (Silvester 2009).

Not long after the release of Witton's book, in 1914 the next chapter in the construction of a distinct Australian identity began with the launch of the Great War, or World War I. At the start of the war in August of that year, the vast proportion of Australians supported the idea of sending soldiers to fight on the side of the British Empire against the Germans. Even before he was elected prime minister, the Labor leader Andrew Fisher pledged to support Britain "to our last man and our last shilling" (cited in Clarke 2003, 185). With few exceptions, most Australians agreed with him. Voluntary enlistment in the armed services remained high through the end of 1915, with the highest figures recorded for July 1915, when 36,600 men joined up (Molony 2005, 224). The historian Gavin Souter argues that "the prevailing emotions in Australia . . . were sheer excitement and a surge of tribal loyalty" (1976, 212).

The first actions taken in the war by Australians involved the navy, which had been established only in 1911 (Welsh 2004, 360). German ships that were in the Pacific to service the country's colonies quickly came under Australian fire, and several wireless stations in Micronesia, New Guinea, and Nauru were captured by the Australians. The most famous of these actions actually took place in the Indian Ocean when the HMAS *Sydney* pursued the German ship *Emden* to the Cocos Islands, where it ran aground and was destroyed (Souter 1976, 205–206). At the time of this battle, the *Sydney,* along with several other Australian ships and their Japanese convoy leaders, were on their way to Egypt. There Australian soldiers were put through desert training before the British attempt to capture Gallipoli, a peninsula in southern Turkey.

The British onslaught against the Turks at Gallipoli began on April 25, 1915, and the first Australians, from the Third Australia Infantry Brigade, landed at 4:30 A.M. at what is now called Anzac Cove, after the Australian and New Zealand Army Corps. As a result of a combination of bad planning and a total misreading of the Turkish forces' capabilities, by evening of that first day more than 2,000 Australians had died, while a further 16,000 were dug into the Turkish hillside for a battle that would last another eight months (Molony 2005, 223). Wave after wave of allied soldiers were sent to their deaths in a vain attempt to take this small coastal territory from the Turks and thus relieve the Russians from Ottoman control of the outlet to the Mediterranean Sea. Finally, just before Christmas 1915, the last 20,000 Australian soldiers were removed from the trenches of Gallipoli under cover of night, with just two deaths, and the Australian "baptism of fire" was over (Molony 2005, 224).

Gallipoli was disastrous for all the armies that participated: Australia lost 8,141 soldiers, New Zealand, 2,431, France 9,798, the British more than 30,000, and the Turks between 80,000 and 100,000 (Welsh 2004, 368). For the Australians, however, Gallipoli became an important national symbol. Many historians argue that it "shocked the country into a new consciousness of nationality, one which was unique, precious and distinct from a sense of being a distant Dominion of the British Empire" (Welsh 2004, 368). The tremendous blood sacrifice on the Turkish shore was seen by many Australians as having given their new nation "equality and acceptance" on the international sphere, where previously there had been just fear and loathing of its convict past. The blood of Australian soldiers had "redeemed" the blood of their convict relatives (Molony 2005, 236; also Welsh 2004, 368).

One of the most important figures in the creation of this foundational national legend was Keith Murdoch, father of News Corp's Rupert Murdoch, publisher of the *Australian* and 17 other Australian newspapers, as well as the *Wall Street Journal, New York Post,* and five British papers (News Corporation 2009). In 1915 Murdoch senior was a journalist who had been sent to Gallipoli "to investigate Australian Imperial Force mail services and associated matters" (Serle 1986, 624). As part of his brief before leaving, he had to sign "the standard official declaration to observe the rules of censorship" (Serle 1986, 624). Despite this, after seeing the impossible position in which the Anzacs found themselves, he broke his pledge. Rather than submitting his article for publication, Murdoch "composed an 8000-word letter to [Prime Minister Andrew] Fisher which he sent on 23 September. It was a remarkable document which lavishly and sentimentally praised the Australians and attacked the performance of the British army at all levels, including many errors and exaggerations" (Serle 1986, 624). He compared the masculine "physique and fighting qualities of the Anzacs" with the "feeble, childlike youths" of the British army (Welsh 2004, 368). This report, as well as Murdoch's later dispatches from the war's European theater, contributed greatly to Australians' nationalistic pride and, as did the legend that developed around Breaker Morant, provided an opportunity for Australians to see themselves as victims of the British, who had sent Australian soldiers to their deaths. As was the case with Morant, the early 1980s saw the production of an Australian film, Peter Weir's *Gallipoli,* which encouraged this view of valiant Australians being sacrificed by incompetent British leaders.

After the massive defeat of the Anzacs and other Allied forces at Gallipoli, hundreds of thousands of other Australian soldiers fought for the British in World War I, and nearly 60,000 of them died (Souter 1976, 209). In summer and fall 1916, some 23,000 Australians died just at the battles around Pozières, France, while in late 1917 another 38,000 died in a few months of fighting around Ypres, Belgium (Molony 2005, 227, 230). Altogether some 59,342 Australian soldiers lost their lives, while a further 152,171 were wounded in action, leaving only 120,267 to return home physically unscathed from their time on the

Melbourne's monumental World War I memorial, the Shrine of Remembrance, built between 1928 and 1934 to honor the memory of the 114,000 Victorians who served in the military during the 1914–18 period (Neale Cousland/Shutterstock)

battlefield (Clark 1995, 235). Today this tremendous national sacrifice, where one in five Australian men between 18 and 45 died, as well as the centrality of this sacrifice to Australian national identity, are still evident in the Great War memorials of almost every Australian town and city, approximately 2,000 spread throughout the country (Inglis 1989, 36). The grandest of these monuments is Melbourne's Shrine of Remembrance, "possibly the most massive 1914–1918 monument in the world" (Inglis 1989, 37).

Sport

While the battlefields of South Africa, Turkey, and Europe provided some of the most significant opportunities to create an Australian national identity in the early 20th century, they were not the only ones. Australian sporting prowess was also, and indeed continues to be, an important arena for the construction of a unique Australian identity. With each sporting victory on the international stage, Australians became more attached to the idea of their common identity and purpose. Victories over English rivals or on English soil were particularly important, for they highlighted Australians' unique place in the empire. For example, in 1914 the Australian Norman Brookes won the English tennis championships at Wimbledon; he also led the men's national team in taking home tennis's Davis Cup four times between 1907 and 1914 (Souter 1976, 208–209). At London's summer Olympics in 1908 Australia won its first medals, one gold for its defeat of England in rugby, two silver, and a bronze (Australian Olympic Committee 1). Four years later in Stockholm Australians dominated the swimming events and took home a total of six medals, placing them sixth on the medal tally list, two of each color (Australian Olympic Committee 2). These games also gave Australians their first female international sporting hero, Sarah "Fanny" Durack, who defeated her teammate Mina Wylie and set a world record every time she entered the pool at the games (Australian Olympic Committee 2).

While tennis, rugby, and swimming continue to be competitions in which Australians are particularly proud of their victories over England, probably the fiercest rivalry between the two countries is on the cricket pitch. Some writers even believe that Australia's victories over England in cricket in 1898 and 1899 contributed to the large majority who voted for federation (Molony 2005, 193). Today when England and Australia line up for the Ashes series, a month-long set of five games of five-day test cricket, millions of viewers in both countries tune in to cheer for their national squad. In the early 20th century this rivalry was already 20 years old, having begun in 1882 when Australia handed England its first defeat in cricket at home. From that point forward, test matches have drawn tremendous interest. In the 1901–14 period, each side won the Ashes trophy four times (Souter 1976, 209); however, from 1882

A fast bowler delivers to the batsman while the wicket keeper and other fielders prepare for action. (Lance Bellers/Shutterstock)

through 2009 Australia won two more series than England, 31 to 29 (Andrews 2006).

Equality

The most important idea that links almost all of the cultural and political forms that contributed to the construction of Australia and Australian national identity through the first two decades of the 20th century is the notion of equality. While Australia has certainly never been an equal society, the idea of equality has been important since at least the 1850s, when Australian nationalists used it in their project. Politically the idea of equality can be seen in the form of government that the Australian state adopted, parliamentary democracy, as well as the substance of many of its laws, particularly the "labour power" legislation.

Culturally there is a national identification with endured hardship, perhaps beginning with the misery of the convicts, and later the plight of the "diggers," poor miners who dragged their dirt-sifting cradles through muddy channels in search of gold, usually with little reward. This image was revitalized by the "diggers" of Gallipoli, who spent eight months living in trenches they had dug into the Turkish hillside. In each of these images the little guy is at the mercy of an authority figure with questionable motives, prone to heavy-handed control and abuse of power. With this in mind Australians tend to be suspicious of authority figures, especially those who have not worked their way up through the ranks and have little firsthand experience of what it means to be "in the trenches." In conjunction with this, inherited power and privilege are not legitimate until validated through honorable action and fairness toward those in less fortunate circumstances, thus acknowledging their equal humanity, regardless of status at birth.

Australian heroes are likely to be working-class "battlers" who quietly achieve success through hard work and irreverent humor directed at anyone putting on airs and graces. This attitude marked a clear departure from their English forebears, who in the early 20th century continued to place considerable importance on ascribed versus achieved entitlements. Australians also experience American culture as very different, with its emphasis on individual accomplishment and bragging. Australians even to this day tend to favor the underdog over the champion; they choose to downplay the accomplishments of self and others over grandstanding. A common metaphor to depict this difference is the tall poppy. As when the tallest poppy in the field is the first to lose its flower, Australians use irony, sarcasm, and other forms of humor to lower people who try to place themselves above others; conversely, Americans tend to revere the tall poppy.

Despite the centrality of this idea, the general myth of equality that emerged as part of an Australian national identity is not borne out by figures from the early 20th century. In 1915 one half of 1 percent of the adult male population owned 30 percent of the country's wealth; a full two thirds of all wealth was owned by just 5 percent of the adult male population (Thompson 1994, 163–164). Aboriginal Australians were not even citizens in the country that had been established on their ancient territory, and other nonwhites could not migrate there. The development of greater political and cultural maturity throughout the 20th century began to address some of these contradictions, but many remain today to be worked out in both the political and the cultural spheres.

Conclusion

The creation of Australia in both its political form as a semi-independent state and its cultural form as a community of national members was still far from complete by 1919, but great strides had been made by politicians and nationalists. A constitution had been written and ratified and enough people had pledged their loyalty to the idea of the new state and its political forms that coups and bloody civil wars were highly unlikely. There were still many questions about what cultural forms best represented this new national community, but, despite their common language and head of state, there was no question in most Australians' minds that they were not English (or Irish), but Australian. Australian courage on the battlefield and victories on the sporting field were just two sites in which Australianness could be imagined as distinct from these other identities. The next period of history, 1920–46, provided even more opportunities for these developments, as well as for other changes in the political and national character of the country.

6

REALIGNMENT (1920–1946)

The transformation of Australia from a cluster of six competing British colonies to an autonomous nation is still a work in progress, given the remaining formal tie to the British monarchy. Nevertheless, the context of two world wars and the volatile interlude between them produced many changes in Australia and the Australian people that pushed them closer to independence. Electoral modifications were made and a challenge to federation from the west established the form the nascent democracy would take. The new capital city was opened by the future King George VI, and the future cricket king, Donald Bradman, had his most productive years in the crease against England. In 1930 21-year-old Donald Bradman stunned the cricket world on the Australians' tour of England by scoring 974 runs in just seven turns at bat, with an average of 139 and a high score of 334 (Molony 2005, 262). Economic depression and a world war that was fought in Australia's Pacific neighborhood challenged the country and its leaders to seek new alliances, while a few white women and Aboriginal men gained access to national positions and power previously monopolized by white men.

War's Aftermath

New Guinea

Australia emerged from World War I as a young country, brimming with confidence about its place in the international sphere. As part of his country's coming of age, Prime Minister Billy Hughes was eager to claim Germany's colony in northeast New Guinea and add it to Australia's existing territory of Papua in the southeast; the western portion of the island was a Dutch colony until 1962. The Australian "coconut lancers" had captured the German territory in 1914 and Hughes saw an expanded Australian colony on the island as a kind of reward or recompense for Australia's devastating war casualties; at 65 percent they were the highest per capita of any country—the figure for Britain was 51 percent; Canada, 50 percent; and New Zealand, 59 percent (Clarke 2003, 193).

Hughes's persistence at Versailles was rewarded, much to the chagrin of the U.S. president Woodrow Wilson, who opposed any postwar annexations. As a latecomer to the war, however, the president held little sway over Australian aspirations. In the end, Australia was given a C class mandate over New Guinea, which allowed it to rule under the supervision of the League of Nations, rather than full ownership. Securing a place in the Pacific beyond Australian borders was a significant foreign affairs victory for Hughes, who had long been concerned about Japanese expansion in the region.

The history of Australian intervention in New Guinea had begun in 1906 when Australia formally accepted administrative responsibilities of the British colony of Papua on the southeast of the island; the British colony of Queensland had actually annexed Papua in 1883 but did not retain administration in the area. In the late 19th century both the British and the Germans were interested in exploiting the resources of their respective territories, but it was the Germans who created economically viable industries and infrastructure to support them; the British, by contrast, built almost nothing. By the early 20th century German coconut plantations had become relatively lucrative in meeting European demand for copra, the dried flesh of coconuts from which coconut oil is extracted. Villagers were obliged to toil on the plantations in return for social services such as schools and medical treatment. Strict discipline was expected and harsh punishments were meted out for any breach of conduct.

Despite the fact that the former German colony was adjacent to the existing Australian colony of Papua, the two regions were under very different administrations after the war. Papua continued to be administered by the benevolent but economically disinterested lieutenant governor, Hubert Murray, who had been in the colony since 1904, while the new mandate was under the rule of Australian generals. The generals' style of colonial rule was to leave the German plantation owners in place to exploit and mistreat local workers. Copra production remained high and, aside from the ascendance of English over German as the official language, little changed in northeast New Guinea. As a result of this management scheme, the newly formed League of Nations repeatedly cited Australia's poor governance of the region, but to little avail. Only the threat posed by Japan in the early 1940s roused the Australian administration to make any significant changes, almost none of which benefited the local population. In 1942 the Australian military amalgamated the two regions under the Australian New Guinea Administrative Unit (ANGAU), which survived the Japanese invasion to last until 1946. Papua New Guinea finally attained independence from Australia in 1975.

Domestic Change

While Australia was changed at the end of the war by becoming a colonizer of other peoples, domestically, too, the war and its aftermath had produced changes in politics, economics, and social life. Some of these changes were the result of greater national maturity and thus greater separation from the British, while others were dictated by global trends.

One of the areas of social and political change in this period was the advancement of women's rights. After winning suffrage earlier in the century, Australian women remained outside political life until the early

Portrait of Dame Enid Lyons. *Lyons (1897–1981) has the distinction of both being the first woman in Australia's House of Representatives and serving in a cabinet position.* (nla.pic-an23259539/National Library of Australia)

1920s. For many feminists during this era and beyond, remaining outside the formal political sphere was actually a choice willingly made. They believed that lobbying on behalf of equal pay and women's and children's benefits, a cluster of issues referred to as maternalism, would be more beneficial than serving the needs of a political party, where other issues would by necessity occupy them and compromises would have to be made on women's issues (Lake 1999).

The first person to break this outsider trend for women in Australian politics was Edith Cowan, who in 1921 became the first woman to be elected to any Australian parliament. Cowan entered the Western

Australian Legislative Assembly as a Nationalist who occasionally allied herself with the government, occasionally with the opposition. Her three years in the state parliament were a capstone for Cowan, who was in her sixties when she entered parliament and had long been an activist for women's and children's rights. This previous experience made her a highly effective parliamentarian, who was able to focus her attention on reforms most urgent for women, including changes in divorce court proceedings, guardianship of children, and inheritance law.

Although these were groundbreaking achievements for Cowan personally, they did not usher in swift social and political changes for women more generally. In fact, 22 years elapsed before a woman reached the next milestone of entering the federal parliament. During the 1920s women's participation in the workforce dropped slightly and many focused their attention on homemaking rather than on competing with returned soldiers and married men for jobs. Women became housewives in greater numbers and at a younger age than ever before, though a few remained in public life to lobby against the social ills they believed threatened the stability of family life, particularly the sale of alcohol (Summers 2002, 434).

Electoral Change

While the British foundation of Australia began with the arrival of the First Fleet in 1788, Australia is really a 20th-century nation, with the federation of the separate colonies in 1901. As such, many aspects of the political system were still being worked through less than two decades later, when World War I came to an end. One of the most important of these was the voting system used in local, state, territory, and federal elections.

Australia is one of just 20 countries in the world today that require its citizens both to enroll to vote once they have turned 18 and to vote in all elections; this is often called compulsory voting (Compulsory Voting in Australia 2008). At federation in 1901 neither of these aspects of the electoral system had been written into the Constitution. It was a full decade before mandatory electoral enrollment was enacted at the federal level, although before this police constables did visit each household to try to establish a complete electoral roll (Hirst 2004, 114). In 1911 "enrolment became a continuing obligation on citizens" (Hirst 2004, 114); at that time, however, actually voting was not mandatory.

Compulsory voting emerged first in Queensland in 1915 as a result of the opposition party's attempt to limit the Labor Party's strength in that year's election. The tactic did not work, but Labor retained the law and the idea soon spread. A royal commission in 1915 recommended that compulsory voting be adopted at the federal level as well. The first step was the Compulsory Voting Act 1915, which required all Australians to vote in constitutional referenda. The idea of compulsory voting for all elections at the federal level, however, did not attract enough support after it was introduced in 1918 to become law. This changed after the 1922 election, when "apathy was widespread" (Welsh 2004, 389) and the turnout much lower than in previous elections; it dropped from 71.59 percent in 1919 to 59.38 percent in 1922 (Enrolment, Voting and Informality Statistics 2008). Because of the low voter turnout in his state, a Tasmanian senator introduced the compulsory voting bill, which passed through both houses "without much discussion or division" (Welsh 2004, 391).

Although it has been the law of the land since 1924, compulsory voting continues to attract considerable discussion at every federal election. Critics claim it is undemocratic since citizens, aside from those serving jail terms of five or more years, those who have been convicted of treason, and those who are "incapable of understanding the nature and significance of enrolment and voting" (Compulsory Voting 2008), have no choice to opt out of the system. Others claim that it allows the political parties to ignore those districts where they have a safe margin of victory (Bennett 2008, 1). Many more Australians, however, continue to support their compulsory system, claiming it makes them feel Australian and increases voter turnout generally, thus guaranteeing a legitimate democratic government (Bennett 2008, 1).

While it took 23 years after federation to establish this electoral policy, the second distinctive feature of Australian elections emerged a few years earlier. In 1918 when compulsory voting was rejected by Parliament, a preferential voting system was supported and put in play through the Commonwealth Electoral Act 1918. Most countries in the world use what is called a first-past-the-post election system, whereby the candidate with the largest number of votes wins. In Australia, however, the winning candidate must receive at least 50 percent plus one of all votes cast. When more than two people are running for a position, as is usually the case, there is a very good chance that no candidate will receive the required 50 percent plus one vote. This problem is solved by requiring constituents to vote not for a single candidate but to rank all the candidates running for any given position. In the first round of counting, only voters' first preference votes (called primary votes) are counted. If no one achieves the necessary number, then the candidate who received the fewest first preferences is dropped from the election and all of his or her votes are redistributed according to voters' second choices. This process continues until the necessary threshold has been reached and a winner declared.

Aboriginal Affairs

In 1924 the first politically organized Aboriginal activist group, the Australian Aboriginal Progressive Association (AAPA), was established in New South Wales by Fred Maynard. The main objectives of the group were to "improve the material conditions of Aboriginal people and to end political oppression" (cited in Maynard 1997, 2). Maynard and the other members of the AAPA believed the key impediment to Aboriginal people's living healthy, independent, and productive lives was the loss of their reserve lands. In New South Wales such land had been successfully cultivated and independently farmed for many decades, until it was seized and the people removed at gunpoint. Between 1913 and 1927 New South Wales confiscated some 13,000 acres (5,261 ha) of prime coastal land from Aboriginal reserves, about half the total of reserve land available (Maynard 1997, 2). As in the case of Coranderrk in Victoria, the Indigenous people of New South Wales had demonstrated that with land and the ability to make decisions for themselves, they could navigate the parameters of white society with success equal to that of any other population in the country. Without the rights and protections of citizenship, however, Indigenous people were systematically denied equal opportunities until 1967. Communities were broken up and children, primarily girls, were forcibly taken from their families to work for white farmers throughout the state as part of the apprenticeship scheme.

Fred Maynard was aware of many instances of abuse of these stolen children, and one of the activities of the AAPA was to lobby for the abolition of the scheme. The AAPA also attempted to change the legal structure of the remaining reserves to grant their Aboriginal residents control over production, consumption, and decision making more generally. In their attempt to protect their sphere of interest and power, the Aboriginal Protection Board tried numerous tactics to prevent AAPA board members, even the one non-Aboriginal member, from accessing the reserves (Maynard 1997, 6). For their work, the AAPA was highly regarded by Indigenous populations both inside and outside New South Wales, but its existence threatened the official policy of white racial superiority. By 1927 under the weight of institutional repression, especially police harassment, lack of funds, and racism, the organization collapsed.

Not long after the AAPA folded in New South Wales, the last recorded mass murder of Aboriginal people in Australia took place in the Northern Territory, near Alice Springs. This event is today known as the Coniston Massacre. It began as a series of "punitive expeditions" against the Warlpiri people led by Mounted Constable George Murray

REGINALD WALTER SAUNDERS

While this period was very difficult for many Aboriginal people in Australia, a few individuals were able to rise above the institutional racism. One such person was Reginald Saunders, Australia's first Aboriginal commissioned military officer. Saunders joined the Australian Imperial Force (AIF) in April 1940, soon after Australia entered World War II, and was quickly identified as a natural leader. Within six weeks he was promoted to lance corporal; three months later he was a sergeant.

Saunders was sent first to Libya and then to Greece, withdrawing to Crete in July 1941. When the allies were forced to evacuate Crete, leaving behind several hundred troops, Saunders was driven into hiding for almost a year. His dark complexion, however, enabled him to pass as Mediterranean until he was secretly taken off the island by a British submarine.

Soon after his return home in 1942, Saunders was sent to fight in the Owen Stanley Range in New Guinea. It was during this time that he was nominated for promotion to a commissioned rank, a level never before offered to an Indigenous Australian. After 16 weeks of officer training in Victoria, Saunders was redeployed in New Guinea in November 1944 and spent the remainder of the war in command of a unit of 30 other Australians. After the war Saunders took a break from the life of a soldier and worked various jobs, until 1950 and the start of the Korean War, when he returned to the army. He was captain of the Third Battalion and fought with distinction at Kapyong and Maryamsam.

After the war Saunders left the army. He eventually moved to Sydney, where he took up the position of liaison and public relations officer for the Australian Government's Office of Aboriginal Affairs. In 1971, decades after Saunders's service to Australia, he was awarded the honor of Member of the Order of the British Empire (MBE). In 1985, five years before his death, he was also appointed to the Council of the Australian War Memorial.

in retaliation for the killing of a white dingo trapper. The official number of Aboriginal people killed is 32, while the unofficial count is at least twice that number (Wilson and O'Brien 2003). Such retaliatory expeditions began early in the colonial period (1790) under the direction of Governor Arthur Phillip "to infuse an universal terror" (Wilson and O'Brien 2003) in response to Aboriginal attacks on white people or property. By 1928 police and vigilante acts of retribution had become so common and disproportionate that the government was increasingly required to respond with lengthy public investigations. As a result of this delayed government action, the 1928 Coniston Massacre stands as the last recorded massacre in Australian history. Though all Europeans involved in the Coniston killings were cleared of any wrongdoing, the Northern Territory no longer officially supported "punitive expeditions," opting instead that white courts settle disputes with Indigenous people. Unfortunately, in the vast majority of instances, these courts proved no more just to Aboriginal people.

The Depression

The global financial and political landscape shifted dramatically after World War I. Power swung to the United States, while the creation of new nations in Europe dramatically changed the flow of trade and exchange of currency. One result of this transformation was a short but deep recession in Australia, in 1920 (Murray in Masson 1993, xv). Although the economy quickly rallied on the back of the sheep and steady wheat production, notice had been served: Australia was too dependent on external demand for its raw materials and international loans for maintaining its public works. With the stock market crash of 1929, the country's export- and loans-driven economy stood no chance of shielding itself from the events sweeping most of Europe and the United States. The economic depression of the 1930s saw massive unemployment, poverty, and deprivation in all Australian cities and rural communities.

This major world event had its roots in the war. On both the winning and the losing sides, many countries funded the cost of the war by abandoning gold as the standard by which they valued their currency and instead simply printed money. Such measures led to inflation that continued far beyond the conflict, even when the gold standard was reinstituted. After the war Germany again tried to solve its financial problems by printing more money, setting off hyperinflation. In addition, the defeated Axis powers of Austria-Hungary and Germany were unable to pay the unrealistically high reparations required of them under the Treaty of Versailles. This failure to pay also contributed to budget problems in the recipient countries, Britain and France. Another problem for Britain was a return to the gold standard at too high a rate, which rendered exports too expensive and overseas demand too low to continue production. With a widespread slump in manufacturing, unemployment rose and remained high in the years leading up to the depression. In contrast, the U.S. dollar was undervalued, encouraging exports and contributing to an unsound economic boom and a credit bubble that resulted in the crash of the stock market in 1929 (Pettinger 2009).

Australia was inextricably caught up in these events because of the sudden slump in prices for its two main exports, wool and wheat, and the drying up of loans from London. In the 1920s wool accounted for 40 percent and wheat 15 percent of total exports, with other agricultural products making up the remainder (Murray 1993, xvi). Gold was no longer being found at prewar rates and other mineral industries were not yet fully developed. With little self-generated revenue, the newly elected Labor prime minister, James Scullin, faced a difficult task in 1929–30 in convincing conservative London financiers, who had lost significant investments on Wall Street, to fund public works projects in a former colony where strong union sympathies often clashed with the interests of investors.

In rural areas small towns built around the business of supplying farms had no buyers for their goods. Thousands in the country and city went bankrupt and various large companies went into liquidation. Unlike that today, the system of unemployment insurance was woefully inadequate to support individuals or keep families together, and retirement benefits were nonexistent except for government or bank employees. Australia at the time did not yet have a federal social welfare system; rather, each state administered its own scheme separately. Only Queensland provided monetary unemployment insurance, but residency had to have been established for six months to be eligible. The other states provided vouchers that allowed the unemployed to collect small amounts of food (Murray in Masson 1993, xii). In addition, in all states unemployment aid was not given to young people living at home if the family had any other form of income. As a result, many people took to the road in search of work with nothing more than the clothes on their back and a "swag," or sleeping bag, for sleeping under the stars (Murray in Mason 1993, xiii).

Despite our knowledge that life was difficult for many in Australia in this period, it is a complex matter to give exact figures of the number of poor and unemployed. Defining who constituted the Australian

PHAR LAP

During the height of the depression, Australians turned to various forms of entertainment to cushion the difficulties caused by the worst financial downturn in the modern history of capitalism. One of the greatest of these diversions was Phar Lap, a racehorse with an astounding 73 percent win rate, whose name means "lightning" in Thai.

Phar Lap's story begins in New Zealand, where he was born, but continues in Australia where the trainer Harry Telford took him after his purchase by an American, David Davis, for the paltry sum of about US$130. On April 28, 1929, Phar Lap proved his purchase price was a bargain when he won his first race, the relatively minor Rosehill Maiden Juvenile Handicap. From there Phar Lap's reputation grew along with his prize money. After making his owners just AU£182 in his first year of racing, Phar Lap went on to earn a total of AU£70,125 over the course of four years, with major wins in the Melbourne Cup, Victoria Derby, AJC Derby, W. S. Cox Plate (twice) in Australia, and the Agua Caliente Handicap in Tijuana, Mexico. Along with Phar Lap's

(continues)

The jockey Jim Pike riding Phar Lap at Melbourne's Flemington Racetrack, circa 1930 (Pictures Collection, State Library of Victoria)

PHAR LAP *(continued)*

numerous victories, the "big, plain looking, cheap-priced underdog" (Equal Marketing 2006) became a phenomenon during the depression because both he and his trainer, Telford, were seen by the Australian public as "battlers." With their victories over wealthy owners and horses that had been purchased for 10 times the price, the pair represented to Australians that hard work and perseverance could prevail in the end, even during times of depression.

Phar Lap's reputation only increased when his life was tragically cut short after his miraculous win at Agua Caliente. Phar Lap died a painful death in Menlo Park, California, just days after this victory. At the time Australians suspected that Americans had poisoned their beloved horse after he defeated their best entrants at Agua Caliente. Hair analyses in 2006 confirming that Phar Lap had a large amount of arsenic in his system at the time of death only confirmed what many Australians had suspected.

Source: Equus Marketing. "The Phar Lap Story" (2006). Available online. URL: http://www.pharlap.com.au/thestory. Accessed May 21, 2009.

workforce in the 1930s entailed simply counting the number of trade union members in each state. Unemployment statistics were collected by counting the number of union members out of work. This method, while straightforward, was far too simplistic to capture the true picture of the economic downturn because it left out various sectors of the population, including school leavers not yet registered with a union, part-time workers who would have preferred to be working full time, most women, and Aboriginal people. Nonetheless, these figures do give some insight into the startling trends. For example, unemployment in the 1920s averaged around 7 percent, while by the early 1930s the figure was around 32 percent. Unemployment was most severe in New South Wales, where 34 percent of trade union members were out of work, and South Australia was not far behind, at 32.5 percent. Of all the states agricultural Queensland was the least affected, with 18.8 percent unemployment (Murray in Mason 1993, xxvii).

In order to gain the confidence of London investors and get his country's economy moving again, Prime Minister Scullin allowed a delegation from the Bank of England, led by Otto Niemeyer, to enter Australia in late 1930 to assess the country's financial situation for themselves. At the same time Scullin sailed to the United Kingdom to participate in the 1930 Imperial Conference from which the Statute of Westminster, which abolished Britain's power to supersede Australian law, emerged; unfortunately, it proved to be an inopportune time for Scullin to be absent. Just prior to his five months overseas the government's deputy leader and treasurer, Edward Granville (Ted) Theodore, was forced to step down while under investigation for fraud; simultaneously, Niemeyer's presence caused resentment and suspicion from the Left faction within the Labor Party. As the depression worsened, Australia was without its leader, deputy leader, and treasurer, while overseas bankers were making decisions about investments that could make or break the economy.

Scullin returned from the Imperial Conference in January 1931 and reinstated his deputy, but the factional fighting over this and other issues had left the party in disarray. Some cabinet members supported Niemeyer's assessment that Australia was living beyond its means and needed to scale spending back significantly. Others demonized Niemeyer as a representative of callous bankers, intent on sucking the working classes dry.

The combination of losing a quarter of an Australian generation in World War I, followed by the Great Depression a mere decade later, left those who rejected Niemeyer's assessment significantly disillusioned with distant powers' ability to manage world events and, indeed, with Australia's involvement in them. One of the key figures representing those who felt betrayed and resentful of these distant financiers was the Labor premier of New South Wales, John Thomas (Jack) Lang. Lang wielded a great deal of influence as the premier of the country's largest state by population. He argued for postponement of debt repayments to overseas bondholders, some of which was war debt to be paid to Britain. This position was very popular with the general public, especially traditional Labor voters from the union movement.

On the other side, several cabinet members argued that Australia had to limit spending. One of those who put forward this case most vehemently was Joseph Lyons, minister for posts, works, and railways, who supported Niemeyer's recommendations wholeheartedly. Lyons was joined by the majority of state premiers, aside from Lang, whose "Premiers' Plan" called for significant cuts in government expenditure in the areas of greatest financial drain, especially wages and pensions for government workers.

Scullin was in a bind, torn between supporting the "Langites," on one side, and the majority of Australian state premiers in their endorsement of Niemeyer's recommendations, on the other. In the end, not wanting to risk the country's ability to attract future loans, Scullin sided with the premiers and began cutting back on infrastructure projects and payments to government employees. For example, the railways at this time suffered huge financial losses with the fall in business and so were forced to make large-scale wage and staff cuts; job losses for nonpermanent government staff were also very high. Other areas of government spending, including pensions for the elderly, war widows, and dependents, were reduced, and government bonds lost much of their value.

In many ways the "Premiers' Plan" marked the end for Scullin. His own party was irreparably split between pro-Lang union demands to increase government spending and postpone overseas debt repayment, on the one side, and the financially conservative premiers demanding exactly the opposite, on the other. Eventually, although Scullin had taken up Niemeyer's plan, Joseph Lyons and several other conservatives abandoned the party and, along with the National Party, formed the United Australia Party (UAP), the predecessor of today's Liberal Party. And then, on November 21, 1931, five Labor Party members who had supported the Langites over the government crossed the floor of the federal parliament in a vote of no confidence in their own government and brought the troubled Scullin administration to an end. In the federal election that followed in December 1931, Joseph Lyons became the new prime minister as head of the UAP. In coalition with the conservative Country Party, the UAP held a comfortable majority in parliament. Lyons went on to lead Australia through the depression; he died in office in 1939, on the brink of World War II.

Western Australia's Challenge to National Unity

Although Western Australia federated with Australia in 1901 on the heels of a successful referendum, very early on many in the state, especially farmers, began to suspect that they had made the wrong choice (Molony 2005, 263). From 1906 when the Western Australian legislature first voted in favor of secession, through the 1930s "the 'yell of the secessionist' was loud" in that state (Molony 2005, 263). The two issues that contributed most directly to the dissatisfaction felt by many Western Australians were the distance from the "business and power interests of its eastern cousins" and tariffs that made "it hard for WA to sell its primary exports on a world market where it had no protection" (Constitutional Centre of Western Australia 2008). Organized protest began anew in 1926 with the formation of the Secession League and continued with the more successful Dominion League of Western

Australia after 1930. The secessionists were opposed by the state's few industrialists in the Federal League, formed in 1931, and by those who lived in the gold districts. Both of these constituents benefited from their ties to the commercial centers in the country's east and saw little benefit in aligning themselves with farmers and graziers.

Finally, when a scapegoat was being sought for the economic difficulties of the depression in 1933, the conservative Western Australian government, which had supported the secessionists, called for a referendum on the issue. The issue passed with 68 percent of the 237,198 votes cast. With more than 91 percent of eligible voters participating, only gold miners rejected the notion en masse (Constitutional Centre of WA 2008). Interestingly, at the same election the conservative and prosecessionist government of James Mitchell was swept from power and replaced by the Labor Party under Philip Collier, which had opposed secession (National Council for the Centenary of Federation 2008).

Despite the overwhelming vote in favor, Western Australians' bid for independence did not eventuate. A delegation of prosecessionists was dispatched from Western Australia in 1934 to present the case for "'restoration' of the State to 'its former status as a separate and distinct self-governing colony in the British Empire'" (Constitutional Centre of WA 2008). They spent two years in London trying to gain access to a full parliamentary review of their argument, but a joint committee from the Houses of Commons and Lords rejected the "petition on the grounds that the British Parliament could not act without the Australian Federal Parliament's approval" (Constitutional Centre of WA 2008). After this failure the secessionist movement largely disintegrated; however, even today small numbers of Western Australians continue to chafe at the financial and legal bounds of remaining in the Commonwealth.

Australian Landscape

In the years between 1920 and 1946 Australians compounded the effects of European migration on the continent's fragile environment with larger and larger infrastructure projects, leading to further degradation of indigenous flora and fauna. Certainly dozens of smaller marsupials were already under threat with the introduction of the domestic cat at an unknown time prior to the First Fleet in 1788, probably from Dutch ships; the wild rabbit in 1839; and the fox in 1845; sheep and cattle also successfully competed for food and water in much of the continent, further damaging indigenous flora and fauna. In this later

Thylacines were also known as Tasmanian marsupial wolves and Tasmanian tigers before their extinction in the 1930s. (Pictures Collection, State Library of Victoria)

period, however, "the destruction of habitat accelerated spectacularly as the twentieth century's technological revolution got under way" (Andrewartha and Birch 1986, 182).

A key symbol of this destruction was the death in 1936 of the last Tasmanian tiger, or thylacine, the largest carnivorous marsupial to have survived into the 20th century. Starting in 1830 the various colonial and state governments that administered Tasmania (Van Diemen's Land) put bounties on the tiger, mainly because of the threat it posed to household animals and stock. In 1909 after 2,184 bounties were paid, the practice was finally ended and the tiger sought primarily by zoos wanting an example of the animal for their collections; the last one was captured for this purpose in 1933. The last known survivor died in captivity at the Hobart zoo in September 1936, chained outside and dying of the cold (Tasmania Parks and Wildlife Service 2008). Occasionally people in both Tasmania and on the mainland, where they are believed to have become extinct about 7,000 years ago, claim to have seen a thylacine, but no sighting has been verified since the 1930s.

A second important ecological development occurred in the mid-1930s with the introduction of a prolific nonnative species. In 1935 the Australian Bureau of Sugar Experimental Stations imported 100 cane toads, *Bufo marinus,* from Hawaii in an attempt to control several species of beetle that were damaging Queensland's lucrative sugar industry.

The first release of 100 toads near Cairns, Queensland, was followed a month later by release of 3,000 more onto sugar plantations throughout northern Queensland, despite the lack of evidence that they did anything to limit the beetle population. It has since been proven that the toads have no effect on the beetle problem.

Even at the time several environmentalists, such as the museum curator Roy Kinghorn and the government entomologist W. W. Froggatt, protested the introduction, but to no avail (Australian Museum Online 2003). Today their warnings seem prescient. The toad population, in the millions and spreading around Australia at a rate of about a mile per year, endangers indigenous wildlife in three ways: competition for food, eating small animals, and poison glands, which cause everything that eats the toad itself to die very quickly of heart failure (National Heritage Trust 2004). So far, efforts to control the toad have met with almost no success, and it remains one of the most dangerous of the continent's invasive pests.

In addition to this kind of experimentation, the first half of the 20th century saw the completion of many large infrastructural projects that further symbolized European Australians' desire to control and tame their fragile environment. The Hume Dam was begun in November 1919 in an effort to control flooding from the Murray River and to harness water for irrigation and domestic and industrial use. In 1936 the completed dam was the largest in the Southern Hemisphere and second largest in the world at the time, at 131 feet (40 meters) high and 5,300 feet (1,615 meters) long; the resulting reservoir held 407 billion gallons (15,420 Gl) of water. Since that time, however, changes to the dam and drought have affected the water levels and led to a perception that the lake is "dry and empty," despite the nearly four square miles (10 sq. km) of water available for boating, water skiing, fishing, and other recreational activities (Border Mail 2008).

The dam and resulting lake have also been blamed for significant environmental damage along the course of the Murray River. The river's natural cycle is to run very high and cold in winter and then peter out to almost nothing in the hot, dry summer months. Indigenous fish and plant life were adapted to that cycle, and with its disruption such native species as the Murray cod and mangrove swamps have come under threat. The multistate management of the entire Murray basin, which is located in New South Wales, Victoria, and South Australia, has also led to considerable disagreement over how best to deal with the environment, as well as water disputes, and the threat to the basin and its ecology continues to this day.

Another significant infrastructural project completed during this period is the iconic Sydney Harbour Bridge, which opened in March 1932 after more than 100 years of discussion, planning, and building. From 1924 through 1932 1,400 laborers used nearly 117 million pounds (530,000 kilograms) of steel held together by six million rivets to create the world's largest steel arch bridge, which stands 440 feet (134 meters) above the water. While the bridge did not disrupt the ecology of the region significantly, about 800 families who were living in its path were forced from their homes without compensation in the late 1920s (Sydney Harbour Bridge 2008).

By the 1920s Australians also began to stitch together their far-flung cities and towns with a national road system. In 1922 the federal government had allocated half a million dollars toward the development and maintenance of this system, to be built and managed by each of the states and territories. A year later the Commonwealth spent a million dollars on road construction, mostly in the far north of Queensland and the Northern Territory. This was followed by the Federal Aid Roads Act of 1926, which "establish[ed] a basis for the development of Australia's first national roads program" (Farmer 2007). By 1926 each state also had its own state road authority to oversee both federal funds and those collected through automobile licensing fees. The onset of the depression in the 1930s slowed road development somewhat, especially at the state level, since lower car ownership rates meant fewer funds to spend on road development and repair. However, federal dollars continued to be spent on rural road development as part of a larger employment scheme, the Federal Aid Road and Works Act 1937. With the start of the war, road development once again picked up in order to facilitate the movement of supplies and troops to defend the country's long and almost uninhabited northern coastline.

In conjunction with the expansion of the national highway system from 1920 through the mid-1940s, Australian automobile production exploded. Domestic car assembly was dominated by the Holden Motor Body Builders Limited, which built bodies for such imported brands as Ford, Chevrolet, Dodge, and Studebaker. In 1925 the American automobile maker Ford opened a plant in Geelong, about an hour southwest of Melbourne, and in 1931 General Motors took over Holden. These two car companies began as rivals for the Australian market and remain so to this day, although additional competition from Toyota and other Asian brands has diminished the rivalry somewhat. Nonetheless, the automobile remains both an important symbol in Australia and a necessity for most Australians since tire and auto companies lobbied for the dismantling of most urban public transport systems in the mid-20th century. Only Melbourne, too poor at that time to dismantle its tram system, has retained a viable network.

In addition to the great changes wrought on the Australian mainland, Tasmania, and other offshore islands, in 1936 Australian territory expanded exponentially. The Australian Antarctic Territory Acceptance Act 1933, which went into effect on August 24, 1936, passed British control of all land south of 60 degrees south and between 160 east and 45 degrees east, except Adelie Land, to Australia (Office of Legislative Drafting 2000). This came about largely as a result of the scientific and exploratory efforts of the Australian Douglas Mawson, who accompanied Ernest Shackleton on his South Pole expeditions and later headed the first Australian Antarctic expedition, in 1911–13. In 1926 this work by British and Australian scientists allowed Britain to assert its right to more than two thirds of Antarctica without dispute from either other European countries or the United States. By 1933 Britain was ready to share responsibility for this huge amount of territory with Australia, which received nearly half the continent, and New Zealand (Welsh 2004, 416–417). Through this acquisition, today Canberra is responsible for a greater amount of the Earth's surface than any country except the Russian Federation (Welsh 2004, 416).

Old and New Alliances

While the influx of American companies such as Ford and General Motors increased during this period, there were other signs that Australia was developing a core relationship with the United States, in addition to that with Britain. Talking pictures arrived in Australia in 1928, along with American accents, while the spread of gramophones and radio put American pop music in every Australian home (Clark 1995, 254). In 1937 a regular airmail route was established between Sydney and the United States, and a year later Canberra and Washington, D.C., were connected via telephone (ABC Archives 2002).

Politically, as well, Australians were beginning to look to Washington nearly as often as they turned to London. The new relationship was solidified in 1940 when Richard Casey, who had formerly served as Australia's chief diplomat in London and at the League of Nations in Geneva, Switzerland, was recruited by Prime Minister Menzies to serve in the country's first diplomatic role in Washington, D.C. This was Australia's first diplomatic mission outside Britain. Casey was recalled to Australia with the election of John Curtin and the Labor Party in

1941, but the ties he helped establish continued to develop during the war and have rarely been strained since.

Despite the new closeness to the United States, which strengthened further during the war, Australia remained aligned to Britain throughout the entire period. Regardless of the relative drop in immigration during the depression, during this period several schemes to attract British migrants were begun or maintained. Just after the end of World War I, former British servicemen benefited from priority migration. This was followed by the Empire Land Settlement scheme in 1922, under which the British government provided assistance for immigrants willing to settle on the land in Australia. In part because of these and a variety of other schemes, more than 260,000 British migrants arrived on Australia's shores between 1921 and 1931 and contributed to the production of wheat on more than 18 million acres (7 million ha) of land, up from nine million (3.6 million ha) in 1920 (Welsh 2004, 393).

Australia's long-standing connection to Britain was also highlighted with the buildup to war in the late 1930s. In his first days in office, Australian prime minister Menzies said of this relationship that "Britain's peace is precious to us because her peace is ours. If she is at war we are at war" (cited in Welsh 2004, 422). After World War II, during much of which the American alliance took precedence over that with Britain, Australia's British connection was again highlighted when Prime Minister Curtin nominated King George VI's brother, the duke of Gloucester, to serve as governor-general.

Perhaps the most symbolic feature of this dual relationship Australia had with Britain and the United States in this period can be seen in the design and building of the country's new capital city, Canberra. In 1908 the site of the Australian Capital Territory was carved out of New South Wales as a compromise capital situated between the two largest cities, Sydney and Melbourne. In 1911 a design competition was held and a year later it was announced that the American architect Walter Burley Griffin had been chosen to design Canberra. Burley Griffin found throughout his nearly seven years on the project that Australian bureaucrats and budgets continually hampered the fulfillment of his vision for the new city. By 1920 he had given up, under protest, and turned the project over to a local management team, who completed it without many of the features Burley Griffin had included to make the city attractive and functional. Seven years later, the city was finally completed and the new Parliament officially opened, not in the presence of the American designer but with the blessing of the British duke of York, who was to become King George VI in 1936.

World War II

Australia entered World War II on September 3, 1939, when Prime Minister Robert Menzies, who had risen to power only five months earlier after the death in office of Joseph Lyons, announced: "It is my melancholy duty to inform you officially that, in consequence of a persistence by Germany in her invasion of Poland, Great Britain has declared war upon her and that, as a result, Australia is also at war" (cited in Clarke 2003, 233).

Although Australia was at war, the young country's military was inadequately prepared for what lay ahead. Compulsory military training had ceased in 1930, and the armed services were divided between the Australian Imperial Force (AIF), which could be utilized only overseas, and the militia, for defense at home. The two units were managed separately, and the two chains of command often disagreed with one another (Welsh 2004, 423). The other branches of the military were not in much better shape; the Royal Australian Navy (RAN) was made up of just six light cruisers, while much of the Royal Australian Air Force (RAAF) had to train and fly with the British air force because of its lack of planes (Welsh 2004, 423–424).

Despite these institutional and personnel problems, Australians began seeing wartime duty almost immediately. The first Australian casualties were probably two RAAF members ferrying materiel to Darwin on September 5, 1939, when their plane crashed. The first Australian killed in action was Wing Commander Ivan Cameron, who was shot down over Kiel, Germany, while serving with the British Royal Air Force (RAF) on September 28, 1939 (Department of Veterans' Affairs 2007). Despite these early deaths, by March 1940, 68,000 Australians had volunteered for the RAAF and 20,000 for the army (Welsh 2004, 424). In October 1939 Menzies instituted the draft for the militia, which required single 20-year-old men to train for three months in order to create battle-ready soldiers in case Australia was invaded (Clarke 2003, 235–236).

Australia's contribution to the land war in World War II began in early January 1941 with the Sixth Division AIF's participation in an Allied defeat of the Italians at Bardia, Libya (Department of Veterans' Affairs 2007). The Sixth Division remained in Libya after this victory and took Tobruk from Italian forces a few weeks later. After this Axis loss, Germany sent Erwin Rommel and the Afrika Korps to assist the Italians in North Africa, and by April Tobruk was largely surrounded. Australians of the Ninth Division defended the important port for eight months and thus succeeded in stopping the Axis powers from completely surrounding the Mediterranean and shortening their supply lines to the Middle East. In the meantime, Australians were also fighting alongside their British and New Zealand allies in Greece, the country's first land battles against the Germans since World War I. In one month of vicious fighting in May–June 1941, 39 percent of Australian soldiers were killed, wounded, or taken prisoner; eventually the Allies withdrew from Greece, leaving the Germans to occupy the country for more than four years (Department of Veterans' Affairs 2007). A third battlefront for Australians in mid-1941 was the Middle East, where about 18,000 Australians from the AIF, RAAF, and RAN fought alongside British and Free French forces against the German-allied French Vichy government. The most significant battles took place in Syria and Lebanon through the months of June and July. The Allies captured Damascus, Syria, on June 21, 1941, and the port town of Damour on July 9 (Department of Veterans' Affairs 2007).

Australia's contribution to the Allies' effort in the Middle East continued into 1943. In early September 1942, an Australian force crossed a minefield near El Alamein, Egypt, but was forced to retreat, with 64 either dead or missing and 100 wounded (Department of Veterans' Affairs 2007). On the basis of information provided by this early reconnaissance team, on October 23, 1942, a much larger force of the British Eighth Army and Australian Ninth Division, aided by the British and Australian air forces, engaged a total of 12 German and Italian divisions in the battle of El Alamein. For 10 days the two sides engaged in the Egyptian desert before the Axis powers turned and fled; the Allies pursued the combined German and Italian forces from November 4, 1942, through May 1943, when Rommel and the Afrika Korps surrendered. Australians lost 2,694 soldiers in this effort, about one fifth the Allies' total (Department of Veterans' Affairs 2007).

While Australians were fighting overseas, the political situation at home changed the priorities of the Australian armed forces. After the disintegration of the coalition government headed by Robert Menzies in early 1941, the Labor Party under John Curtin was able to form a government on October 7. Curtin did not share Menzies's blind faith in the ability of the British to defend Australia; he also desired a stronger alliance with the United States (Serle 1993, 554). After the Japanese bombing of Pearl Harbor, Hawaii, on December 7, 1941, Curtin went public with this intention when he published a letter in the *Melbourne Herald,* stating, "Without any inhibitions of any kind, I make it quite clear that Australia looks to America, free of any pangs as to our traditional links or kinship with the United Kingdom" (Welsh 2004, 433).

Curtin's Australia also immediately declared war on Japan, without waiting for Britain to act.

Curtin moved swiftly after Pearl Harbor to evacuate Darwin, Northern Territory, in anticipation of a Japanese attack and to begin calling AIF divisions home to defend the Australian continent. Despite British prime minister Winston Churchill's reluctance, on February 17, 1942, Curtin called for Australian troops to be returned from overseas to attend to the immediate threat closer to home. Churchill initially diverted the homeward-bound Seventh Australian Division midcourse to serve in Burma (Myanmar), but Curtin, outraged, insisted they be returned immediately. Eventually, the AIF Sixth and Seventh Divisions returned to the Australian mainland (Welsh 2004, 433) and assisted their militia colleagues in the defense of Papua New Guinea.

In further efforts to bolster Australia's ability to defend itself, Curtin allowed for the use of conscripted militia soldiers, who were legally allowed to fight only on home soil, to fight overseas. He did this by expanding the definition of *home* to include all territories held by Australia, including the mandated territory of Papua. The term *home* eventually included the entire Southwest Pacific area with the exception of the Philippines and portions of Borneo and Java (Welsh 2004, 435).

On February 19, 1942, four days after the fall of Singapore to the Japanese, Curtin's nightmare came true when mainland Australians were attacked for the first time since the British descended on the Aboriginal people in 1788. The Japanese air force launched two devastating raids on Darwin using 188 aircraft from the same unit that attacked Pearl Harbor. The raids killed at least 243 people, sank eight ships, and destroyed 20 aircraft and most civilian and military amenities (Commonwealth of Australia 2009). While this attack was the most devastating, with more bombs dropped than on Pearl Harbor, Darwin was bombed another 63 times by November 1943. Other towns in northern Australia were also bombed by the Japanese during this time, including Katherine in the Northern Territory, Townsville in Queensland, and Broome, Port Headland, Wyndham, and Derby in Western Australia (Commonwealth of Australia 2009). In all there were approximately 100 air raids on Australia.

Coupled with the fall of Singapore, a huge strategic defeat only a few days earlier, the attacks on Darwin had the potential to destroy Australian morale, a very effective weapon of war (Commonwealth of Australia 2009). Hoping to neutralize this strategy, the Australian government censored the real toll of the attacks, claiming that only 17 people had been killed. To this day many Australians remain unaware of the severe peril that faced Darwin and of the bombardment of other Australian towns. One of the few dramatic depictions of the first bombings of Darwin can be seen in the motion picture *Australia*, released in 2008.

The Japanese entry to the war had ramifications for Australians other than the bombings on the Australian mainland and the exit of Australian forces from the European theater. Thousands of Australian soldiers in Malaya, Singapore, New Guinea, Timor, Java, and Borneo were killed or captured between January 14, 1942, and the end of the Pacific war in August 1945 (Department of Veterans' Affairs 2007). In Singapore alone, more than 15,000 Australian troops were taken prisoner and more than 3,000 were killed or wounded (Clark 1995, 268). Australian sailors and fliers were also lost in battles for these islands, as well as in the Pacific more generally.

The other significant consequence for Australia of the war in the Pacific was the further tightening of the relationship with the United States. In March 1942 General Douglas MacArthur arrived in Australia, after a bitter defeat in the Philippines, to take command of the entire South West Pacific Area. As part of his brief in mid-April 1942 MacArthur assumed command of the entire Australian military. After a difficult start, in which MacArthur underestimated the Japanese threat to New Guinea and northern Australia, the alliance secured the country's safety and allowed Australian soldiers to participate in battles in New Guinea and the Dutch East Indies through August 1945. With the country secure, Australians began demobilizing as early as June 1944, when other Allied troops were only beginning their assault on the beaches of Normandy in France (Welsh 2004, 436–437).

While the June 4–6, 1942, battle of Midway is probably the most iconic battle of the Pacific war because it signaled the end of Japanese dominance in the region, for Australians the New Guinea battle of the Kokoda Trail is the most symbolically important. By early March 1942 the Japanese had already landed on the east coast of New Guinea at Lae and Salamaua and proceeded through dense jungle along the Kokoda Trail toward the capital at Port Moresby. The trail is a muddy foot track approximately 100 miles (161 km) long that climbs the Owen Stanley Range through extremely rough terrain and connects the north coast of Papua with the south coast at Port Moresby. By June the Australians had landed the 39th Battalion, young, poorly trained, and inexperienced militia troops who had not been trained in jungle warfare and were not prepared for the oppressively hot, malaria-infested climate. Almost immediately they faced an undefeated, battle-hardened Japanese force fresh from victories in China, the British colony of Malaya, and the American colony of the Philippines.

The key objective for both sides in this battle involved gaining control of the strategically important plateau village of Kokoda and a small airstrip nearby. Getting there, however, was a logistical nightmare. With few transport aircraft available, the only way in was with the help of local Indigenous men as bearers. The journey involved an eight-day march, but these Indigenous bearers could carry only enough food for one man for 13 days; thus most of the supplies were consumed in transit. Local native men formed the Papuan Infantry Battalion (PIB), without whom forward troops would not have received supplies and the wounded could never have survived the grueling journey back to base (Department of Defence 2004a).

From July to September 1942 the pathetically outnumbered Australian forces kept the Japanese in check. One battle is estimated to have involved a mere 100 Australians against 2,000 Japanese (Department of Defence 2004a). From September 1942 to January 1943 the 39th Battalion of militia soldiers was reinforced by more experienced AIF soldiers, forcing the Japanese back up the Kokoda Trail toward their landing beaches on the north coast. Eight months of intense fighting reduced the Japanese army from 35,000 to 13,500, with Australian losses at 2,165 and 3,350 wounded; this was the first victory without the involvement of British troops and thus was an undeniable Australian triumph (Welsh 2004, 435).

After securing the Kokoda area from the Japanese, Australian soldiers retook the rest of the island over the next 15 months and then moved to New Britain, and in May 1945 to Borneo. The last significant battle of the war for Australia was an eight-week assault on the Prince Alexander Range in Borneo, in which the Japanese were finally defeated in July 1945, just weeks before their final capitulation after the nuclear bombings of Hiroshima and Nagasaki.

Wartime at Home

The effects of World War II were not limited to those areas in northern Australia that were bombed by the Japanese or those Australian soldiers who served in the Middle East, Europe, and the Pacific. Australians who remained at home likewise experienced rapid change, both at the hands of the federal government, which tried to consolidate powers previously held by the states, and at the hands of internal and external social forces. For example, the National Security Act 1942 devised a "new manpower plan" that organized the Australian workforce down to the last person (Clarke 2003, 243). The act forbade men working in "'reserved' occupations," such as iron, munitions, and other heavy industry, from enlisting in the military and controlled the labor of all other available men and women for use in the most appropriate wartime capacity (Clarke 2003, 243).

As more and more men in nonmilitary industrial occupations were called to serve in the armed services, women soon filled positions that had previously been denied them. Under the National Security Act, "all 'unoccupied' women—defined as those single or divorced or childless between the ages of 18 and 45—were liable to be conscripted into industry" (Welsh 2004, 437). Urban women worked in factories, drove taxis, and volunteered in a large number of other roles, such as the Women's Auxiliary National Service, while rural women in the Women's Land Army maintained agricultural outputs at nearly their prewar level (Clarke 2003, 243). Women also served in a variety of military roles, including the Women's Auxiliary Air Force, Women's

AAMWS (Australian Army Medical Women's Service) privates Gladys Ware, Ursula McHaffie, Thelma Cuddy, and Doris Aitken, probably members of the first group of AAMWS to serve overseas when they were sent to Koitaki in the hills behind Port Moresby, New Guinea. (Pictures Collection, State Library of Victoria). Thanks to Keith Rossi, RSL (Returned and Services League) historian, for additional information about the AAMWS and probable location of this photo.

Royal Australian Naval Service, and Women's Army Service (Welsh 2004, 437). Almost half a century after gaining the right to vote, women in this period also entered both houses of the federal parliament; in 1943 Enid Lyons was elected to the lower house from the United Australian Parties and Dorothy Tangney was elected to the Senate from the Labor Party.

In addition to government-dictated employment, Australians at home suffered under higher income taxes, the restriction of luxury items such as tobacco and imported alcohol, and the rationing of even the most basic food items (Clarke 2003, 243). Nonetheless, life at home was not all drudgery. Workers in all industries were receiving higher wages than before the war, and farmers had a guaranteed market for everything they could produce. Life in the capital cities was more exciting, even with the mandated 6:00 P.M. closing time for pubs, with 24-hour public transport and nightclubs filled with both American soldiers and locals with their overtime wages to spend. The black market also provided a place for people to spend those wages, especially on illicitly brewed alcohol and cigarettes obtained from American soldiers who had ready access through their post exchange (PX) stores; clothing, food, and many other items were also available on the black market for those with the money to spend (Clarke 2003, 244–245).

While the presence of thousands of American soldiers meant access to cigarettes and a good time for many, it also presented something of a challenge to Australian society. The first challenge was to the white Australia policy, which in the 1940s remained very important to many Australians. In January 1942 the Labor government of John Curtin tried to prevent African-American soldiers from being stationed in Australia. When this failed in the context of wartime necessity, limitations were placed on where African Americans could spend their time, and mixing with white Australians was curtailed as much as possible (Horne 2003, 180–183). Of course, the segregation African-American soldiers experienced in Australia was not very different from what they knew at home, especially in the Jim Crow South. Indeed, many African Americans' experience on the ground in Australia was much better than expected, especially after they had overcome the prejudices established in Australia by their own white commanding officers (Brawley and Dixon 2002).

In addition to race, other problems were caused by the presence of American soldiers in Australian cities; despite their common English language, the culture of the two groups was, and remains to this day, very different. Americans appeared arrogant and disrespectful to their Australian counterparts, while Australians appeared submissive. Numerous fights between the two groups broke out when the Americans first arrived in 1942 and continued until the end of the war. One of the worst of these began on the Americans' Thanksgiving Day 1942, with a small scuffle turning into a major riot. The so-called battle of Brisbane started with a brawl between a drunken Australian soldier and an American military police officer and ended several days later with about 80 men hospitalized for their wounds and the death of one Australian private at the hands of an American (Clarke 2003, 245).

Despite these difficulties, dating between Australian women and American soldiers was not uncommon, and many marriages took place. Several thousand Australian wives migrated to the United States after the war and a substantial number of American soldiers remained in Australia. Exact numbers are difficult to find, but an American newspaper article on the subject from 1944 claims the number of marriage between American soldiers and Australian women during the war averaged 200 per week (Detroit Free Press 1944).

Conclusion

As was the case after World War I, the end of World War II made many Australians reflect on their global position. After the Great War, Australia under Billy Hughes pursued colonialism with a much greater fervor than before the war and secured German New Guinea at the Treaty of Versailles. World War II had a similar effect in focusing the Australian government on issues beyond the country's borders. Rather than foreign territory, however, the threat of Japanese invasion led many Australians to look to European migrants as a way of bolstering their defense against an aggressive power from Asia. Prime Minister Chifley, who replaced John Curtin at his death in early July 1945, and then Robert Menzies through the remainder of the 1940s and beyond pursued a policy of "populate or perish" that continued until the global economic crisis of the 1970s.

As occurred after World War I, Australian women were also retired from many of the positions they had taken up during the next world war. By June 30, 1947, all women's branches of the military had been disbanded and many factory workers, taxi drivers, and other laborers had returned home. By the end of 1951, however, all women's military units had been reestablished in light of the Korean War. Many women who had a taste of the financial independence gained by working outside the home also refused to return there after the war. For the most part they worked in "female" jobs such as nursing, teaching, and domestic service and earned just 75 percent of their male counterparts' pay at best; nonetheless, they remained an important part of the rapidly expanding postwar Australian economy.

7

POPULATE OR PERISH
(1947–1974)

The decades that followed World War II moved Australia into what the historian John Molony calls the "third phase" of the country's history, following establishment from 1788 to 1850 and consolidation from 1850 to 1945 (2005, 286). This third phase had many contradictory aspects. On the one hand, Australians experienced a very long period of sustained economic growth and considered themselves happier than did the citizens of any other country (Molony 2005, 290). On the other hand, all the governments and most politicians of the time spoke and acted as if the country were under constant siege, particularly from Asians and communists. Public policy in these years was mostly dedicated to these two, contradictory themes: keeping "the forgotten people," as Robert Menzies referred to the middle class, happy and at the same time safe from perceived external harm. Many of the most important political, social, and economic events of the period illustrate the centrality of these two impetuses.

Assisted Migration
Although Robert Menzies, Australia's longest-serving prime minister, spent most of his nearly 20 years in office after World War II, probably the most important figure in this period for setting the stage for contemporary Australia was Arthur Augustus Calwell. Calwell began his public service immediately after high school when he joined Victoria's Department of Agriculture in 1913. During World War I he served in the militia and then continued in public service, first at the Treasury in 1923, and later in various positions in the Labor Party. In 1940 he was elected to the federal parliament from the seat of Melbourne and remained there until his retirement in 1972 (Freudenberg 1993, 241–244).

Calwell was the prime mover in the postwar policy to "populate or perish," a phrase first uttered by Billy Hughes in 1937 (Jupp 2002, 11). From as early as the 1930s, Calwell was concerned that Australia's small population could not survive. He rightly understood that natural increase could not grow the country and, in fact, that after 1970 there would be a net decrease in population (Kunz 1988, 11). His answer to this dilemma was that immigration be expanded. However, Calwell, as did many Australians of the time, still believed in the importance of maintaining a "white" Australia. In one of his most self-contradictory actions, he expelled nonwhite residents in 1948, despite the country's desperate need for labor, and forbade the Japanese wives of returned Australian servicemen and their children to enter the country because "they are simply not wanted and are permanently undesirable" (Kunz 1988, 11).

For Calwell population growth through European immigration had to be the country's defensive bulwark against "the nations to the north of us [as they] cast covetous eyes on Australia and fight a way into it" (cited in Kunz 1988, 11). While Calwell uttered these particular words in a 1930s speech, the events of World War II and its immediate aftermath made this impetus in Australia even stronger. The bombing of Darwin and close call with Japanese forces in New Guinea had frightened many Australians and opened the door to far greater immigration than the country had experienced before. The success of China's communists in 1949 only increased concern about what was called the "yellow peril" and pushed the government into further action. Calwell himself believed that "white" immigration was as central to the country's defense as were its land, sea, and air forces (Kunz 1988, 13).

Nonetheless, immigration on the scale that Australians experienced in the 1947–70 period was unprecedented (2.5 million people) and required somebody who was fully committed to the idea, outspoken on the topic, and well prepared to begin the process. Calwell was an ideal candidate because his many years of experience in the Labor Party and in public service generally had prepared him to sell his idea to even the most skeptical of Australians: union leaders and members who had been working against increased immigration for nearly 100 years as a way of keeping wages high. Calwell became Australia's first minister for immigration in July 1945 and immediately began "the most remarkable and far-reaching" changes of the postwar period (Molony 2005, 284).

The planning stage of Calwell's population scheme took nearly two years to complete. In that period, he worked out that an increase of 2 percent per annum, 1 percent through natural increase and 1 percent through immigration, or about 70,000 people (Kunz 1988, 15), was required to populate the continent to a defensible 20–30 million "within a generation or two" (Kunz 1988, 12). The second part of the planning stage was finding transportation to Australia for tens of thousands of European migrants. The third and perhaps most difficult part of his plan was gaining Australians' acceptance of thousands of migrants. Toward that end, Calwell used the media to create "interest in and sympathy for" newcomers (Kunz 1988, 14). He coined the phrase "new Australians" to indicate that, regardless of their origins, these new residents would quickly become contributing members of the old society. He wanted to prevent both segregation imposed by established Australian society and separation by new arrivals and hoped that an Australian label would facilitate mixing.

In the end, the first and second aspects of this plan pointed to the same solution. Calwell's aim in the first planning stages was that the majority of this new population was to be from Britain, and a ratio of 10 Britons to one continental European was "mentioned in his first ministerial statement" (Kunz 1988, 18). The British and Australian governments worked out a scheme in 1947 whereby voluntary migrants from Britain would pay just £10 per person for passage, with the remainder subsidized by the two governments. Housing and employment would be provided by the Australians on the condition that migrants agreed to work at an assigned position for a period of two years. Nevertheless, there was a dearth of volunteers, which required Calwell and his growing immigration department staff (from 46 to 5,000 people over three years) to look beyond Britain (Clarke 2003, 253). While British subjects were believed to have the greatest chance of assimilating into Australian society—Australians, after all, were British citizens until 1949—other Europeans were soon deemed equally acceptable. In September 1945 Australia's delegation to the International Labour Conference in Paris was instructed to "look around north-western Europe for potential sources of immigrants" (Kunz 1988, 15); the Dutch and Scandinavians were believed to be the most suitable. Nonetheless, these small countries could not provide the large numbers of people Australia desired and transport remained a concern. Calwell soon began to look farther afield.

In 1947 Australia became a signatory country to the International Refugee Organization (IRO) and Calwell's boss, Prime Minister Chifley, encouraged his immigration minister "to investigate the DP [displaced persons] situation" (Kunz 1988, 18). At his meeting in June with the Preparatory Commission of the IRO, Calwell finally found the answers

While single, able-bodied white men were the preferred class of migrant in Australia, not all ships contained as great a percentage of men as the SS Partizanka, *arriving from Malta in 1948.* (Pictures Collection, State Library of Victoria)

to his two most pressing problems in his plan to populate Australia with Europeans: people and transportation. If Australia agreed to resettle about 12,000 Europeans per year who had been living in refugee camps in Europe since the end of the war, the IRO would provide their transport. Suddenly Calwell's goal of 70,000 "white" able-bodied migrants seemed attainable.

Between 1947, when the IRO took control of the European refugee camps formerly administered by the United Nations Relief and Rehabilitation Administration, and 1951, when the IRO ceased to exist, nearly two million displaced peoples passed through the system (Kunz 1988, 29). Italians, Yugoslavs, Hungarians, Poles, Germans, Greeks, Russians, and the citizens of almost every other continental European country spent months and even years waiting in former military camps in Italy, Austria, and Germany for third-country resettlement. Those who had been driven from their homes early in the war spent up to 14 homeless years before being resettled, while some of those who fled Hungary, Czechoslovakia, Poland, and the other Soviet bloc countries just as the borders were being solidified in 1948 were homeless for only a few months (Kunz 1988, 133).

While food, clothing, and housing were provided by the IRO, frequently one of the most precious objects obtained by these refugees was their IRO eligibility card. This international identification card "certified a politically blameless past, safeguarded the holder from repatriation, guaranteed continued minimum maintenance and opened the door to possible emigration" (Kunz 1988, 31). Generally third countries were willing to resettle only card holders as a way of blocking entrance to former enemy combatants; however, 485 former Nazis and Nazi officials were allowed to resettle in Australia (Franklin 2005).

Even before the agreement between the IRO and Australian government had been signed, Calwell's agents began the process of scouring Europe's camps for suitable candidates for resettlement (Kunz 1988, 35). Australia was competing against the United States, Canada, Argentina, and even Britain and Belgium in this, with most countries preferring young, able-bodied single men and women with at least some secondary education. Australia also put light skin color very high on its list of important traits, especially for the first migrants, who were to create a good first impression on the Australian people.

These first migrants arrived in Fremantle, Western Australia, in November 1947 aboard the USS *General Stuart Heintzelman*. In all it carried 843 people from the Baltic countries of Lithuania, Latvia, and Estonia, most of whom continued on to Melbourne, where they were transferred to the newly established migrant camp at Bonegilla, northern Victoria, to learn some rudimentary English and begin the four-week induction process (Kunz 1988, 38). With the success of this first shipload, other nationalities were soon welcomed to Australia's shores, though it was another two years before all Europeans were deemed suitable (Kunz 1988, 38). Married couples and even some children also made the journey to Australia in these years when other categories of people began to dry up. Altogether, about 150 trips were made to Australia in decommissioned military ships, carrying about 170,700 people, or 16 percent of all Europe's refugees, to Australia's shores, the largest number per capita in the world and the second largest in total after the United States (Kunz 1988, 40–45).

Despite the Australian government's preference for refugees with some secondary or even tertiary education, most new arrivals were unable to take up positions commensurate with their skills, qualifications, and experience, especially in their first two years (Kunz 1988, 49). The majority were put to work in unskilled positions, often in rural or provincial regions where many Australians were reluctant to live. Some of the most common jobs were in the sugarcane fields of

About 320,000 migrants passed through this camp at Bonegilla, Victoria, on their way to permanent settlement in Australia. (Pictures Collection, State Library of Victoria)

Queensland, refineries and automobile plants, and the large infrastructural projects envisioned by the Australian government, especially the Snowy Mountains Scheme (see below). This aspect of their migration often rankled those with advanced degrees and qualifications, who made up a significant proportion of the Hungarians, Czechoslovaks, and Baltic peoples. Interviews with elderly migrants 50 years and more after their arrival indicate that many had been misled into believing that they would be allowed to continue teaching, practicing medicine or law, or working as scientists. In fact, this was generally not the case. The most closed of the professions, which required starting all over again at an Australian university, was medicine, leaving many doctors and even experts in their research field left to work as orderlies, while engineering proved to be the most open field (Molony 2005, 285).

Aside from the lack of recognition of their advanced education, the "new Australians" found a great deal else to give them culture shock. The most obvious difficulties were with the English language, rural Australia's primitive conditions in comparison with prewar Europe's cities, and entirely different ways of life. Lack of housing was a problem for many, who were forced to live in Quonset huts for months at a time while entirely new suburbs were built with materials imported from Europe. With the memory of the war close at hand, many of these new suburbs were named after Australia's fallen soldiers, such as the industrial Geelong suburb of Norlane, built for migrant workers at nearby Ford and Shell plants and named after Norman Lane, who had been killed in Singapore.

Mid-20th-century Australian eating habits also caused considerable consternation and are still remembered in the 21st century for the horror they caused. Such Australian delicacies as canned spaghetti and the concoction of leftovers known as "bubble and squeak" continue to be sources of amusement for those who arrived on the earliest refugee ships. In reaction, Europeans in all Australian cities and many rural areas began to open cafés and restaurants and to grow their own, preferred food items (Thompson 1994, 84). In 1952 the Andronicus brothers introduced the first espresso machine to Australia and began the country's long period of transition from primarily tea drinkers to one of the coffee capitals of the world (Gee and Gee 2005).

People who had been accustomed to living in such art, literature, and music capitals as Paris, Budapest, and Prague also found Australia's cities drained of life after 5:00 P.M. and on weekends. In the early 1950s when they arrived from Paris, Georges and Mirka Mora found Melbourne to be devoid of entertainment, a common sentiment among migrants to all Australian settlements (Johnson 2007, 141). Rather than complaining in their own language over a cream cake and cup of espresso, as Andrew Riemer describes his experience with Sydney's Central European migrant population (1992), the Moras established a variety of institutions and organizations to fulfill their need for stimulating conversation, good food, and wine. In 1954 they, along with their Australian-born friends John and Sunday Reed, formed the Contemporary Art Society upstairs from the Moras' café, Mirka. That same year the Mirka's owners put tables and chairs in front of their café, the first in the city to do so, and thus was born the "Paris End" of Collins Street in downtown Melbourne. A few years later, when they could no longer accommodate the crowds that their art shows, other events, and food and drink attracted, the Moras opened Melbourne's

MIRKA MORA

Parisian Mirka Mora, born Madeleine "Mirka" Zelik, was nearly killed at age 14 when in 1942 she and her mother were captured by the Nazis. During the train journey to Pithiviers concentration camp, Suzanne Zelik asked her daughter to peer through a crack in the carriage to see the names of the stations they passed through. Suzanne then wrote this information in a letter to her husband, sealed it in an envelope, and had Mirka push the envelope through the crack when they slowed to pass through a station. Somebody found the note, put a stamp on it, and posted it to Leon Zelik, who was able to free his family just a day before they were scheduled to be deported to Auschwitz. For the next three years, the Zelik family escaped further detection by the Nazis through the kindness of friends and strangers in the French countryside.

The second pivotal moment in Mora's life occurred when she and her husband, Georges Mora, migrated from cold war Paris. They arrived in Melbourne in 1951 and almost immediately set up a studio where Mirka could paint and where they could entertain other artists and intellectuals. Over the next few years they opened a number of cafés and restaurants, hosted art shows and other exhibitions, restarted the Contemporary Art Society with John Reed, and generally tried to re-create the intellectual life they had known in Paris.

Mora's life changed again in 1970 when she and her husband split up, and she moved to a small studio of her own with nothing but her art work and supplies from her old life. Georges went on to remarry and have another child at the age of 72, while Mirka maintained her life as an artist. She added doll making and mosaics to her drawing and painting resumé and maintained her status as an icon of the bohemian life in Melbourne. Today she lives and works at the Mora Complex, a combination studio, gallery, business office, and home for the extended Mora family, including her gallery-owning son William.

first restaurant licensed to serve alcohol until 10:00 P.M.—the previous closing time was strictly 6:00 P.M. and alcohol and food could not be served on the same premises (St. Kilda Historical Society 2005).

According to the social historian Murray Johnson, "the standard view [in Australia] is that socially the 1950s was dull, conservative, inward-looking and complacent" (2007, 137). This may have been the case in the early part of the decade, but by the end of the 1950s tens of thousands of food-loving, wine-drinking, and entertainment-seeking European migrants had begun to change the cultural core of the country. The "cultural cringe" of the old Australians, a belief that "anything Australian was second-rate at best," had not yet fallen by the wayside, and many "writers, artists, musicians, and others were forced to flee overseas in a bid to establish their reputations, or even to be noticed by their fellow Australians" (Johnson 2007, 137). However, conditions were changing.

Unfortunately for many migrants Australian culture did not change quickly enough. Even for many who spoke English as their first language, the struggles of adaptation, or what was called assimilation at the time, contributed to considerable distress. One in five migrants from this period actually chose to leave the country after the two-year employment contract ended or as soon as he or she had the money to purchase a ticket back to the Northern Hemisphere (Welsh 2004, 444). For many thousands of others who remained, life in Australia was a constant struggle with depression, drug addiction, or alcoholism (Thompson 1994, 85). Women from non-English-speaking backgrounds who did not enter the workforce were in the most difficult situation because their opportunities for social mixing and integration into Australian society were very limited and usually mediated by English-speaking husbands or children (Molony 2005, 286). Men and women who suffered loss of social and economic status through migration also fared worse than those with a peasant background, who gained access to the Australian middle class.

Perceived Communist Threats

Although the population issue remained central to Australian security policy throughout the 1947–74 period, even with the election of the newly formed Liberal Party in 1949, it was not the only concern that attracted government attention. Following the United States, many Australians were also extremely concerned about the global spread of communism. This began immediately after the war, when the Soviet Union took control of most of Eastern and Central Europe; continued with the Chinese Communist Party's takeover on the mainland in 1949; and exploded into war in 1950 when communist North Korea invaded the military dictatorship established in South Korea by Syngman Rhee and his American supporters.

Three days after this invasion, on June 28, 1950, Australia's new Liberal-Country Party coalition prime minister, Robert Menzies, committed Australian naval forces to the U.S.-led United Nations (UN) force that was to defend Rhee's Korea against the communist incursion. A month later Australian ground troops from the Third Battalion, Royal Australian Regiment (3RAR), joined the police action, as it was called, as part of the 27th British Commonwealth Brigade, along with soldiers from Britain and New Zealand. They were joined by a second Australian battalion in 1952, when Australian brigadiers took over command of the entire Commonwealth Brigade. During the three-year conflict, 276 Australians were killed or died of wounds inflicted on the battlefield, while a further 1,210 were wounded; 30 Australians were taken prisoner of war, one of whom died in captivity (Department of Defence 2004).

The alacrity with which Menzies contributed forces to this anticommunist war in the Korean Peninsula is not surprising in light of the context in which his coalition gained power. Just prior to the 1949 election, Australia suffered through one of the most difficult industrial strikes of the decade. The communist-led Miners' Federation walked off the job in New South Wales to demand better wages and conditions and quickly threw the country into chaos. Other miners immediately followed, forcing electricity rationing, layoffs, and further disruptions throughout the country (Molony 2005, 291). Despite Prime Minister Chifley's attempts to control the situation by sending the military in as strike-busting workers, Labor's traditional ties to the communists proved difficult to disavow. In addition, in the immediate postwar period, the ruling Labor Party had tried its hand at nationalizing both the banking and the medical systems as part of its wider project of increasing social welfare. As a result, despite the Labor government's prosecution for sedition of a communist leader, Labor was made to pay in October 1949, when Menzies's five-year-old Liberal Party took power in coalition with the Country Party.

One of the first actions taken by the new government was to try to ban the Communist Party in Australia, despite its relatively small size of just 20,000 members (Clarke 2003, 257). The legislation would also have forbidden any individual who had associated with the Communist Party to take a position in either the public service or a trade union, creating the context for McCarthyite witch hunts in Australia (Welsh 2004, 451). Fortunately, anticommunist fervor, while strong in some sectors of Australian society, did not reach the pitch that it did in the United States, and the country's highest court quickly ruled the law unconstitutional. Menzies and his government tried again to ban the Communist Party, this time through the mechanism of a federal referendum, in September 1951. The measure failed by the narrow margin of 50.6 percent to 49.4 percent (Welsh 2004, 458).

This failure was still not enough for Menzies and the Liberals to lay the communist threat to rest. In 1954 what has come to be known as the Petrov Affair exploded on to the pages of the Australian press. On April 3 Vladimir Petrov, who had worked at the Soviet embassy in Canberra, defected to Australia, and his wife was dramatically rescued at Darwin airport from the hands of KGB kidnappers trying to take her home. Menzies appointed a royal commission to look for Australian spies, as Petrov had named names in exchange for his and his wife's safety. As had been the case previously, Menzies's most vocal opponent in this action was Herbert Vere Evatt, leader of the Labor Party since 1951 and in 1948 president of the UN General Assembly. Evatt had been the loudest among those campaigning for a no vote in the referendum on the Communist Party and used his legal experience to serve as primary defense attorney for those accused of espionage as a result of Petrov's denunciations.

In addition to these domestic affairs, Menzies's anticommunism contributed greatly to Australia's foreign policy at this time. In 1950 Australia joined Canada, New Zealand, Britain, India, Pakistan, and Sri Lanka (then called Ceylon) as signatories to the Colombo Plan. Each of these countries pledged to contribute £8 million over three years to educate and train people throughout Southeast Asia as a way of countering Chinese Communist influence in the region. As part of the Colombo Plan, Australia by 1968 had spent tens of millions of dollars; sent more than 1,500 teachers, trainers, and other experts to the developing world; and welcomed more than 9,400 students (Clark 1995, 286).

Perhaps the most significant action to fight communism taken by Australian governments in the postwar era was to support the U.S. war in Vietnam. This action, taken by Menzies in 1965, a year before he retired, was perhaps the clearest signal that Australia had finally forsaken its long foreign policy alliance with Britain in favor of the United States. This process had begun with Curtin's giving control of Australia's forces to the U.S. general Douglas MacArthur during World War II, was continued with the signing of the ANZUS (Australia–New Zealand–U.S.) Treaty in 1951 despite British protest, and concluded in the jungles of Vietnam. Nonetheless, for most years these two alliances could be maintained with little to no contradiction. After all, Britain had supported U.S. action in Korea by providing military forces, and all three countries were signatories to the South-East Asia Treaty

Organization (SEATO) when it took effect in 1954 (Clark 1995, 294). In Vietnam, however, Menzies was forced to make a choice between the nay-saying British and the "domino-theory"-touting Americans. Menzies, one of the most ardently royalist Australians to serve as prime minister, quickly took up the American position, sent advisers in the early 1960s, instituted the draft in 1964, and deployed 1,500 troops to Vietnam in April 1965. By 1967 there were 6,300 Australians on the ground in Vietnam, despite loud protests at home, and by withdrawal in 1971, more than 8,500 Australians had served (Australian War Memorial, Vietnam War). Total Australian casualties were minuscule compared to those of the Americans and Vietnamese but make up more than 42 percent of those who served, 3,629 missing, injured, or killed on the ground (Australian War Memorial, Statistics).

New Weapons

Although Australia began to turn its foreign policy away from Britain even before the cold war, there continued to be close cooperation between the two countries in many areas of both foreign and domestic security in the following years. For example, from 1950 to 1963, the Australian Air Force and several battalions of ground troops participated in the Malayan Emergency, Britain's fight to maintain control of the Malayan Peninsula.

As part of this security initiative in 1948 Australia also allowed Britain to build a rocket-testing range at Woomera, South Australia, and to test atomic weapons in several locations throughout the country during the 1950s and early 1960s. Britain began its atomic weapons program in 1947 in the context of the cold war, when the U.S.S.R. and France similarly acted quickly to join the United States as possessors of such weapons. As a strong ally, Britain tried at first to work with the United States, both in the development of such technology and in its testing. U.S. legislation at the time, however, banned such cooperation and Britain was forced to turn to its own scientists for development and to locate a sparsely populated area to test the new weapons. In 1950 the British prime minister, Clement Atlee, "sent a top secret personal message" to Prime Minister Menzies, who, without even consulting his cabinet, gave permission for atomic testing on the Monte Bello Islands, Western Australia (Australian Institute of Criminology 1989). After this informal communication, the British formally applied for permission to test their first atomic weapon, code-named *Hurricane*, which was granted after Menzies's reelection in 1951. The first tests were conducted on

October 3, 1952, without "any official Australian watchdog to observe them, or to ensure the hazards were kept to a minimum" (Cross 2001, 33). The Hurricane test was followed by 20 more major tests at Emu Field and Maralinga in South Australia, further tests at Monte Bello, and the final tests in 1958 on Christmas Island, this time with a local Atomic Weapons Test Safety Committee in place (Cross 2001, 33). In addition, hundreds of so-called minor tests were staged at Maralinga through 1963, resulting in "far more radiation than the major tests" being spread throughout the Australian continent (Cormick 1991).

Throughout 1956 the Australian public was informed of these activities largely through progovernment newspaper reports that highlighted the dual benefits of increased economic activity and security. Seemingly only as an afterthought did these papers comment on the safety of the atomic tests, such as the brief statement in March 1956 by Sir Oliver Howard Beale, minister for supply and defense production, that "the impending nuclear explosions would not 'harm the nation or the population'" (Cross 2001, 31). The *Adelaide Advertiser,* which had been owned by Keith Murdoch and his heirs since 1929, was particularly supportive of the British atomic testing and throughout the first half of 1956 "carried a series of optimist reports on the nuclear theme" (Cross 2001, 30). The sale of uranium was the economic highlight of these reports, but infrastructure development in South Australia, such as a £1 million renovation of Adelaide's Edinburgh Airfield, was also reported as a benefit of Australia's participation in the tests at Maralinga (Cross 2001, 30). On the security side Australians were reassured that the nuclear tests would present "the possibility of closer ties between the UK and USA over rocket research, using the Woomera Range" (Cross 2001, 31).

Nevertheless, almost from the beginning there was disquiet in some sectors of Australian society about the potential risks of nuclear fallout on the population. The first to speak up publicly were trade unions concerned about their members' health (Cross 2001, 40). After the June 1956 tests on the Monte Bello Islands, however, this protest became much more widespread. It began just a few days after the tests on June 19, when a uranium prospector in outback Queensland found extremely high Geiger counter readings and proceeded to make them public. This was followed by a call from the Labor Party leader, Herbert Vere Evatt, for a review of the testing and for the Labor Party generally to begin voting against any further funding or tests (Cross 2001, 42). Evatt later attempted to censure the government over its handling of the testing matter but was defeated when nobody from the government's side would cross the floor (Cross 2001, 66).

Despite these concerns, initial cleanup of the testing sites did not take place until more than a decade later, when the Woomera rocket range closed in 1967. But a royal commission in 1985 found that significant amounts of radiation remained at Maralinga, and today, more than 50 years after the tests took place, the concerns of antinuclear activists continue to be aired in public: More than 800 people have taken the British government to court over the effects of radiation exposure suffered at the Australian testing sites (Tasker 2009). Nevertheless, for many hundreds of others who were affected by nuclear fallout, there will be no justice. While the Safety Commission overseeing the tests in the 1950s and 1960s claimed that Aboriginal people had been moved from the region, the 1985 royal commission found that many nomadic and seminomadic groups had experienced fallout firsthand. Yami Lestor was a 10-year-old boy when in October 1953 his band was "engulfed" by a black mist resulting from the explosion of Totem 1, the first full-scale atomic bomb detonated in the South Australian desert. He says of the experience, "I can't say how many died. All I can remember is that we moved camp many, many times after the black mist came. In our culture, we always move camp when someone dies" (cited in Cormick 1991).

Bread and Circuses

The impetus to keep Australia secure in the postwar world, whether through nuclear deterrence, fighting communism at home and abroad, or populating the country with tens of thousands of "new Australians," was only one side of the equation that kept the country relatively peaceful and stable. The other side was the provision of bread and circuses: the expansion of domestic infrastructure and the welfare state, and both public and private expenditures on entertainment and entertainment infrastructure.

Infrastructure

The history of the Snowy Mountain Hydroelectric Scheme goes back to 1944 and a Labor government inquiry into how best to utilize and harness the large amount of water that flowed off the Australian alpine region of southern New South Wales and northern Victoria. This inquiry resulted in the passing in July 1949 of the Snowy Mountains Hydroelectric Power Act 1949, which set the foundation for not only the construction of the project but also the management of the vast works after its completion (Snowy Hydro, The History, 2007). The project was to generate huge amounts of electricity for Australia's developing industrial economy as well as carry extra irrigation water to the dry southeast corner of the country. Construction began on October 17, 1949, and 25 years later 90 miles (145 km) of tunnels, 50 miles (80.5 km) of aqueducts, 16 major dams, seven power stations, and a pumping station were all completed on time and on budget for AU$820 million.

Internationally the Snowy Scheme was heralded in 1967 as "one of the seven civil engineering wonders of the modern world" by the American Society of Civil Engineers and remains one of the most complex water projects in the world, with just 2 percent of its features visible aboveground (Snowy Hydro, Engineering Facts, 2007). Domestically the Snowy Scheme was important as both a technological wonder, utilizing the country's first large computer from 1960 to 1967 (Snowy Hydro, The History, 2007), and an employer for the large number of migrants arriving in the country during its construction; about 70 percent of the labor consisted of migrants. At any one time about 7,300 people were working on the scheme, and overall more than 100,000 people contributed their technical skills and labor (Snowy Mountains Scheme 2008).

In retrospect, the Snowy Scheme has been viewed as an economic and engineering wonder (Lunney 2001) as well as an ecological disaster, diverting 99 percent of the Snowy River to reservoirs and other rivers (Gale 1999, 304). This has affected all of the rivers in the region in terms of increased salinity, erosion, and weed growth along with decreases in fish, insect, and other invertebrate life and wetlands (Gale 1999, 308–309). As a result, after 24 years of operation, the Commonwealth, Victoria, and New South Wales governments called for an inquiry into the environmental impact of the project, with the final report issued on October 23, 1998. This report called for an increase in water flow through the Snowy River in order to balance the needs of the electricity plants, irrigators, and nature (Gale 1999, 311). As a result, in late 2000 the three governments agreed to commit AU$375 million "to restore 21% of average natural flows, equivalent to 56 billion gallons (212 gigaliters) in the Snowy River" plus a further 18.5 billion gallons (70 Gl) to the Murray and other important rivers in the system (Vanderzee and Turner 2002). Unfortunately this commitment was not upheld, and in 2007–08 the Snowy River received just 3.5 percent of its natural flow and the water situation in southeastern Australia remains as tenuous today as it did when the Snowy received just 1 percent (Le Feuvre 2008).

In addition to the Snowy Scheme, the decades between 1947 and 1974 produced many other infrastructural developments in Australia, funded largely by state and federal governments enjoying the pros-

The vast majority of work on the Snowy Scheme was done on tunnels such as these, built to carry millions of gigaliters of water in and out of the hydroelectric power plants that were at the center of the scheme. (Pictures Collection, State Library of Victoria)

perity of near-full employment and the wool and mineral booms. For example, the Commonwealth Aid Road (CAR) Acts, starting in 1947, saw the development of most of the country's interregional highways as well as the improvement and sealing of thousands of secondary roads and thoroughfares (Infrastructure Australia 2006). By 1966 motorists could drive along the coast from Melbourne to Sydney on entirely sealed roads, and by 1969 the problem of the multigauge rail-ways had been overcome with the completion of a "standard gauge transcontinental connection" (Farmer 2007, 5). Indoor plumbing was also a luxury in many Australian homes until the wealth of the 1950s and 1960s moved the toilet indoors. Another development in this period was the introduction of myxomatosis to rid the country of its plague of rabbits, which had been breeding out of control since being introduced a century earlier. Unfortunately the virus affected only about 99 percent of rabbits, and the last 1 percent has gone on to repopulate the country to nearly the level before 1950. The Menzies government also earned the praise of many rural families in this period, for it is largely credited with the electrification of the Australian bush, or countryside.

Wages and Welfare

In addition to infrastructure, Australian governments in the postwar era spent much more money on social welfare than previously. According to the Australian government's own history of welfare provision, "the Australian welfare state was officially established in 1943" (Department of Families, Community Services 2004) and expanded generously for many years afterward. Chifley's Labor government introduced a wid-ows' pension in 1942 and funeral benefits a year later, and in 1944 "unemployment, sickness, and pharmaceutical benefits schemes" took effect (Castles and Uhr 2007, 106). The Australian High Court rejected this legislation on the grounds that it was unconstitutional and over-reached the Commonwealth's specific tasks, but a 1946 social services referendum changed the country's Constitution, one of only eight successful referenda in the 20th century, and a long history of govern-mental payouts began. The electoral defeat of the Labor Party in 1949 slowed the addition of benefits to what Labor had called the "'national welfare scheme'" (cited in Castles and Uhr 2007, 106), but it did not stop existing social payments. In fact, each decade saw a tremendous increase in social spending as a percentage of gross domestic product (GDP), from 5.2 percent in 1940–41 to 12 percent in 1970–71, just one year before Labor finally regained power for the first time since 1949 (Castles and Uhr 2007, 99).

Additionally, wages rose in the postwar period, in part as a result of high demand for Australian wheat, wool, and minerals but also with the 1950 decision by the Arbitration Court to raise the minimum wage for men by 15 percent, from seven pounds two shillings to eight pounds two shillings; women's wages were set at 75 percent those of men. By June 1953, when quarterly adjustment of wages was ended in a bid to decrease inflation, men's wages had risen to 11 pounds 16 shillings (Carroll 1977, 37).

A Bit of Fun

With these higher wages Australians in the 1950s turned their aspirations toward the increasingly vast array of both imported and domestic consumer goods available in the local marketplace. The first entirely Australian-built Holden automobile rolled off the assembly line on November 29, 1948 (Carroll 1977, 43), and by June 1961 Australians had one car for every five people (Symons 1982, 178). Refrigerators went from being a luxury item to a necessity in Australia, and by 1955, 73 percent of households had at least one (Symons 1982, 178). Television arrived in Australia in 1956, and by the end of that same year 5 percent of households in Melbourne and 1 percent in Sydney had acquired a set (History of Australian Television, 2008). By 1960 all the state capitals had their own television channels, and in 1962 many rural areas had as well, so that about 75 percent of the population had access to some form of television broadcast (Carroll 1977, 133).

Other forms of entertainment also absorbed Australians' new wealth, especially films from Britain and Hollywood, and the new sounds of rock and roll. At first, rock and roll was seen by many adults as a scourge to be eradicated as quickly as possible, especially after the country's "first serious rock 'n' roll riot" in Brisbane on November 21, 1956 (Evans 1997, 114). However, the genre fairly quickly moved into the mainstream, and soon Australian television hosted several music-oriented shows, including *Bandstand, Six O'Clock Rock,* and later *Countdown,* on which both domestic and overseas acts appeared live and in the first music videos. When the Beatles arrived in Melbourne in 1964, thousands of people turned out to greet them and about 350 people had to be treated for "fainting, hysteria and minor injuries" (Carroll 1977, 156). A local supergroup, the Easybeats, formed by a group of British and Dutch migrants at the Villawood Migrant Hostel, also attracted enormous crowds and had 15 Top 40 hits in the five years they played together (1965–70), including their biggest hit, "Friday on My Mind."

While rock and roll was exciting the vast majority of Australia's younger population, new forms of entertainment were being introduced or expanded for the older generations, as well. In 1957 Sydney hosted a competition to design a new entertainment complex for the city's harbor. The Danish architect Jørn Utzon won the international tender and work began right away. Although not completed until 1973 and without Utzon, who had resigned in protest over government interference in 1966, the Sydney Opera House can be seen as a vital component of Australia's postwar economic boom and social expansion.

Postwar prosperity also contributed to a tremendous increase in the number of sporting events, feeding Australians' traditional love of sports. In 1956 Melbourne hosted the games of the XVI Olympiad. This was the first Olympics to be held outside Europe or North America, the first to be televised live, and even the first in which all athletes joined to close the event. From November 22 to December 8, 1956, 3,314 athletes from 72 countries participated in 145 summer events spanning 17 sporting disciplines, including swimming, rowing, and track and field. Competing at home gave Australians a great advantage at these games, where they participated in several team sports for the first time, including soccer and basketball, and earned more medals, 35, than an Australian team was able to win again until 1996 (Australian Olympic Committee 3).

Although the Olympics graced Melbourne for just a short period in the early summer of 1956, the infrastructure and attitude toward sport the games symbolized and engendered remained. And, as had been the case earlier in the 20th century, sport was an important arena for defining Australian identity. One discipline where Australians were particularly strong in the postwar period was men's tennis. The 1956 Wimbledon men's singles finals from 1956 to 1958, in which one Australian defeated another for the trophy, provide a good case study. In 1956 New South Welshman Lew Hoad defeated his countryman Ken Rosewall in front of a packed British center court audience; Hoad then won the next year over his Australian rival Ashley Cooper, who then defeated his fellow Aussie Neale Fraser in 1958. Altogether between 1946 and 1970 there were 10 all-Australian men's singles finals at Wimbledon and another 10 years in which one finalist was Australian. In addition to Hoad, Fraser, and Cooper, the list of Australian finalists during this period includes Geoff Brown, John Bromwich, Ken McGregor, Frank Sedgman, Fred Stolle, Rod Laver, Marty Mulligan, John Newcombe, Tony Roche, and Roy Emerson (AELTC, Men's 2008). While Australian women were not as prolific as their male counterparts, among them Margaret Smith Court, Evonne Goolagong Cawley, and Judy Tegart won the Wimbledon women's singles trophy four times in nine finals, including one all-Australian final in 1971 in which Goolagong defeated Court (AELTC, Ladies 2008).

In addition to tennis, Australians did very well in a number of other individual sporting events in the period, especially swimming, cycling,

Lew Hoad and Ken Rosewall, two of Australia's postwar tennis stars, making their Wimbledon debut as 17-year-olds in 1952 (Pictures Collection, State Library of Victoria)

and track and field. In team sports the Australian men dominated the cricket pitch during the postwar period, winning the Ashes trophy seven times to England's four between 1946 and 1974; the contest was a draw four times. Australia's international rugby squads in this period were likewise successful over their English counterparts, winning three test matches and losing two (Rugby Union Archives, personal communication 2009). Australia's women were also at the top of international competition in their most popular sport, netball, a modified version of basketball that remains the country's most popular team sport for women (Taylor 2001).

It's Time! Harold Holt

While Menzies's conservative Liberal Party with its Country Party partner ruled Australia for an unprecedented 23 years in the postwar period, in January 1966 it was time for Menzies to step down to allow his deputy, Harold Holt, time to consolidate support for the general election in November of that year. The coalition won the election, despite Australians' dismay with the escalating war in Vietnam, and Holt began to make the prime minister's office his own. Even small changes were important at the time because large numbers of Australians, both young people and those who had arrived from Europe after 1949, had never known any head of government besides Menzies. Holt, at 57 years old, was not a member of the younger generation, but his interests in fashion and physical fitness and personable character meant that he was embraced by old and young alike. He began holding weekly press conferences, which his predecessor had avoided, and entered Parliament by the front door, rather than the side to avoid the press (Australia's Prime Ministers, Holt).

As well as these important symbolic acts, the short period of Holt's leadership produced many other significant changes in Australia. As part of the country's continuing distancing from Britain, the Holt administration introduced a new decimal currency, the Australian dollar, to replace the former British system, whereby pounds were divided into 20 shillings, which in turn were divided into 12 pence. The distancing from Britain can also be seen in Holt's overt and long overdue recognition that his country was located in the Asia-Pacific region rather than Europe or the rest of the North Atlantic. While Menzies had not visited Asia during his long rule, in just a year Holt made two extended trips there, first to Southeast Asia in early 1966 and then to East Asia a year later. In addition, numerous Asian leaders made their first trips to Australia to meet with Holt to discuss regional trade, security, and immigration issues.

As part of Holt's embrace of Asia, 1966 also marks the start of the abolition of the "white Australia policy." There was still plenty of work to be done throughout the 1970s and beyond, but in 1966 "Holt's first prime ministerial statement announced the relaxation of restrictions that had blocked the entry of non-European migrants for 65 years. The *Migration Act 1966* increased access to migrants other than those from Europe, including refugees fleeing Vietnam" (Australia's Prime Ministers, Holt). This set the stage for about 26,000 people from the "Australasian neighbourhood," as it was called by the Holt administration, to enter Australia by 1970 (Jakubowicz). Immigration from the region expanded even more in 1975, when large numbers of Vietnamese refugees arrived, and has continued ever since. By the early 1990s about half the immigrants to Australia originated in an Asian country, and today about 7 percent of the population is of Asian descent.

A fourth long overdue issue to be tackled by the Holt administration was recognition of Aboriginal people as citizens of Australia, a country the vast majority of them had never left. While suffrage had been extended to Aboriginal people in Victoria, New South Wales, Tasmania, South Australia, and the Australian Capital Territory in 1949; in Western Australia and the Northern Territory in 1962; and in Queensland in 1966, in most other respects Aboriginal people remained outside public life in Australia until the referendum in 1967. They were denied access to most public spaces, including swimming pools, pubs, and hotels, and in many areas continued to live under the administration of state-run protection boards. Aboriginal war veterans were not even allowed to enter their local Returned and Services League halls, except on ANZAC day (National Museum of Australia 2007–08).

The push for Aboriginal rights in Australia was not new by the time of the 1967 referendum but had been slowly gaining momentum throughout the 20th century. In the second decade of the century the Association for the Protection of Native Races was formed in Sydney and, although moribund for a number of years, gained prominence in 1928 when its members pushed for "a Royal Commission to look into the Commonwealth taking control of Aboriginal dealings" (Dawkins 2004). Several similar organizations were established in the interwar years, all of which advocated an examination of the citizenship problem by the Commonwealth government. Two sections of the Australian Constitution had to be changed in order to provide equal rights to Aboriginal people. The first was Section 127, which stated, "In reckoning the numbers of the people of the Commonwealth, or of a State or other part of the Commonwealth, aboriginal natives shall not be counted." The second was Section 51 (xxvi), which stated, "The Parliament shall, subject to this Constitution, have power to make laws for the peace, order, and good government of the Commonwealth with respect to: The people of any race, other than the aboriginal race in any State, for whom it is deemed necessary to make special laws."

The first public mention of a referendum to change these sections of the Constitution was in 1957, when Jessie Mary Grey Street advocated this course of action during her work with both the British Anti-Slavery Society and the Australian Federation of Women Voters (AFWV) and had her petition presented at Parliament. A year later the Commonwealth government under Menzies established the Federal Council for the Advancement of Aborigines and Torres Strait Islanders, which likewise spent most of its political capital on pushing for a referendum to change the Constitution.

A number of important Aboriginal people contributed to the referendum process. Perhaps most important was Charles Perkins, whose Freedom Rides throughout western New South Wales in 1965 moved the plight of Australia's Aboriginal people into the living rooms of the country's non-Indigenous majority. As a result, when Harold Holt became prime minister and quickly signed the United Nations International Accord for the Elimination of All Forms of Racial Discrimination, the majority of the country was ready to follow him. When the question of

CHARLES NELSON PERKINS

C harles Perkins was born in 1936 in the Northern Territory city of Alice Springs. He resided with his mother at the Alice Springs Telegraph Station Aboriginal Reserve until he was 10, when he was taken to the St. Francis Home in Adelaide to complete his schooling. At 16 he was provided a trade as a fitter and turner but far preferred life as a soccer player. After playing for various teams in Australia, he wound up in the English professional league, training with Everton and playing for an amateur team, Bishop Auckland. In 1959 he turned down an opportunity to play for Manchester United and homesickness sent him back to Australia.

Upon arriving home, Perkins moved to Sydney and became the second Aboriginal person to complete a bachelor of arts degree in Australia. In 1965 Perkins organized the first Australian Freedom Ride, taking students and the national media from Sydney to various country towns throughout New South Wales, highlighting the discrimination against Aboriginal people. In 1967 Perkins also worked tirelessly to highlight the need for a yes vote on the referendum. From this period until his death in 2000, Perkins held almost every possible public position related to Indigenous affairs in Australia (papers of Charles Perkins [1936–2000]).

When Perkins died an untimely death at age 64, his friend the journalist John Pilger wrote of him that *"Charlie Perkins was, in many ways, Australia's Mandela. Indeed, had the Australian racial composition, been reversed, as in South Africa, he would have surely fulfilled that role"* (Pilger 2000; italic per original text). The Australian public mourned Perkins at an elaborate state funeral, "in recognition of his dedicated work for Indigenous Australians" (National Museum of Australia, 2007–08), but there is no doubt that he would have preferred state recognition for his cause in the form of an apology, a treaty, and reparations for hundreds of years of land theft and abuse at the hands of whites and their governments.

Sources: "Papers of Charles Perkins (1936–2000)." National Library of Australia. Available online. URL: http://nla.gov.au/nla.ms-ms8047. Accessed February 12, 2009; Pilger, John. "Charles Perkins: A Tribute." Johnpilger. com (October 19, 2000). Available online. URL: http://www.johnpilger. com/page.asp?partid=166. Accessed February 12, 2009; National Museum of Australia. "Charles Perkins" (2002–2008). Available online. URL: http:// indigenousrights.net.au/person.asp?pID=983. Accessed February 9 and 12, 2009.

legal equality was posed in the May 27, 1967, referendum, it received an overwhelming 90.7 percent approval vote. Overnight Aboriginal people, whose ancestors had lived on the Australian continent for some 60,000 years, became citizens of the country established on their land in 1901. A federal organization, the Council for Aboriginal Affairs, with Charles Perkins as a founding member, was established to oversee Aboriginal policy at the Commonwealth level. Improvement to individual people's lives was not immediate, and many are still waiting today to experience some form of social and economic equality, but one of the legal barriers to equality had finally been breached.

Another important Aboriginal concern to emerge during this period related to land rights. Even before their existence was recognized in the Australian Constitution, many Aboriginal people and Torres Strait Islanders had believed that it was time to redress the loss of their land since colonization and settlement had begun in 1788. One of the first actions toward this end took place in Arnhem Land, Northern Territory, in 1963. At the time that region was being explored by mining companies, and bauxite, an important form of aluminum, was found in abundance. In the face of this threat to their territory, the Yolngu people composed a petition combining both traditional and modern forms of communication, bark painting and legal text, and presented it to the House of Representatives (AIATSIS and Pascoe 2008, 110). The Yolngu

Aboriginal land rights demonstration, Parliament House, July 30, 1972. Protesters demonstrate in Canberra in conjunction with the establishment of the first Aboriginal tent embassy. (Ken Middleton/nla.pic-vn2356023/National Library of Australia)

were unsuccessful, but their actions set the stage for numerous court cases that did finally produce changes in the law in the 1980s.

Another important moment in the fight for recognition of Aboriginal land rights in this period was the establishment on January 26, 1972, of an Aboriginal tent embassy on the front lawn of the old Parliament House in Canberra. The protesters presented the government a five-point plan leading to full recognition of their land rights and stated that they would not give up their protest until they were successful. This was a historic moment, for the largely Sydney-based Aboriginal protesters were joined by thousands of non-Aboriginal supporters in their march to Parliament. The embassy has been revived numerous times since 1972 and has been a continuous presence in the capital since 1992. At the start of 2010 it remained on the grounds in Canberra because, although various legal and political goals have been met, full recognition of prior ownership of the land has yet to occur through the signing of a treaty or other formal recognition.

Sadly for Australia's Indigenous and non-Indigenous populations alike, Harold Holt had less than two years in the prime minister's office to continue the work he began in recognizing both Aboriginal rights and Australia's location in the Asia-Pacific region. On December 17, 1967, Holt went for a swim off the southern Victorian coast and disappeared.

He was a strong swimmer and had frequently taken a dip in the ocean to revive his mind and energy, but on this day a strong current and windy conditions were too much for him. His body was never found, and as a result speculation in the country was rampant. While some contended that the Russians had kidnapped him, others said it was the Chinese. Still others maintained that he had committed suicide over the war in Vietnam or some difficult domestic issue. There has never been any solid evidence to support such theories; however, even today it is not uncommon to hear Aus-

The irony of Prime Minister Harold Holt's death while swimming is evident not only in the number of times he was photographed in and around water but also in a swim center in Melbourne having been named after him. (AAP)

tralians debating the topic. In October 2008 the national broadcaster ABC Television aired a miniseries, *The Prime Minister Is Missing*, which explored the idea of suicide but seemed to conclude with the more prosaic verdict that Holt, who had been suffering from shoulder pain, overestimated his swimming ability in rough seas and was swept away by a strong current.

Gough Whitlam

With the news that the prime minister had gone missing, Australians' security concerns reemerged, setting the stage for a Liberal Party victory in 1969, with John Gorton in the leadership position. As is often the case, the Australian electorate was reluctant to usher in a new political era so soon after their national loss, although the Liberal majority in the House was diminished by 17 seats. By 1972 the majority of Australians had embraced the Labor Party's campaign slogan, "It's time!" for a change in leadership and governing ideology. Certainly after 23 years in power, the Liberal coalition was seen to be running out of ideas, and the leadership change from Gorton to William McMahon after the future prime minister Malcolm Fraser's defection from the cabinet did not help the situation. The real impetus for change, however, was from the Labor Party itself. In 1967 its long-serving leader Arthur Calwell, architect of the postwar immigration policy, stepped down in favor of the younger, more dynamic Gough Whitlam. Whitlam lost his first election in 1969 but in gaining 17 seats for Labor set the stage for the party's historic victory in 1972.

Whitlam spent his three years in office bringing about numerous changes to Australian society. Symbolically he continued the drift away from Britain by replacing "God Save the Queen" as the country's national anthem with "Advance Australia Fair." On the practical side he introduced free tertiary education and a national health insurance policy, ended the draft, and helped create numerous bureaucratic and legal structures and organizations, including the Law Reform Commission, the Social Welfare Commission, the Aboriginal Land Rights Commission, the Women's Affairs Office, the Australian National Parks and Wildlife Service, the Australian Heritage Commission, and the Family Court. Australian consumers saw increased protection under the Trade Practices Act 1974 and all people of non-European background became equal under the law in the Racial Discrimination Act 1975. As part of its commitment to dignity and social welfare, the Whitlam government also accepted the terms of the Woodward Report, which recommended turning over the Northern Territory's Aboriginal reserves and missions to their Indigenous owners. Internationally Whitlam had this same determination to legislate for equality and fairness. In 1974 his government oversaw the granting of independence to Australia's overseas colony on New Guinea.

While in retrospect many of the Whitlam era reforms can be seen to have conferred great benefits on the country, such as greater equality for women, Aboriginal people, and those with working-class backgrounds; longer life expectancies due to health care for all; and increased protection for the environment, families, and consumers, at the time he often struggled because the Liberal-Country Party coalition controlled the Senate. His government passed a record 507 bills during their period in office, but another 93 were rejected by the Senate, 15 more than had been rejected in the previous 71 years (Molony 2005, 352). In the context of this stymieing by the Senate, in May 1974 Whitlam called for a double dissolution of Parliament, in which all members came up for early election, to try to gain control of the intransigent Senate. While his measure failed in the Senate and Labor even lost two seats in the House, the election did give his government some ability to act. The government continued its reform agenda for the next 17 months with this diminished majority but in the context of high unemployment, political scandal, and foreign interference lost office on November 11, 1975, in what has been called "the most dramatic event in the history of the Australian federation" (Farnsworth 2001).

Conclusion

The postwar period generated many changes in Australia: hundreds of thousands of migrants from non-English-speaking countries, social welfare, infrastructural development, and Aboriginal rights. By the mid-1970s the long global economic boom that supported these changes had finally ended, and Australians were feeling the effects of unemployment and inflation for the first time in a generation. Unfortunately for the Labor Party, its election in 1972 coincided with this downturn. Having been out of power for 23 years, party leaders had also been denied a forum for experiencing national leadership and made them, perhaps, overeager to pursue their agenda for change. As a result, the few short years in the early 1970s when Labor controlled the Commonwealth government were turbulent and ended abruptly in the most dramatic political events in Australian history.

8

CONSTITUTIONAL CRISIS
(1975-1983)

Nation-building in Australia has always been a project of attempting to bridge deep-seated social divisions. In the early years, settlers and emancipists often viewed each other across a vast social, political, and economic chasm. While this distinction faded toward the end of the 19th century, class divisions, racial divisions, and political divisions between conservatives and reformers continued to disrupt the factors that created a common national identity. In late 1975 another vast division emerged to disturb national unity, that between people who supported the governor-general's actions in sacking the government on November 11 and those who, following Whitlam's advice, "maintain[ed] their rage" about it.

Dismissal

Although the Whitlam government was reelected in the double dissolution election in 1974, the following months were not easy for Whitlam or the Labor Party. Following the international trend, unemployment ballooned from just 4.5 percent in December 1972, when Whitlam first took office, to 14.4 percent in mid-1974 and 16.9 percent by the middle of 1975 (Clark 1995, 318). Deep social and political divisions in Australian society, which had been emerging since the late 1960s, also moved to the fore in this period. Many Liberals and their traditional supporters—generally social, political, and economic conservatives—were outraged at changes in Australian society since Menzies's retirement in 1966. Even prior to Whitlam's election they had "misgivings about the moral effects of some of the goods transported to Australia by the multinationals," including rock and roll; American publications, television, and films; and youth fashion (Clark 1995, 303). During the Whitlam era, with government support of women's and

Aboriginal rights, free university education and health care, and even the early phases of multiculturalism under the immigration minister Al Grassby, the conservative establishment found a tangible enemy they could attack in their quest to turn back the clock. The most important mouthpiece for this camp was Malcolm Fraser, who became Liberal Party leader in March 1975.

Some of the material used by Fraser to oppose the government was clearly nonsense, such as the cries of "favoritism" and "politicisation of the public service" (Clark 1995, 315) against several Whitlam appointees; after all, what government does not appoint its supporters and allies to key positions? Other changes, however, were based on some serious errors of judgment by Whitlam and other important figures in the government. Two of the most important of these concerns, the "loans affair" and the "Junie Morosi scandal," involved some of the same set of circumstances: Jim Cairns, a leading left-wing economist and deputy prime minister, treasurer, and later minister for environment, embroiling himself with individuals whom the media attacked for their non-Australian "exotic" background and supposed connections to shady business deals. In retrospect, nothing illegal is likely to have taken place in either of the affairs, but bad decisions were made and in the political context of Australia at the time, this was all that was necessary to keep the pressure on Whitlam and his government.

One of the first scandals of the Whitlam period, the "loans affair" or "Khemlani affair," was a botched attempt by Jim Cairns and the minister for minerals and energy, Rex Connor, to raise a AU$4 billion loan for the government. They were going to use the money to bail out the sinking Australian economy by buying back many of the formerly state-owned oil and mineral companies that Menzies and the Liberals had sold to foreign multinationals (Clarke 2003, 299). The recession that plagued most of the globe in this period meant that former sources of cash in the West had dried up. As a result, the two senior ministers broadened their search to the Middle East, into which petrodollars were flowing continually. When the Liberals and media found out about this policy initiative, as well as the activities of "certain businessmen of dubious reputation" who were to serve as middlemen in the deal (Clarke 2003, 299), Whitlam and Connor were forced to face the House of Representatives and assure them that no activity of this sort would move ahead. After their public statement, however, a Pakistani banker by the name of Tirath Khemlani was discovered to have continued his attempts at securing a Middle Eastern loan for the government. Fraser and the media jumped on this information, embarrassing Whitlam and forcing him to fire Connor and demote Cairns to the environment ministry.

The second Cairns scandal surrounded his appointment of a woman purported to be his mistress to the position of principal private secretary. The woman, Junie Morosi, excited the public imagination with her exotic background—part-Chinese, part-Italian, part-Portuguese, born in Shanghai, and raised in Manila—and her beauty. These two factors, along with her being a woman in a position of power, made for a very juicy story to sell to the Australian people. As she said in an interview with *Woman's Day*, "If I had been a white Anglo-Saxon male there would have been no story at all" (cited in Australian Politics Books 2009c).

Cairns first appointed Morosi in December 1974 after she had spent some time working as an assistant in the commissioner for community affairs' office. Perhaps because of her Asian background or her inexperience, the media began immediately to attack her and her husband with claims that their businesses were benefiting from her access to politicians. Cairns refused to cave in to media pressure and fire his private secretary, but Morosi quit within days of her initial hiring. A later investigation into the claims of business improprieties found no evidence and Cairns rehired Morosi, much to the chagrin of many of his friends and supporters (Australian Politics Books 2009c).

While even the allegations of having hired his mistress were enough to instigate the combined Fraser-conservative media attack machine, events in July 1975 seemed to support their claims that Cairns was not fit to control the country's finances. After having seemingly put the disastrous loans affair behind him, Cairns was found to have continued trying to raise money for the government, this time through George Harris, a well-known businessman in Melbourne and the Carlton Football Club president. "Harris claimed that Cairns had given him a letter authorising him to investigate overseas loans, and promising him a 2.5% commission. Cairns denied having given him such a letter" (Australian Politics Books 2009b). Unfortunately for Cairns, Harris produced the letter with his signature on it, leaving Cairns to claim, feebly, that he did not remember signing it. The media seized on Morosi's mishandling of the minister's office, isolating Cairns from colleagues and advisers, and creating a situation of "poor communications in his office" (Australian Politics Books 2009c). For the second time in just six months Morosi was out of a job, and this time so was her boss. Whitlam fired Cairns for cause but could not stop the Fraser attacks on his government.

As a side note, for many years Cairns and Morosi denied that there was any sexual relationship between them and even fought several defa-

FURTHER SCANDAL

While the "loans affair" and "Junie Morosi scandal" were two important events that rocked the Whitlam government, they were not the only ones. On March 16, 1973, not long after taking office, Whitlam's attorney general, Lionel Murphy, raided the offices of the Australian Security and Information Office (ASIO) in an attempt to uncover "a plot to withhold information from him" (293). The raid was a fiasco in which Murphy used one of his own agencies to raid another agency under his purview, a situation that contributed to the whole event being played in the media as a farce. "Whitlam himself later admitted that this fiasco was probably his government's greatest mistake" (293). It certainly caused doubts among U.S. Central Intelligence Agency (CIA) officials concerned with Australia that the Whitlam government could be trusted to maintain secrets it deemed vital to American and other international security interests.

Another error in judgment made by the Whitlam administration is known as "the Gair Affair." In March 1974 Senator Vincent Gair, member of the Democratic Labor Party, which split from the Labor Party in 1955, expressed interest in taking up an overseas diplomatic position. According to opposition and media portrayal afterward, Whitlam seized the opportunity of a half-Senate election to stack the upper house with Labor members and appointed Gair to serve as ambassador to Ireland. The Liberal leader at the time, Billy Snedden, was publicly outraged at the Gair appointment and threatened to "block supply," the Australian term for withholding funds to the government. In reaction, Whitlam requested that the governor-general call a double-dissolution election, in which the entire lower and upper houses of Parliament would be dissolved and all members forced to campaign to regain their seats. The resulting election did not give Labor the Senate majority it sought, though a few more pieces of legislation were passed in the immediate aftermath, and the bad press that resulted from the entire affair only contributed to the public sense that Whitlam had lost control of the political agenda.

Source: Clarke, Frank G. *Australia in a Nutshell: A Narrative History.* (Dural Delivery Centre, N.S.W.: Rosenberg, 2003), p. 293.

mation suits in court against Australian media outlets for making this claim. Nevertheless, in 2002, Cairns admitted in an ABC Radio interview that the two had slept together, thus ending decades of speculation.

From this period in mid-1975 there appeared to be no way the Whitlam government could survive another election. For example, in June a safe Labor seat in Tasmania was lost with an enormous 13.8 percent swing in the vote in an election to replace a Labor member of Parliament (MP) who had accepted an ambassadorial position. But Fraser and the conservatives, including the premiers of New South Wales and Queensland, were not willing to wait the one to one and a half years before the next full election and set the wheels in motion for a more immediate change of government. Instead of replacing Labor senators with fellow Labor Party members when one left the Senate to become an ambassador and another died, the premiers of New South Wales and Queensland replaced them with their own supporters, snubbing long-standing Australian tradition. Subsequently, in October 1975 the conservatives in control of the Senate, which "had ceased to act as a house of review and had taken on the role of the defender of the established order of society against the Labor government" (Clark 1995, 312), "blocked supply." In other words, the government was denied access to funds and would have to cease functioning. Whitlam thought he could outmaneuver the Senate and even gain enough support from dissenting Liberals to regain control of the budget. But he did not realize that John Kerr, whom he had appointed governor-general, would side with Fraser and the Liberals.

On November 11, 1975, Kerr summoned Whitlam to his residence and used his privilege as representative of Queen Elizabeth II to sack the democratically elected government. He immediately asked Malcolm Fraser to name a caretaker government and set a date for an election.

Whitlam and the rest of the country were shocked that the (until that time) representative of the ceremonial head of state could do such a thing, and without either the permission or even the knowledge of the queen herself. Constitutionally, the governor-general did have the ability to act with "reserve powers" and without the prime minister's permission in emergencies. But in their claim that Kerr had acted unconstitutionally, Whitlam, Labor supporters, and many constitutional scholars have continued to note that the government had not yet run out of money and thus there was no emergency (Hirst 2002, 199). For his part, Kerr disagreed, drawing on his conversations with Garfield Barwick, Australia's chief justice at the time and former Liberal Party minister (Clarke 2003, 303). Against Labor cries that democracy had been thwarted, the Liberals said there was nothing more democratic than an election, which was held on December 13, 1975. The Liberals won this election with a landslide victory.

Gough Whitlam speaking to the press and country from the steps of Parliament House after his dismissal. The most famous line from this speech is "Long live the queen, because nothing will save the Governor-General." (nla.pic-an24355082/National Library of Australia)

In the postdismissal period, numerous explanations have been put forward as to why Kerr acted when and how he did. For example, CIA meddling in the affair has been postulated by many interested in this question (Pilger 1992). The journalist John Pilger and others cite evidence from Christopher Boyce's espionage trial in the United States, in which he testified that he saw top secret papers documenting CIA interference in Whitlam's government. Boyce's story, as well as that of his accomplice Daulton Lee, is told in the 1980 book by the *New York Times* journalist Robert Lindsey *The Falcon and the Snowman* and the 1985 Hollywood film by the same name.

The circumstantial evidence for CIA meddling in the affair largely relates to the Whitlam government's exposure of U.S. spy operations on Australian soil at Pine Gap, near Alice Springs, and Whitlam's contemplation of refusing the Americans further access to the site (Clark 2000). In his interview with Bill Morrison, the Australian defense minister, in 1975 the Australian journalist Andrew Clark discovered not only that Kerr had asked for and received a high-level defense briefing just days before he sacked the government, but that this briefing included CIA warnings about further Australian revelations and actions related to Pine Gap (Clark 2000). Warren Christopher, secretary of state under Bill Clinton and assistant secretary of state under Jimmy Carter in 1977, also reportedly told Gough Whitlam in Sydney in 1977 that "the US administration would never again interfere in the domestic political process of Australia" (cited in Clark 2000). The U.S. government has denied participating in the dismissal but, according to Clark, has not "directly rebutted" (2000) Christopher's words, and thus the implication remains that there was interference at one time.

Malcolm Fraser

Malcolm Fraser's election on December 13, 1975, created the largest parliamentary majority ever held in Australian history, 91 to 36. The Liberal–National Country Party coalition also controlled the Senate with an eight-seat majority. Nonetheless, for the next eight years "Australian politics revolved around the personalities of the protagonists in . . . [the] great drama" of the dismissal (Clarke 2003, 306). Rather than thoughtfully addressing the economic problems Australia was suffering at the time, inflation and unemployment, Fraser's government was in a frenzy of impatience that failed to take constructive advice (Stone 2007, 13). According to one Fraser government insider, Deputy Secretary of the Treasury John Stone, "the Prime Minister was at loggerheads with his own Treasurer (and Deputy Leader of his party), whose views were supported by all the [relevant] agencies" (2007, 15). As a result of Fraser's stubborn adherence to policy opinion, Australia's economy failed to improve. Unemployment skyrocketed from 275,400 in December 1975 when Fraser became the elected prime minister to 674,000 in December 1982 (Clarke 2003, 309). Quite a number of Whitlam-era policies that might have mitigated this economic disaster were also rolled back, including funding for Aboriginal and women's issues, education, and the arts (Clarke 2003, 307).

Although in many areas of policy Fraser wanted to be the anti-Whitlam, there were two important issues on which Fraser was as progressive as Whitlam, if not more so: immigration and multiculturalism. According to the immigration specialist James Jupp, "The Fraser government is best remembered for its humane approach to refugees and its creation of the institutions of multiculturalism" (2007, 39). While Whitlam greatly reduced immigration in response to the economic downturn, Fraser reversed that trend almost immediately by increasing numbers from 55,000 in 1975–76 to 70,000 in 1976–77 (Franklin 2007); by 1981 the number of entering migrants was up to

120,000 people per year (Betts 2003, 39). Included in the populations allowed into Australia for the first time in this period were almost 56,000 Vietnamese refugees and several thousand Lebanese Muslims fleeing the civil war in that country in 1976; previously, a population of Lebanese Christians had arrived and settled in the largest cities.

Fraser's government also followed the path set by Harold Holt and Gough Whitlam to recognize the multicultural nature of Australian society. In 1977 Fraser announced the need for a review of Australia's migrant programs and services, which was to be undertaken by the well-known Melbourne lawyer Frank Galbally. When Galbally's committee presented its work a year later, its report was "the first occasion on which a report commissioned by the Commonwealth Government . . . [was] tabled . . . in languages other than English"; the other languages were Arabic, Dutch, German, Greek, Italian, Serbo-Croatian, Spanish, Turkish, and Vietnamese (Fraser 1978). The review called for far more public expenditure on English language and migrant settlement programs; the availability of more translation, child care, preschool, and aged care services; and greater involvement in the provision of these services by migrant communities themselves (Fraser 1978). The reverberations of this report were enormous and continue today with the existence of a series of Migrant Resource Centres, Adult Multicultural Education Services centers, and the Special Broadcasting Service, with its range of television and radio stations that disseminate news and entertainment in many different languages.

Despite the failure of his policies to perform the economic miracles Australians had hoped for, elections in 1977 and 1980 returned Fraser to power. The first of these victories is generally seen as a continuation of the poisoned election in 1975. Whitlam remained the leader of the Labor Party and campaigned mainly on the theme of the undemocratic nature of the dismissal. Fraser focused almost entirely on the economic mismanagement of the Whitlam years and thus held on to most of his vast majority in both houses. After this loss, Whitlam resigned both from his leadership position and from Parliament. He has gone on to a productive postparliamentary career as a speaker, writer, and campaigner for the issues he considers most important, such as republicanism. Perhaps because of Labor's dissociation from Whitlam, in 1980 the Liberals' margin of victory was much smaller and Fraser's Senate majority began to evaporate.

Finally, in 1983 Fraser called an early election in the hope that his Labor adversary would remain Bill Hayden, over whom Fraser maintained a lead in the polls. Rather than take his party to another defeat, however, Hayden stepped down from the leadership, to be replaced by the popular and gregarious Bob Hawke, who had entered Parliament just three years earlier. The leadership change, in conjunction with enormous unemployment figures and the bitterness of the events of 1975, gave Hawke the chance to put Labor back into government, and on March 5, 1983, he did just that.

Politics of a Different Variety

Although the 1975–83 period can best be characterized by the dismissal of the Whitlam government and the failure of the Fraser government to address the underlying economic crisis in Australia, these were certainly not the only political events to capture Australians' imaginations at this time. Environmental, gay and lesbian, Aboriginal, and women's political movements also received much greater public prominence in the mid- to late 1970s than ever before.

Franklin-Gordon

In 1973 environmentalists in Tasmania lost their six-year campaign to save Lake Pedder from being flooded as part of a hydroelectric scheme supported by the Tasmanian government. Rather than give up their cause, this loss motivated many in the movement to work even harder. In 1976 a number of these disappointed activists met in the living room of Dr. Bob Brown to form the Tasmanian Wilderness Society (TWS), which in 1984 became the Wilderness Society.

In 1979 the Tasmanian Wilderness Society and its allies went into action when the Hydro-Electric Commission (HEC) proposed a massive $3 billion scheme to dam the Lower Gordon River, which included flooding large sections of the Wild Rivers National Park and destroying much of the Franklin River (Brown 2003, 8). For four years TWS, the Australian Conservation Foundation, Friends of the Earth, and 16 other local, national, and international organizations worked together as the South West Coalition to fight for the Franklin. The first stages of this fight entailed negotiation with state and local governments, campaigning during state and Commonwealth elections, and raising grassroots awareness of the issue (Brown 2003, 9). In 1980 Norm Sanders even won a seat in Tasmania's parliament as a Democrat with a platform of fighting the Franklin dam project (Brown 2003, 8).

In the early stages, Tasmania's Labor premier, Doug Lowe, remained neutral on the issue and even tried in 1979 to propose an alternative site, the so-called Gordon above Olga site, to that put forward by the

HEC. This site would have saved the Franklin River, but the issue became deadlocked in Tasmania's upper and lower houses of parliament. In 1981 Lowe became frustrated by this situation and took matters into his own hands: He would "nominate the area for World Heritage Listing" (Brown 2003, 9), thus opening the possibility of federal intervention on behalf of the conservationists. Lowe subsequently lost his position as Labor leader and state premier over the issue, which led him to cross the floor and sit the remainder of his 23 years in the state parliament as an independent.

After Lowe's exit from the premier's office, Tasmanians voted in a referendum he had initially proposed to decide the matter. Much to the consternation of the conservationists, a "no dams" option did not appear on the ballot; the only two choices concerned the placement of the dam. From the day the referendum was announced, conservationists poured their energy into campaigning for a write-in vote saying "No Dams." They were successful, with the "no dams" option collecting 44.89 percent of all votes. Nevertheless, this was not enough to halt the proposal altogether (Dwyer 2008). The inconclusive vote, in which no option received more than 50 percent, led both the prodam and the antidam coalitions to step up their campaigns.

While most of the activists who began campaigning to save the Franklin did so because its loss meant the destruction of many thousands of acres of undisturbed wilderness, in 1981 greater impetus to save the area was found when Aboriginal caves were discovered in the region. "They contained the remains of campfires, stone tools and animal bones which dated back to 24,000–8,000 years BP (before present). . . . Similar caves were subsequently discovered which would have been flooded by the Gordon above Olga scheme" (Wilderness Society 2008).

In 1982 matters came to a head when the prodam government of Liberal Robin Gray was elected and proceeded to pass legislation to start the dam project at its originally nominated site. Work to construct a road through pristine rain forest to reach the site began almost immediately. In response, thousands of conservationists and their supporters demonstrated throughout Australia; 14,000 turned out in Melbourne in November and many more thousands watched the conservationists' films throughout the country (Wilderness Society 2008).

Starting on December 14, Bob Brown and TWS staged a massive blockade of the Franklin River site, during which 1,272 people were arrested for trespassing on HEC property (Wilderness Society 2008). Among those jailed was Brown, who actually left his cell to take up

The beauty of southwestern Tasmania's wilderness area was one of the driving forces behind the fight to stop the Franklin-Gordon dam project. (Pictures Collection, The State Library of Victoria)

a seat in Tasmania's parliament on Norm Sanders's resignation over the dam issue, and the British botanist David Bellamy. "Footage of his [Bellamy's] arrest was shown in 32 countries around the world" (Dwyer 2008) and called greater international recognition to the environmentalists' cause. The blockade remained in place until March 1983, when federal elections delivered the federal government to the antidam Labor leader Bob Hawke; he defeated the staunchly prodam Malcolm Fraser, in part through the actions of the 70 TWS branches throughout the country, whose supporters worked tirelessly to deliver lower house seats to Labor and Senate seats to antidam Democrats (Wilderness Society 2008). One of Hawke's first actions upon taking office was to sign a bill ending development in the Franklin-Gordon area.

This seemingly decisive move, however, did not put an end to the issue. The Tasmanian premier, Gray, refused to abide by the federal legislation and stop the project. The issue moved to Australia's High Court, where the five judges had to decide whether the Commonwealth's foreign policy prerogative, in play in this case because the area had been deemed a World Heritage Listed site in 1981, outweighed the state's rights to define its own development. On July 1, 1983, "the majority [of judges] accepted the main Commonwealth arguments and held that the 1972 UNESCO Convention for the Protection of the World Cultural and Natural Heritage which established 'a World Heritage List' imposed a legal obligation on Australia" (Dwyer 2008). This time Premier Gray agreed to follow the law and stop the project.

The effects of the environmentalists' victory have been felt throughout Australia and the world since the early 1980s. Bob Brown has remained an important political figure in the subsequent 26 years, working to create the world's first Green Party in Tasmania (Brown 2003, 8). From there he took his party to the national and then the international level, hosting the First Global Greens Conference in Canberra in 2001. Today he is leader of the Australian Green Party and a federal senator from Tasmania. In addition, one global ramification of the worldwide media coverage of the Franklin blockade was that environmental issues were seen to be important electoral issues. After the blockade ended and David Bellamy returned to Britain, he was invited to discuss the affair with Prime Minister Margaret Thatcher, who, Bellamy recalls, said "there are votes in this green business" (ABC Hobart 2008).

Mardi Gras

While many of Australia's environmentalists were jailed for making a stand against destructive development in Tasmania, other Australians were likewise experiencing the inside of jail cells as a result of standing up for their beliefs. In 1978—the ninth anniversary of the Stonewall Riots in New York City when a group of lesbians and gays for the first time stood up publicly against police brutality—a group of like-minded people in Sydney wanted to mark the date with a parade. For some the night ended in a jail cell rather than at the scheduled party in the heart of the city's gay neighborhood, Kings Cross.

The lesbian and gay rights movement in Australia emerged in the 1970s after several decades of silence among lesbians and gays themselves and repression and censorship by society at large (Willett 1997). In 1970 the American lesbian rights organization Daughters of Bilitis opened a chapter in Australia; it was the first openly lesbian or gay group in the country and soon took the name the Australasian Lesbian Movement (ALM). The following year saw Sydney's CAMP (Campaign against Moral Persecution) hold Australia's first lesbian and gay demonstration. By the mid-1970s a number of other political and social organizations had emerged alongside the ALM and CAMP, including Society Five in Victoria, Campus Camp in Queensland, and Sydney Gay Liberation in New South Wales, as well as several lesbian and gay religious groups.

In 1975 the activists who risked their jobs and family relationships to start these organizations began to see concrete evidence that their work was both galvanizing the lesbian and gay community's support and reaching a wider audience. In that year South Australia became the first Australian state to legalize homosexual sex between consenting adults; the Australian Capital Territory followed in 1976. At the same time an Australian court ruled in favor of CAMP in their fight with the Catholic Church over whether they should be allowed to submit a report to the 1975–77 Royal Commission into Human Relationships, which was looking into a wide range of issues, from immigrant settlement to single-parent families (Marsh and Galbraith 1995, 302). CAMP was joined by Society Five and Campus Camp in shedding some light on the nature of homosexual relationships at the time. Additionally, the first National Homosexual Conference took place in Melbourne in 1975 and was followed by conferences in Sydney and Adelaide in 1976 and 1977, respectively.

In addition to these public successes, gay men in particular at this time were beginning to identify with a particular geographic space in the heart of Sydney. "By June 1978 around 50% of the recognised gay venues were in and around Oxford Street, the majority between Whitlam and Taylor Squares" (Marsh and Galbraith 1995, 302). As a result, when in April 1978 the San Francisco Gay Freedom Day Committee contacted lesbian and gay rights organizations throughout the world to suggest "a worldwide demonstration for gay rights" to recognize the ninth anniversary of the Stonewall Riots (Marsh and Galbraith 1995, 302), the infrastructure, organization, and location were already set in Sydney. Ken Davis and Ann Talve had received the letter from San Francisco and set events in motion with the Gay Solidarity Group for a two-part day of events: a lesbian and gay rights march and a political forum with police harassment and legal reform on the agenda. Later a nonpolitical social event, the Mardi Gras party, was added to celebrate lesbian and gay culture.

June 24, 1978, began in Sydney with the International Gay Solidarity March, when about 400 people took to the streets of the central business district with banners and placards demanding equal rights for lesbians and gay men (Ross 2008). In the public meeting that followed the political issues of the day—legalizing homosexual sex and ending discrimination and police harassment—were discussed. Next was the evening Mardi Gras parade, when "close to 2000 people joined in, singing along and chanting 'out of the bars and into the streets, join us' as they headed for Kings Cross" (Ross 2008). Lance Gowland sat in the driver's seat of a sound truck, leading the group of exuberant dancers through Sydney's gay district, until the New South Wales police decided that, despite their legal permission to parade in Sydney, the homosexuals must be stopped. Police officers pulled Gowland from his truck and confiscated both it and the public address system he was using to lead the parade (Ross 2008). The crowd kept marching, but more police turned out, tried to prevent the parade from continuing on its designated route, and then began beating and arresting marchers as they tried to turn back on the route that had led them into the Kings Cross area (Ross 2008). While they wielded their batons and truncheons, injuring dozens of marchers, many police were not wearing their badges and nametags so that they would not be identifiable later.

Altogether 53 people were arrested at the parade site that night, but this action did not deter many of the remaining marchers from following the paddy wagons back to the local police station and continuing their chanting. Numerous protests followed in the subsequent months, and by the end of that year, 478 lesbians and gays had been arrested for protesting (Marsh and Galbraith 1995, 302). Eventually almost all the charges were dropped, police claimed to have lost the files, and New South Wales even changed the law that had been used to arrest the marchers. For many of those who were arrested, however, the incident did not end happily. The conservative tabloid newspaper the *Herald Sun* published the names of all 53 people arrested on June 24 and many of those who were arrested in the later protests as well, leading to job losses and ostracization by friends and family.

Drawing upon their experiences in 1978, lesbian and gay activists in 1979 held a second Mardi Gras in the streets of Sydney. Politics remained on the agenda, with about 800 people participating in a rally

In contrast with the early parades and Mardi Gras events, in 2008 the parade was all about showing off. (Khoo Si Lin/Shutterstock)

and forum, but this time the police did not harass participants, and 23,000 people gathered for the evening Mardi Gras party (Marsh and Galbraith 1995, 303). By 1981 politics was largely off the agenda at Mardi Gras, and lifestyle celebration had come to the fore. In that year the event was moved to Sydney's summer holiday season in February, to attract a larger crowd, and continued the march toward commercial success. While the event still attracted tens of thousands of domestic and international visitors, management problems in 2002 contributed to the organizing company's declaring bankruptcy. A change in management saved the annual event, which continues to inject many tens of millions of tourist dollars into Sydney's economy.

The political action taken in the late 1970s also began to have an effect on Australia's legal system. Following South Australia and the Australian Capital Territory, Victoria legalized gay sex in 1981, New South Wales in 1984, Western Australia in 1989, Queensland in 1991, and finally Tasmania in 1997. Even prior to legalizing homosexual sexual activity, however, New South Wales had outlawed discrimination against lesbians and gay men in 1982. Other legal rights followed, including the right to sponsor a non-Australian partner's immigration to the country in 1991. In 2008 the most far-reaching legal reforms were enacted by Kevin Rudd's Labor government in which 84 Commonwealth laws were changed "to eliminate discrimination against same-sex couples and their children in a wide range of areas, including social security, taxation, Medicare, veteran's affairs, workers' compensation, educational assistance, superannuation, family law and child support" (Attorney-General's Department 2008). Gay marriage and same-sex adoption continue to be areas in which discrimination remains legal, but at least in the case of the latter, several Australian states began inquiries into the matter in 2009.

Aboriginal Politics

The highly politicized culture of the 1970s extended not only to environmentalists and lesbians and gay men, but to Australia's Aboriginal population. After the resounding yes vote in the 1967 referendum, a number of Aboriginal organizations and individual Aboriginal people emerged as important spokespeople for Indigenous Australians.

In December 1971 a small group of Aboriginal activists formed the Black Panther Party of Australia (BPPA) as an offshoot of the global Black Power movement. Many of the leaders of both the party and the movement were young urban Aboriginal people who had been disappointed after the 1967 referendum to find that the government's attitude toward their people was "business as usual" (Lothian 2005, 182). They rejected the black-white coalitions of their parents' generation and turned to African-American, Caribbean, and African models of self-determination to underpin their cause (Lothian 2005, 183–184). The most outspoken was Dennis Walker, a founding member of the BPPA and son of the Aboriginal writer and activist Oodgeroo Noonuccal (Kath Walker). With his family legacy of activism and Black Power advocacy, Walker saw the American Black Panther Party's "revolutionary ideology, along with the right of armed self-defense of the Black community and the eventual 'overthrow of the system,' . . . [as] the backbone of the Australian Party" (cited in Lothian 2005, 186). Walker himself served as the party's defense minister and was the primary advocate in the group for violence in order to achieve their goals of "land, bread, housing, education, clothing, justice, and peace," as well as an "education that teaches us our true history" and "an immediate end to POLICE BRUTALITY" (cited in Lothian 2005, 187). In the end, the BPPA did not initiate any violence; nor did they achieve most of these stated goals. Nevertheless, they were an important voice in Australian Aboriginal politics in the 1970s, especially for those whose anger had been building since the 1967 referendum (Lothian 2005, 190).

Even so, Black Power ideas imported from the United States did take hold in Australia and lead to the establishment of numerous organizations by the core group of BPPA members. The first was the Aboriginal Legal Service of New South Wales, which in 1970 was "the first organization in that state to be conceived, established, and controlled by Aborigines [sic] since the 1930s" (Lothian 2005, 193). After the success of this project in Sydney, by 1974 similar organizations had opened in all the other Australian states, providing services and advice to Aboriginal people at low or no cost. The Aboriginal district in Sydney in which this legal support organization is located, Redfern, was also soon home to an Aboriginal-run medical center, food programs for adults and children, and an Aboriginal preschool center (Lothian 2005). The self-determination of the BPPA was being played out for the benefit of thousands in Sydney, whether they advocated the revolutionary ideology of the party or not.

While the radical Black Panther Party of Australia was forming in 1971, more conservative Aboriginal politics was also finding its voice. In that year Neville Bonner became Australia's first Aboriginal member of Parliament as a Liberal Party senator. He entered the Senate with organizing experience gained as a member and later president of One People of Australia League (OPAL), a moderate social welfare organization dedicated to helping Aboriginal people access their rights in the areas of health, education, and welfare. After his nomination to the Senate in 1971 to fill the seat of the retiring Queensland Liberal Annabelle Rankin, Bonner went on to win elections in 1972, 1974, 1975, and 1980. In 1983 he stood for his seat as an independent after having angered Queensland Liberal Party leaders by speaking out against them on Indigenous affairs and voting against them 23 times. He narrowly lost that race but continued his work for Aboriginal and Torres Strait Islander people until his death in 1999.

Bonner was conservative by nature and a strong opponent of a number of progressive ideas that emerged in Australia at the time, including republicanism and most of Gough Whitlam's reformist agenda from 1972 to 1975. He also "found much of Aboriginal protest unruly" and strongly rejected any form of separatism (Rowse 1997, 97). At the same time he was a passionate spokesperson for his people from within the parliamentary system. He raised issues in Parliament in the 1970s that to this day are current in Australian society, such as the use

After his maiden speech on the Senate floor, Senator Neville Bonner then gave a boomerang throwing display on the grounds of Parliament House, 1971. (Pictures Collection, The State Library of Victoria)

of skin color as a marker of Aboriginality and the inability of patent and copyright laws to protect Aboriginal craftspeople (Ridgeway 2003). While rejecting the methods of those who set up the Aboriginal tent embassy in 1972, he fully understood the cause of their frustration and often served as a mediator between them and the government (Rowse 1997, 97).

Bonner was not the only Aboriginal leader during the 1970s and early 1980s to try to bridge the chasm between his people and the white establishment. Galarrwuy Yunupingu was also able to work with both communities to fight for his people's rights. Yunupingu began his life as an activist in 1971, while serving as a translator for his father and others of that generation as they fought the government and mining industry for land rights in Arnhem Land; their bark petition was rejected. Four years on, Yunupingu was a manager at the Northern Land Council (NLC) and fighting for native title for Aboriginal people in the Northern Territory. He served as chairman of the NLC from 1977 to 1980 and then continuously from 1983 to 2001, being reelected every three years. In 1978 he was the first Aboriginal person to receive the Australian of the Year award for having negotiated an agreement between his people and the government over uranium mining. Rather than standing against mining altogether, Yunupingu "sees it as a way for Aboriginal people to escape the welfare trap if it is conducted on the traditional owners' terms. These include a fair distribution of the economic benefits and respect for the land and specific sacred sites" (Australian of the Year Awards 2008). As did Bonner, Yunupingu rejects separatism and sees both his Australian of the Year and later Order of Australia awards as "recognition for Aboriginal people as the indigenous people of this country who must share in its future" (Australian of the Year Awards 2008).

While the Black Panthers and Neville Bonner were busy on the mainland, in Tasmania the skeleton of the woman commonly known as "the last Aboriginal Tasmanian," Trugannini, was taken from the state museum and cremated. One hundred years after her death, Aboriginal elders in that state ceremonially scattered Trugannini's ashes off Bruny Island, one of the areas she called home during her life. The fight to have their ancestors' remains returned from both Australian and overseas museums gained greater force after this highly symbolic event. The British Museum returned samples of Trugannini's hair and skin in 2002, and thousands of other artifacts, bones, and biological samples have been returned to Aboriginal communities, especially in Tasmania.

For many Aboriginal people at this time, these very important symbolic and political actions were far from their daily experiences. Lower life expectancies, higher rates of unemployment and poverty, lack of education and job skills, and the strong effects of institutional racism meant that survival was foremost on many individuals' minds. Nonetheless, these role models from the 1970s and 1980s have inspired today's generation of Aboriginal activists, from Noel Pearson in the Cape York area of Queensland to the filmmaker Warwick Thornton, director of *Samson and Delilah* (2009).

The Women's Movement

Australia's women also continued their long struggle for equal rights in the 1970s and early 1980s. While women had been voting in Australia for almost three quarters of a century by this time, the repressive nature of postwar Australian society meant that many other rights had been denied them. This condition began to change, slowly, in the 1960s and gained speed as the 1970s progressed. For example, in 1972 the Conciliation and Arbitration Commission granted women "equal pay for work of equal value" (Summers 2002, 549), and in 1977 they were granted the right to maternity leave. Unfortunately, these changes have not resulted in women in Australia actually receiving equal wages—the differential in 2007 remained 15 percent (Horin 2007)—and the struggle continues. Women in the 1970s also gained a more direct political voice. While the first female parliamentarian and senator at the federal level both took their seats in 1943, not until 1976 did a woman hold a cabinet position "with portfolio responsibilities," when Prime Minister Fraser named Senator Margaret Guilfoyle minister for social security (Summers 2002, 554).

This political change accompanied a number of legal reforms in Australia benefiting women and families more generally. No-fault divorce was introduced in 1975 by Whitlam's newly created Family Court, and South Australia passed the country's first sex discrimination legislation in the same year (Summers 2002, 558); New South Wales and Victoria followed in 1977 (Summers 2002, 559). South Australia remained on the cutting edge of women's issues in 1976 when it became "the first jurisdiction in the world to make rape in marriage a crime" (Summers 2002, 558).

This period also introduced changes for women related to fertility and other medical services. The first legal abortion clinic in the country opened in Sydney in 1974, after a series of court rulings in the late 1960s and early 1970s that allowed for limited legal access to abortion (Summers 2002, 557). Sydney was also the site of the opening of the country's first women's clinic, the Leichhardt Women's Health Centre, and Elsie, the first refuge in the country for women escaping violent relationships (Summers 2002, 228). Single mothers also gained access to state support in 1973, thus recognizing the reality of some women's lives.

Life Isn't All about Politics

While this era remains one of the most politicized in Australian history, public life of course was not only about politics. In 1977 the long tradition of secularism in Australian society took its toll on a number of mainstream Protestant churches. Because of their low numbers, the Methodists, Presbyterians, and Congregational Unionists merged under the banner of the Uniting Church. Today the Uniting Church is reaping the reward of their ecumenism in the 1970s and is the third-largest Christian community in Australia, behind the Roman Catholics and the Anglicans (Uniting Church of Australia 2009).

A number of intense media spectacles also riveted the country and took advantage of the introduction of color television in 1975. The earliest was the first airing of the Swedish pop group Abba's music videos on the ABC Television show *Countdown* on August 3 and 10, 1975, just a few months after the arrival of color television. Abba had three number-one hits in Australia in the latter months of that year and all three were simultaneously in the top 10 (Palm 2002, 271). Many hits later, Abba made their only down under tour in early 1977, when for two weeks they performed live before more than 1 percent of the entire Australian population, filmed a movie of their experiences, and dodged the enormous crowds that turned out at every location where there was potential for seeing them in person (Palm 2002, 330). This

"THE WIFE WANTS TO KNOW IF YOU CAN FIX IT FOR A COUPLE OF TICKETS TO 'ABBA'?"

Abba's popularity in Australia is humorously depicted here, with Prince Philip requesting concert tickets for Queen Elizabeth II from Prime Minister Malcolm Fraser and his wife, Tammy. Governor-General John Kerr is depicted far left. (Stewart McCrae Cartoon collection/nla.pic-vn3102566/National Library of Australia)

set the stage for their continued popularity through the present day. As late as 2002–03 Melbourne audiences were able to watch five different television specials documenting some aspect of the supergroup's rise and fall.

In the midst of Abba's two-week sojourn in Australia, the country experienced the arrival of a second royal entourage, this time the Silver Jubilee visit of Queen Elizabeth II and her husband, Prince Philip. In March 1977 they spent nine days in Australia, stopping in every state and territory to mark the queen's 25 years on the throne. This was a very short visit compared to her 1954 two-month tour, the first by a reigning monarch to Australia, but tens of thousands of visitors and well-wishers still turned out at each event.

As the 1970s gave way to the 1980s, the Australian media continued to create spectacles in order to sell magazines and newspapers and attract television and radio audiences. One example of this is the tragedy that befell the Chamberlain family as they camped near Uluru in the Northern Territory in mid-August 1980. The couple, Michael and Lindy, with their two sons and infant daughter, Azaria, were camping near what was then called Ayers Rock (Uluru) when Lindy saw a dingo exit the tent where

d found her innocent. The fina
her freedom and her reputatio
8 when the Northern Territor
her and her husband's crimina

dy
numerous political and pop cul-
one touched as many Australians
lay bushfires. The period up to
driest periods in recorded history
. Winter rainfall in 1982 had been
bruary summer rainfall was down
inability and Environment 2009).
early February 1983, Victoria and
ignificant bushfires, alerting all rel-
at this would be a more dangerous
ously experienced. To make matters
ed with strong winds to create a mas-
which more than 90 million pounds
ifted into the air, blocking out the sun
e efforts of firefighters throughout the
inability and Environment 2009).
16 southeastern Australians woke to
days in a week. A biting north wind
country's central desert region and tem-
(40.5°C); humidity dipped below 15
d by sparks from power lines, arson, and
ng in narrow strips from north to south,
Burning debris from these initial fires lit
of the day more than 100 fires were burn-
stralia (Department of Sustainability and

re very difficult for the various fire authori-
not unfamiliar. The most severe problem of
e afternoon, when the hot northerly wind
and a strong west wind blew in from the
in terms of loss of life, property, trees, and
latively narrow bands of fire moving north to
moving rapidly west to east. The change was

AUSTRALIAN MUSIC IN THE 1970S

While in the 1970s the Swedish band Abba was selling mi[llions] of singles and albums in Australia, being watched by mil[lions] on *Countdown,* and attracting more than 1 percent of the popula[tion] to their live shows, several Australian bands and individuals we[re] making it big overseas. While Olivia Newton-John and the Gi[bb] brothers were all born in England, their immigration to Austral[ia] in childhood has always marked Newton-John, the Bee Gees, and Andy Gibb as Australian acts. All three were huge pop stars in the 1970s and provoked greater awareness of Australian culture in the rest of the world.

Although very different from Newton-John and the Gibbs, Australian music of the 1970s is incomplete without at least a mention of AC/DC. The group formed in 1973 through the effort of the brothers Malcolm and Angus Young, who had migrated to Australia from Scotland as children. When they began playing together in Australian malls, pubs, and clubs, Angus was just 18, and to play on his youth, he always performed in a school uniform, made up of shorts, long socks, blazer, tie, and cap. The group put out their first album, *High Voltage,* in 1975; it was released outside Australia the following year. Their following albums had considerable international success with the lead singer Bon Scott, a fellow Scottish migrant. After Scott's death in 1980 the band was forced to regroup, this time with the lead singer Brian Johnson. They had their greatest success in 1980 with Johnson on lead vocals with *Back in Black,* which sat at the top of the charts in England for months. Numerous albums followed in the 1980s and beyond, including another chart-topping album, *Black Ice,* in 2008. The news of this success has not been welcomed in some corners of the English press, however, because every time the group has been number one on the English charts, the country has been on the verge of economic collapse; in 1980 unemployment neared 20 percent.

Source: Petridis, Alex. "Things Must Really Be Bad—AC/DC Are No. 1 Again." Guardian (October 27, 2008). Available online. URL: http://www. guardian.co.uk/music/2008/oct/27/acdc-music-recession. Accessed February 20, 2009.

the media frenzy and endless rumors, a[nd] piece of the puzzle in reclaiming both was granted Lindy in September 198[ ] Court of Criminal Appeal quashed bot[h] convictions entirely.

Trage[dy]

While Australians had experienced ture events in the 1974–83 period, [na]- directly as the 1983 Ash Wednes[day] February 16, 1983, was one of the in the southeastern state of Victoria well below average, and by mid-F[ebruary] 75 percent (Department of Susta[inability] From November 25, 1982, throug[h] South Australia experienced five [ ] evant agencies and individuals th[ ] fire season than had been previ[ous] worse, the dry conditions combin[ed] sive dust storm on February 9, i[n] (40.8 million kg) of topsoil was [ ] in Melbourne and hampering th[e] two states (Department of Susta[inability]

On the morning of Februar[y] clear skies for one of the first [ ] was blowing heat in from the [ ] peratures soared above 105°F[ ] percent. Numerous fires, cause[d] other causes, were pushed al[ong] advancing toward the coast. [ ] other fires, so that by the end[ ] ing in Victoria and South A[ustralia] Environment 2009).

While these conditions w[ere] ties to deal with, they were the day emerged later in th[e] suddenly changed directio[n] coast. This was disastrous wildlife because it turned n[ ] south into miles-wide fires

so sudden that 47 Victorians and 28 South Australians were unable to get out of the fires' path and died. Significant property damage occurred in both states as well, with 2,080 families left homeless in Victoria and a further 383 in South Australia; in the 892 square miles (2,310 km^2) directly affected by fire were farms, stock, equipment, forest plantations, towns, and other resources worth between AU$350 and AU$400 million (Department of Sustainability and Environment 2009).

In the aftermath of the fires, soil erosion, fears for the survival of native wildlife, and even the fear that revegetation could not occur because of their severity played in the minds of many Australians. Nonetheless, the Australian landscape proved itself to be as tough as the people who reside there. Homes were rebuilt, farms and plantations reestablished, and within a week of the fires' being extinguished, small green shoots could be seen emerging from the blackened soil and tree trunks. Unfortunately this rejuvenation in 1983 meant that fuel has been readily available for subsequent major bushfires in these regions, with none as severe as the February 2009 fires, which surpassed the death and destruction of the Ash Wednesday fires many times over.

Conclusion

Politically, the year 1983 marked the transition from the bitterness of the Whitlam–Fraser years to 13 years of consecutive Labor rule in Australia. Economically, the 1980s also witnessed important changes, since Fraser's government had been unable to deal with the upward spiral of unemployment with its concomitant downward spiral in Australians' standard of living. Socially and culturally, the 1980s and early 1990s also ushered in significant changes, for in this period bipartisan support for multiculturalism, which had been introduced by Harold Holt and then nurtured by the Whitlam and Fraser governments, began to wither. The contradictions and changes wrought by these changes are the subject of the following chapter, which looks at the years 1983–96.

9

CONTRADICTION AND CHANGE (1983–1996)

fter Gough Whitlam's dismissal in 1975 and eight years of Liberal government under Malcolm Fraser, the Australian Labor Party under Bob Hawke won its first of a record-breaking five elections in a row, which kept them in power until 1996. In their 13 years in government, Labor oversaw the first phases of the country's "fundamental economic restructuring" toward a more unfettered capitalism (Painter 1998, 2). Unlike their contemporaries in the United States and the United Kingdom, however, the ruling party in Australia did not take up right-wing social policies; Asian immigration, Aboriginal rights, and multiculturalism more generally remained on Labor's agenda during the entire period. Labor in these years also reintroduced universal health care, a Whitlam-era policy that had been abandoned by Fraser. Perhaps in reaction to Labor's almost wholesale adoption of traditionally Liberal economic policies, the Liberal opposition gave up its prior support for the tenets of multiculturalism and turned its social policies rightward.

Economic Rationalism

Bob Hawke and the Labor Party took over the Commonwealth government in 1983 during a period of prolonged economic difficulty. Unemployment was 10.4 percent and had been high for nearly a decade; the national deficit was more than AU$9.6 billion (Welsh 2004, 532). During the previous eight years, few if any of the solutions to these economic problems attempted by Malcolm Fraser had done much good and Australians were hungry for change. Bob Hawke stepped into the prime minister's office in March 1983 and immediately began to speak "of 'bringing Australians together,' . . . about 'the kids in despair,' of kids using drugs, and of the break-up of family life in Australia" (Clark 1995, 324). He "believed Labor could reduce unemployment, inflation, and the number of industrial disputes" (Clark 1995, 324) and set his government to work on these tasks. With his "man of the people" persona, Hawke is said by many commentators to have maintained a love affair with the Australian people that kept him in office through four federal elections and several internal challenges (Mills 1993, 2).

Although the Hawke government benefited from good luck, such as the end of the multiyear drought immediately after the 1983 election, they should be credited with going beyond the charisma of their leader and achieving many of their early aims. Within six months unemployment figures had finally dropped, inflation was decreasing, and the number of industrial disputes declined (Clark 1995, 325). Hawke's politics of consensus have largely been credited for his early success. As a Labor prime minister, Hawke was able to draw the most powerful Australian unions to the bargaining table and convince them with the Prices and Incomes Accord that lower wages were an acceptable trade-off for rising employment (Clarke 2003, 316). Additionally, Labor under Treasurer Paul Keating floated the Australian dollar—that is, its international value was determined by the balance of payments rather than at a fixed percentage of the U.S. dollar—and allowed foreign-owned banks to operate in Australia for the first time. These modernizing tactics were deemed necessary to recover from the decades since World War II, during which the Liberals had allowed the economy to stagnate (Robins 1989, S5).

While these fiscal policies contributed to positive changes in the Australian economy over the next decade and beyond, Hawke and Keating did not stop there. By the end of Labor's reign in 1996, the government had instituted a series of free-market reforms that robbed the Liberals of their economic platform and "for the most part[,] would not [have been] at odds with those of Mrs Margaret Thatcher" (Robins 1989, S6). In 1985 Paul Keating tried to institute a general goods and services tax and, when that failed, reformed the tax system to lessen the burden on the highest-earning individuals and corporations. Protective tariffs on Australian goods were also lowered, from an average of 34 percent in 1983 to less than 10 percent when Labor left office in 1996 (Welsh 2004, 533). The Hawke government also began two decades of asset sales, whereby publicly owned property such as banks, utility companies, and even roads and police stations either were sold to private interests or had their maintenance and building costs paid for by private companies. The first of these sales was of a lucrative property in Tokyo that had once housed the Australian embassy, which netted the government nearly AU$700 million in revenue over several years (Hawker 2006, 250). While all of these changes were highly symbolic of Labor's new economic "ideology of free trade and economic rationalism" (Clarke 2003, 328), perhaps the most important symbol was the use of the government's Hercules troop planes to break an airline pilots' strike in 1989 (Douglas and Cunningham 1992, 5). Labor, the party of the union movement and working people more generally, turned to the military to break a strike.

Even immigration, which had dominated postwar Australia, was transformed during the Hawke-Keating years on the basis of the ideology of economic rationalism. The turning point in this process was in 1988, when the Committee to Advise on Australia's Immigration Policies released its report, "Immigration—a Commitment to Australia," sometimes also called the Fitzgerald Report. Claiming to be responding to the concerns of a large number of Australians about high immigration rates, the report argued that Australia's immigrant "selection methods need a sharper economic focus, for the public to be convinced that the program is in Australia's interests" (Committee to Advise 1988, 1). In the aftermath, and especially after Keating took office in 1991, fees were introduced for migrant services, such as visa applications and the appeals process, and new migrants themselves were denied access to health care for their first six months of residence in the country (Jupp 2002, 55–56). As a result of these and other policies, the number of immigrants radically decreased in this period (Jupp 2007, 46).

Many economists would have agreed with Paul Keating when he stated, after a 20 percent fall in the value of the Australian dollar in 1986, that Australia was at risk of becoming little more than a banana republic and needed economic restructuring to favor free markets and other neoliberal reforms (Robins 1989). Nonetheless, there is another side of the story. Labor's adoption of traditional right-wing economic policies lowered the unemployment rate but also increased income inequality (Harding 1995, 31) and the poverty rate, which, according to an OECD estimate, rose from 14.4 to 16.1 percent between 1981–82 and 1989–90 (cited in Department of Families, Community Services 2000, 6.3). Real wages in Australia fell significantly from 1984 through 1989, and then more slowly (Clarke 2003, 318), to result in a lower standard of living for most of the middle class. The Australian political scientist Michael Hogan argues that "the great losers from the Keating years have not been the potential underclass, but the great bulk of middle-income earners, especially those at the lower end of that scale" (1995, 183).

While Labor was sacrificing the middle class on the altar of economic rationalism, the Left's traditional concern for the poor did not diminish. Instead, the welfare state itself was transformed from one in which "welfare entitlements are meant for all citizens" (Hogan 1995, 183) to one that in many ways became more progressive, or what the economist Ann Harding calls more "pro-poor" (1995, 30). The most affluent members of Australian society lost access to a number of welfare benefits, including free university education, a benefit lost to all Australians in subsequent years, while targeted social welfare was directed toward the poorest percentage of the population. This targeting mitigated some of the effects of wage inequalities that developed in this period, at least for the poorest segment of society, but also resulted in a middle-class backlash against Labor in the second half of the 1990s and first half-decade of the new millennium.

Another area in which traditional Left politics were not abandoned was in the reintroduction in 1984 of a single-payer health insurance scheme, Medibank, which had been introduced by Whitlam and dismantled by Fraser. Under the Hawke-Keating system, every taxpayer was required to contribute 1 percent of his or her taxable income to the scheme and in return every Australian would receive low or no-cost health care. In subsequent years incentives for wealthier Australians to take out private health coverage have been added to the system, but the Labor dream of health care for all has not been abandoned.

Symbolic Politics

For many Australians in 2009, the Hawke-Keating years do not call up memories of economic rationalism or Ronald Reagan–inspired theories of the trickle-down effects of neoliberalism. The further tack to the Right of the following Howard Liberal government (1996–2007) meant that Labor's complicity in this process has been somewhat erased from public memory. What has not disappeared, however, are the other aspects of the Hawke-Keating years, "the non-measurable arena of symbolic politics" (Hogan 1995, 187). One of the symbols of the dawning of a new age was the 1988 opening in Canberra of the country's new AU$1.1 billion Parliament House, built into a hillside overlooking Lake Burley Griffin. Another important symbol for the times was the entrepreneur Alan Bond's victory in the 1983 America's Cup yacht race with *Australia II,* a 39-foot (12-m) yacht captained by John Bertrand. Bond's

The new parliament building nestles into the hillside and gives the impression of being part of the landscape. (Clearviewstock/Shutterstock)

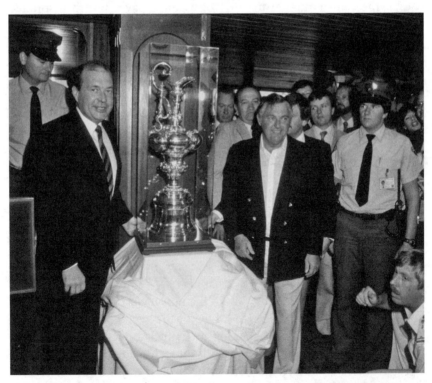

Brian Burke, premier of Western Australia, and Alan Bond showing off the America's Cup at the Royal Perth Yacht Club in 1983. (National Archives of Australia: A6135, K3/11/83/36)

combination of business acumen and patriotic sporting flair seemed to issue forth "a national awakening of a sort" (Australianbeers.com 2006). His later conviction for fraud, jail term, and bankruptcy proceedings have tainted his personal image, but not the America's Cup victory.

For the Labor government the two most important symbolic arenas of the time were an increased openness to Asia and dialogue on Aboriginal rights. During the Keating years the Australian republican movement, which aims to replace the British monarch as head of state with an Australian, also gained new impetus. As with Labor's economic policies, however, even some of these symbolic arenas were sites of contradiction in the 1980s and early 1990s.

Asia

While of the two it is Paul Keating who is most remembered for his focus on Australia's relationship with other Asia-Pacific countries, as prime minister, Bob Hawke was similarly interested in pursuing an Asian agenda. At the time he argued "that finding Australia's 'true place in Asia' would be one [of] Australia's most important challenges" (cited in Lovell 2007, 9).

One of the most important of the Hawke government's legacies in the area of engagement with Asia was the creation in 1989 of the Asia-Pacific Economic Cooperation (APEC) group. Today APEC is made up of 21 countries located in or on the border of the Asia-Pacific region, contains about 40 percent of the world's population, and accounts for nearly 55 percent of global GDP (About APEC 2009). In 1989, however, the group that met in Canberra was much smaller; it consisted of representatives from just 12 countries and did not include such important players in the region as China, Hong Kong, Taiwan, or Russia. In addition, while the United States was a founding member of APEC, it was not until 1992 and the election of Bill Clinton that the United States became actively engaged in it. By then Paul Keating had replaced Bob Hawke as prime minister of Australia and the two new leaders began the tradition of a yearly APEC Economic Leaders' Meeting (About APEC 2009). Indeed, APEC is often listed as a Keating initiative and success story because of his ability to draw the United States into the core decision-making process and strengthen the group's ties more generally.

Aside from his treasurer's love of Asia, much of the driving force for Bob Hawke's engagement with Asia prior to June 1989 was China's economic liberalization, which he believed was "the single most important thing that [was] happening in the world" (Mills 1993, 180). On the basis of this belief, he traveled to China twice during his time in office and hosted Chinese leaders in Australia three times. As a result of these relationships and the Hawke government's attempts at "enmeshing" Australian mining with Chinese steel production, China made its two largest overseas investments at the time in Australian mining and smelting companies. Politically, as well, the Hawke government saw itself as a broker between an emerging China and the rest of the world. In his first year in power, Hawke served as a middleman between China and the United States on the issue of technology transfer, and a year later, on his first visit to China, he raised the issue of China's becoming a signatory to the Nuclear Non-Proliferation Treaty, which finally came about in 1992 (Mills 1993, 181).

Perhaps because of his grand dreams of an Australian-Chinese axis of power in Asia, Hawke was particularly disturbed by the Chinese government's military response to student democracy demonstrators in Tiananmen Square on June 3–4, 1989. Hawke "wept openly for the victims of Chinese repression . . . [and] for the death of his dreams of a powerfully beneficial relationship with China" (Mills 1993, 182). More pragmatically, the Labor government allowed an initial 27,000 and eventually, about 42,000 Chinese students who were studying in Australia to remain permanently in the country, rather than "be sent back to face the wrath of their country's leaders" (Fairfax Online 2003). With chain migration over the subsequent decade, this decision led to the migration of more than 100,000 Chinese to Australia by the mid-1990s, a larger number than at any time other than the 1850s gold rush (Fairfax Online 2003).

Despite the centrality of China in the Hawke government's Asia focus, other Asian countries were also important to Australia's foreign policy initiatives, both before and after 1989. With its legacy of having fought with the Americans in Vietnam, Cambodia, and Laos in the 1970s, Australia under Hawke and his foreign ministers Bill Hayden and Gareth Evans sought to create peace in this region of the world. In 1986 Hayden advocated for the trial of Pol Pot on genocide charges, which was rejected by the United States (Totten, Parsons, and Charny 2004, 352), and left his successor, Evans, to work with the global community in subsequent years to find a lasting peace in the country.

Today though he remains one of Australia's longest-serving foreign ministers, Evans is best known globally as a central player in the drafting of the UN's Cambodian peace plan in 1990. He was a prominent member of the international team that met in Jakarta in 1988 and in the penning of a proposal in February 1989 for the demilitarization and normalization of Cambodia after the period of the Khmer Rouge killing fields and subsequent invasion of Vietnam. The 1990 UN agreement, which resulted from meetings in New York and Paris, borrowed heavily from Evans's initial document, including the watering down of language on genocide and the Khmer Rouge (Totten, Parsons, and Charny 2004, 351). The Evans document and subsequent UN agreement also allowed the Khmer Rouge back into the world of legitimate governance, despite their refusal to disarm or give up violence as a means to power (Kiernan 1994).

One of the many contradictions between Labor's policy and actions in this period concerned its guidelines on the Cambodian refugees who arrived by boat in Australia between 1989 and 1994. Although Hawke, Hayden, and Evans were all active parties in the eventual signing of the 1990 UN peace agreement, when 19 boatloads of Cambodians arrived in Australian waters fleeing from the exact conditions deplored by these leaders, they were largely vilified by them. In reaction to the boat people's arrival, Hawke stated, "We have an orderly migration programme. We're not going to allow people just to jump into that queue by saying we'll jump into a boat, here we are, bugger the people who've been around the world" (cited in Socialistworld.net 2003).

Labor policy toward the refugees also contradicted its policy of engagement with Asia and reflected its economic rationalist approach to immigration, based on the mistaken belief that refugees cost a country more than they contribute. The Labor government built Australia's first detention center for migrants at Port Hedland, Western Australia, a policy for which the later Howard government was severely criticized. Labor also legislated that all refugee status claimants arriving on Australian soil between December 1989 and December 1992 were to be held in detention until their status had been determined by the Department of Immigration. One potential reason for this contradiction is that, as active contributors to the UN solution in Cambodia, the Australian government could not then acknowledge that the solution was not working and that large numbers of Cambodians were being forced by their own government to flee (Socialistworld.net 2003). Regardless of the reason, this reflected badly on Labor and contradicted its traditional position as the political party of the Left in Australia. According to Labor's own human rights commissioner, Christopher Sidoti, "no other western country permits incommunicado detention of asylum-seekers—it is incomprehensible that a country with such a proud record of commitment to finding durable solutions to refugee issues should resort to measures denying the basic rights of an individual" (Socialistworld.net 2003).

Although these Cambodian affairs were a setback to Labor's desire to engage more with Australia's Asian neighbors, the policy of engagement was not abandoned by Paul Keating when he became prime minister in 1991. Indeed, one of the strongest legacies of his five years in office was Australia's deeper commitment to that region. His first overseas trip as prime minister was to Indonesia in April 1992, followed up with trips to Japan, Cambodia, and Singapore in September and October of that same year. These trips were aimed mainly at strengthening the ties among APEC countries and calling these countries' economic ministers to the table each year. Their success was celebrated with more Asian travel—to Laos, Thailand, Vietnam, and Indonesia in 1994, and to Japan in 1995, when Keating received an honorary doctorate based on his work in unifying the region (Australia's Prime Ministers 2002).

While Bob Hawke drew on the economic potential of China in his discourse on why Asia was so important to Australia and Australians, Paul Keating focused his attention on one of the country's nearest foreign neighbors, Indonesia. In 1995 he and Indonesian president Suharto signed what was then a secret defense treaty with the goal of securing both countries' borders and security interests. The treaty was extremely important for Keating, as it was Australia's first reciprocal security treaty with an Asian nation; in retrospect it has been labeled second only to the ANZUS treaty with the United States in terms of importance to Australian security issues at the time (Acharya 2001, 192). The treaty was subsequently torn up by the Indonesians over Australian support for East Timorese independence in 1999 but was replaced by a new treaty in 2005.

Aboriginal Rights

A second important arena for symbolic politics in the 1983–96 period was the relationship between the federal government and the country's Aboriginal people. In 1983 the new Labor government's position on Aboriginal rights was more progressive than that of any previous Australian government. Its electoral platform supported implementing *"national, uniform Land Rights legislation"* with a promise to "achieve this by overriding state governments by Commonwealth legislation if necessary" (Foley 2001). By the middle of 1985, however, Land Rights legislation was a dead issue with the Hawke government, having been sacrificed on the altars of economic rationalism and political expediency. Numerous mining and pastoral organizations had lobbied heavily against any Aboriginal land rights during Hawke's first years in power, and Western Australia's Labor premier, Brian Burke, threatened to quit the party and lead his state as an independent if land rights moved ahead (Foley 2001). In addition, Hawke's first minister for Aboriginal affairs, Clyde Holding, was kept at arm's length from the locus of real power in the government, the cabinet, and thus was unable to alter its economics-focused agenda. The result was government backpedaling on almost all promises for Aboriginal reconciliation, although these were part of the keystone of Hawke's electoral promises: "Reconciliation, Recovery, Reconstruction" (cited in Welsh 2004, 531).

Despite this disappointing start, the Hawke years were not entirely without progress in the area of Aboriginal rights; a few small but highly symbolic gestures were made. For example, in 1983 Uluru, then known by most whites as Ayers Rock, was given back to the Anangu people, from whom it had been taken in 1958 to become part of a national park; the area in which Uluru and neighboring Kata Tjuta (the Olgas) are located had been carved out of the South West Aboriginal Reserve for tourism purposes. In 1985 the official handing over ceremony occurred, with Australia's governor-general, Ninian Stephens, and Clive Holding, then minister for Aboriginal affairs, handing a land deed to

Since the mid-20th century, when tour operators began taking groups to see it, Uluru has been the most iconic symbol of the Australian outback. For the Anangu people, it is also an important sacred site, a fact that was only somewhat recognized by the historic return ceremony in 1985. (Brooke Whatnall/Shutterstock)

Nipper Winmatti, an elder of the Mutitjulu community, in a highly ritu-alized and moving ceremony (see Innes 2008). In return, the Anangu were required to sign a 99-year lease giving Uluru back to the national park system in exchange for AU$75,000 annually and 20 percent of the income from entrance fees (Whittaker 1994, 316). Since that time, "the tourism industry [has] tend[ed] to dominate much decision-making in the national park despite a supposed Anangu majority on the board of management" (Curl 2005).

In July 2009 the issue was raised at the federal level when Parks Australia released a management plan that stated, "'For visitor safety, cultural and environmental reasons, the director and the board will work towards closure of the climb'" (Ricci 2009). Unfortunately for the Anangu people and those who undertake the arduous climb without the proper level of fitness, the call to ban climbing was subsequently dropped in late October 2009 following statements by the prime min-

TO CLIMB OR NOT TO CLIMB

In 1983 Prime Minister Bob Hawke promised the local Aboriginal community, the Anangu, that by leasing Uluru back to the National Park Service they would be allowed to ban people from climbing the rock but rescinded the promise when the agreement was put forward in 1985. Therefore, there is no white law against climbing Uluru. Nevertheless, the Anangu request that tourists not climb it for a number of reasons, including the sacredness of the site. In their worldview, only adult men who have undergone elaborate initiation rituals in their society have the right to climb to the top, and for any-body else, climbing is unthinkable. Perhaps more important, however, is the Anangu sense of responsibility for people on their land and their personal sadness when someone is injured or dies, and indeed about 40 people have died in falls since the mid-1960s. Awareness of the Anangu's wishes is growing, among both Australians and foreign tourists, but in 2004, 50 percent of tourists still expressed a desire to climb the rock (James 2007, 399); by 2008, when the author visited the area (and did not climb), a park ranger estimated that that number had decreased to 25 percent. The ranger, like many other Aboriginal people, was hopeful that this number would continue to decrease and that tourists would no longer act like *"minga just"*—lots of ants—to be pitied rather than scorned (cited in Whittaker, 1994, 316).

ister and numerous tourism officials on the impact of instituting the prohibition (Alexander 2009).

Another symbolic event during the Hawke years in the area of Aboriginal rights was the 1990 creation of the Aboriginal and Torres Strait Islander Commission (ATSIC), an elected body that replaced several earlier elected Aboriginal committees to advise the government on Indigenous affairs. The history of elected bodies to represent Aboriginal issues in Australia goes back only to 1973, when the Whitlam government established the National Aboriginal Consultative Committee (NACC), which, as its name suggests, existed only to consult with the government and minister for Aboriginal affairs on issues relating to Aboriginal people. The NACC existed for four years before being disbanded by Malcolm Fraser in 1977 because of its members' activism in seeking greater control of resources, as well as some concerns about the electoral process. The NACC was replaced with the National Aboriginal Conference (NAC), a similarly elected organization that "was to serve as a 'channel of communication' between Indigenous communities and the Commonwealth Government, and to provide advice to the federal minister" (Pratt and Bennett 2004). As Whitlam had with the NACC, Fraser struggled to find a place for Aboriginal consultation in the real workings of his government and the body floundered as a result of a lack of power and financial problems. After a review of the NAC in its first years in power, Hawke followed the same path as that of his predecessor; he disbanded the organization and replaced it with his own "experiment in . . . government-sponsored Aboriginal representative structures" (Pratt and Bennett 2004).

As with Labor's initial promise of land rights legislation, ATSIC's stated aims were progressive and sought to provide the structure for positive government-Aboriginal relations. The 1989 bill stated that ATSIC's objectives were to

- ensure maximum participation of Aboriginal and Torres Strait Islander people in government policy formulation and implementation
- promote Indigenous self-management and self-sufficiency
- further Indigenous economic, social and cultural development, and
- ensure co-ordination of Commonwealth, state, territory and local government policy affecting Indigenous people. (cited in Pratt and Bennett 2004)

Unfortunately, despite Liberal Party fears of creating a separate locus of Aboriginal power in Australia, ATSIC's funding model kept the organization highly constrained. Only about 15 percent of its budget was actually controlled by the elected counselors, while the rest was quarantined by the government for particular programs (Pratt and Bennett 2004). Few people outside ATSIC realized the contradiction between the organization's stated objectives and its financial constraints, and thus "many of ATSIC's elected representatives complained that it was the scapegoat for the inadequacies of *all* levels of government in Indigenous affairs" (Pratt and Bennett 2004). As had happened with the NACC and NAC, a change in governing party in 1996 eventually led, in 2004, to the disbandment of ATSIC. Unlike that of his predecessors, however, John Howard's Liberal government did not seek to replace ATSIC with its own elected Aboriginal organization and instead advocated the "mainstreaming" of all Indigenous service provision (Pratt and Bennett 2004). The present Rudd Labor government, elected in 2007, began work in 2009 to establish "a new national representative [I]ndigenous body, . . . to include an eight-member executive and 128-person national congress" (Berkovic and Rintoul 2009).

In addition to the creation of ATSIC and handing over of Uluru, Hawke and many of his government ministers spoke eloquently about Aboriginal issues on numerous occasions. In 1988 Hawke himself promised that the treaty process, which Fraser had begun in earnest in 1979 with the creation of the Aboriginal Treaty Committee, would be completed during his time in government. After a royal commission into the deaths of 99 Aboriginal people and Torres Strait Islanders in Australian prisons, Commissioner Elliott Johnston likewise spoke of the need for reconciliation between the two peoples in order to end "community division, discord and injustice to Aboriginal people" (Reconciliation Australia 2007). As a result, in 1991 the government passed the Council for Aboriginal Reconciliation Act with unanimous support in both the House and the Senate, and in one of his last acts before losing a power struggle to Paul Keating, Hawke appointed the first members of the council (Reconciliation Australia 2007).

When Paul Keating became prime minister at the end of 1991 he was determined to push the reconciliation process forward to make positive changes in the lives of the country's Indigenous people. He stated this most clearly in his now-famous Redfern speech, delivered in December 1992 to kick off the UN's International Year of the World's Indigenous People. While the speech covers with broad brushstrokes many of the wrongs done to Aboriginal people since 1788, perhaps the most moving section is Keating's identification of non-Aboriginal Australians' responsibility for those wrongs:

> *Recognition that it was we who did the dispossessing. We took the traditional lands and smashed the traditional way of life. We brought the disasters. The alcohol. We committed the murders. We took the children from their mothers. We practised discrimination and exclusion. It was our ignorance and our prejudice. And our failure to imagine these things being done to us. With some noble exceptions, we failed to make the most basic human response and enter into their hearts and minds. We failed to ask—how would I feel if this were done to me?*
> *(Keating 1992)*

Keating was assisted in his goals by Australia's highest court when, in 1992, it decided in favor of the plaintiff in the case of *Mabo v. Queensland*. The case began when a gardener at James Cook University, Eddie Koiki Mabo, a member of the Meriam nation, bristled at the information given him by a historian on campus that the land he believed he had inherited from his father on Murray Island was not actually his (Perkins episode 7, 2008). In response, Mabo read all that he could about a prior land rights case, in which the judge had ruled against the Yolngu people of the Northern Territory at least in part because of the Yolngu's communal land tenure system. After organizing a land rights conference in Townsville in 1981, at which he described the individual land tenure system on his native Murray Island in the eastern Torres Straits, Mabo and four other claimants gave instructions to a legal aid lawyer to start a case on their behalf. The case was first heard in May 1982 and set off a decade of legal and political fighting between those who supported it and those who feared the repercussions of granting any form of native title to Australian land.

The streets of Brisbane, Queensland, became one of the first battlegrounds outside the courtroom when in October 1982 thousands of protesters marched in support of native title and Aboriginal reconciliation during the Commonwealth Games. The protesters took advantage of the presence of thousands of media outlets from around the globe to highlight the lack of basic human rights in Queensland for Aboriginal people (Perkins episode 7, 2008). Another important site of the political battle waged at this time was Sydney in 1988, when 10,000 Aboriginal and Torres Strait Islander people descended on the city in the hope of hearing Prime Minister Hawke fulfill his promise of a treaty to mark the 200th anniversary of the First Fleet (Perkins episode 7, 2008). The moment passed without the promise being fulfilled and

The last family photo taken of Eddie Koiki Mabo before his death from cancer in 1992. (Newspix)

with that, black communities all over the country placed even greater hope in the *Mabo* case.

The *Mabo* fight took several legal twists and turns during the decade before a final decision was reached. At first, Queensland's lawyers, legislators, and Premier Joh Bjelke-Petersen attempted to thwart the case entirely by passing a state law granting freehold title to local councils; the state made a similar move in 1985, with the Queensland Coast Islands Declaratory Bill. If enacted, this bill would have "extinguish[ed], retrospectively and without compensation, any and all traditional rights to land that might exist throughout the Torres Straits" (Keon-Cohen 2000). This required that, in the midst of their case, Mabo's lawyers take the state of Queensland to court on a second matter to try to have the bill thrown out on the basis of racial discrimination, for if the bill were enacted, the *Mabo* case would have been legislated out of existence (Perkins episode 7, 2008). Mabo's lawyers won the battle when Australia's High Court threw out the law in 1988.

The next phase was for the Supreme Court of Queensland to meet on Murray Island for the first time, in order to hear local witnesses talk about their system of law, called *Malo's law* after the god who delivered it to the Meriam ancestors. The plaintiffs, including Mabo himself, also walked the perimeters of their traditional property to show the judges the generations-old pointers that marked their property lines (Perkins episode 7, 2008). Unfortunately after years of legal battles, in 1990 the Supreme Court of Queensland, under Judge Moynihan, ruled against Mabo on a technicality, on the ground that Mabo's adoption was not legal and thus he was not the legal heir to his adoptive father's land.

With this decision in mind, lawyers for Mabo asked whether he would withdraw his own claim from the case, leaving just two of the original five claimants to take it to Australia's High Court; two other claimants had died since the case began in 1982 (Perkins episode 7, 2008). Mabo accepted this advice and withdrew his claim, leaving James Rice and the Reverend Dave Passi as the sole claimants in a case that continued to bear Mabo's name. The arguments before the High Court were made in the early 1990s, and on June 3, 1992, the High Court ruled in favor of the plaintiffs, making history in Australia as the first legal recognition of Indigenous ownership of the land prior to English colonialism (Perkins episode 7, 2008). Sadly, Mabo had died on January 21, 1992, five months before the celebrated victory that inspired the conservative newspaper the *Australian* to name him, posthumously, Australian of the Year.

With this legal precedent, the Keating government was able to act with renewed purpose in the area of Aboriginal land rights, although critics charge that Keating was moving to protect the status quo against Aboriginal land claims. In 1993 after nine months of negotiating, compromise, and more than 50 hours of debate in Parliament, the government passed the Native Title Act 1993, sometimes also referred to as the Mabo Act. The act granted some land rights to Aboriginal people, allowing groups and individuals to make claims for unclaimed Crown land, without entirely challenging the mining and agricultural interests that opposed such legislation. For example, the act protected deeds and leases made prior to its passage, regardless of whether those deeds and leases had been legally enacted.

While the passage of the Mabo Act was deemed by many as an important victory for Aboriginal rights in Australia, not all Aboriginal people or groups agreed. In the events leading to this, one group of Aboriginal leaders presented the government with its own version of a right and just agreement, which they called the Aboriginal Peace Plan. This plan, put forward in June 1993, called for the Commonwealth to have the authority to override the states and territories in order to protect Aboriginal and Torres Strait Islander rights and land claims (Aboriginal Law Bulletin 1993). Another group of 400 Aboriginal people met in August 1993 to discuss their concerns that the Mabo Act would not provide the kind of land security they envisioned. The document that resulted from their conversations, called the *Eva Valley Statement,* reiterated the Peace Plan's call for the Commonwealth to "take full control of native title issues to the exclusion of the States and Territories" and then called for the Commonwealth to "agree to a negotiating process to achieve a lasting settlement recognising and addressing historical truths regarding the impact of dispossession, marginalisation, destabilisation and disadvantage" (ATNS 2007). Neither group's interests were given serious consideration by the government, and the final draft of the Mabo Act is considered by critics merely to have "established mechanisms aimed at 'validating' the land titles of the occupiers which may have been called into question by the *[Mabo]* decision" (Hagen 1999). While symbolically the act may have been useful for Keating and Labor to separate themselves from the Liberal opposition, for many Aboriginal people it represented business as usual by an occupying government.

Another important piece of symbolic politics enacted during Paul Keating's years as prime minister was the inquiry begun by the Human Rights and Equal Opportunity Commission (HREOC) on the Aboriginal Stolen Generations. For two years starting in 1995, the HREOC engaged in the National Enquiry into the Separation of Aboriginal and Torres Strait Islander Children From Their Families. Eventually, the report found that widespread human rights abuses had taken place and that an apology and compensation were due to thousands of Indigenous Australians. Unfortunately by that time Keating was out of office and the report's recommendations were not taken up by the subsequent government, an issue that will be addressed in the next chapter.

In the main, Labor during this period "supported policies of indigenous self-determination . . . but the politics of land rights, treaty and reparation for colonial policy seemed to be a greater challenge than expected and impeded by economic rationalist members of the Hawke-Keating ministries" (Lovell 2007, 10). Political will turned out to be insufficient to the task, and Indigenous Australians today are still waiting for most of the promises of the 1980s to be honored; reconciliation remains a distant dream and recompense has been rejected outright by the current government.

Republicanism

The third highly symbolic arena in which Labor acted in the 1980s and 1990s was exploring the ramifications for Australia of changing its form of government from a constitutional monarchy to a republic, with an Australian head of state replacing the British queen (or king). This began in 1985 when the Hawke government signed the Australia Act, which finally separated the British legislature and courts from those in the Australian states. The most noted of these connections had been the ability of the British Privy Court to overturn decisions of the supreme courts of all the Australian states; the Australian High Court had already been separated from such overruling in 1975. Before Australia and the United Kingdom enacted their parallel bills, the Australian states and territories had been legal British colonies, although Australia itself had not had that designation since 1901 (Australia Act 1986).

Republicanism began to gain real momentum in Australia in 1991 when the Labor Party placed it on its platform. Within a few months the

Australian Republican Movement (ARM) was formed by such notable Australians as the novelist Thomas Keneally, author of *Schindler's Ark*; the cricketer Ian Chappell; and the former head of the Liberal Party, Malcolm Turnbull. In 1993 other symbolic changes were enacted, including the elimination of references to the queen in the citizenship oath and the loss of voting rights for British citizens living in Australia.

When Paul Keating replaced Bob Hawke as the head of the Labor Party and federal government, republicanism received an even greater boost. It was Keating who moved to have references to the queen removed from the citizenship oath, which succeeded, and to remove the Union Jack from the corner of the Australian flag, which failed. Keating also appointed a republican advisory committee, a group of prominent republicans, including Malcolm Turnbull, who explored the constitutional changes required to establish a republic. In 1995 Keating gave a speech outlining the path toward constitutional change, which began, "It is the Government's view that Australia's Head of State should be an Australian and that Australia should become a republic by the year 2001" (Keating 1995). As was the case with several other initiatives begun under Labor in these years, the election of a Liberal government in 1996 stalled the republican movement. The issue has not died, however, and there is much speculation that the reelection of a Labor government in 2007 may lead to a resurgence in republican activities.

Multiculturalism

While the turn toward Asia and greater Aboriginal rights were two important issues that at least symbolically separated Labor from the Liberal opposition during the Hawke and Keating years, from 1983 to 1996, multiculturalism more generally remained an issue about which both political parties maintained a steady dialogue. Dialogue, however, does not mean consensus. During this period, Labor maintained its stance that multiculturalism was an appropriate agenda for governing Australia. In 1987 the Hawke government established the Advisory Council on Multicultural Affairs and the Office for Multicultural Affairs to manage "the vision of multiculturalism as a national identity" (Lovell 2007, 8). This vision was even more clearly elucidated in 1989 in the government's National Agenda for a Multicultural Australia, prepared by the Advisory Council. Before leaving power in 1996, Labor even expanded the definition of multiculturalism to add sex (1984) and disability (1992) as protected categories against discrimination; racial discrimination had been outlawed by the Whitlam government in 1975.

Despite, or perhaps because of, Labor's commitments to its tenets, the opposition during this period gradually moved away from the strong support for multiculturalism espoused by its leader, Malcolm Fraser, just a few years earlier. Most people who followed this dialogue concur that by 1988 "bipartisan agreement on multiculturalism [had] ended" (Jupp 2007, 106). In June of that year John Howard, leader of the Liberal Party, gave a speech to the party faithful in Western Australia in which he questioned the basic tenets of multiculturalism as government policy or agenda. In this and a host of other speeches, "he argued that multiculturalism could not possibly be an 'all-embracing national cement' for Australia" (cited in Lovell 2007, 12). In so doing, he "used the public ambivalence towards multiculturalism strategically . . . to 'shatter' the cross-party consensus on the value of multiculturalism" (cited in Lovell 2007, 12). At first, Howard lost his leadership position in the Liberal Party, at least in part for his views on multiculturalism (Jupp 2007, 107). Nevertheless, after another federal election loss in 1993, the Liberals reelected Howard, and his antimulticultural views took hold throughout the party.

While 1988 was a watershed year in the debate on multiculturalism, in which the political consensus between the two main parties was broken, it was not the first time that multiculturalism had been under fire. Throughout the 1970s and 1980s

> there were increasing rumblings about "buying the ethnic vote" and "pandering to the ethnic lobby." . . . Ethnicity should not be given priority over class according to those on the left, nor over gender argued feminists. Aboriginal leaders had never accepted that the special status of indigenous people could be properly acknowledged by multiculturalism. (Galligan and Roberts 2003, 9)

From the very beginning, when Whitlam's minister for immigration Al Grassby used the term, *multiculturalism* was little understood outside the public service and often misrepresented as putting white, Anglo-Celtic Australians at a disadvantage.

Perhaps the best starting date for the backlash against multiculturalism, however, is 1984, when the historian Geoffrey Blainey gave a talk to the Rotary Club of Warrnambool, in far western Victoria, in which he struck "a cautionary note" about immigration policy, which, he feared, was creating a large number of resentful Australians (Macintyre and Clark 2004, 73). Blainey's remarks, at the end of a speech in which he had spoken about immigration and multiculturalism only in positive terms, polarized Australia's intellectual class. The Department of History at the University of Melbourne, where Blainey taught and served as the dean of the Faculty of Arts, was torn apart. Twenty-three of its members "wrote to the press two months after the controversy began to dissociate themselves from his views on immigration policy," and protesters disrupted Blainey a month later when he delivered an address in Sydney (Macintyre and Clark 2004, 73). However, rather than clarify his remarks and place them in the context of his wider praise for immigration and multiculturalism, the maelstrom caused Blainey to push his ideas even further. Macintyre and Clark argue that "the misrepresentation of his views and the vehemence with which they were condemned strengthened his resolution. Rather than let the media tire of the dispute, he pursued it in articles, interviews, speeches, and statements" (Macintyre and Clark 2004, 73). Indeed, the Australian media covered Blainey and his immigration debate for about a year and then moved, along with him, to other topics, including "Aboriginal land rights, the environment, the monarchy, trade unions, [and] judicial activism" (Macintyre and Clark 2004, 75). By then Blainey had left his academic positions to become a full-time "controversialist" (Macintyre and Clark 2004, 73), and as such he reached great prominence in the years after Labor's defeat in 1996.

Other Changes

While Labor was installing a new economic regime in Australia and the Liberals were questioning the orthodoxy of multiculturalism, a number of other changes were occurring throughout Australia to galvanize the period as one of tremendous transformation.

In 1987 Queenslanders experienced one of their most important changes as the country's longest-serving premier, Sir Joh Bjelke-Petersen, finally retired in the face of corruption charges. Bjelke-Petersen entered Queensland's state parliament in 1947 and was elected premier in 1968 as leader of the state's National Party. During his extraordinary 40 years in state politics he "always seemed to have a problem with the concept of conflict of interest" (Dempster 2005). As early as 1957 he used a ministerial colleague to gain permission to search for oil in north central Queensland, and just three weeks after he became premier, two companies in which he held shares were given permission to search for oil on the Great Barrier Reef (Dempster 2005). While never convicted of bribery or corruption charges, Bjelke-Petersen was implicated in several other high-profile cases in the 1980s and 1990s. In

1989 the Australian Broadcasting Tribunal found that Bjelke-Petersen had blackmailed Alan Bond for $400,000, while a 1992 defamation trial ruled that Bjelke-Petersen had taken bribes from the industrialist Leslie Thiess "on a large scale and on many occasions" between 1981 and 1984 (Dempster 2005).

At the same time as he was using his political positions for economic gain, Bjelke-Petersen maintained an iron grip on most aspects of public life in Queensland, from the parliament to the police force (Dempster 2005). The Fitzgerald Report, which eventually brought the massive police corruption in the state to light and resulted in Bjelke-Petersen's retirement, highlighted the connections among the state's government, police force, prostitution, gambling, and organized crime. Bjelke-Petersen himself was charged with perjury after giving evidence to Fitzgerald, but, with the lone dissent of a Young National Party member on the jury, he was acquitted with a hung jury.

Despite these obvious weaknesses, Bjelke-Petersen's combination of social conservatism and laissez-faire economics remained popular in Queensland almost to the end of his political career. His stance on issues ranging from abortion to native title was that of the ultracon-servative Right and provided little to no room for compromise. For example, in speaking out against the Hawke government's commitment to native title rights, Bjelke-Petersen blamed "'gays,' 'heathens,' unions, and 'forces of the Left including communists, the World Council of Churches and other forces for revolution'" (cited in Whittaker 1994, 323). For many voters in far north Queensland at the time, Bjelke-Petersen was speaking common sense. In addition, Queensland's economy during this period grew immensely. Bjelke-Petersen elimi-nated Queensland's inheritance tax and thus attracted retired people from all over the country to the state's booming new high-rise develop-ments on the Sunshine and Gold Coasts, north and south of Brisbane, respectively. Environmental issues were all but ignored, as were claims for heritage listed buildings, in order to move forward on the building of new airports, ports, electricity stations, coal mines, dams, freeways, and buildings (Australian Politics Books 2009a). As a result, Bjelke-Petersen is not entirely reviled today and remains in the minds of many Queenslanders their greatest politician to date.

While Queenslanders were freeing themselves from the corrupt gov-ernment of Bjelke-Petersen, Western Australians saw the ascendance and downfall of the first female premier in Australian history. In 1990 Western Australia's premier, Peter Dowding, stepped down from his position as a result of a financing scandal and his party elected Dr. Carmen Lawrence to replace him. She had been in the state parliament for four years and had served as both minister for education and minister for Aboriginal affairs. Upon taking over from Dowding, Lawrence not only became premier but also held the portfolios of treasurer and minister for Aboriginal affairs, public sector management, women's interests, family, and multicultural and ethnic affairs. Rather than for this overwhelming workload, however, Lawrence's brief three-year period at the helm of Western Australia is best known for the "Easton affair." In 1992 Penny Easton committed suicide after documents relating to her divorce from the public servant Brian Easton were read aloud in the state parliament. In the documents Brian claimed that the Liberal opposition leader Richard Court had illegally provided Penny with information that would damage him in their divorce settlement. After winning the 1993 election, in 1995 Premier Richard Court established a AU$7 million royal commission to explore whether or not Lawrence had been aware of the plan to release the private divorce papers in the parliament and thus was culpable in Penny Easton's suicide. The commission concluded that Lawrence had been aware of the plan and had lied to them about that knowledge; the result was her trial for perjury two years later. Despite the testimony of several other cabinet members, Lawrence was acquitted of all charges in that trial and moved on to a position in the federal Parliament. Nonetheless, most commentators agree that the "Easton affair" damaged Lawrence's once-bright political career and eliminated her chances of becoming Australia's first female prime minister.

In addition to Carmen Lawrence, other Australian women were making history in the 1983–96 period. Bob Hawke appointed Susan Ryan minister for education in 1983, the first woman to serve at ministerial level in a Labor government, and in 1986 Joan Child was elected as the first and so far only woman Speaker of the House of Representatives. The following year Mary Gaudron became the first woman justice on the High Court and Macquarie University named Di Yerbury the first female vice chancellor of an Australian university. Women graduated as pilots in the Royal Australian Air Force for the first time in 1988 and took up some combat positions in the Australian Defense Force in 1992 (Summers 2002, 559–561). In 1990 voters in the state of Victoria elected their first female premier, Joan Kirner of the Labor Party, who served for slightly more than two years before a swing to the Right delivered the government to Jeff Kennett and the Liberals.

GLORIA JOAN LILES CHILD

Joan Child was a pioneering Australian woman on two fronts. In 1974 she became the first woman to sit in federal Parliament for the Labor Party when she won the Melbourne seat of Henty. Just one year later when Malcolm Fraser swept into power, she lost her seat, but the tenacious Child was reelected in 1980. After serving in a number of important parliamentary and committee positions, including as deputy Speaker from 1984 to 1986 and chair of the House of Representatives Standing Committee in 1986, Child became the first (and so far, only) woman elected by her peers to serve as Speaker of the House. She served in that role for three years, including the period when Parliament moved into its new home in Canberra. In 1989 Child retired from her position as Speaker and one year later, at the age of 69, retired from politics entirely when her electorate was eliminated in an electoral redistribution. In the year after her retirement, Child's political accomplishments were celebrated with her appointment as an Officer of the Order of Australia, the second-highest award within the Order of Australia system.

Child's life before entering into parliamentary politics was a combination of domestic necessity and local political action. Widowed at a young age, she was left to raise her five sons on her own, often cleaning houses in order to make ends meet. In the late 1960s and early 1970s she became politicized in the wake of the Vietnam War. She joined the Draft Resisters' Union (DRU) and worked to shield resisters from prosecution and put an end to national service. Her experience with the DRU led to a career-long interest in the Vietnam War, including working for restitution for soldiers exposed to Agent Orange while serving in Southeast Asia. Her DRU experience also contributed to Child's decision to stand for Parliament in the historic 1972 election that delivered the government to Gough Whitlam and the Labor Party for the first time since World War II. In this first run Child lost by just 300 votes.

Conclusion

After living through 13 years of contradiction and change under the Labor government, in March 1996 the Australian people rejected a sixth term for Labor and elected the Liberal–National Party coalition led by John Winston Howard. This was largely a personal rejection of Paul Keating, who had been experiencing "hysterical and vituperative" attacks from the opposition for most of his years in power (Clarke 2003, 355). By the end, however, Keating's love of Italian suits, French clocks, and classical music was repeatedly used to depict him as elitist and un-Australian, while his counterattacks on the opposition as "old-fashioned and backward-looking" were further evidence of his "unduly combative" nature (Clarke 2003, 356). The fact that the unemployment rate was about the same in 1996 as it had been in 1983 when Labor was first elected, 9 percent, and the national debt had increased from 28 percent to 59 percent of national income likewise contributed to the Liberal argument that it was time for a change (cited in Jones 2004). A large number of former Labor voters "who had been left behind by the pace of change and had become frightened and resentful," a cohort labeled "Howard's Battlers" by the media (Clarke 2003, 359), delivered a large majority to the coalition.

10

THE HOWARD YEARS
(1996–2007)

The Howard years were in many ways the logical extension of the changes begun during the previous 13 years of Labor government. Free markets and free trade remained bipartisan causes, while the unleashing of reactionary social policies to stoke the fear in Howard's battlers kept the coalition, and John Howard in particular, in power, despite the breaking of numerous Liberal campaign promises. The ironic nickname "Honest John," which Howard had earned during his time as Malcolm Fraser's treasurer, was revived in this period with Howard's differentiation between "core" and "noncore" promises, the latter being lies told in order to win elections (Clarke 2003, 359). One such noncore promise was the election pledge in 1996 that he would "never, ever" revive the question of a goods and service tax (GST), which the Liberal candidate John Hewson had campaigned for in 1993 and lost, thus delivering Paul Keating the unwinnable election. By 1997 a GST was on Howard's agenda and in July 2000 the new tax system took effect.

Fear and Loathing in Australia

When Paul Keating adopted the free market policies of the Liberal Party and essentially made the two parties identical in their underlying economic ideology, the Liberals had to find some issue on which to fight electoral battles. With one important exception, gun control, the direction in which Howard took his party and government ideology was backward, what has been called "Howard's '1950s throwback'" (cited in Singleton 2005, 5). Rather than embracing the new relationships Labor had developed in Asia, taking responsibility for centuries of Aboriginal dislocation, and recognizing the vast diversity in multicultural Australia, "the party he led looked back to the Menzies' era for its ideological underpinnings and its social policies" (Clarke 2003, 358).

Immigrants, Muslims, and Aboriginal people, in particular, were used as scapegoats for the economic and social changes that were the natural outcomes of the laissez-faire economics both parties had embraced.

Pauline Hanson

Even prior to the 1996 election, multiculturalism, immigrants, and Aboriginal people had been under fire in some corners of the Liberal Party. It was 1988 when John Howard first expressed his desire to roll back the clock on multiculturalism. In early 1996 Pauline Hanson, a fish-and-chips shop owner and little known Liberal Party candidate from the city of Ipswich, Queensland, gained prominence with the publication of a letter to a newspaper railing against government assistance to Aboriginal people. Two weeks prior to the 1996 election she was dropped by the Liberals for this but startled many Australians when she went on to win the election quite handily as an independent. Hanson used her brief time in Parliament to speak about a variety of populist issues, from Aboriginal affairs and multiculturalism to immigration

Pauline Hanson, seen here delivering her maiden speech in the House of Representatives in 1996, is one of Australia's most controversial politicians of the late 20th century. (©Newspix/ News Ltd/3rd Party Managed Reproduction & Supply Rights)

and privatization. Her first speech in Parliament made Hanson a star, at least temporarily, as pundits, academics, and politicians argued whether or not her racist diatribe deserved recognition as an accurate reflection of the state of the nation. As a result of this coverage, the Australian author Donald Home has said that "Pauline Hanson's speech in 1996 may have been the most effective maiden speech ever made in the Australian parliament" (cited in *Economist* 2001, 14).

Many in Australia were horrified at the racist, xenophobic content of the speech. Parliament censured Hanson on an almost unanimous vote, but, just a month later, John Howard himself began the process of absorbing some of her views into the Liberal mainstream. He said, "I thought some of the things she said were an accurate reflection of what people feel" (cited in Murphy 2002). At the same time, Hanson herself maintained an antipathy for the Liberal Party that had dropped her in 1996. Even after losing her own seat in 1998, her political party, One Nation, which she formed in 1997, continued to contest seats in rural regions throughout Australia by running against the more traditional conservative candidates from the Liberal and National Parties. In 1998 One Nation took 11 seats in Queensland's unicameral parliament and frightened the coalition into absorbing even more of her ideas into its own platform. Three years later One Nation held just three Queensland seats but captured nearly a fifth of the vote in some rural areas of Western Australia and in so doing delivered the election to Labor. Hanson was vindicated and claimed that "the results showed 'people are fed up with Johnny Howard'" (cited in *Economist* 2001, 14).

It is hard to believe, however, with the benefit of hindsight, that Howard was fed up with Hanson, or at least some of her ideas. For it was Howard who first pushed the Liberal Party to disavow multiculturalism and later used many of the issues Hanson had raised in her maiden speech to retain his hold on the Australian government. As framed by his political opponent Michael Danby, Labor MP for Melbourne Ports:

> Hanson said that ATSIC [the Australian and Torres Strait Islander Commission] should be abolished—Howard abolished ATSIC. Hanson said that native title should be restricted— Howard gutted the Native Title Act. Hanson said that immigration should be restricted—Howard gave us the Pacific Solution and the Cornelia Rau and Vivian Solon [immigration] scandals. (cited in Kohn 2006)

This same process has been called in a more neutral analysis John Howard's "embracing [of] a brand of what looks like 'soft Hansonism'" and "flirting with Mrs Hanson's ideas as a means of accommodating the politically disenchanted" (*Economist* 2001, 14).

While the fear and loathing Hanson unleashed were drawn into the mainstream in Australia over the next decade, she herself could not maintain her early momentum. After losing her parliamentary seat in 1998, Hanson continued to campaign for One Nation. By 2001, however, the support she had garnered by speaking out against Aboriginal funding, immigration, and other issues had withered away with the Liberals' adoption of these policies. In 2003 Hanson reentered electoral politics and ran for the Senate as an independent and lost. In 2007 she created a new political party, Pauline's United Australia Party, to contest one of Queensland's Senate seats, losing again. In 2009 again as an independent, Hanson tried to win a seat in Queensland's state parliament and failed. Between her runs for political office, Hanson kept herself in the media spotlight in 2004 with a season on *Dancing with the Stars,* where she finished second, and in 2007 published her autobiography, *Untamed and Unashamed: Time to Explain.*

Refusing Refugees

While the steady creep of the Liberal Party toward positions held by One Nation remained somewhat muted in John Howard's first two terms as prime minister, as the 2001 election neared it became much more obvious. In March 2001 the coalition trailed behind Labor by nearly 20 percentage points (Clarke 2003, 374), enough to deliver the government to the Labor leader, Kim Beazley, with a landslide margin. Broken election promises on GST and cleaning up government corruption, as well as failed leadership on Aboriginal issues and formation of a republic, all contributed to widespread rejection of the Liberals and Nationals. Nevertheless, by the time of the election in November all of these issues had disappeared when John Howard's Hanson-like response to several refugee crises won back his frightened "battler" constituency. Fear and loathing had proved to be election winners, and Howard skillfully took advantage of the opportunities he was handed to stir up both of these emotions.

The first incident took place in late August when a Norwegian container ship, *Tampa,* rescued 433 Middle Eastern asylum seekers from a sinking people-smuggling ship in the Indian Ocean. As dictated by international law, the captain of the ship made for the nearest port, Australia's Christmas Island, and tried to land. He was prevented from doing so when members of the Australian Special Air Services illegally commandeered the ship and took it to the island nation of Nauru, a former Australian colony whose economy had collapsed when its phosphate reserves were exhausted in 2000. This was the first action in what eventually became known as the "Pacific Solution" to the arrival of refugees on Australia's outer shores.

One month after the *Tampa* incident, the government, with Labor support, passed the "Migration Amendment (Excision from Migration Zone) Bill 2001, [which] amended the *Migration Act 1958* to excise Christmas, Ashmore, Cartier and Cocos (Keeling) Islands from the migration zone. As a result, any unlawful non-citizen attempting to enter Australia via one of these islands [was] now prevented from making an application for a protection visa" and instead had to await processing in a detention center on Nauru or Manus Island, New Guinea (Phillips and Millbank 2003). Nauru was paid more than AU$30 million in rent for the first two years of the solution; by the time it was abolished in 2005, more than AU$1 billion had been spent on the illegal, inhumane system.

While the Howard government's actions over the *Tampa* incident breached international law and were considered "shameful" by Australia's own human rights ombudsman (Welsh 2004, 566), they were politically popular. Many Australians had been dismayed for years at the actions of a very small minority of first- and second-generation Muslim migrants, who "stood accused of a long list of antisocial behaviours," including drug dealing, violence, and rape (Clarke 2003, 375). As a result, 77 percent of Australians supported Howard's actions (Kelly 2001). Even the Labor Party eventually supported the Pacific Solution in the

Refugee claimants must await their processing in Australia behind fences and razor wire in detention centers, far from friends and community support and often with little regard for their health and mental well-being. (A Turner/Shutterstock)

Senate, despite its many legal flaws, leaving the Democrats and Greens as the sole voices of opposition. Even at the time, the Australian media began to talk about how these political victories may have improved the coalition's chances of pulling out an impossible electoral win later in the year (Kelly 2001).

While the *Tampa* incident began the political revival of the Liberals in 2001, the falsified "children overboard" case in October helped to seal the deal. The situation was very similar to the *Tampa* case: Muslim Iraqis were caught by the Australian military in their attempt to land on an Australian offshore island and request asylum. Twenty-four hours after the refugees had been approached by the HMS *Adelaide* and their ship had begun to sink, photographs of people in life jackets were taken and broadcast throughout Australia with commentary by Howard's minister of defense, Peter Reith, claiming that "the desperate survivors had demonstrated their barbarity by throwing children into the water" (Welsh 2004, 566–567). Officers on the *Adelaide* immediately contradicted the claim and later documents have proven that "the Australian Defence Force (ADF), Australian Public Service (APS) and even the office of the Defence Minister knew the incident had not occurred" (Herd 2006). Nonetheless, the Howard government refused to recant on the children overboard claim, and, in the climate of fear and loathing already whipped up by Hanson, Howard, and their supporters, the accusation stuck and helped support both the Pacific Solution and the Liberal election campaign.

Of course, while they had nothing at all to do with Australia or its immigration policies, the terrorist attacks on the United States in September 2001 served as perhaps the final nail in the coffin for Labor in November 2001. John Howard's statements against multiculturalism and overt actions against the unauthorized arrival of Muslims on Australia's shores seemed to be justified in the context of the international situation. For many Australians, this entirely unrelated incident, halfway around the world, validated Hanson and Howard's "leadership" in working toward limiting Asian and Muslim immigration at home. The result was that John Howard "swept in on coded racism in 2001" and kept himself in power for six more years using the same tactics (Jupp 2005, 173).

War on Terror Comes Home

Just one month after the September 11 terrorist attacks, the United States invaded Afghanistan in an attempt to rout out Osama bin Laden and his supporters. In December that year David Hicks, a young Australian who had converted to Islam after a trip to Albania in 1999, was captured in Afghanistan by Northern Alliance forces, along with many other Taliban fighters, and held in a local jail. In January 2002 Hicks was transported to Guantánamo Bay, Cuba, and held there for more than five years, often in solitary confinement. In the meantime, several citizens of U.S. allies Spain, Sweden, and Britain who were being held at Guantánamo were released when their governments negotiated on their behalf. Hicks and his fellow Australian detainee Mamdouh Habib, however, remained at the mercy of the flawed U.S. military justice system for years when the Howard government refused to intervene on their behalf. Habib was finally released without charge after three years of detention and torture at Guantánamo, including being tied up

MAMDOUH HABIB

Mamdouh Habib was born and raised in Egypt but spent much of his early adulthood traveling the world, working in such diverse places as Jordan, Turkey, Italy, and Bulgaria. In 1982 he settled in Sydney, married, and was granted Australian citizenship. Until 2001 he ran his own cleaning business to support his wife and growing family.

The Habibs' quiet life changed in 1993 when the Australian Security Information Organisation (ASIO) began harassing him on suspected connection to the World Trade Center bombing that year. The harassment continued after the 2001 attacks in the United States, when agents tried to induce Habib to spy on other Australians during a business trip he took to Egypt and Dubai. Habib did not cooperate and continued his trip through the Middle East. The trip, however, ended in disaster when a Saudi companion was killed while the two were in Pakistan and Habib, not knowing where to turn, escaped to Afghanistan. After hearing about the September 11 attacks in the United States, Habib called his wife in Australia to ask about the events and subsequently tried to reenter Pakistan. After this call, his family home was searched by ASIO officials and he was arrested by U.S. drug enforcement agents on a bus as he tried to cross the Afghan-Pakistani border.

In the nearly 40-month period of Habib's capture, he was first hooded and tortured in Pakistan, while being questioned by both ASIO and the Australian Federal Police (Taylor 2005). He was then "kidnapped by the US and sent to Egypt under the CIA's rendition program" (O'Brien 2008). He remained in Egypt for five months and claims that at this time "he was drugged and tortured with electric while a prostitute menstruated on him and being told his family had been killed (*Sydney Morning Herald* 2005c).

David Hicks's case was an even greater travesty than that of Habib for the length of time he was held. It was also particularly troubling for many Australians because even his U.S. Marine lawyer, Major Michael Mori, found his client's treatment by the American and Australian governments to be unjust. Hicks was held for two and a half years and repeatedly tortured (*Sydney Morning Herald* 2004) before the U.S. government even charged him with a crime. Two years later in June 2006, the U.S. Supreme Court ruled that the military commission that would have tried Hicks for conspiracy, attempted murder, and aiding

shocks, was threatened with sexual attacks by dogs and hung by his feet and beaten" (O'Brien 2008).

After months of torture at the hands of the Egyptians, Habib was returned to the Americans and taken to Guantanamo Bay, Cuba, where his incarceration continued for a further two and a half years. During this period Australian officials from ASIO, the Federal Police, and the Department of Foreign Affairs and Trade questioned Habib; American officials also continued their interrogations. Finally, after having laid no charges against Habib or finding any evidence of participation or collusion in terrorist activities, Habib was released in January 2005.

Habib returned to Australia a broken man, having missed out on years of his children's upbringing and the support of his wife and siblings. Despite the complete lack of evidence for any wrongdoing and the years of abuse and detention, Habib was greeted back in Australia by the news that Prime Minister Howard was refusing to issue an apology or pay compensation and that Attorney-General Philip Ruddock was seeking to prevent him from selling his story. Habib's passport was cancelled and he remained a "security interest" in Australia. Despite the challenges, Habib published his story in 2008 and continues to seek compensation from the U.S. and Australian governments for his mistreatment.

Sources: Taylor, Stephen. "Transcript of Interview with Ex-Guantanamo Bay Detainee Mamdouh Habib." Broadcast on February 13, 2005, Channel 9, 60 minutes. Available online. URL: http://freedetainees.org/924. Accessed May 8, 2009; O'Brien, Natalie. "Voyage to the Darkest Side for Mamdouh Habib." Australian, October 25, 2008. Available online. URL: http://www.theaustralian.news.com.au/story/0,25197,24547702-5001561,00.html. Accessed May 8, 2009.

the enemy was itself illegal. And so Hicks remained in solitary con-finement, where he had been since March 2006, without an end to his imprisonment in sight.

In November 2006 nearly five years after his capture, Amnesty International also took up Hicks's case, and a month later thousands of Australians marched in the country's major cities in an attempt to force the Howard government to intervene on Hicks's behalf. Nonetheless, despite the international and domestic furor caused by his jailing, neither the Howard nor the Bush governments would act to right the wrongs done to Hicks (*Age* multimedia). Finally, in March 2007 Hicks pleaded guilty to terrorism charges before a U.S. military commission and was sentenced to seven years' prison, with all but nine months of the sentence suspended. Not long after, Hicks was returned to Adelaide, South Australia, where he served the remaining months of his sentence at Yatala prison.

According to Hicks's father, Terry Hicks, the Australian Greens sena-tor Bob Brown, and the Amnesty International Australia spokesperson Katie Wood, the terms of Hicks's release illustrate the unfair nature of the entire affair. As part of the conditions of his release, Hicks was not allowed to discuss his imprisonment for a year nor pursue any of his prior claims of torture or illegal imprisonment against the U.S. govern-ment. To Brown and many other of Hicks's supporters, these terms seemed to reflect an agreement between the Bush and Howard govern-ments to keep Hicks quiet until after the November 2007 Australian federal elections. While Wood and Amnesty International were also concerned with the Howard government's having "wholeheartedly abandoned one of its own citizens to an unfair process," they were largely critical of the apparent disregard for Hicks's human rights (*Age* multimedia). "If he can't pursue allegations of torture and other ill treatment and can't also talk about his experience in Guantánamo Bay, then this basically means that human rights scrutiny can't be made to what happened to him" (*Age* multimedia).

Despite the fact that he was not convicted of any crime in his home country, immediately upon his release from Yatala in December 2007, Hicks was placed under a one-year control order by the Australian Federal Police, which allowed officials to keep a close eye on him. The order was lifted a year later, and David Hicks, who had abandoned his Muslim faith, was allowed to reintegrate into Australian society.

David Hicks and Mamdouh Habib were not the only Australians to suffer loss of rights and freedoms in the international war on terror and the domestic climate of fear. In 2001 the Melbourne taxi driver "Jihad"

Jack Thomas took his family to Afghanistan, where the Muslim convert is said to have trained with al-Qaeda and been instructed to return to Australia to commit terrorist acts. Thomas was captured in Pakistan in 2003, questioned and allegedly tortured by the Pakistani authorities, and later interviewed by Americans and the Australian Federal Police, who denied him the right to have his lawyer present (Neighbour 2006). During his five months of detention in Pakistan, Thomas confessed to training with al-Qaeda and to the plan for setting up a terrorist cell at home. However, his confession was disallowed in Australian courts, because of lack of due process and legal representation, and Thomas was returned to Australia in June 2003. For the next 17 months Thomas resumed his life in Australia, living quietly in a Melbourne suburb and working three jobs to support his Indonesian wife and two children (Neighbour 2006).

Despite the evidence that Thomas had fully reintegrated into Australian society and his own claims that he had confessed merely to end his detention and mistreatment, the Australian Federal Police raided the Thomas home in November 2004 and arrested him for events related to his arrest in Pakistan years earlier. He was later found not guilty on two serious terrorism-related charges, but guilty of traveling on a falsified passport and of receiving funds from a terrorist organization (Neighbour 2006). Thomas was sentenced to five years in prison but was released just a few months later, after successfully appealing his conviction.

Thomas was then placed on a control order, which set a midnight curfew and allowed him to make phone calls only with police permission, despite having his conviction overturned and not having broken any Australian laws during his time in Afghanistan and Pakistan. According to the circular logic of Philip Ruddock, the Howard government's attorney general at the time, the lack of conviction should not matter because "if you work on the assumption that only those people who could be convicted of an offence could be the subject of a control order, you wouldn't have control orders" (ABC News Online 2006). The government followed the control order with a second trial, on the same terrorism charges that had been successfully appealed just a few months earlier. Thomas was found guilty only of falsifying his passport, sentenced to nine months imprisonment, but was spared from having to serve any extra time because of the long period of his legal ordeal. After more than six years of torture, uncertainty, and government harassment, Thomas walked out of court a free man on October 29, 2008. Nevertheless, the antiterrorism laws that the Howard government rushed through the Parliament, which allowed these control orders to be placed on people who had not been convicted of a crime, remain in place to this day.

While Hicks and Thomas were Australian citizens by birth and entered conflict with the Howard government because they associated with a Muslim military organization, a third case illustrates the extent to which the Hanson-Howard climate of fear had taken over Australia in the post-2001 period. In July 2007 a Muslim Indian doctor who had been working in Australia, Mohammad Haneef, was arrested at the Brisbane, Queensland, airport and held without charge for 12 days on suspicion of having participated in the 2007 bomb attack at Glasgow airport. The evidence presented for the arrest was that Haneef is related to one of the Glasgow bombers, he left one of them his cell phone SIM card when he left Britain, and he was attempting to leave Australia on a one-way ticket. His explanation for the ticket, which was supported by his family's circumstances, was that he did not have the funds to purchase a return ticket at the time and was returning to India to visit his wife and newborn daughter, who was born by cesarean section and was suffering from jaundice. His father-in-law was going to purchase tickets for the entire family to return to Australia.

After nearly two months of legal limbo, the case against Haneef was dropped for lack of evidence. But the Howard government was not satisfied and cancelled the doctor's visa. The cancellation was later found to have been illegal and Haneef's visa was reinstated in August 2007. As a sign of their respect for the man and his work, the Gold Coast, Queensland, hospital where Haneef had been working at the time of his arrest offered him a permanent position. In 2008, the Clarke Inquiry looked into one legality of the Federal Police (AFP) and government actions in the Haneef case and found their case significantly lacking (Clarke 2008).

Abrogating Aboriginal Rights

While the Howard government opposed Labor on multiculturalism and immigration, a third area of Labor policy prior to 1996 also came under fire after 1996: reconciliation with Australia's Aboriginal people. According to Will Sanders, a specialist in Aboriginal economic affairs, "John Howard, as Prime Minister, has never even been adequate" in the areas of reconciliation and Indigenous affairs (2005, 152). After the *Mabo* case and the passage of even the watered-down Native Title Act, many Australian pastoralists became fearful that they would lose access to the nearly 42 percent of the continent covered by grazing leases (Northern Land Council 2003a). A December 1996 judgment by Australia's High Court in *Wik Peoples v. the State of Queensland (Wik)* added to that fear, which John Howard exacerbated with his comment that "the pendulum had swung too far towards Aborigines and had to be reset" (cited in Clarke 2003, 364).

The decision that so frightened pastoralists and mining companies was that "a leasehold grant did not necessarily extinguish native title" (Welsh 2004, 559). At the same time, the judges determined that in the situation of coexistence of title, pastoralists' rights would take precedence over those of Aboriginal peoples (Northern Land Council 2003a). In other words, the court had handed down a symbolic victory for Aboriginal people and given them the right to take their claims to court, but in fact very little would change. Nonetheless, the Howard government vowed to "reset" the pendulum and take away even the symbolic victories gained by Aboriginal people. It did so with its "ten point plan" and subsequent Native Title Amendment Act 1998, which effectively stripped Aboriginal people of native title on pastoral land, suburban and urban land, vacant government land, and both air and seaways (Northern Land Council 2003b).

Another arena in which even symbolic recognition of Aboriginal people's rights was denied by the Howard government was its reaction to the May 1997 parliamentary tabling of *Bringing Them Home: Report of the National Inquiry into the Separation of Aboriginal and Torres Strait Islander Children from Their Families*. The report had been commissioned by the Keating government in 1995 and undertaken by Mick Dodson, the Aboriginal and Torres Strait Islander social justice commissioner, and Sir Ronald Wilson, president of the Human Rights and Equal Opportunity Commission. The final 700-page account highlighted the damage done to Aboriginal individuals, families, and communities over nearly a century of Australian governments' taking Aboriginal children from their parents to be raised in institutions or fostered out to white families. Reconciliation for these acts was determined to require, at minimum, compensation to the "Stolen Generations" in the form of both an apology and financial restitution (Dow 2008). By 2001 the governments of all the states and territories had issued apologies to the Stolen Generations, but the federal government refused to do so, issuing instead a statement of "regret" (Dow 2008).

This refusal, in conjunction with the minister of Aboriginal affairs's denial that the Stolen Generations even exist, unleashed a torrent of criticism. The Aboriginal activist Charles Perkins stated, "Reconciliation is

On May 28, 2000, an estimated 200,000 Australians walked across the Sydney Harbour Bridge as part of a Reconciliation Walk aimed to move the Howard government to apologize for the Stolen Generations. (Thorsten Rust/Shutterstock)

finished now. . . . We are now facing major confrontation between black and white in this country" (cited in Welsh 2004, 560). Even the somewhat conservative historian Frank Welsh has argued that "at a time when sensitivity and generosity were called for . . . the Howard government's response seemed . . . to be poor-spirited and mean" (2004, 560). The response from Australians over the next few years was also highly critical. In May 2000 nearly a quarter of a million Australians participated in a March for Reconciliation over the Sydney Harbour Bridge, displaying their displeasure with government inaction. However, this displeasure did not damage the Howard government in the long run, since *Tampa* and "children overboard" came to the rescue in late 2001.

Late in the Howard administration's tenure, another situation arose in the relations between black and white in Australia that required "sensitivity and generosity," neither of which was forthcoming. The occasion was the tabling of a report by the Northern Territory Board of Inquiry into the Protection of Aboriginal Children from Sexual Abuse, commonly referred to as "Little Children Are Sacred." The investigation and report had been commissioned by the Northern Territory's government in August 2006 after it was alleged on the ABC television news program *Lateline* that pedophilia was rampant in Aboriginal communities in the Northern Territory. The investigation had been carried out by an Indigenous public servant, Patricia Anderson, and a white lawyer, Rex Wild, over the course of nine months in 2006–07. Their 320-page report (Wild and Anderson 2007) substantiated that sexual abuse did occur among a portion of Aboriginal children in the Northern Territory and made a variety of recommendations on how to combat the poverty, social disruption, and alcohol abuse that contributed to it.

With the tabling of this report in April 2007 the governments of both the Northern Territory and the Commonwealth immediately went on the offensive. However, because the Northern Territory does not have the political status of an independent state, the Commonwealth's reactions took precedence. As John Howard said, "We're very happy to work with the Northern Territory Government, but it will need to be on the terms that I am about to announce" (cited in Hunter 2007). Those terms outlined a series of actions, together called the Northern Territory Intervention, which took into consideration almost none of the recommendations made by Anderson and Wild. For example, in the area of policing, the report suggests recruiting more Aboriginal officers and more female officers for remote areas and conducting "effective, meaningful and ongoing consultations with individual Aboriginal communities" (Hunter 2007). In response, the government stationed secondees from other police forces and the army to serve in the Northern Territory and required that the state government "remove customary [traditional] law as a mitigating factor for sentencing and bail conditions" (Hunter 2007). In the area of housing, the report recommends building more houses and units in rural communities and training Aboriginal people in home repair and other maintenance skills. Instead, the government came forward with an "introduction of market based rents and normal tenancy arrangements" (Hunter 2007). Similar gaps exist between the report's recommendations and the terms set down in the intervention in the areas of access to pornography and alcohol and in Aboriginal schooling (Hunter 2007).

The governmental response has drawn criticism from such diverse sources as Aboriginal leaders, Amnesty International, and the United Nations, which cite racial discrimination and disregard for Aboriginal people's civil and political rights (ABC News 2009). Nonetheless, since taking power in late 2007 Kevin Rudd's Labor government has continued to pursue many of the means and ends established by the Howard government earlier that year. Among the policies being continued is "income quarantining," which is supposed to prevent adults from spending government money on alcohol, cigarettes, gambling, or pornography. Unfortunately, the measure has not been shown to improve child health in the territory; one of its main goals, anemia, for example, rose among Aboriginal children in the Northern Territory, from 20 percent in December 2006 to 55 percent in June 2008 (Fisher 2009). In addition, "income management" has been imposed on thousands of Aboriginal people for whom its purpose is irrelevant, including "aged pensioners without children, functional families, those who neither drink nor take drugs and families in which school attendance is high" (Fisher 2009).

Perhaps the most troubling aspect of this bipartisan discriminatory policy is that it targets Aboriginal people in the Northern Territory, where the federal government has far more power than in the states, for a problem that is widespread throughout the country. For example, in Queensland substantiated child abuse among non-Indigenous children takes place at the exact rate of that among Indigenous children in the Northern Territory: 13.7 cases of abuse per 1,000 children. But this is nowhere near the rate of abuse of Aboriginal children in most other Australian states and territories. Aboriginal children in Victoria suffer abuse at the rate of 63 cases per 1,000, 56 per 1,000 in the Australian Capital Territory, 43.2 per 1,000 in South Australia, and 27.1 per 1,000 in New South Wales; only Western Australia (12.2 per 1,000) and Tasmania (5.8 per 1,000) have lower rates than the Northern Territory (cited in Hunter 2009). Despite warnings by the United Nations, racism has trumped both logic and human rights, and the politics of fear and loathing continues, at least in this arena.

Port Arthur

In the late 1980s Australia began to experience an increase in gun violence, including two separate mass murders in Melbourne in 1987 in which Julian Knight and Frank Vitkovic killed seven and eight people, respectively; a further 24 people were wounded in these incidents. In 1996, however, Martin Bryant made Australian history when he killed 35 people and injured 18 others during an eight-minute shooting spree in Port Arthur, Tasmania.

Bryant was a 28-year-old who had suffered lifelong mental problems, including autism and schizophrenia, and received a pension because he was unable to hold a regular job. In the years prior to the shootings he had lost his best friend, Helen Harvey, a wealthy misfit who left him most of her inherited fortune, and his father, who committed suicide. According to many of the reports written about Bryant both before and after the massacre, as well as the opinions of his teachers and psychologists, his father had been the sole restraint on him, and "when he died he didn't have that restraining influence any longer" (cited in Wainwright and Totaro 2009, 15). Building on a love of guns he had developed at an early age, Bryant was able to use some of his inherited wealth to purchase assault weapons without a license or any training. After the massacre, many Australians were horrified at a system that had allowed Bryant to purchase both guns and ammunition despite the revelation of one of the psychologists who evaluated him during his early life: "Martin tells me he would like to go around shooting people. It would be unsafe to allow Martin out of his parents' control" (cited in *Sydney Morning Herald* April 24, 2009).

While the Howard government was adept at stirring up fear in the Australian populace where compassion might have been appropriate, in the case of gun control, fear seems to have been appropriate. Many Australians feared the ability of the mentally ill to purchase automatic and semiautomatic weapons without a license, as Bryant had. Despite massive protests in Sydney, Melbourne, and throughout the country over the new restrictive laws, Howard acted on a sentiment he had expressed a full year before the massacre: "Every effort should be made to limit the carrying of guns in Australia" (Megalogenis 2006, 197). By 1997, the Howard government had championed "some of the world's toughest gun laws" and instituted a buy-back system in which the government removed about 600,000 guns from circulation (Garnaut 2007). As a result of Howard's tough stance on guns, Australia has had 250 fewer deaths per year than prior to the National Firearms Agreement, or just "0.27 firearm-related homicides per 100,000 Australians—about one-fifteenth of the U.S. rate" (Garnaut 2007).

International Relations

While fear and loathing were central to the development of much domestic policy in the years between 1996 and 2007, on the international scene Australia sometimes presented a very different face to the world. This began in 1998, when Australia supported East Timorese independence after 23 years of support for the Indonesian annexation of the half-island in 1975, and continued in 2000 with the success of the Sydney summer Olympics. However, these actions were followed by more controversial affairs, such as Australian deployment in Afghanistan and Iraq in support of the Bush administration's war on terror and the Australia–U.S. Free Trade Agreement.

East Timor

In 1975 when the Portuguese pulled out of East Timor and Indonesia invaded the small, half-island nation, the Australian government under Gough Whitlam sided with the Indonesians, refusing to go to the aid of the independence-seeking East Timorese. Indeed, Australian government documents released in 2000 reveal that Whitlam encouraged the Indonesians to invade, telling the Indonesian president, Suharto, in 1974 that East Timor was "too small to be independent" (cited in Lane 2000). After that period, Whitlam and the subsequent governments of Fraser, Hawke, and Keating were all strongly criticized by both the Left and the Right for their support of Suharto's military dictatorship, invasion of Timor, and human rights abuses. Finally, in 1998 the Howard government turned around 23 years of Australian policy on Indonesia and supported some degree of self-determination in East Timor.

This about-face is said to have driven Indonesia's new president, Dr. Habibie, to push for a plebiscite in the region in 1999 (Dalrymple 2003, 205). Despite the presence of heavily armed Indonesian-trained militia, the East Timorese voted for independence by a margin of 78 percent in August 1999 and thus unleashed violence by both anti-independence forces and those of Falintil (Armed Forces of National Liberation of East Timor). Thousands were killed or injured in the onslaught and a quarter of the new country's population fled, most to West Timor (BBC News 2009). Alone in the international community, the Howard government had been prepared for the plebiscite's aftermath by having amassed troops and supplies in northern Australian bases and chartered a transport ship to be ready in the waters off Australia's north coast to move these troops and supplies into East Timor (Dalrymple 2003, 206). Nonetheless, Howard refused to deploy Australian forces without Indonesian support and thus convinced the Habibie government to accept a UN international peacekeeping mission.

With Resolution 1264 the UN Security Council created the International Force for East Timor (INTERFET), on September 15, 1999. The mission of the 7,500-soldier force was to "restore peace and security in East Timor, protect and support the United Nations Assistance Mission East Timor (UNAMET) in carrying out its tasks, and within force capabilities, facilitate humanitarian assistance operations" (INTERFET 2000). Just five days later INTERFET, with its 4,500-strong contingent of Australians and led by the Australian major general Peter Cosgrove, deployed on the island and began the work of restoring peace to the region. During its five months on East Timor, INTERFET was able to supervise the Indonesians' largely peaceful withdrawal and experienced no combat deaths (Paterson 2000). On February 23, 2000, INTERFET formally ceased to exist, and Major General Cosgrove handed control of East Timor to UNTAET, the United Nations Transitional Administration of East Timor, under the Filipino lieutenant general Jaime de los Santos. Nineteen of the 23 countries that had contributed forces to INTERFET had forces in UNTAET, including Australia.

Despite the Howard government's support for East Timorese independence, as well as the granting of asylum to 43 West Papuans in Australia in 2006, Australia and Indonesia have been able to resume ministerial-level discussions and other important diplomatic relations. In 2005 the Indonesian president, Yudhoyono, traveled to Australia, and the two countries signed the papers to form the Australia Indonesia Partnership for Reconstruction and Development (AIPRD) joint commission, under which Australia provided AU$1 billion to assist in the rebuilding of Aceh and other Indonesian regions after the 2004 tsunami that ravaged the area. In the following year the two countries began talks on a new security agreement, which was signed in 2006 as the Lombok Agreement. By 2007 they were engaged in nearly AU$10.5 billion in trade, and bilateral trade and diplomatic ties had been normalized.

Sydney Olympics

In September 1993 Sydney was elected by the International Olympic Committee to host the 2000 summer Olympics, or the Games of the XXVII Olympiad. For the next seven years parts of the city were transformed to house athletes and stage sporting events as diverse as swimming, trampoline, basketball, and softball. Building costs to create the infrastructure for the 18-day event were estimated to have been AU$2.185 billion (Sport Business International 2001), while the total cost of staging the event was AU$6.6 billion, more than double the Australian Olympic bid committee's original estimate of AU$3 billion (cited in Liebreich 2003).

Despite the financial burden to Sydneysiders and Australians more generally, whose tax dollars contributed between AU$1.7 billion and AU$2.4 billion to the games' final costs (cited in Liebreich 2003), the Sydney games were considered a great success. After the close of the games, they were even dubbed "the best Games ever" by Juan Antonio Samaranch, president of the International Olympic Committee at the time (Sydney Olympic Park Authority 2008). More than 10,000 athletes representing 199 countries had participated in 28 sporting disciplines and 300 separate events. North and South Korea entered the Olympic Stadium for the opening ceremony together for the first time, marching

CATHY FREEMAN

Catherine Astrid Salome Freeman was born in February 1973 in Mackay, Queensland. During childhood she became well known for her athletic ability, with local newspapers calling her "the 'wonder girl' from Mackay" (quoted in Sports Card World 2006). In 1987 Freeman began working with a professional coach, Mike Danila, who believed that at 16 she had a chance to compete for Australia at the Commonwealth Games. Danila was right; Freeman was chosen to run for Australia on what turned out to be the gold-medal-winning 4 × 100 meter relay team.

After this victory, Freeman left Queensland and moved to Melbourne, where better training facilities and coaching were available. She also continued to receive significant national attention as the Young Australian of the Year in 1991. After her feat of being the first female Aboriginal Australian to win a gold medal at the Commonwealth Games, in 1992 Freeman was the first to represent Australia at the Olympics. In 1994 at the Commonwealth Games in Victoria, Canada, she received two gold medals, in the 200- and 400-meter races, and two years later at the Atlanta Olympics took silver in the 400 meters. She followed this with gold medals in the same event at the World Championships in Greece in 1997 and Seville in 1999. In between Freeman was again honored in her home country by being awarded Australian of the Year in 1998.

The 400-meter final at the Sydney Olympics was to be Freeman's last great international stage; she won in 49.11 seconds. Prior to the games, a few Aboriginal leaders in Australia had urged Freeman not to run in protest of government treatment of Aboriginal people, but Freeman refused; she did, however, use her international prominence to denounce the Howard government's disavowal of the Stolen Generations with her grandmother's story of having been taken from her family. Subsequently, it was Freeman's athletic ability and carrying of both an Aboriginal and an Australian flag during her victory lap that gave the issue of reconciliation prominence for Australians and the global audience alike.

Source: Sports Card World. "Tribute to Cathy Freeman" (2006). Available online. URL: http://users.chariot.net.au/çbyoung/freeman.htm. Accessed May 8, 2009.

under a unity flag bearing the outline of the Korean peninsula, and East Timor, though it did not yet have an Olympic committee, was allowed to send four athletes to the games. Part of the glory for Australians were

Cathy Freeman with both Aboriginal and Australian flags on her victory lap after her gold medal race at the 2000 Sydney Olympics. (AAP)

the performances by a young swimmer named Ian Thorpe, who took home three gold medals and two silvers in addition to several world records, and the runner Cathy Freeman, who both lit the Olympic flame at the opening ceremonies and took home a gold medal in the 400-meter event (Australian Olympic Committee 5).

For some Australians the Olympics was an opportunity not only to host a world-class event, but also to draw global attention to some of their country's and the world's most pressing problems. Antiglobalization activists as well as those who wanted to highlight the plight of the homeless engaged in public events in Sydney during the games (Lenskyj 2002). Performing at the opening ceremony, the 1980s rock band Midnight Oil highlighted the Howard government's refusal to apologize to the Aboriginal Stolen Generations by having *Sorry* emblazoned in large white letters on their all-black outfits. Aboriginal activists themselves used the opportunity to take their case to the court of global public opinion, establishing a 100-tent embassy in Sydney's Victoria Park (Morgan 2003, 27). Cathy Freeman used her victory lap after the 400-meter race to highlight the need for Aboriginal reconciliation by wearing an Aboriginal flag around her shoulders in addition to the Australian flag.

War

Even before the September 11, 2001, attacks on the United States drew much of the world into at least temporary alliance with the Americans, John Howard was "portraying Australia as a loyal follower of the United States" (Baldino 2005, 191). "The Howard Doctrine," as it came to be known, was for Australia to serve as "a kind of 'deputy sheriff' to the United States, in Asia" (Baldino 2005, 191). Australia under Howard also followed U.S. unilateralism in this period by withdrawing from international arbitration tribunals, such as the International Court of Justice, and distancing itself from the UN Declaration on Human Rights, despite having been one of the eight countries to have participated in its drafting in 1948 (Baldino 2005, 194). The Howard government also refused to sign the UN Convention on the Elimination of All Forms of Discrimination against Women and the Kyoto Protocol on climate change.

Perhaps the clearest sign that Australia in this period had stepped out of the bounds of international law was in 2003 when John Howard agreed to send troops to Iraq, despite not having gained the UN Security Council's authority to do so (Baldino 2005, 194). Several former prime ministers, including the Liberal Malcolm Fraser, "urged Howard not to go to war without Security Council consent" (Baldino 2005, 194), but their plea was ignored. In the first year of the Iraq war, 2,000 Australian Defense Force soldiers served in the region, in logistics, maritime support, and battle. By the time Kevin Rudd fulfilled a 2007 election promise to bring most Australian soldiers home in June 2008, only one Australian soldier had died in Iraq (al-Nasrallah 2008). Nonetheless, the illegal nature of the war and lack of clarity in both its purpose and its cause meant that about 80 percent of the Australian public remained adamantly opposed to Australia's participation (al-Nasrallah 2008).

While the US.-led war in Iraq has had limited global support and drawn significant criticism for the false pretenses under which it was begun, the war waged in Afghanistan since October 2001 has been on much clearer legal grounds. After the September 11, 2001, attacks, the UN Security Council passed Resolution 1386 (2001), which "calls upon Member States to contribute personnel, equipment and other resources to the International Security Assistance Force" (Nautilus Institute 2009). Australia answered that call immediately, deploying the Special Forces Task Group to Afghanistan and Royal Australian Navy ships to the Persian Gulf in late 2001. The task group was withdrawn a year later but redeployed for 12 months from September 2005, and then again from March 2007. In addition to these forces, the Reconstruction

Task Force entered Afghanistan in March 2006, while a helicopter detachment served for 13 months from March 2006. The navy has remained in the Gulf consistently since late 2001, supporting troops in both Afghanistan and Iraq (Nautilus Institute 2009). Kevin Rudd did not withdraw Australian forces from Afghanistan and in April 2009 increased Australia's commitment to 1,550 soldiers from 1,100 (Sun 2009). In mid-October 2009 the Rudd government announced that it had no intention of increasing its troop numbers and would bring home the last 1,500 or so soldiers stationed in the country once their mission to train the Afghan national army in Oruzgan had been completed (Larkin 2009).

On October 12, 2002, Australia's participation in the "war on terror" was felt in force by the civilian population. That evening, 88 Australians were killed in two separate bomb attacks in nightclubs in Kuta, Bali, Indonesia. The bombings are sometimes referred to as "Australia's September 11" because of the large number of Australians killed and injured in attacks that were clearly targeting foreign tourists (Australian Federal Police 2008). The first hit, at Paddy's Bar, was by a suicide bomber who wore explosives in a backpack, while the second, larger blast involved about 2,000 pounds of explosives in a van parked outside the Sari Club (Australian Federal Police 2008). A third bomb was also detonated that night, at the U.S. consulate, but caused minimal damage and injured just one person. After the attacks, Bali's hospitals were quickly filled to capacity and dozens of injured people from all of the 18 countries represented on the list of wounded were flown by Royal Australian Air Force planes to Australian hospitals in Darwin and elsewhere in the country (Australian Federal Police 2008).

Interpretations of the cause and effect of the Bali bombings in 2002, as well as a 2005 bomb attack that killed and injured far more Indonesians than foreigners, differ. John Howard claimed that these attacks "were a reminder that the War on Terror required resolute action and must persist" (Baldino 2005, 201). For many Australians, however, the confessions of two of the bombers, in which they stated Australians were targeted for their support of the U.S. war in Afghanistan (*Age* 2003), indicated that distancing the country from the United States might be a safer option (*Age* 2002). Some Howard critics also believe that the government's lack of prior information about the bombings pointed to "systemic failures in Australian intelligence collaboration as well as its politicisation" (Baldino 2005, 201). Prior to the bombings, the Australian Security and Intelligence Organisation (ASIO) apparently ignored warnings about Jemaah Islamiyah and al-Qaeda activities in

Indonesia that might have alerted it to the danger for Australians and other foreigners in Bali (Baldino 2005, 201).

Trade

In exchange for the Howard government's support of the Bush administration's war in Iraq, Australia was able to negotiate a free trade agreement with the United States. After more than a year of negotiations, the Australia–United States Free Trade Agreement (AUSFTA) was signed by both governments in May 2004 and took effect on January 1, 2005.

According to the Howard government, which enthusiastically sought this closer bilateral tie with the United States, AUSFTA "offered substantial benefits for Australian business" (Baldino 2005, 202). The Australian government body responsible for trade relations, Austrade, asserts on its Web site that the agreement "ensures greater access to the United States market for Australian products . . . [and] enhances prospects for Australian services, trade and investment, improves the regulatory and investment environment between the two countries, and promotes increased business mobility" (Austrade 2009). Critics of the agreement, however, claim otherwise. For example, an Australian National University (ANU) study found that "the government's estimates on economic gains had been overstated" (cited in Baldino 2005, 203). The economist Ross Garnaut, also from ANU, feared not only the direct economic loss to Australian businesses but also the "terrible signals" it sent to Australia's Asian trade partners, who "purchased over half of Australian-based exports" (cited in Baldino 2005, 203). Even the former Liberal Party leader John Hewson was critical of the Howard government's efforts toward bilateralism, claiming "we have consistently seen that our maximum benefits would flow from success in multilateral trade negotiations" (cited in Baldino 2005, 2004).

Many industry organizations in Australia likewise thought their government had sold them out in order to rush through a deal with the Bush administration. Australian farmers criticized not only the relaxation of quarantine rules that had protected Australia's fragile landscape but also the inability of Australia's negotiators to open U.S. markets to Australian sugar, beef, dairy, and other agricultural products (Baldino 2005, 202–3). Australia's media and software industries decried the agreement, which they feared would swamp local products with unregulated American products (Baldino 2005, 202–203). Most serious for many older Australians was the concern over higher prices for many medications. Australia's Pharmaceutical Benefits Scheme allows Australians to purchase tax-subsidized medications for between three and 10 times less than prices paid by Americans (Ranald and Southalan 2005). Other concerns with the treaty included weaker government regulation of essential services, including water use, food labeling, and the introduction of genetically modified organisms; the potential loss of jobs from tariff cuts; and inability to protect the small Australian film and television market (Ranald and Southalan 2005). The Australian medical establishment was also concerned with the local blood supply, which was forced to open its doors to foreign suppliers with potentially weaker oversight and health rules (Bambrick, Faunce, and Johnson 2006, 320).

Three years after the implementation of AUSFTA, the best evaluation given to the treaty on the Australian side was that it was "patchy" (Clarke and Gao 2007, 845), while numerous independent analyses found that the agreement has been largely negative for Australia. The International Monetary Fund and National Institute of Economic and Industry Research (NIEIR) both found that AUSFTA would cost Australia billions of dollars and hundreds of thousands of jobs, thus shrinking the Australian economy (Priestley 2008). At the same time, the Australian Department of Foreign Affairs and Trade officials urged a "long term view" of the situation (Clarke and Gao 2007, 845). Most Australians hope that this long-term view is more positive than the short-term one, in which in 2007 their country suffered an AU$13.6 billion trade deficit with the United States and overall trade between the two countries fell dramatically over the 2002 benchmark (Priestley 2008).

Beginning of the End

As a result of the October 2004 election, John Howard's Liberal-National coalition of parties had control of both the lower and the upper houses of Parliament from July 1, 2005, through November 2007. This was the first time since 1981 in Australia that the government party had controlled both houses and thus had no need to negotiate with any other party in order to pass bills. The most important and far-reaching legislation passed by the coalition in its unfettered two-year period was referred to as WorkChoices. This new industrial relations law changed a number of important aspects of the relationship between employer and employee, including unfair dismissal laws, minimum wages, vacation time, leave loading (extra vacation pay), and aspects of contract negotiation. Most central, according to the bill's sponsor, then–workplace relations minister Kevin Andrews, "was to encourage the spread of Australian Workplace Agreements (AWAs), or individual contracts, which will be negotiated between workers and their bosses" (*Sydney Morning Herald* 2005). This individual negotiation was to replace long-standing Australian tradition and workplace law whereby contracts were negotiated for groups of employees, such as teachers, clerks, or truck drivers. As is the case with this last point, all aspects of the WorkChoices bill favored employers over employees by allowing employers to reduce the wages and benefits of many employees (ABC News 2007).

Hardest hit by the new laws were women and young people, who had less bargaining power than male and older employees and were thus forced to accept conditions that prior to WorkChoices would have been illegal, such as no overtime pay, less vacation time, and an inability to join a union. Others were fired for refusing to sign an AWA or requesting a collectively bargained contract rather than an individual one (Stitt and O'Neil n.d.). While it was women and young people who suffered most under the new regime, according to Peter McIlwain, "the man who approve[d] the agreements for the [Howard] Government," "All AWA's expressly excluded at least one protected award condition" (Long 2006). In other words, all Australians who signed employment contracts after the implementation of WorkChoices lost a benefit that they would have received if they had signed their contract prior to their implementation.

As might be expected, the response of a majority of Australians to the WorkChoices law was negative. At their one-year anniversary, 59 percent of Australians opposed the new laws, while just 24 percent supported them (ABC News 2007a). Despite the Howard government's spending AU$121 million to advertise and promote the scheme, as stories began to emerge of people losing their jobs, benefits, or wages, more and more Australians rejected it (Marris 2007). By November 2007 the Labor Party was able to campaign on the back of WorkChoices and John Howard was swept from power.

The overreach of power that the Howard government implemented with WorkChoices in 2006 was not the only sign to many Australians that it was time for a change in government. On December 4, 2005, a group of four Lebanese-Australian men and three Anglo-Australian life guards on Cronulla Beach, Sydney, had a fight. According to the Lebanese-Australian men, the lifeguards had started the fight by verbally taunting them about their ethnic background; the lifeguards claim that the others had begun the fight by verbally abusing Anglo-Australian women (Kabir 2007, 1). In response to this event, the conservative talk back radio host Alan Jones used his Sydney morning radio program as a forum for fanning the flames of racial and ethnic mistrust. He and numerous other Anglo-Australians had received an anonymous text message after the December 4 fight urging that Anglo-Australians "Come to Cronulla this weekend to take revenge. This Sunday every Aussie in the Shire get down to North Cronulla to support the Leb and wog bashing day" (cited in Marr 2005). Jones read this message on his show several times between December 4 and December 11 and consistently supported callers who expressed a desire for violence (cited in Marr 2005).

On Sunday, December 11, "about 5,000 young [Anglo-]Australians converged on Sydney's Cronulla beach, many draped in Australian flags, singing *Waltzing Matilda* and *Advance Australia Fair* and chanting 'Kill the Lebs', 'no more Lebs', 'get Lebs off the beach', 'F . . . k off, Lebs' and 'F . . . k off wogs'" (cited in Kabir 2007, 1). They threw bottles at police and stomped on their cars, closed off streets, and bashed both men and women who appeared to have a Lebanese or other Middle Eastern background (*Sydney Morning Herald* 2005a). A handful of people were arrested on the day, while many others were taken to hospitals to have their injuries treated. Contrary to Jones's prediction the week prior to the riot, that if you "Shoot one, the rest will run" (Marr 2005), a number of Lebanese-Australian young men did not flee the violence. Instead, through the night of December 11 and the following day, many individuals supported their community with the same vigilante violence that had ruled the Anglo-Australian crowd earlier. They carried "guns, machetes, baseball bats, knives, chains and iron bars and launched a reprisal attack by smashing shops and cars and threatening people who got in their way" (Kabir 2007, 1–2).

In the days and weeks leading up to Christmas 2005, these events were given top priority on many Australian television and radio news and current events programs. Politicians also weighed in heavily on the topic of ethnic violence; the New South Wales premier, Morris Iemma, declared "What it showed on the weekend was the ugly face of racism in this country" (Davies and Peatling 2005). Prime Minister John Howard, while reacting with disgust to the mob violence, rejected both the idea that Australian society was racist and that his policies and anti-multiculturalism had provided the context for the events (Davies and Peatling 2005). The controversial historian Keith Windschuttle even blamed Australia's multicultural policies for the violence, claiming "the incidents were 'multicultural riots' and should be blamed on the 'multiculturalist policies and ideas' that had created and ghettoised ethnic communities within Australia" (Reporting Diversity 2007, 69).

Many Australians, however, disagreed and saw a logical continuum from Howard's antimulticulturalism and anti-immigration positions to the alcohol-fused violence at Cronulla. This connection was made clear in several newspapers, which ran a cartoon showing an Anglo-Australian rioter wearing a T-shirt that proclaimed, "We will decide who comes to this beach and the circumstances in which they come," paraphrasing Howard's statement after the *Tampa* incident, "We will decide who comes to this country and the circumstances in which they come" (Strom 2006).

A third set of events that may have contributed to Howard's defeat in 2007 concerned serious errors made by the immigration department under his watch, which deported an Australian citizen to the Philippines and locked up an Australian permanent resident in a refugee detention center. Both cases were disturbing in that the women involved, Vivian Alvarez Solon and Cornelia Rau, had forms of disability that were exacerbated by their immigration ordeals. Solon was deported to the Philippines in 2001 after months of hospitalization for serious physical and mental trauma when her claims of being an Australian citizen were not believed; she was found without a passport in her possession. Despite her family's effort to find her, including filing a missing person report with Australian police, she spent four years living as an indigent in the Philippines. An investigation into the case afterward found that the immigration department had discovered their error in the months after her deportation but chose to ignore their mistake. She was eventually found living in a hospice for the destitute and dying near Manila and was allowed to return to her family in Australia in 2005 (Barlow 2005). Rau, who had lived in Australia as a permanent resident since she was a teenager, was locked up, first in prison despite having committed no crime, and then in a detention center, when her mental illness prevented her from revealing her real name. During her 10 months of detention, Rau did not receive an accurate diagnosis or any form of treatment for her schizophrenia, from which she had suffered off and on for several years.

After the discovery of these errors, the government hired a former Australian Federal Police officer to make an inquiry into the Rau and Solon cases, as well as immigration department policies and procedures more generally. The Palmer Inquiry damns every level of the department, from poorly trained officers who overstep their positions to a government concerned more with numbers than with humanity. Palmer writes in one of his 34 conclusions: "There are serious problems with the handling of immigration detention cases. They stem from deep-seated cultural and attitudinal problems within DIMIA [Department of Immigration and Multiculturalism and Indigenous Affairs] and a failure of executive leadership in the immigration compliance and detention areas" (Palmer 2005, 15). During the course of his investigation, Palmer was also given case notes on more than 200 other examples of error and mistaken identity leading to wrongful immigration detention, pointing to a systemic problem of incompetence and abuse.

Conclusion

While many Australians had supported the Hanson-inspired changes to immigration policy in 2001, by 2007 they had grown weary of the inhumane and draconian policies enacted to protect them. In conjunction with Howard government failures in the area of industrial relations and multiculturalism, this was one more piece of evidence that voters used in their judgment against the incumbents in November 2007.

In addition to these issues, exit polls that followed the Howard government's loss on November 24, 2007, indicate that global warming, water, education, and health were key factors in the large swing toward Labor that day (Watson and Browne 2008, 4). Kevin Rudd and the Labor Party won with 83 seats in the lower house of Parliament to the Liberals' 65 seats; the Liberals also lost their outright majority in the Senate, or upper house, a change that took effect on July 1, 2008.

This election was historic for several reasons. First, it introduced Australia's first female deputy prime minister, Julia Gillard, who also became the minister for employment and workplace relations, education, and social inclusion. Second, it was also the first time since 1929 that a sitting prime minister lost his own seat in Parliament. John Howard was defeated by the former ABC journalist Maxine McKew by a swing of 5.5 percent of the vote in his home district of Bennelong, located in the northern suburbs of Sydney.

11

RECONCILIATION AND REPUBLICANISM? AUSTRALIA SINCE 2007

Implementation of Kevin '07 Promises

Many Australians thought the election of a Labor government in 2007 would mean a change in direction for their country. Conservative ideologies underpinning Aboriginal, immigration, and social policies would be repudiated; climate change would be addressed more seriously; and workplace relations would reflect the needs of both employees and employers. Many thought the country would once again look forward rather than back, perhaps even toward a republican form of governance and reconciliation between Indigenous and non-Indigenous citizens. Eighteen months into Labor's first term, the evidence was mixed on progress toward the attainment of these goals.

Since taking over the government in early December 2007, Kevin Rudd and the Labor Party have made good on several of the campaign promises that led to these expectations but sometimes have failed to deliver in the aftermath. For example, on December 3, 2007, Kevin Rudd signed the Kyoto Protocol, which John Howard had rejected outright. This act was praised by many voters, who had named climate change as one of their top concerns in choosing Labor over the coalition. In the subsequent period, however, many have been disappointed by the government's actions to combat climate change. A December 2008 White Paper on the subject called for just a 5 to 15 percent reduction in the 2000 level of carbon emissions by the year 2020; thus the protocol's target of a 60 percent reduction on 2000 levels by 2050 will be very difficult to achieve. In May 2009 the government proposed revising the 2020 figure to 20 percent of 2000 levels. But as this would occur only if a global agreement were made in Copenhagen in December 2009 "to stabilise levels of CO_2 equivalent at 450 parts per million or lower by mid century" (Wong 2009), the plan was dropped. In yet another blow to Australians concerned about the environment, the government in early May 2009 both postponed the start of its already-weak carbon trading scheme until July 2011 and lowered the cost of polluting from AU\$40 per metric tonne (2,205 lbs.) of emissions to AU\$10 per metric tonne (Coorey 2009). Business leaders cheered the move, while environmentalists were dismayed at the prime minister's apparent lack of commitment. Whether or not this will hurt the Labor Party at the next election, which must occur by November 2010, remains to be seen.

The pattern of early symbolic action followed by weak follow-up is also evident in the Rudd government's Aboriginal policy. At the opening of Parliament on February 13, 2008, Kevin Rudd made a public apology to Australia's Aboriginal population for the Stolen Generations, which had been rejected by the Howard government since receiving the *Bringing Them Home* report in 1997. In front of Aboriginal guests and every media outlet in the country, Rudd tabled a parliamentary motion to apologize "for laws and policies which had 'inflicted profound grief, suffering and loss on these our fellow Australians'" (Sorry Day 2007). In return he received a glass coolamon, or carrier, from Lorraine Peeters, a member of the Stolen Generations, bearing the message: "We have a new covenant between our peoples—that we will do all we can to make sure our children are carried forward, loved and nurtured and able to live a full life" (cited in ANTAR 2009).

All over the country, tens of thousands of people gathered to watch the prime minister's speech, in which he not only apologized for past wrongs but promised to establish "a policy commission to close the gap between Indigenous and non-Indigenous Australians in life expectancy, educational achievement and economic opportunity" (cited in ANTAR 2009). It was an extremely moving day for most Australians and seemed to set the stage for an entirely different relationship between government and Indigenous people than had prevailed for the previous 200 years.

Unfortunately for Australia's Aboriginal population, very little has actually changed, for further discussion of compensation as called for in the *Bringing Them Home* report was precluded by Labor as far back as the 2007 election campaign. In an interview two weeks before issuing the apology, Kevin Rudd stated: "We will not be establishing any compensation fund. I said that before the election, I say it again" (cited in Robson 2008).

In addition to lack of compensation, the practical follow-up to the apology has been less than many Australians had hoped, especially the country's Indigenous population. An important policy direction pursued by Paul Keating, the Labor prime minister prior to Kevin Rudd, was reconciliation. The election of a Labor government in 2007 prompted many Australians to conjecture whether or not it was too late for this idea to flourish again. With just two years of evidence to draw on it is difficult to make any final decisions in 2009, but there are some indicators that after 11.5 years of conservative rule in Australia reconciliation will remain on the back burner, at least for the foreseeable future.

Paul Keating initiated the reconciliation discussion at the Commonwealth level in Australia in 1992 during his Redfern speech marking the start of the UN's Year of Indigenous People. "For Keating, reconciliation was about reconciling past atrocities through the recognition of Indigenous rights," especially native title and other recognition of land rights (Howard-Wagner 2008, 5). Looking back, apologizing, making up for destruction in the past, and providing both the symbolic and the financial ways forward were the keys to advancing the process of reconciliation. If Keating had won the election in 1996, it seems likely that reconciliation on that model would have moved forward. However, from 1996 to 2007 reconciliation under John Howard meant mainstreaming Aboriginal services and "uniting the nation" (Howard-Wagner 2008, 9). Apologies, native title to land, and compensation were all seen as "special rights" that discriminated against Australia's non-Indigenous people and thus were off the table.

Since taking office, Kevin Rudd's government seems to be trying to bridge the gap between these two disparate points of view. By apologizing for the Stolen Generations at the opening of Parliament in February 2008, he turned back the clock to 1992, when Keating acknowledged white Australia's history of dispossessing Aboriginal people of their land, removing their children, and introducing alcohol, petrol, and drugs (Keating 2009 [1992]). At the same time, by refusing compensation in favor of "put[ting] more funds into solving the serious problems of Aboriginal disadvantge [sic]" (Robson 2008), Rudd in 2008 sounded a lot like John Howard in 1996, when he said: "We want higher living standards and greater economic independence for Aboriginal and Torres Strait Islander people. We will work with states and territories and with ATSIC to achieve practical outcomes designed to overcome the undoubted social and economic disadvantage of our indigenous people" (cited in Howard-Wagner 2008, 6).

In his 2008 apology Rudd promised the Australian people that each year he was in government he would present a report card on the progress made toward solving Aboriginal disadvantages in housing, education, health, and life expectancy. As with Howard, there was no mention of continuing to address past wrongs in the area of Aboriginal culture, identity, or land rights, and little work has been done in these areas at the Commonwealth level. In fact, some Aboriginal groups in the Northern Territory are very angry with the government for threatening "to withdraw the funding for teaching [the local Aboriginal] language and culture" in schools (cited in ABC Indigenous 2009). Even the fact that 2009 was the UN's International Year of Reconciliation went relatively unmentioned in the places where real government power is held in Canberra and the state and territory capitals.

Judging the Rudd government's view of reconciliation on its own criteria does not create a better picture of the current process than using Keating's criteria, and the problems at the end of 2009 appear to be as intractable as they were prior to the apology. In his February 2009 first report card on how the government's "closing the gap" policies were doing 12 months on, Rudd mentioned some small progress, such as the commitment of an additional AU$58.3 million for fighting eye disease for the 20,000 Indigenous children who suffer from trachoma (*National Indigenous Times* 2009). He also mentioned that the government "had built houses, carried on the Howard government's intervention in the Northern Territory, supported the Australian Employment Covenant led by mining magnate Andrew Forrest, and invested billions more in health initiatives" (*National Indigenous Times* 2009).

These rather vague benchmarks were applauded by some government supporters but drew stark criticism from the opposition, Greens, and many Indigenous groups and individuals. For example, a Sydney Indigenous group, Stop the Intervention Collective in Sydney (STICS), "condemned" Rudd's report for being nothing but "deceit and hypocrisy" (Gibson 2009). For example, while Rudd stated that the government had built 80 new houses for Indigenous Australians, STICS claimed that these were built not for Indigenous families but for government officials (Gibson 2009). The sharpest criticism, however, was of the government's continuation of the Howard-era Northern Territory Intervention, especially the suspension of the Racial Discrimination Act (RDA), until at least spring 2010. Suspending the RDA allows racially discriminatory government policies, such as income quarantine, to continue for at least another year.

If reconciliation includes such concepts as "respect and toler-ance . . . truth and justice," as per the UN document announcing the International Year of Reconciliation (UN General Assembly 2006), the "forcible acquisition of Aboriginal Land under the NT Intervention and the ongoing suspension of the Racial Discrimination Act" (cited in Gibson 2009) hardly seem to fit the criteria. On the brief evidence so far, reconciliation between Indigenous Australians and the federal government does not seem to have a bright future.

A second priority of the Keating government that was largely aban-doned by Howard was looking toward making Australia a republic with a local head of state to replace the constitutional monarchy nominally headed by the British monarch. Howard allowed the referendum on the issue to go through in 1999, but it was defeated by 54.4 percent, largely because Australians wanted an elected head of state rather than one chosen by the prime minister or Parliament. Many Australians believed that the election of a known republican such as Kevin Rudd would mean some movement toward constitutional change.

In July 2007 four months before being elected prime minister, Kevin Rudd used the campaign trail to promise that if Labor were elected, a second referendum on the republic issue would be held (News.com. au 2007). At the same time, he stated that he did not think it was "a 'first order concern'" (News.com.au 2007) for most Australians and thus could not put a time frame on when it would be raised. What he did indicate was that he thought "the time will come before too much longer when we do have an Australian as our head of state" (News. com.au 2007). In March 2009 while visiting Queen Elizabeth II in London, Rudd's comments on the topic had not changed significantly since his campaign trail interpretation of the situation 20 months ear-lier. In response to reporters' questions, he stated, "Is it (the republic) a top priority issue? No" (News.com.au 2009), and "Her Majesty is well loved in Australia and Australia will become a republic and we'll have a referendum in due season" (News.com.au 2009). When that "due season" will arrive, however, remains to be seen.

Two indications that the formation of a republic remains at least several years in the future emerged in April 2009. The first was a state-ment by the Australian governor-general, Quentin Bryce, who on April 3 agreed with Kevin Rudd that Australia would eventually become a republic. Nevertheless, in her statement she used the phrase a "devel-opment of our democracy in future *decades*" (italics added) (cited by Women for an Australian Republic 2009), rather than future months or years. A second indication that the republic remains a distant priority emerged on April 22, the day the government announced actions it would take on nine of the recommendations made at the Australia 2020 Summit in 2008; action toward creating a republic was not on the list. In response to questioning about the issue, a government spokesperson would only say that "it is 'committed to constitutional reform'" (cited by Women for an Australian Republic 2009).

Despite this relative inaction by the government, other actors in Australian politics have begun to move ahead on the issue. In November 2008 Bob Brown, senator from Tasmania and leader of the Green Party, introduced a bill in the Senate, Plebiscite for an Australian Republic Bill 2008, calling for a vote on whether or not Australia should change the Constitution. The issue that confused the 1999 referendum, the election or selection of the head of state, was not mentioned in the bill, as this vote was designed to ascertain whether or not Australians desired a republic at all. The question as stated by the bill is "Do you support Australia becoming a republic?" (Brown 2008, 6). The bill was sent to committee two days after being read in the Senate and was returned by the Senate Finance and Public Administration Committee on June 15, 2009. Rather than address the plebiscite issue directly, the committee recommended that the government establish "an ongoing public awareness campaign on Australia's constitutional system" and "that if any further process advocating constitutional change is undertaken, including that of a republic, it seek to encourage Australians to engage meaningfully in the debate" (Senate Finance and Public Administration Legislation Committee 2009).

Another policy area that Labor used in their 2007 election campaign was ending the Howard-era "Pacific Solution" for asylum seekers who arrive by boat at Australia's offshore islands. As promised, the last 21 refugees held in an Australian detention center on Nauru, all Sri Lankan men fleeing civil war in their country, were removed from detention in the first few months of 2008. However, some aspects of the Pacific Solution have continued, much to the consternation of Australians concerned with their country's human rights record. For example, asylum seekers who attempt to reach Australia by sea are still housed and processed on an offshore island rather than on the Australian mainland. In addition, depending on where they are apprehended, many are still treated according to Howard-era laws that excised some offshore islands from the country's regular migration rules.

Gay and lesbian Australians have also had a somewhat mixed first term under Kevin Rudd's Labor government. In November 2008 a bipartisan effort to end discrimination passed through the Parliament providing same-sex couples with most of the federal rights granted to heterosexual couples. Included among the changes were pension and retirement benefits, veterans' entitlements, hospital visitation rights, and inheritance of pension funds, which had previously been denied same-sex partners. While lesbian and gay rights groups were very happy with the changes, most also pointed out the one glaring exception: Same-sex marriage was not included and at the time the bill passed, "Attorney-General Robert McClelland reaffirmed that same-sex marriage was not on the agenda" (Dennett 2008).

Many women's groups were elated when John Howard was finally defeated in November 2007, and the Rudd government has worked hard to maintain this key constituency. His choice of Julia Gillard as his deputy prime minister and minister for workplace relations pleased many, as did his appointment of Australia's first female governor-general, Quentin Bryce. The March 2009 overturn of a Howard-era law that, as did the Mexico City Policy in the United States under Republican presidents, withheld Australian foreign aid from agencies that provided abortions and some forms of contraception to the developing world, also received praise from women's organizations. The government's proposal for a new parental leave bill in May 2009, the first of its kind in the country, and AU$41.5 million toward fighting violence against women were also seen as positive steps toward attaining gender equality.

Of course, no government is able to please even its key supporters all the time, and this is true of the Rudd government, as well. For example, very early in the Rudd administration, an important policy conference, the Australia 2020 Summit, was held in which 1,000 people were chosen from around the country to discuss policy options in 10 different categories, including security, education, the arts, and climate change. Leading Australians were chosen to chair each of the 10 panels, and when the final announcements were made, only one of those 10 people was female: The actress Cate Blanchett was to chair the panel on the arts. Single mothers also lost out in the 2009 budget, which raised pensions for all other categories of recipients to acknowledge sharp rises in the cost of living during the global economic downturn.

A second policy area in which the government has almost entirely made good on its election promises is to rid Australia of Howard's industrial relations laws, WorkChoices. This took quite a bit longer than some had hoped, in part because the coalition retained a hold on the Senate until July 1, 2008, and in part because of the complex nature of undoing the multifaceted array of legislation covered by WorkChoices. Nonetheless, on March 20, 2009, Deputy Prime Minister

QUENTIN BRYCE

Quentin Bryce, Australia's 25th governor-general since federation in 1901, was raised in rural Queensland in the 1940s and 1950s, a time and place in which girls were largely expected to marry and dedicate their time to family life. Bryce defied her society's expectations by graduating from the University of Queensland in 1962 with a B.A. She went on to marry in 1964, and, while pregnant with her first child in 1965, finish her law degree at the same university. Immediately upon graduation, she became just the seventh woman to be admitted to the bar in her home state. Bryce spent the next three years living in London with her young family and then was the first woman to be offered a teaching position in the law school at her alma mater; she took the position and held it from 1968 through 1983.

Although she did not leave the University of Queensland until 1983, five years earlier Bryce began the work that was to make her a nationally prominent figure by serving on Prime Minister Malcolm Fraser's National Women's Advisory Council. By the mid-1980s Bryce moved permanently from teaching to government service, starting with an appointment as the director of the Queensland Women's Information Service. She remained in that position until 1987, when she became the director of the Human Rights and Equal Opportunity Commission in Queensland. From 1988 to 1993 Bryce was the federal sex discrimination commissioner. Moving from gender equality to children's welfare issues, from 1993 to 1996 Bryce helped found and served as CEO of the National Childcare Accreditation Council.

In 2003 Bryce was nominated by Premier Peter Beattie to serve as governor, the queen's representative in Queensland. After nearly five years of success in the role, Beattie's successor, Anna Bligh, had hoped to keep Bryce on in her position. In April 2008, however, Bryce was nominated by Prime Minister Kevin Rudd for governor-general and she was sworn in on July 29. Many hope she is to be Australia's last governor-general and is even allowed to move into the role of president with the transition to a republic sometime in the future.

and Minister for Workplace Affairs Julia Gillard announced that Labor's own Fair Work Bill had finally passed through the Senate, and thus WorkChoices was officially dead and buried. Labor's new set of workplace laws are based on very different principles from the individualism and employer-centric emphasis of WorkChoices; they guarantee the right to collective representation and bargaining, minimum wage, and at least 10 other benefits such as overtime pay, holidays, and the right to ask for a flexible schedule (Gillard 2008).

Outside the Government Sphere

From December 2007 through late 2009 the Labor government acted to change some of the more draconian of the Howard-era policies on Aboriginal reconciliation, industrial relations, and refugees; women, lesbians, and gay men have largely benefited, as have those who choose to be represented by a union. At the same time, Australians have experienced a number of important events since 2007 that are far from the

VEGEMITE

Vegemite was invented in 1922 by the Fred Walker Cheese Company. Seeking a way to utilize the nutritious but unpalatable spent yeast left over after the brewing of beer—which contains high amounts of riboflavin, niacin, folate, and thiamine—Walker called upon his chemists to create a tasty food product. Dr. Cyril Callister concocted the best version, which combined the processed yeast concentrate with liquid onion, celery seed, salt, and a small amount of caramel; the new product hit shelves in 1923 (Kraft Foods Australia 2009). For 86 years Callister's recipe was the only form of Vegemite available, but in 2009 Kraft Foods announced that a more spreadable form of Vegemite was being made available, after 300,000 Australians answered questions about what they liked, loved, and disliked about the iconic product.

Kraft made the change with an important nod to the food's long history. In 1923 Walker offered a large monetary prize for naming the new food; Kraft did the same in 2009. In 2009, however, the process did not go nearly as smoothly as it had in the 1920s. From amongst about 50,000 submissions, Kraft's marketing team chose iSnack 2.0 as the name for their new product, a combination of Vegemite and cream cheese. In response tens of thousands of Australians complained about the gimmicky name in such diverse forums as letters to the editors of all major newspapers and even Facebook pages. Almost immediately Kraft moved to save their new product, conducted a telephone poll of about 30,000 Australians, and iSnack 2.0 became Vegemite Cheesybite practically overnight. The alacrity with which control of any government. In February 2009 bushfires in Victoria killed 173 people and injured more than 500 others in Australia's worst fire emergency in history. Three months later Queensland's seven-year drought was declared officially over when the state received a year's worth of rain in just two days. The rainfall would have filled the equivalent of half of Sydney Harbour, and flooding caused damage throughout the state (Marriner and Macey 2009). In the same month, the Tasmanian devil, the world's largest surviving carnivorous marsupial, was listed as an endangered species due to a facial cancer that has killed about 70 percent of the species since 1996 (Nguyen 2009).

The global economic downturn also began to affect Australia's previously booming economy when prices in such primary industries as

---

Kraft responded indicated to many Australians that the entire exercise had been a publicity stunt to put the product on the news; Kraft's spokespeople deny the charge (Daily Telegraph 2009).

In 1923 when Vegemite failed on the market, Walker persevered with his product and its name by offering free Vegemite and coupons with his other food products; he even gave away several cars in contests meant to lure consumers to Vegemite during the depression. After many years of struggle and financial loss, he finally had a winner on his hands by the mid-1930s. Word of mouth combined with his outrageous give-aways had finally bolstered sales. By the time Australian soldiers were shipping out to fight in World War II, Vegemite had become so popular it was included in their rations.

The Australian Fred Walker Cheese Company merged with the American food giant Kraft in 1926 and became known as the Kraft Walker Cheese Company. In 1950 the Walker name was dropped entirely to reflect the fact that Kraft had purchased the product and process rights after Walker's death. Despite this change, the only Vegemite factory in the world remains in Port Melbourne, very near the laboratory in which Dr. Callister invented his concentrated yeast product.

Sources: Kraft Foods Australia. "Vegemite Discovery." 2009. Available online. URL: http://www.vegemite.com.au.vegemite/page?siteid=vegemite-prd&locale=auen1&PagecRef=670. Accessed May 21, 2009; Daily Telegraph, The. "Kraft Backflips on Vegemite Name iSnack 2.0" September 30, 2009. Available online. URL: http://www.dailytelegraph.com.au/news/kraft-backflips-on-vegemite-name-isnack20/story-e6freuy9-1225781188006. Accessed October 25, 2009.

iron, coal, and wool dropped in the wake of diminished worldwide demand. On April 20, 2009, Prime Minister Rudd uttered the words *recession* and *inevitable* in the same breath during a speech in Adelaide, South Australia, and thus brought the crisis home. Nonetheless, Australia did not suffer from the downturn as much as the United States or the United Kingdom, in part because banks remain more regulated in Australia than in these other countries and the cost of housing has been maintained at an artificially high level with the implementation of larger first-time home buyers' grants. Despite the usual pattern, the economic slump, from which Australia recovered by late 2009, did not affect Rudd's popularity as the preferred prime minister; in early April 2009 he retained a 65 percent preference rate over his main rival, the Liberal Malcolm Turnbull, whose rate was just 18 percent (*Sydney Morning Herald* 2009a). Nonetheless, by January 2010 a change in Liberal leadership to Tony Abbott had begun to reverse the trend, with Rudd's preference rate down to 57 percent and Abbott's up to 25 percent (ABC News 2010).

Conclusion

Depending on your vantage point, Australian history can be seen as very long or relatively short. A few rural communities of Aboriginal people have kept alive the world's oldest continuing culture for some 60,000 years, living off the driest and most inhospitable continent on Earth, other than Antarctica. The formation of a modern nation-state by migrants to this continent, however, did not take place until the start of the 20th century. In addition, until the mid-20th century, most, although certainly not all, of the migrant population in Australia were from Britain or Ireland, spoke English, and at least nominally practiced some form of Christian faith. Since the arrival of Calwell's migrants starting in the late 1940s, the migrant community in Australia has diversified greatly, with the addition of northern and then southern and eastern Europeans in the 1950s and 1960s, then Asians and Middle Easterners starting in the 1970s, and small populations of Africans today.

This mix of Indigenous and migrant, as well as old and new migrants, has meant that the formation of an Australian national identity has been complex and continual. The first migrants defined themselves in opposition to the continent's Aboriginal population, with the lasting ramification that today reconciliation between Aboriginal and migrant societies is fraught with difficulties stemming from institutional racism, cultural misunderstanding, and endemic poverty. With the addition of great migrant diversity in the latter half of the 20th century, the identity problem was compounded. The first decades of this history saw assimilation as the order of the day; identity issues were believed best approached by subsuming the new entirely into the old migrant patterns. When this failed to lead to a cohesive, unified national community, multiculturalism and integration replaced assimilation as the underlying ideology. Again, certain segments of the national community rejected the status quo and began searching for new concepts to take Australia into the 21st century.

Despite the lack of consensus on the nature of Australianness, Australians will start the second decade of the 21st century with much to recommend their society. Parliamentary democracy provides a smooth and stable transition between governing parties every few years. The economy in 2007 provided a healthy GDP per capita of AU$37,564, which is somewhat more equally distributed than in the United States (OECD 2009). Life expectancy is one of the highest in the world, at 81.4 years (UNDP 2009). Potential challenges to the continuation of these trends, however, do exist. Global warming and drought are probably the two most serious challenges that Australians now face. Maintaining the country's first-world standard of living on the back of a third-world-style primary exporting economy may also prove difficult if new caches of iron, coal, and other minerals are not discovered. And, of course, the complex and continual project of defining Australian identity will continue unabated.

Appendix 1

Basic Facts About Australia

Official Name
Long form: Commonwealth of Australia
Short form: Australia

Government
Australia is a constitutional monarchy with the British monarch serving as the titular head of state. The monarch's representative in Australia is the governor-general, who is nominated by the prime minister and accepted by the monarch, usually for a term of five years. The governor-general is advised by an executive council, made up of all current government ministers and parliamentary secretaries.

Actual governance in Australia is undertaken by the party or coalition of parties with the majority of seats in the 150-seat House of Representatives. The leader of this party or coalition is the head of government, or prime minister. The prime minister works with his or her cabinet, consisting of the most senior members of government, and ministers, or those in the government responsible for policy areas such as immigration, health, and workplace relations. Prime ministers must call elections for the House at least every three years but can call them more frequently in special circumstances, such as when an opposition-dominated Senate blocks the government's access to funds to run the country, called blocking supply.

In addition to the House of Representatives, Australia has a 76-person parliamentary house of review, or Senate. While members of the House of Representatives are elected within electorates of about 86,000 people each, which means that states with larger populations send more people to the House, every state, regardless of population, sends 12 members to the Senate; the territories each send two. Senators are elected for a term of six years and every three years, half the Senate must run for reelection.

The Commonwealth of Australia was formed in 1901 when six separate British colonies, Tasmania, Victoria, New South Wales, Queensland, South Australia, and Western Australia, federated under a single constitution. Because of this history, each of these states also has a governor who serves as the British monarch's representative in the state, while an elected premier serves as the head of each state parliamentary government. Two federal territories, the Northern Territory and Australian Capital Territory, have similar parliamentary structures but are governed by chief ministers rather than premiers; they also lack a governor and their laws can be overruled by the Commonwealth government.

Australian shires, cities, and towns have a system of local governance in which elected councils and lord mayors make decisions about local issues, such as zoning, licensing, infrastructure development, and some areas of social welfare.

Australia's democracy is unique in the English-speaking world in its requirement that all citizens, with a few exceptions such as those convicted of treason or without the ability to understand their rights and responsibilities, must both register to vote and participate in all local, state, and federal elections, including referenda. Not doing so incurs a fine; thus most elections have a participation rate of at least 95 percent.

Political Divisions

Capital
Canberra

States and territories, capital cities, areas, and populations
Australian Capital Territory, Canberra: 907.88 square miles (2,351.4 km²) with 347,800 people

New South Wales, Sydney: 309,389.61 square miles (801,315.4 km²) with 7,041,400 people

Northern Territory, Darwin: 522,078.11 square miles (1,352,176.1 km²) with 221,700 people

Queensland, Brisbane: 669,568.67 square miles (1,734,174.9 km²) with 4,349,500 people

South Australia, Adelaide: 380,441.24 square miles (985,338.3 km²) with 1,612,000 people

Tasmania, Hobart: 26,221.82 square miles (67,914.2 km²) with 500,300 people

Victoria, Melbourne: 87,805.65 square miles (227,415.6 km²) with 5,364,800 people

Western Australia, Perth: 977,442.21 square miles (2,531,563.7 km²) with 2,204,000 people

Geography

Area

Australia is the only continent-sized country and is located in an area of about 3 million square miles (more than 7.6 million sq. km). In addition to the mainland, Australia controls 8,223 other islands, from the large island state of Tasmania to tiny specks of land in the Torres Strait and the Indian and Pacific Oceans.

Boundaries

Australia, as the national anthem states, is girt by sea: the Pacific Ocean to the east, the Indian Ocean to the west, the Southern Ocean to the south, and the Arafura Sea to the north. Its nearest neighbor is Papua New Guinea to the north, located about 124 miles (200 km) away at the two countries' closest points.

Topography

Australia is one of the oldest landmasses on Earth and as such has no significantly high mountain ranges. The Great Dividing Range, which runs from Australia's top end in the Cape York Peninsula all the way south to the Grampians in Victoria, with an eastern spur that reemerges from Bass Strait to form the highlands of Tasmania, is low by global standards. At 7,310 feet (2,228 m) the highest mainland peak, Mount Kosciuszko, is not even half the height of Mont Blanc, Europe's highest peak. In the west, the Western Plateau rises even less significantly, to about 984 feet (300 m), while the vast central region of the continent is a lowland where millions of years ago ancient seas flourished; the lowest point is at Lake Eyre, at 52.5 feet (16 m) below sea level.

Climate

Australia's climate is largely warm and very dry, though western and central Tasmania and the alpine region of Victoria and New South Wales can be cold at any time of year; the southern Victorian coast ranges from cold and damp in winter to hot and dry in summer. North of the tropic of Capricorn the climate is generally warm, with humid and wet periods throughout the year. The hot, dry central desert regions see very little rainfall at any time of year and have average temperatures between 90°F and 100°F (the high 30s°C). The oscillation between El Niño and La Niña wind patterns in the Pacific creates years of drought and years of above-average rainfall throughout the continent. The highest recorded temperature in the country of 128°F (53.1°C) was at Cloncurry, Queensland, in 1889, while the lowest of -9°F (-23°C) was at Charlotte Pass, New South Wales, in 1994.

Demographics

Population

Australia has a relatively small population, estimated on January 22, 2010, to be 22,023,101. Population density is also very low at about 7.5 people per square mile (2.6 people per sq. km). About 85 percent of the population live in a belt of territory running from Adelaide and Tasmania in the south; through all of Victoria, the Australian Capital Territory, and New South Wales; and up to Brisbane in the northeast, representing less than a quarter of the total area of the country.

Urban versus Rural

Australia is a largely urban country with 88 percent of the population living in cities; nearly three quarters of inhabitants live in the capital cities alone.

Capital Cities

Sydney is the country's largest city, with about 4.2 million people. In 2009 Melbourne was the country's fastest-growing city, adding about 150,000 people in just two years, with a projected population of 4 million by the end of 2009. The other capital cities are considerably smaller. In June 2008 Brisbane was estimated at 1.95 million, Perth at 1.6 million, Adelaide at 1.17 million, Canberra at 345,000, Hobart 209,000, and Darwin at 120,000. Outside these capital cities, only Newcastle, New South Wales, and the Gold Coast, Queensland, have populations of more than half a million.

Languages

English is the national language in Australia. However, as a result of the country's large proportion of migrants, with 24 percent of the population born overseas and another 26 percent with at least one overseas-born parent, at least 200 languages and dialects are spoken in the country's 8.1 million households, representing about 16 percent of the population. Italian, Greek, Arabic, Cantonese, Mandarin, and Vietnamese are the most commonly spoken of the non-English languages.

Religions

Six percent of the population adheres to a wide variety of non-Christian faiths, including Islam, Buddhism, and Judaism, and another 30 percent professes no faith at all. Of the Christian faiths, the largest percentage are Roman Catholic, at 26 percent; 19 percent are Anglican; and 19 percent are of other Christian faiths such as Greek and Russian Orthodox, Uniting, and Baptist.

Economy

Gross Domestic Product

In 2009 Australia's GDP was estimated at US$819 billion (PPP), or $38,500 per person. During the global financial crisis in 2008–09, Australia avoided the sharp downturn experienced in many other Western democracies, largely because of exports of primary goods such as agricultural products, coal, and other minerals. As of October 2009, the country had not experienced a formal recession, defined as two successive quarters of declining GDP, in more than 17 years, and had already raised interest rates in response to strong economic growth in the previous months.

Currency

Since 1983 the Australian dollar has been a floating currency that ranges in value from near-parity with the U.S. dollar to an all-time low in 1999 of just US$0.49.

Agricultural Products

Major agricultural products are wheat, barley, sugarcane, cotton, rice, fruit, beef and dairy, wool, lamb and mutton, poultry, and wine.

Minerals

Australia is a mineral-rich country containing 50 percent of the world's titanium, 40 percent of its bauxite, 33 percent of its diamonds, 22 percent of its uranium, 20 percent of its zinc-lead, 12.5 percent of its iron ore, and 95 percent of its opal. Australia is also among the world's leading sources of copper, nickel, silver, and gold.

Industrial Products

The mining, agricultural, and education industries dominate the Australian economy on the back of high exports in all three areas.

Trade

Australia's economy is largely dependent upon external trade, with a slight imbalance of payments favoring imports. In 2008 exports of coal, iron, gold, meat, wool, bauxite, wheat, and timber products contributed about US$178.9 billion to the economy; another important export is education, with a large influx of international students contributing US$13.7 billion to the economy. In the same year imports of machinery, computers, telecommunication equipment, oil, petroleum products, and manufactured goods cost the country about US$187.2 billion. Despite a bilateral trade agreement with the United States that took effect in 2005, Australia's largest trade partners are mainly in Asia. Exports to Japan, China, South Korea, and India together constituted 46.6 percent of all exports, while imports from China, Japan, Singapore, and Thailand constituted 35 percent of all imports.

APPENDIX 2

CHRONOLOGY

B.C.E.

ca. 68,000–56,000	Possible date of some archaeological sites in far northern Arnhem Land
ca. 45,000	Date used by conservative prehistorians and archaeologists as the founding of Aboriginal culture in Australia. Some experts also give this period as the one in which Australia's megafauna became extinct.
ca. 20,000	Aboriginal societies are now evident in every corner of Australia.
ca. 17,000	The end of the Last Glacial Maximal produces a distinct change in Aboriginal prehistoric culture, with more widespread use of tools, increased populations, and greater exploitation of natural resources.
ca. 11,000	Rising sea levels as the last ice age ends; separation of Tasmania from the mainland
ca. 10,000	Australia and New Guinea are separated by rising sea levels, creating the Torres Straits Islands.
ca. 5000	The dingo arrives from Asia and as a result Australia sees more ecological changes.

C.E.

15th century	Chinese traders from Java, Timor, and elsewhere in the Indonesian archipelago probably land in northern Australia.
1606	The Dutch explorer Willem Janszoon is the first European to land in Australia.

The Spanish explorer Luis Váez de Torres sails through the passage between Australia and New Guinea that now bears his name.

1622   The British ship the *Tryall* is wrecked off the coast of Western Australia at the Tryall Rocks.

1642   Abel Tasman discovers the island he calls Van Diemen's Land (Tasmania).

1644   Tasman charts about three quarters of Australia's coast.

1687   The French captain Abraham Duquesne-Guitton captains the first French ship to enter Australian waters.

1688   The British pirate William Dampier sails to New Holland (Western Australia) and lands to make repairs to the captured ship, the *Cygnet*.

ca. 1720   Macassan trepang hunters arrive in Australia.

1770   Captain Cook charts Australia's east coast, lands at Botany Bay, and takes possession of Australia for Great Britain at Possession Island; he names the new British colony *New South Wales.*

1772   The French captain François de Saint-Allouarn sails along Australia's west coast, lands at Dirk Hartog Island, and claims western New Holland for France.

The French captain Marc-Joseph Marion Dufresne lands in Tasmania, and his sailors kill an Aboriginal man, the first lethal black-white violence on the island.

1776   The revolution in the United States forces Britain to seek new territory for a penal colony; Joseph Banks, who had sailed with Cook, recommends Botany Bay.

1786   King George III decides on Botany Bay as his country's new penal colony.

1788   The First Fleet arrives under Governor Arthur Phillip and establishes a settlement at Port Jackson, New South Wales.

1790   The New South Wales colonists nearly starve to death when rations from England are delayed. Phillip begins attracting free settlers to New

	South Wales and granting freed convicts land to help the new colony survive.
1792	Arthur Phillip is replaced at Port Jackson by Major Francis Grose.
1803	Matthew Flinders circumnavigates Australia. Convicts and soldiers sent by the New South Wales governor, captain Philip King, begin settling the south coast of Van Diemen's Land (Tasmania) at the Derwent River.
1804	The settlement on the Derwent River is named *Hobart Town*. Whites in Van Diemen's Land are authorized to shoot Aboriginal people on sight.
1806	Governor King is replaced by William Bligh, who in 1808 experiences the second mutiny of his career when the officers at the Sydney Cove colony rise up against him.
1810	Lachlan Macquarie takes over as governor of the New South Wales colony. The first Aboriginal missions are established to "civilize" the Indigenous people and train them in domestic and other forms of labor.
1819	Macquarie seconds Matthew Flinders's suggestion that the entire continent be named *Australia*.
1821	The age of Macquarie ends, largely because of his emancipist ideals; he is replaced by Thomas Brisbane as governor of New South Wales.
1823	The British Parliament changes the status of New South Wales from penitentiary to a Crown colony.
1824	White settlers massacre more than 100 Aboriginal people at Bathurst, New South Wales, after the murder of seven whites; Governor Brisbane declares martial law, which allows for almost indiscriminate slaughter of Aboriginal people.
1825	Van Diemen's Land becomes a separate British Crown colony under George Arthur.
1829	The former territory of New Holland is taken by the British and renamed *Western Australia*. Charles Sturt "discovers" and "names" the Darling River.

1830	Establishment of both Port Arthur, the recidivist penal colony in Van Diemen's Land, and the Black Line in that colony.
	Sturt "discovers" and "names" the Murray River.
1834	Governor Stirling of Western Australia leads the police and others in committing atrocities at the Pinjarra massacre; at least 30 members of the Bindjareb Bilyidar Nyungars are killed in what is also known as the battle of Pinjarra.
1835	John Batman negotiates two treaties with Aboriginal peoples in Port Phillip, the area of contemporary Melbourne. These treaties are later deemed illegal by the colonial authority and the rental agreements disallowed.
1836	South Australia is founded as a free province rather than a penal colony.
	Captain William Lonsdale is appointed administrator in the Port Phillip area.
1837	The British Parliament recommends the creation of a protector of Aborigines position for Australia in light of the actions of whites against the native peoples, especially in the Bathurst or Wiradjuri wars.
	The Roman Catholic Church begins its mission work among Aboriginal people.
1838	Myall Creek massacre of 28 Aboriginal people by whites; seven of the murderers are convicted and hanged for their crime.
	Violent raids against Aboriginal groups throughout New South Wales, especially the Namoi, Gwydir, and Big Rivers regions.
1839	Robert Hoddle draws up the plans for Melbourne.
1840	Edward Eyre explores central Australia in the hope of finding suitable grazing land.
	Transportation of convicts to New South Wales is discontinued.
	Long Lagoon massacre of at least 100 Aboriginal people who may have been poisoned with strychnine.

	Start of a three-year depression caused by land speculation and drought
1841	"Assignment" of convicts as laborers for free settler ends in Van Diemen's Land.
	Rufus River massacre in South Australia of at least 30 Aboriginal people in retaliation for sheep plundering
1843	Invention of a mechanized reaping machine reduces the need for convict labor at the same time that the overinflated, extractive economy collapses in conjunction with a six-year economic depression in the United States.
1844	Charles Sturt's last inland exploration takes him into the Simpson Desert and, as does Eyre's, fails to find either an inland sea or good pastureland.
1845	Copper is discovered at Burra, north of Adelaide in South Australia, which quickly becomes the largest mine in Australia.
1846	Transportation of convicts to New South Wales is reinstated but without the "assignment" system, thus leading to significant antitransportation sentiment in the colony.
1848	Introduction of dual religious and secular education systems in New South Wales and Victoria, which leads to significant quarreling over limited government funds; South Australia avoids this conflict by introducing solely secular schooling from the start.
	New South Wales police raid and kill Aboriginal people in Queensland to open up new lands for settlement.
	Australia's first non-English publication is the Adelaide-based German paper *Die Deutsche Post für die Australischen Kolonien*.
1849	An antitransportation rally of 4,000–5,000 people turns out at Circular Quay, Sydney, to meet the transportation ship the *Hashemy*.
	An antitransportation league is formed in Van Diemen's Land.

The colonies' first Chinese migrants arrive from southern China.

1850 All colonies have their own antitransportation league, except Western Australia.

Western Australia begins accepting convicts from Britain.

1851 The Australian Colonies Government Act separates Port Phillip (Victoria) from New South Wales.

The start of the New South Wales and Victorian gold rushes

1853 The last convicts transported to Van Diemen's Land arrive from Britain.

1854 The Eureka Stockade miners' rebellion in Ballarat, Victoria.

1855 Van Diemen's Land is renamed *Tasmania* after the first European to have landed there.

Constitutions drafted by legislative councils in 1852 in New South Wales, Victoria, South Australia, and Tasmania are ratified by the British Parliament.

Large numbers of Chinese miners arrive to seek their fortunes in the Victorian goldfields.

Victoria imposes a £10 poll tax on Chinese arriving in the state.

1856 The first sitting of Parliament in Melbourne.

Sea travel between London and Australia is reduced to 65 days by new shipping technology.

1857 The Buckland riot pits white miners against Chinese.

Aboriginal people attack whites at Dawson River, Queensland. Violent reprisals by both police and settlers result.

1858 Melbourne, Sydney, and Adelaide are connected by telegraphic wires.

The non-Aboriginal population of Australia reaches one million people.

1859 In the north Queensland separates from New South Wales and becomes its own colony.

	Thomas Austin introduces rabbits to Australia in Geelong, about one hour from Melbourne.
1860	Indian, Pashtun, and other Muslim cameleers ("Afghans") arrive to explore the continent's interior with Burke and Wills.
	"Blackbirding" transports kidnapped Pacific Islanders to Queensland to work in the sugarcane fields.
1861	The Emerald, Queensland, massacre of 170 Aboriginal people in retaliation for the murder of 19 settlers
1862	Victoria and New South Wales allow any citizen, except children and married women, to purchase land; Queensland follows suit in 1869, South Australia a year later.
1863	The Northern Territory is created as a dependent territory, to be governed from Adelaide in South Australia.
	The inhabitants of the Torres Strait Islands are first affected by white diseases and policies.
1867	Henry Lawson is born at the Grenfell gold fields in New South Wales.
	The first Australian cricket team to tour overseas is an all-Aboriginal team that plays 47 matches in England; after each match they are required to display their talents with boomerangs and spears.
1868	The last convicts arrive in Western Australia from Britain.
	Aboriginal people resist arrest in the Kimberley region and 150 are murdered.
1869	Victoria establishes Australia's first Board for the Protection of Aborigines. Other colonies follow in 1883 (New South Wales), 1897 (Queensland), 1905 (Western Australia), and 1911 (South Australia).
1877	Settlers in far north Queensland's Daintree River area are murdered by Aboriginal people.
1880	The cultural icon Edward "Ned" Kelly is captured at Glenrowan, Victoria; he is later hanged in Melbourne.

1882	Australia's cricketers defeat England for the first time in test cricket, the long, five-by-five-day version of the game. This is the start of an almost yearly event called the Ashes series.
	The McKinlay River massacre, after which the white murderers are exonerated by the Northern Territory's official inquiry
1888	"The White Australia Policy" first appears in print in the Brisbane newspaper the *Boomerang*.
	Australia's first mosque is built in Adelaide by "Afghan" cameleers.
1889	The Australian Women's Suffrage Society is formed.
1891	The "Monster Petition" containing signatures from more than 30,000 women, about 10 percent of the state's total number, is presented to the Victoria state parliament to support the claim that Victorian women want the vote.
1892	Australia's first French newspaper, *Le Courier Australien*, begins publication; today it is the oldest continuously published non-English paper in the country.
1894	South Australia is the first Australian colony to grant women the right to vote and stand for election.
1895	"Banjo" Paterson writes "Waltzing Matilda."
1897	Queensland effectively bans all Aboriginal people from towns and cities, confining them to reserves and missions.
1897	Australia's first Orthodox church is built in Sydney by Greek and Lebanese migrants.
1898	Western Australia grants women the right to vote.
1900	Queen Victoria signs the act creating the Commonwealth of Australia.
	The Stolen Generations commence with a change in government policy concerning Aboriginal children.
1901	Federation
	Sir Edmund Barton is elected the new country's first prime minister.

	The Immigration Restriction Act restricts immigration to whites and formalizes the White Australia policy.
1902	Aboriginal people in New South Wales and South Australia lose the right to vote with the enactment of the Commonwealth Franchise Act; white women gain that right at the federal level.
	The British execute Australian Harry "Breaker" Morant in South Africa.
1903	Alfred Deakin replaces the retiring Edmund Barton as prime minister; Barton moves to the newly established Australian High Court.
1904	The Lawn Tennis Association is established in Melbourne, helping to establish the city as the sporting capital of Australia.
1905	Women in Queensland gain the right to vote.
1906	South Australia puts an end to the Macassan trepang trade in the Northern Territory.
	In Melbourne the Tait Brothers film company premieres its film, *The Story of the Kelly Gang,* the first of five films produced in the past century chronicling the life of the bushranger hero and possibly the world's first full-length feature film.
	Outside Sydney the iconic Bondi Surf Lifesaving Club is established.
1907	In Western Australia a 2,036-mile rabbitproof fence begun in 1902 to protect grazing land is completed.
	The 1907 Exhibition of Women's Work in Melbourne contains 16,000 exhibits of women's work and attracts about a quarter of a million visitors.
1908	Victoria is the last state in the Commonwealth to grant women the right to vote.
	Australia's rugby team defeats England to take gold at London's summer Olympics.
1911	The Australian Capital Territory, home of the new capital, Canberra, is carved out of land formerly held by New South Wales.

	The federal government takes control of the Northern Territory.
1912	Walter Burley Griffin, an architect from Chicago, wins the competition to design Canberra, Australia's new capital city.
	Fanny Durack and Mina Wylie swim for gold and silver, respectively, at the summer Olympic games in Stockholm; Durack sets a number of world records.
1914	With the start of World War I Australia offers to support Britain to the last man and shilling.
	The HMAS *Sydney* destroys the German cruiser *Emden* in the Indian Ocean.
1915	Anzac (Australian and New Zealand Army Corps) troops spend eight months dug into the trenches at Gallipoli, Turkey.
1918	By war's end the Australians have lost 59,342 soldiers.
1918–1920	The Spanish flu kills thousands of Australians at home.
1919	Prime Minister Billy Hughes guarantees that racial equality is not enshrined in international law by obstinately refusing to support the creation of the League of Nations if this Japanese proposal is accepted.
1921	Edith Cowan is elected Australia's first female member of a state parliament in Western Australia's seat of West Perth.
1922	Henry Lawson dies after penning such Australian classics as *Song of Australia* and *The Drover's Wife*.
1924	The Sydney Harbour Bridge is begun; it officially opens eight years later.
	Fred Maynard starts the Australian Aborigine Progressive Association.
1927	Canberra becomes the official national capital.
1928	The Coniston massacre of more than 30 Aboriginal people north of Alice Springs is the last recorded massacre in Australia.
	A waterside workers' strike in Melbourne turns violent after scab labor is brought on-site.

1929	Stanley Bruce is the first Australian prime minister to lose his government and his seat in Parliament at the federal election in October.
1930	Phar Lap wins the Melbourne Cup horse race; he dies in California just two years later.
1931	Sir Isaac Isaacs becomes the first Australian-born governor-general.
	The Statute of Westminster is passed by the British Parliament, formally renouncing any legislative authority in its overseas dominions of Australia, New Zealand, Canada, South Africa, and the Republic of Ireland; Australia ratifies the act in 1942.
	Talking movies introduced to Australian cinemas
1932	Joseph Lyons becomes prime minister as leader of the newly established United Australia Party.
	Prime Minister Joseph Lyons establishes the ABC, the Australian Broadcasting Commission; its successor, the Australian Broadcasting Corporation, is a leader in noncommercial radio and television broadcasting to this day.
1933	Western Australians vote 2 to 1 to secede from the Commonwealth; the British government refuses even to hear their case and the matter goes no further.
	Phar Lap's body goes on display at the National Museum of Victoria in Melbourne, where his remains can be seen to this day.
	As the effects of the depression wear on, assisted passage for British migrants ceases.
	Billy Hughes warns that Britain is no longer in a position to protect Australia by sea.
1934	Melbourne's massive World War I memorial, the Shrine of Remembrance, is dedicated.
	The Sydney Harbour Bridge is opened.
1935	Cane toads are released in Queensland.
1936	Keepers at the Hobart zoo allow the last known thylacine, or Tasmanian tiger, to die of the cold while chained outside.

	The Hume Dam outside Albury, Victoria, opens. Australia becomes responsible for almost half of the land area of Antarctica.
1937	Regular airmail service between Australia and the United States is established.
1938	Immigration numbers are boosted when assisted passage from Britain is reintroduced. Canberra and Washington, D.C., are connected by direct radio-telephone.
1939	Prime Minister Joseph Lyons dies in office. Robert Menzies becomes prime minister for the first of his 18 years in office. Menzies declares that as a consequence of Britain's being at war, Australia is also at war.
1941	The Japanese attack Pearl Harbor, Hawaii. Menzies loses a cabinet election and is replaced by the Country Party leader, Arthur Fadden. Fadden loses his majority in the House of Representatives, allowing the Labor Party leader John Curtin to become prime minister. Prime Minister Curtin's letter of unequivocal alignment with the United States appears in the *Melbourne Herald.* Women's branches of the air force, navy, and army are formed and women are hired as tram conductors in Melbourne for the first time.
1942	Britain loses its Asian colonies to Japan. The Kokoda Trail campaign The Japanese bomb Darwin's harbor and kill 243 people. John Curtin makes the U.S. general Douglas MacArthur head of Australia's defense forces. The Statute of Westminster is ratified in Australia.
1943	John Curtin's Labor Party wins the general election with a wide margin. The first woman federal parliamentarian, Dame Enid Lyons, is elected; she is the widow of the former prime minister, Joseph Lyons. The first woman senator, Dorothy Tangney, is also elected this year.

1944	Reginald Saunders becomes the first Aboriginal soldier to attain the rank of a commissioned officer.
	The Liberal Party of Australia is formed.
1945	John Curtin dies in office.
	The treasurer, Ben Chifley, becomes prime minister.
	Introduction of the welfare state with the inauguration of federal unemployment and sickness benefits
1946	Despite their service during the war, Melbourne bans women taxi drivers.
1947	The immigration minister, Arthur Calwell, begins accepting European displaced persons.
	Workers are granted the 40-hour workweek by the Commonwealth Arbitration Court.
1948	Calwell expels all nonwhite war refugees from Australia; 48 Chinese refugees are deported a year later when the High Court upholds the order.
	The British Long Range Weapons Organisation begins building its rocket range at Woomera, despite Aboriginal protests the previous year.
1949	Robert Menzies is reelected prime minister; he serves until 1966.
	The Australian cricketer Donald Bradman is knighted by King George VI.
	Aboriginal servicemen are granted the right to vote.
	The Snowy Mountains Hydro Electric Authority is established.
1950	Australia sends troops to the Korean War.
	Menzies attempts to ban the Communist Party from operating in Australia, and federal police raid the party's headquarters in Sydney, Melbourne, Hobart, Perth, and Darwin.
1951	Australia signs the ANZUS Treaty with New Zealand and the United States.
	The introduced virus myxomatosis kills 99 percent of the country's rabbit population.

1952	Iron ore is discovered in the Hamersley Range of the Pilbara region, Western Australia.
	Britain tests its first nuclear bomb, the Hurricane, on the Monte Bello Islands, Western Australia.
1953	Britain tests three nuclear bombs at Emu Field, a site near Woomera.
1954	Australia establishes Mawson Base, the southernmost human settlement, on Princess Elizabeth Land, Antarctica.
1955	Australia welcomes its millionth postwar migrant, Barbara Porritt, a 21-year-old bride from Yorkshire, England, who lands with her husband, Dennis, on November 8.
	Edna Everage enters Australian public life with her stage debut.
1956	Melbourne hosts the XVI Summer Olympic Games.
	Victoria and New South Wales see the birth of Australian television.
	Britain begins a series of nuclear tests at Maralinga that last until October 1957.
1957	A competition to design Sydney's opera house is won by Jørn Utzon of Denmark.
	Drought in Australia's wheat belt in the west leads to the need to import wheat from Canada.
1958	Lake Eucumbene in New South Wales exceeds Lake Hume as Australia's largest reservoir.
1959	The country's population reaches 10 million.
	The Snowy Mountains Scheme puts its first electricity plant online.
1961	The tennis player Rod Laver wins his first of four Wimbledon singles finals; he wins the grand slam of tennis the following year with victories in the Australian, French, and U.S. Opens, plus Wimbledon.
1962	Aboriginal Australians are allowed to vote in federal elections with the enactment of the Commonwealth Electoral Act 1962.
1963	The remaining members of the Mapoon Aboriginal community on Cape York Peninsula, far north Queensland, are evicted and their

homes destroyed by police to allow the Comalco company to mine bauxite on their land.

Australia endorses the Nuclear Test Ban Treaty, the first country to do so.

1964   The Mount Isa mining strike is the most disruptive and wide-reaching industrial action since before World War II.

1965   Australia commits troops to the war in Vietnam.

The Labor Party deletes the phrase "White Australia" from its immigration platform.

1966   Both Prime Minister Robert Menzies and the Sydney Opera House architect Jørn Utzon resign from their posts; the former is replaced by Harold Holt.

Australia replaces its currency, pounds, shillings (20 per pound), and pence (12 per shilling), for dollars and cents.

1967   A Commonwealth referendum, passed by more than 90 percent of voting Australians, makes Aboriginal Australians citizens of the country established in 1901.

Prime Minister Harold Holt vanishes while swimming off the coast of Victoria.

1968   Possibly the oldest cremated human remains are found at Lake Mungo, New South Wales; carbon-14 dating results indicate they are about 26,000 years old.

Joh Bjelke-Petersen of the Country Party becomes premier of Queensland.

1969   Australia begins its phased troop withdrawal from Vietnam in December, five months after police and 3,000 antiwar protesters clash at Melbourne's U.S. consulate.

The principle of equal pay for women is adopted by the Commonwealth Conciliation and Arbitration Commission just three years after the ban on married women's working in the public service is lifted.

1971   Australian troops complete combat duty in Vietnam.

1972	Gough Whitlam and the Labor Party are elected for the first time in 23 years.
	The Aboriginal tent embassy is set up in Canberra as part of the land rights struggle.
1973	The Migration Act is finally revised to end nearly three quarters of a century of the White Australia policy.
	The Sydney Opera House is opened by Queen Elizabeth II, with the Australian Opera Company's *War and Peace,* by Prokofiev.
	Patrick White wins the Nobel Prize in literature, the only Australian to do so.
1974	Cyclone Tracy destroys much of the city of Darwin and kills 64.
	The Whitlam government hands over all remaining missions and reserves in the Northern Territory to their Aboriginal owners.
	Australia grants independence to its Papua New Guinea colony.
1975	The Whitlam government introduces a universal health insurance scheme, which has been changed over the decades but continues to provide guaranteed health care for all Australians today.
	Gough Whitlam's government is sacked by the governor-general, who represents the queen.
	Malcolm Fraser and the Liberal Party are elected a month after the sacking of the Whitlam government.
1976	The Tasmanian Wilderness Society is formed at the home of Bob Brown.
	The remains of Trugannini, who died in 1876 as supposedly the last Aboriginal Tasmanian, are cremated and her ashes are scattered off Bruny Island, Tasmania.
1977	The Methodist, Congregational, and Presbyterian Churches of Australia merge as the Uniting Church.
	Queen Elizabeth II and Prince Philip tour Australia as part of the queen's Silver Jubilee.

1978	Australia's first gay and lesbian Mardi Gras parade is held in Sydney.
	The Special Broadcasting Service (SBS) begins airing non-English-language news, movies, and other programming.
1979	The Hydro-Electric Commission (HEC) chooses the Franklin–Gordon River system in Tasmania as an appropriate place for a dam project.
	Galarrwuy Yunupingu is named Australian of the Year; he is the chairman of the Northern Land Council.
	Women working in the private sector are granted the right to maternity leave.
1980	10-week-old baby Azaria Chamberlain disappears from a campsite near Uluru (Ayers Rock) in the Northern Territory. Lindy Chamberlain, her mother, is later convicted of the baby's murder.
	Australian athletes attend the Moscow Olympics despite Prime Minister Fraser's recommendations to join the boycott by the United States and other countries to protest the USSR's invasion of Afghanistan.
	UNESCO declares the Great Barrier Reef, the only living thing on Earth visible from space, a World Heritage site.
1981	Sydney sees its first death of acquired immunodeficiency syndrome (AIDS), it is not identified as such until 1993.
1982	In an attempt to nationalize Australian Rules football, the South Melbourne Swans club moves to Sydney.
	The state government of Tasmania approves damming of the Franklin River, leading to a massive blockade of southwest Tasmania by protesters.
	Thomas Keneally wins the Booker Prize for *Schindler's Ark*, the basis for the 1993 film *Schindler's List*.
	Brisbane hosts the Commonwealth Games, a sporting competition for nations that belong to the British Commonwealth.

1983	Ash Wednesday bushfires kill 75 people in the states of Victoria and South Australia.
	The Franklin River dam project is halted by the High Court of Australia after a three-year battle.
	Bob Hawke and the Labor Party win the federal election in a landslide.
1984	New South Wales decriminalizes homosexuality.
1985	Uluru National Park, including the iconic Uluru itself, is handed over to the Mutijulu Aboriginal community.
	The Royal Commission on British Atomic Tests at Maralinga denounces the British for violating safety standards; it also recommends compensation be paid to affected communities and individuals.
	The Tasmanian Aboriginal Centre makes its first request for repatriation of Aboriginal remains from overseas museums and collections.
1986	Lindy Chamberlain is released from prison when Azaria's jacket is found outside a dingo den; convictions of Lindy and her husband, Michael, are quashed two years later.
	The Australian House of Representatives elects its first female speaker, Joan Child.
1987	In two separate incidents, 15 people are killed by automatic weapons fire in Melbourne.
	Premier Joh Bjelke-Petersen retires from Queensland politics.
1988	Canberra's opening of the new Parliament House is attended by Queen Elizabeth II.
1989	Bond University opens on the Gold Coast, Queensland; it is Australia's first private university.
1990	Carmen Lawrence of Western Australia is elected Australia's first female state premier.
	Bob Hawke's Labor government is returned for a fourth term.
	The Aboriginal and Torres Strait Islander Commission (ATSIC) is formed.

1991	The Labor Party replaces Bob Hawke as prime minister with the treasurer, Paul Keating.
1992	The *Mabo and Others v. Queensland* case legalizes native title in Australia.
	The *Australian,* a national newspaper, names Eddie Mabo Australian of the Year.
1993	Paul Keating and Labor win an "unwinnable" election.
	The federal Native Title Act is passed.
1994	In the Blue Mountains outside Sydney a park ranger finds a stand of Wollemi pines, which had previously been thought long extinct.
1995	The parliament of the Northern Territory legalizes voluntary euthanasia only to see it overturned by the Commonwealth government shortly thereafter.
1996	The Liberal Party leader, John Howard, is elected prime minister as head of a coalition of the Liberal and National Parties.
	The Port Arthur massacre in Tasmania; John Howard's new government responds with tough gun control legislation.
1997	Tasmania is the last Australian state to remove laws making homosexuality illegal in the state.
1998	A constitutional convention on becoming a republic is held in Canberra and concludes that, in principle, republicanism is appropriate for Australia and that a referendum on the issue should be held in 1999.
	John Howard is reelected despite a platform of introducing a 10 percent goods and services tax (GST).
1999	The referendum to make Australia a republic with an elected head of state to replace the British monarch fails.
	Australian troops head a UN force in East Timor to quell violence resulting from a positive vote for independence in the small, half-island state.
2000	Sydney hosts the XXVII Summer Olympic Games.

The Liberal government introduces the 10 percent goods and services tax (GST).

More than 500 detainees escape from the Woomera detention center, which houses refugees and illegal immigrants awaiting decisions from the Department of Immigration.

2001   The Norwegian freighter *Tampa* is refused entry into Australian waters.

John Howard pledges Australia to join the United States in the "war on terror."

David Hicks is arrested in Afghanistan.

2002   The "children overboard" claims are proven false.

Eighty-five Australians are killed in a nightclub bombing in Kuta, Bali.

Australia ratifies the International Criminal Court.

2003   John Howard pledges 2,000 armed service people to the U.S. invasion of Iraq; tens of thousands of Australians protest the war in March.

A second year of record-low rainfall threatens crops and results in water restrictions.

2004   The ruling Liberal Party gains control of the Senate.

Water flows into Lake Eyre for the first time in four years.

Australia and the United States sign the Australia–United States Free Trade Agreement.

Peter Garrett, former lead singer of the 1980s band Midnight Oil, becomes a Labor Party candidate for Parliament.

An Aboriginal man dies in custody on Palm Island, Queensland, and about 300 people destroy the police station and other buildings in response.

Tasmanian Mary Donaldson marries Crown Prince Frederik of Denmark.

2005   An Australian permanent resident, Cornelia Rau, is discovered to have spent 10 months being held in detention as an illegal immigrant.

Nine Australians are arrested in Bali for drug smuggling and face the death penalty.

Immigration officials admit they deported Australian Vivian Solon to the Philippines four years earlier and were unable to locate her for years.

The Cronulla riots in Sydney.

2006   Steve Irwin, a.k.a. the Crocodile Hunter, is killed by a stingray off the coast of Queensland.

Australian troops arrive in both East Timor and the Solomon Islands to settle unrest in those two countries.

The 10-year drought has become the drought of the century, sending food prices upward and economic growth forecasts down.

2007   The Labor Party under the leadership of Kevin Rudd defeats John Howard and the Liberal-National Coalition.

John Howard loses his parliamentary seat of Bennelong after 33 years.

The new prime minister, Kevin Rudd, signs the Kyoto Protocol agreement.

2008   The Labor government apologizes to Australia's Aboriginal people for the Stolen Generations.

The federal government abandons some aspects of the former government's asylum seeker policies.

Kevin Rudd appoints Quentin Bryce as Australia's first female governor-general.

Same-sex couples are granted the same rights and responsibilities as those of de facto hetero-sexual couples, except the right to marry.

2009   Bushfires in Victoria kill 173 people.

Drought ends in much of Queensland when dry conditions are replaced by massive floods in May.

Indian students studying in Australia protest against racially motivated violence against them in Melbourne and Sydney, putting Australia's enormous international education market at risk.

Australia's soccer team, the Socceroos, qualify for the World Cup Final 2010 in South Africa, their second consecutive final appearance.

Australia is the first G2O country to raise interest rates following the global economic downturn, signalling strong economic growth in the latter half of the year.

Appendix 3

Australian Prime Ministers since 1901

Edmund Barton, January 1, 1901–September 24, 1903
Alfred Deakin, September 24, 1903–April 27, 1904
Chris Watson, April 27, 1904–August 18, 1904
George Reid, August 18, 1904–July 5, 1905
Alfred Deakin, July 5, 1905–November 13, 1908
Andrew Fisher, November 13, 1908–June 2, 1909
Alfred Deakin, June 2, 1909–April 29, 1910
Andrew Fisher, April 29, 1910–June 24, 1913
Joseph Cook, June 24, 1913–September 17, 1914
Andrew Fisher, September 17, 1914–October 27, 1915
Billy Hughes, October 27, 1915–February 9, 1923
Stanley Bruce, February 9, 1923–October 22, 1929
James Scullin, October 22, 1929–January 6, 1932
Joseph Lyons, January 6, 1932–April 7, 1939
Sir Earle Page, April 7, 1939–April 26, 1939
Robert Menzies, April 26, 1939–August 28, 1941
Arthur Fadden, August 28, 1941–October 7, 1941
John Curtin, October 7, 1941–July 5, 1945
Frank Forde, July 6, 1945–July 13, 1945
Ben Chifley, July 13, 1945–December 19, 1949
Robert Menzies, December 19, 1949–January 26, 1966
Harold Holt, January 26, 1966–December 19, 1967
John McEwen, December 19, 1967–January 10, 1968
John Gorton, January 10, 1968–March 10, 1971
William McMahon, March 10, 1971–December 5, 1972
Gough Whitlam, December 5, 1972–November 11, 1975

Malcolm Fraser, November 11, 1975–March 11, 1983
Bob Hawke, March 11, 1983–December 20, 1991
Paul Keating, December 20, 1991–March 11, 1996
John Howard, March 11, 1996–December 3, 2007
Kevin Rudd, December 3, 2007–present

APPENDIX 4

AUSSIE TERMS AND PHRASES WITH TRANSLATIONS INTO AMERICAN ENGLISH

All words that end in –er are pronounced as if they end in –ah; single middle r's should also be pronounced as if the r is an h or is absent entirely.

ambo   ambulance or its personnel

arvo   afternoon

Aussie   Australian

avo   avocado

banana lounge   reclining deck chair, long enough to stretch out on

barrack   be a supporter of an athletic team, as in "I barrack for the Bulldogs"

bastard   the national adjective, can be positive or negative depending on tone of voice and context

bathers   swimsuit

bevvy   alcoholic drink or beverage

big smoke   large city, such as Melbourne or Sydney

bikkie, biscuit   cookie

bingle   not terribly serious car accident

bitumen   blacktop

bloke   guy

bloody   very

bloody oath   true

blue   fight or argument

Blunnies, Blundstones   iconic workman's boots, now mainstream footwear for men and women

Bob's your uncle   a saying that means "and there you have it"

bogan   usually pejorative or self-deprecating, for a person who is, or is perceived to be, of a lower-class background

bonnet   hood of a car

boogie board   shortened surf board ridden by lying rather than standing on it

boot   trunk of a car; also cleats worn for football, soccer, etc.

bottle shop   liquor store, can be drive-in

break-up   party to kick off the silly season at a workplace

brekkie   breakfast

Brisvegas   Brisbane, Queensland

buck's night   bachelor party before the groom gets married

buggered   completely exhausted

Bundy   Bundaberg rum, made in Queensland

burl   call on the phone

cab sav   Cabernet Sauvignon wine

cappuccino   coffee drink with equal amounts of espresso, steamed milk, and milk froth

cark it   to die

car park   parking lot

chewie   chewing gum

chewie on yer boot   a taunt used in Aussie Rules football to indicate a bad kick

chockas or chocka block   full, as in "The pub is chockas tonight"

chokkie   chocolate

chook   chicken

college   can mean high school or a university dormitory

countery   a meal from a pub where you order at the counter but it is delivered to your table

cozzie, costume   bathing suit

crook   being unwell (to describe a person or animal), or poorly made (to describe an object)

cuppa   cup of tea or coffee

dag   goofball, slightly out of fashion but sweet, both a mild insult and a term of endearment

died in the arse   a car that breaks down might be described by an Australian as having "died in the arse"

divvy van   vehicle police use to transport people they have picked up, usually drunk troublemakers; abbreviated from *divisional van*

dob   tattle

doco   documentary film

dog's breakfast   a mess or confused muddle, as in "to make a dog's breakfast of an assignment"

doona   comforter

dummy   baby's pacifier

dunny   bathroom, toilet

dux   valedictorian at a high school

EFTPOS   Electronic Funds Transfer at Point of Sale direct debit

emcee   master of ceremonies

entree   appetizer

esky   cooler, for the transport of bevvies (see **bevvy**) or food

faculty   a university department, not the people who teach there

fair dinkum   true, real, genuine

fair go   to give a fair chance

fairy floss   cotton candy

fanny   female genitalia

feral   modern version of a hippie, often with dreadlocks

flake   shark fillet, usually battered and deep fried (the standard fish and chip shop fish)

flat   apartment

flat white   coffee drink with steamed milk but no froth

football   in Victoria, South Australia, and Western Australia, Australian Rules Football; in New South Wales and Queensland, rugby

footpath   sidewalk

fortnight   two weeks

fringe   bangs

full as a goog   stuffed, at the end of a meal

garbo   (trash) garbage collector

go bush   to get away from it all

Good on ya!   Well done!

googie, goog   egg, often referred to as a "googie egg"

grog   alcohol

happy as Larry   happy as a clam

hash sign   #, pound sign

hen's night   a party before a woman gets married

hole in the wall   automatic teller machine (ATM)

holls   holidays

hoon   punk, often engaged in drunken antisocial behavior or drag racing

hooroo   bye-bye

hotel   pub, bar

hundreds and thousands   candy sprinkles, as on a cookie or cupcake

Hungry Jacks   Burger King

icy pole   popsicle

idiot box   TV

iffy   questionable, as in "it's a bit iffy"

innings   to have a good innings is to have had a long and successful career, life

jam   jelly

jarmies   pyjamas

jelly   Jell-O

jocks   men's underpants

jumper   sweater

kettle   jug used to boil water, either electrical or stove top

kip   short nap; *see* nana nap

Kiwi   New Zealander

knackered exhausted; *see* buggered

knocker someone who criticizes others

lamington day-old sponge cake cut into squares, dipped in chocolate, and rolled in desiccated coconut

larrikin wild at heart, usually with little regard for authority, often admired by Australians

latte coffee drink with double the amount of steamed milk to espresso, little bit of milk froth on top

lecturer a junior professor

lid hair, used to comment on an unusual hairstyle, as in "check out that lid"

lift elevator

light globe light bulb

li-lo (pronounced "lie-low") blow-up flotation matt for pool or beach

lolly candy, especially hard candy

long black coffee drink with double the amount of hot water to espresso, no milk

loo bathroom

Maccas McDonald's, Mickey D's

main course, main entree

mark (as in Australian Rules Football) a catch

mash mashed potatoes

metho mentholated spirits

milk bar corner shop, deli

mince ground beef

mobile cell phone

mozzies mosquitoes

nana grandmother

nana nap short nap taken during the day

nappy diaper

nature strip tree belt

nip shot, as in alcohol

No worries! No problem!

number plate   license plate

ocker   *see* bogan

opportunity shop, op shop, or oppy   thrift store

Oz   Australia

parma   chicken parmesan, or a fried, crumbed chicken cutlet topped with spaghetti sauce, Parma ham, and tasty cheese; a specialty in Melbourne pubs and hotels

petrol   gas for an automobile

pie   like a pot pie but made with beef or mutton and most often purchased as a take-out snack with sauce

pie floater   in some parts of the country, pie served in restaurants upside down in a dish of thick pea soup

pie night   a social gathering usually organized by a junior sporting club as a fund-raiser where people eat frozen or fresh meat pies heated in the oven for a small donation

piker   someone who is a little lazy or who backs out of an arrangement

pinch   steal

pissed   drunk

pong   bad smell, stench

poofter   formerly derogatory term for a gay man that has been reclaimed by gay men themselves and thus used with affection inside the community

postie   postman/woman

pot   glass of beer (the exact measurements differ by state)

prang   car crash

pressie   present or gift

primary school   elementary school

pusher   stroller for toddlers

queue (pronounced "Q")   to line up, or the line itself

rashy   nylon shirt worn under a wetsuit to prevent a rash

ratbag   silly person

rego   registration, as of your car

rellies   relatives

ripper   fantastic!

rissole   ground meat dish, like a single-serving meatloaf

root   sexual intercourse

rubbish bin   trash can

rug up   to wear lots of warm clothes in the winter

sauce   similar to ketchup

sausage sizzle   selling grilled sausages to raise money for charities and community organizations, often held at hardware stores on weekends, outdoor market days, sports clubs, etc.

scab   strike breaker; also someone who gets things free by taking advantage of others' generosity

schooner   large glass of beer (measurements differ by state)

serviette   napkin

servo, service station   gas station

She'll be right   indicates that something is not exactly perfect but is good enough

shi'touse   very bad

short black   espresso coffee

shout   buy friends' drinks in rounds (in turn)

show bag   a themed plastic bag filled with commercial merchandise purchased at fairs and carnivals; often used tongue in cheek nowadays to refer to the bag of sponsors' merchandise handed out to participants at conferences

sickie   a day off from work or school on the excuse of being ill, but really more of a mental health day

silly season   Christmastime, beginning in early to mid-November and lasting till January 26

skivvy   turtleneck

slab   case of 24 cans of beers

slice   baked bar, like a brownie, but can come in dozens of flavors

smoko   10-minute break from work to have a cigarette, nowadays outside because of strict smoking laws

snag   sausage

sook   crybaby

sparky   electrician

spaz   very derogatory term for someone with a physical disability. (It should *not* be used to mean clumsy)

spew   vomit

spit the dummy   get really upset

stickybeak   nosey person or the act of looking around, as in "have a sticky beak"

stirrer   troublemaker

stubby   bottle of beer

sunnies   sunglasses

swag   bed roll, somewhat old fashioned

take away   take out

tall poppy   successful person who stands out from the crowd, not a good thing in Australia

tall poppy syndrome   Australians tend not to like tall poppies if they are too loud about their success, so, like the tallest poppies in the field, they lop their heads off

Tassie (pronounced Tazzie)   Tasmania

tasty cheese   like a white cheddar; "extra tasty" is sharper

tea   can refer to dinner

telly   TV

term deposit   certificate of deposit (CD) at a bank

the bush   the countryside

thongs   flip flops

tinnie   can of beer

togs   bathing suit

tomato sauce   *see* sauce

top end   far north of the country

torch   flashlight

trackie   tracksuit

trackie bums   track suit pants

tucker   food, sometimes written as tukka

undies   underwear

uni (pronounced "yoonie")   university

up whoop-whoop   far away in the country

ute   pick-up truck, utility vehicle

vejjo   vegetarian

wag skip school, truant

walkabout a time of wandering, originally in reference to Aboriginal people

wanker jerk, only used for blokes

weatherboard clapboard house

wetty wetsuit, for surfing in cold water

whinge to complain/whine a lot

windcheater sweatshirt

yabby inland, fresh water crayfish

yakka hard work, as in "hard yakka"

yobbo a loud person, often drunk

yum cha dim sum

zebra crossing pedestrian crossing marked by white stripes painted on the road

APPENDIX 5

BIBLIOGRAPHY

AAP. "AWB Execs 'Did Not Mean to Do Wrong.'" November 28, 2006. Available online. URL: http://www.news.com.au/story/ 0,27574,20834377-37435,00.html. Accessed May 4, 2009.

ABC Archives. "1930s." 2002. Available online. URL: http://www.abc. net.au/archives/timeline/1930s.htm. Accessed May 22, 2009.

ABC Hobart. "The Franklin Blockade Remembered and Celebrated in Hobart." Available online. URL: http://www.abc.net.au/local/ stories/2008/07/02/2291481.htm. Updated July 3, 2008. Accessed February 17, 2009.

ABC Indigenous. "Govt 'Not Doing Enough' to Close the Gap: NT Groups." February 26, 2009. Available online. URL: http://www. abc.net.au/news/stories/2009/02/26/2502576.htm.?site=indigenous. Accessed May 13, 2009.

ABC News. "More Than 55pc of Australians Oppose WorkChoices: Poll." March 26, 2007a. Available online. URL: http://www.abc.net. au/news/stories/2007/03/26/1881101.htm. Accessed May 6, 2009.

———. "PM Knew WorkChoices Would Hurt Workers.'" July 21, 2007. Available online. URL: http://www.abc.net.au/news/stories/ 2007/07/21/1984522.htm. Accessed May 6, 2009.

———. "UN Report Says NT Intervention 'Discriminatory.'" April 6, 2009. Available online. URL: http://www.abc.net.au/news/stories/ 2009/04/06/2535819.htm. Accessed April 27, 2009.

ABC News. "Rudd's Popularity Takes a Hit in Poll" (January 19, 2010). Available online. URL: http://www.abc.net.au/news/stories/ 2010/01/19/2795398.htm. Accessed January 22, 2010.

ABC News Online. "Hicks's Father Slams Release Conditions." March 31, 2007. Available online. URL: http://www.abc.net.au/news/newsitems/ 200703/s1886478.htm. Accessed April 28, 2009.

———. "Thomas Family Vows to Fight Control Order." August 28, 2006. Available online. URL: http://www.abc.net.au/news/newsitems/ 200608/s1726381.htm. Accessed April 28, 2009.

Aboriginal Law Bulletin. "Effects of Pastoral Leases in Queensland." 1996. Available online. URL: http://austlii.law.uts.edu.au/au/journals/AboriginalLB/1996/9.html. Accessed October 22, 2008.

————. "Mabo: The Aboriginal Peace Plan." 1993. Available online. URL: http://www.austlii.edu.au/au/journals/AboriginalLB/1993/19.html. Accessed April 15, 2009.

"Aborigines and Cricket." Available online. URL: http://www.convictcreations.com/football/aborigines.htm. Accessed August 24, 2008.

"About Apec." January 14, 2009. Available online. URL: http://www.apec.org/apec/about_apec.html. Accessed April 8, 2009.

Acharya, Amitav. *Constructing a Security Community in Southeast Asia: ASEAN and the Problem of Regional Order.* New York: Routledge, 2001.

"Advance Australia!" Excerpts. Available online. URL: http://finch.customer.netspace.net.au/chapter10.htm.l#longlagoon. Accessed August 24, 2008.

AELTC. "Ladies' Singles Finals 1884–2008." Available online. URL: http://www.wimbledon.org/en_GB/about/history/rolls/ladiesroll.html. Accessed February 2, 2009.

————. "Men's Singles Finals 1877–2008." Available online. URL: http://www.wimbledon.org/en_GB/about/history/rolls/menroll.html. Accessed February 2, 2009.

The Age. "Aussies Were Deliberately Targeted in Bali." February 10, 2003. Available online. URL: http://www.theage.com.au/articles/2003/02/10/1044725712936.html. Accessed May 4, 2009.

————. "2,200 Firms Paid Saddam Bribes: Report." October 27, 2005. Available online. URL: http://www.theage.com.au/news/World/2200-firms-paid-Saddam-bribes-report/2005/10/27/113 0382514669.html. Accessed May 4, 2009.

————. "'We Had No Warning': PM Tells Bereaved Father." November 26, 2002. Available online. URL: http://www.theage.com.au/articles/2002/11/26/1038173742338.html. Accessed May 4, 2009.

The Age, multimedia. "The Trials of David Hicks: Interviews: Michael Mori: An Easy Sacrifice." Available online. URL: http://www.theage.com.au/multimedia/hicks/hicks.html. Accessed April 28, 2009.

AIATSIS and Bruce Pascoe. *The Little Red Yellow Black Book: An Introduction to Indigenous Australia.* Canberra: Aboriginal Studies Press, 2008.

Alexander, Cathy. "Uluru Climb Could Stay Open After All." The Age, October 20, 2009. Available Online. URL: http://news.theage.com.au/breaking-news-national/uluru-climb-could-stay-open-after-all-20091020-h5zk.html. Accessed on October 24, 2009.

al-Nasrallah, Haider. "Australia Withdraws Troops from Iraq." Reuters UK, June 1, 2008. Available online. URL: http://uk.reuters.com/article/topNews/idUKL0164801020080601?pageNumber=1&virtual BrandChannel=0. Accessed May 1, 2009.

Alomes, Stephen A. "The Fragile Spring: The Australian Colonies and Imperial Britain 1880–1901." Excerpted from *A Nation at Last? The Changing Character of Australian Nationalism 1880–1988.* In *Australia to 1901: Selected Readings in the Making of a Nation,* edited by Martin Crotty and Erik Eklund, 574–594. Croydon, Vic.: Tertiary Press, 2003.

Anderson, Benedict. *Imagined Communities: Reflections on the Origin and Spread of Nationalism.* London: Verso, 1983.

Andreoni, Helen. "Olive or White? The Colour of Italians in Australia." *Journal of Australian Studies* 77 (2003): 81–92.

Andrewartha, H. G., and L. C. Birch. *The Ecological Web: More on the Distribution and Abundance of Animals.* Chicago: University of Chicago Press, 1986.

Andrews, Lucy. "Ashes History." Behind the News, October 17, 2006. Available online. URL: http://www.abc.net.au/news/btn/v3/stories/s1765802.htm. Accessed October 23, 2009.

"Animal's Peculiar Features Holds Clues to Evolution of Mammals." *ScienceDaily.* Available online. URL: http://www.sciencedaily.com/releases/2008/05/080507131453.htm. Accessed October 1, 2008.

ANTAR. "What Is the Australian Story?" *Sea of Hands,* January 28, 2009. Available online. URL: http://www.antar.org.au/what_is_the_australian_story. Accessed May 14, 2009.

ATNS. Agreements, Treaties and Negotiated Settlements Project. "Eva Valley Statement, 1993." 2007. Available online. URL: http://www.atns.net.au/agreement.asp?EntityID=1742. Accessed April 15, 2009.

Attorney-General's Department. "Overview of the Australian Government's Same-Sex Law Reforms." Australian Government, 2008. Available online. URL: http://www.ag.gov.au/samesexreform. Accessed October 24, 2009.

Austrade. "Australia–United States Free Trade Agreement (AUSFTA): Overview." 2009. Available online. URL: http://www.austrade.gov.au/AUSFTA/default.aspx. Accessed May 4, 2009.

"Australia Act 1986." Available online. URL: http://scaleplus.law.gov.au/htm.l/pasteact/1/973/pdf/AustraliaAct86.pdf. Accessed April 15, 2009.

Australia on the Map. The AOTM Landings List. Available online. URL: http://www.australiaonthemap.org.au/content/view/14. Accessed August 25, 2008.

Australianbeers.com. "Alan Bond." 2006. Available online. URL: http://www.australianbeers.com/history/bond.htm. Accessed April 16, 2009.

Australian Bureau of Statistics. 1301.0 Yearbook Australia 2006. "Religious Affiliation." 2006. Available online. URL: http://www.abs.gov.au/ausstats/abs@.nsf/46d1bc47ac9d0c7bca256c470025ff87/bfdda1ca506d6cfaca2570de0014496e!OpenDocument. Accessed June 3, 2009.

―――. 1301.0 Yearbook Australia—2008. "Country of Birth." 2008. Available online. URL: http://www.abs.gov.au/AUSSTATS/abs@.nsf/bb8db737e2af84b8ca2571780015701e/F1C38FAE9E5F2B82CA2573D200110333?opendocument. Accessed January 7, 2009.

―――. 1301.0 Yearbook Australia—2008. "Geography of Australia." Available online. URL: http://www.abs.gov.au/ausstats/ABS@.nsf/7d12b0f6763c78caca257061001cc588/8826A00C209DDB02CA2573D200106A75?opendocument. Accessed January 21, 2009.

―――. "Migration, 2006–07." Available online. URL: http://www.ausstats.abs.gov.au/ausstats/subscriber.nsf/0/F15E154C9434F250CA2574170011B 45B/$File/34120_2006-07.pdf. Accessed October 25, 2008.

―――. "Population Clock." 2009. Available online. URL: http://www.abs.gov.au/ausstats/abs%40.nsf/94713ad445ff1425ca25682000192af2/1647509ef7e25faaca2568a900154b63?OpenDocument. Accessed January 22, 2010.

―――. "Population Growth: Australia's Population Growth." 2006. Available online. URL: http://www.abs.gov.au/ausstats/ABS@.nsf/2f762f95845417aeca25706c00834efa/e2f62e625b7855bfca2570ec0073cdf6!OpenDocument. Accessed January 8, 2009.

Australian Federal Police, The. "Bali Bombings 2002." May 2, 2008. Available online. URL: http://www.afp.gov.au/international/operations/previous_operations/bali_bombings_2002.htm.l Accessed May 4, 2009.

Australian Government Culture and Recreation Portal. "Australian Fauna." 2007. Available online. URL: http://www.cultureandrecreation.gov.au/articles/fauna. Accessed October 24, 2008.

Australian Government Department of Foreign Affairs and Trade, 2008. "About Australia: Flora and Fauna." Available online. URL: http://www.dfat.gov.au/facts/flora_and_fauna.html. Accessed October 24, 2008.

Australian Heritage Database. "Fort Dundas, Pularumpi, NT, Australia." Australian Government Department of the Environment, Water, Heritage and the Arts, 2002. Available online. URL: http://www.environment.gov.au/cgi-bin/ahdb/search.pl?mode=place_detail;place_id=18163. Accessed January 14, 2009.

Australian Human Rights Commission. "A Statistical Overview of Aboriginal and Torres Strait Islander Peoples in Australia." August 2006. Available online. URL: http://www.hreoc.gov.au/Social_Justice/statistics/index.html. Accessed January 8, 2009.

Australian Institute of Criminology. "A Toxic Legacy: British Nuclear Testing in Australia." In *Wayward Governance: Illegality and Its Control in the Public Sector,* edited by P. N. Grabosky, 235–253. Canberra: Australian Institute of Criminology, 1989. Available online. URL: http://www.aic.gov.au/publications/lcj/wayward/ch16.html. Accessed January 30, 2009.

Australian Museum Online. "Cane Toads, Giant Toads or Marine Toads." 2003. Available online. URL: http://www.austmus.gov.au/factsheets/canetoad.htm. Accessed May 18, 2009.

———. "Indigenous Australia: Timeline—Contact History 1500–1900." 2004. Available online. URL: http://www.dreamtime.net.au/indigenous/timeline2.cfm. Accessed September 3, 2008.

Australian of the Year Awards. "Galarrwuy Yunupingu AM (b. 1948) 1978 Award." National Australia Day Committee, 2008. Available online. URL: http://www.australianoftheyear.org.au/pages/page91.asp. Accessed February 18, 2009.

Australian Olympic Committee (1). "London 1908." Available online. URL: http://corporate.olympics.com.au/games/465/London+1908. Accessed January 5, 2009.

Australian Olympic Committee (2). "Stockholm 1912." Available online. URL: http://corporate.olympics.com.au/games/464/Stockholm+1912. Accessed January 5, 2009.

Australian Olympic Committee (3). "Melbourne 1956." Available online. URL: http://corporate.olympics.com.au/games/7/Melbourne+1956. Accessed January 30, 2009.

Australian Olympic Committee (5). "Sydney 2000." Available online. URL: http://corporate.olympics.com.au/games/2000/Sydney+2000. Accessed April 30, 2009.

Australian Politics Books. "Don't You Worry about That! The Joh Bjelke-Petersen Memoirs." 2009a. Available online. URL: http://www.australian-politics-books.com/ccp0-prodshow/dont-you-worry-about-that-joh-bjelk e-petersen.html. Accessed April 17, 2009.

———. "A Foolish Passionate Man—Paul Ormonde: A Biography of Jim Cairns." 2009b. Available online. URL: http://www.australian-politics-books.com/ccp0-prodshow/a-foolish-passionate-man-paul-ormon de-jim-cairns.html. Accessed February 13, 2009.

———. "Sex, Prejudice and Politics: Junie Morosi." 2009c. Available online. URL: http://www.australian-politics-books.com/ccp0-prodshow/sex-prejudice-politics-junie-morosi.html. Accessed February 13, 2009.

Australian Rainforest Foundation. Available online. URL: http://www.arf.net.au/australias_rainforests.html. Accessed October 24, 2008.

Australian War Memorial. "Case Study: Reginald Saunders." Education Section, 2003. Available online. URL: http://www.awm.gov.au/education/box/casestudy/03.pdf. Accessed June 1, 2009.

———. "Statistics." Available online. URL: http://www.awm.gov.au/encyclopedia/vietnam/statistics.asp. Accessed January 29, 2009.

———. "Vietnam War, 1962–75." 2009. Available online. URL: http://www.awm.gov.au/atwar/vietnam.asp. Accessed January 29, 2009.

———. "Who's Who in Australian Military History: Captain Reginald Walter (Reg) Saunders, MBE." 2009a. Available online. URL: http://www.awm.gov.au/people/302.asp. Accessed May 29, 2009.

Australia's Prime Ministers. "Harold Holt." Copyright 2002. Available online. URL: http://primeministers.naa.gov.au/meetpm.asp?pageName=inoffice&pmId=17. Accessed February 3, 2009.

———. "Paul Keating." Copyright 2002. Available online. URL: http://primeministers.naa.gov.au/meetpm.asp?pmId=24&pageName=inoffice. Accessed April 8, 2009.

Baldino, Daniel. "Australia and the World." In Howard's Second and Third Governments, edited by Chris Aulich and Roger Wettenhall, 189–207. Sydney: University of New South Wales Press, 2005.

Bambrick, Hilary J., Thomas A. Faunce, and Kellie Johnston. "Potential Impact of AUSFTA on Australia's Blood Supply." Medical Journal Australia 185, no. 6 (2006): 320–323.

Barlow, Karen. "Solon Case Included in Palmer Inquiry." ABC News, July 15, 2005. Available online. URL: http://www.abc.net.au/am/content/2005/s1414864.htm. Accessed May 7, 2009.

Barry, John V. "Kelly, Edward (Ned) (1855–1880)." In Australian Dictionary of Biography. Vol. 5. Melbourne: Melbourne University Press, 1974.

BBC News. "Timeline: East Timor." April 4, 2009. Available online. URL: http://news.bbc.co.uk/1/hi/world/asia-pacific/country_profiles/1504243.stm. Accessed April 30, 2009.

Bennett, Scott. "Compulsory Voting in Australian National Elections." Department of Parliamentary Services Research Brief, October 2005, revised March 2008. Available online. URL: http://www.aph.gov.au/library/Pubs/RB/2005-06/06rb06.pdf. Accessed May 19, 2009.

Berkovic, Nicola and Stuart Rintoul. "Probity Check for 'New ATSIC' as Minister Fails to Commit Seed Mondy." *Australian*, August 28, 2009. Available online. URL: http://www.theaustralian.news.com.au/story/0,25197,25991970-2702,00.html. Accessed October 24, 2009.

Betts, Katherine. "Birthplace Origins of Australia's Migrants." *People and Place* 11, no. 3 (2003): 37–42.

Blainey, Geoffrey. *The Tyranny of Distance*. Melbourne: Sun Books, 1966.

Blazey, Peter. "Battler Joan Child Still Takes It All in Her Stride." *Australian*, July 20, 1983, 9.

"Boer War, The." Australian Government Culture and Recreation Portal, 2008. Available online. URL: http://www.cultureandrecreation.gov.au/articles/boerwar. Accessed December 10, 2008.

Border Mail, The. "The Dams." December 24, 2008. Available online. URL: http://www.bordermail.com.au/news/local/news/general/part-6-the-dams/1394912.aspx?storypa ge=0. Accessed May 19, 2009:

Bourke, Colin, Eleanor Bourke, and William Howell Edwards. *Aboriginal Australia: An Introductory Reader in Aboriginal Studies*. St Lucia: University of Queensland Press, 1998.

Brawley, Sean, and Chris Dixon. "Jim Crow Downunder? African American Encounters with White Australia, 1942–1945." *Pacific Historical Review*, 71, no. 4 (2002): 607–632.

Brew, Nigel, Jan Miller, Roy Jordan, and Sue Harris Rimmer. "Australians in Guantanamo Bay: A Chronology of the Detention of Mamdouh Habib and David Hicks." Australian Parliament, 2007. Available online. URL: http://www.aph.gov.au/library/pubs/online/Australians_GuantanamoBay.htm.#2005. Accessed May 8, 2009.

Brown, Bob. "Plebiscite for an Australian Republic Bill 2008." The Parliament of the Commonwealth of Australia: The Senate, November 11, 2008. Available online. URL: http://parlinfo.aph.gov.au/parlInfo/download/legislation/bills/s656_first/toc_pdf/0821820.pdf;fil eType=application%2Fpdf. Accessed May 14, 2009.

Brown, Suzie. "Remote Control." Australian Conservation Foundation. *Habitat Australia*, August 2003, 8–9.

Brownfoot, Janice N. "Goldstein, Vida Jane Mary (1869–1949)." In *Australian Dictionary of Biography*. Vol. 9. Melbourne: Melbourne University Press, 1983.

Bryson, Bill. *In a Sunburned Country*. New York: Random House, 2000.

Bunbury, Bill. *Hindsight* on Radio National. View from the North: A Special Six-Part Series on the History of the Northern Territory.

Episode 1: *Turn the Map Upside Down,* first broadcast on March 9, 2003. Available online. URL: http://www.abc.net.au/rn/history/hindsight/features/north/epis_1.htm. Accessed January 15, 2009.

Buninyong and District Historical Society, Inc. "Remembering the Gold Discoverers of 1851." Newsletter, June–August 2005. Available online. URL: http://home.vicnet.net.au/~buninhis/newsletters/aug_05.htm. Accessed September 30, 2008.

Butlin, N. G. *Forming a Colonial Economy, Australia 1810–1850.* Cambridge: Cambridge University Press, 1994.

Cameron, Kate. "Aboriginal Struggle for Citizenship." Discovering Democracy Discussion Papers, 2000. Available online. URL: http://www.abc.net.au/civics/democracy/struggle.htm. Accessed December 16, 2008.

Carroll, Brian. *The Menzies Years.* North Melbourne, Vic.: Cassell Australia, 1977.

Castles, Francis G., and John Uhr. "The Australian Welfare State: Has Federalism Made a Difference?" *Australian Journal of Politics & History* 53, no. 1 (2007): 96–117.

City of Melbourne. "International Relations: Thessaloniki." 2004. Available online. URL: http://www.melbourne.vic.gov.au/info.cfm?top=161&pg=1643. Accessed January 8, 2009.

Clancy, Brian. "Big Smoke Is Choking Us." *Weekly Times,* January 2, 2009. Available online. URL: http://www.weeklytimesnow.com.au/article/2009/01/02/38131_opinion-news.html. Accessed January 7, 2009.

Clark, Andrew. "Kerr Briefed on CIA Threat to Whitlam." *Sunday Age,* October 15, 2000. Available online. URL: http://archives.econ.utah.edu/archives/pen-l/2001m06.5/msg00016.htm. Accessed February 13, 2009.

Clark, Ian D., and Fred Cahir. *A Critique of "Forgetfulness" and Exclusivity: The Neglect of Aboriginal Themes in Goldfields Tourism in Victoria.* Ballarat: University of Ballarat, 2001.

Clark, Manning. *A Short History of Australia.* 4th rev. ed. Ringwood, Vic.: Penguin, 1995.

Clarke, Andrew, and Xiang Gao. "Bilateral Free Trade Agreements: A Comparative Analysis of the Australia–United States FTA and the Forthcoming Australia-China FTA." *University of New South Wales Law Journal* 30, no. 3 (2007): 842–854.

Clarke, Frank G. *Australia in a Nutshell: A Narrative History.* Dural Delivery Centre, N.S.W.: Rosenberg, 2003.

———. *The History of Australia.* Westport, Conn.: Greenwood Press, 2002.

Clarke, M. J. "Report of the Inquiry into the Case of Dr Mohamed Haneef." Commonwealth of Australia, 2008. Available online. URL: http://www.haneefcaseinquiry.gov.au/www/inquiry/rwpattach.nsf/VAP/(3A6790B96C927794AF1031D9395C5C20)~Volume+1+FINAL.pdf. Accessed October 24, 2009.

Clendon, Mark. "Reassessing Australia's Linguistic Prehistory." *Current Anthropology* 47, no. 1 (2006): 39–61.

Committee to Advise on Australia's Immigration Policies. "Immigration—a commitment to Australia: Executive Summary." Available online. URL: http://www.multiculturalaustralia.edu.au/doc/fitzgerald_2.pdf. Accessed April 6, 2009.

Commonwealth of Australia. "The Australian Gold Rush." Culture Portal, 2007. Available online. URL: http://www.cultureand recreation.gov.au/articles/goldrush. Accessed September 30, 2008.

———. "Fact Sheet 195—The Bombing of Darwin." National Archives, 2009. Available online. URL: http://www.naa.gov.au/about-us/publications/fact-sheets/fs195.aspx. Accessed May 29, 2009.

"Compulsory Voting in Australia." Australianpolitics.com, 2008. Available online. URL: http://www.australianpolitics.com/elections/features/compulsory.shtml. Accessed May 19, 2009.

Constitutional Centre of Western Australia. "1925 to 1950: From Federation to Thoughts on Secession," 2008. Available online. URL: http://www.ccentre.wa.gov.au/index.cfm?event=briefHistory1925To1950. Accessed May 20, 2009.

Contos, Natalie. "The Pinjarra Massacre Site Project: From Doctoral Student to Community Consultant." *Journal of Prevention & Intervention in the Community,* 19, no. 2 (2000): 13–19.

Conway, Jill. "Macarthur, Elizabeth (1763–1850)." In *Australian Dictionary of Biography.* Vol. 2. Melbourne: Melbourne University Press, 1967.

"Cook, James (1728–1779)." In *Australian Dictionary of Biography.* Vol. 1. Melbourne: Melbourne University Press, 1966.

Cooper, H. M. "Flinders, Matthew (1774–1814)." In *Australian Dictionary of Biography.* Vol. 1. Melbourne: Melbourne University Press, 1966.

Coorey, Phillip. "Carbon Bill Burns as Rudd Fiddles." *WA News,* May 5, 2009. Available online. URL: http://www.watoday.com.au/national/carbon-bill-burns-as-rudd-fiddles-20090505-asx2.html. Accessed May 15, 2009.

Coranderrk Mission History, 2004. Available online. URL: http://www. abc.net.au/missionvoices/coranderrk/mission_history/default.htm. Accessed October 24, 2008.

Cormick, Craig. "Maralinga: Who's to Pay for the Clean-up?" *Green Left Online*, November 27, 1991. Available online. URL: http://www. greenleft.org.au/1991/37/116. Accessed February 5, 2009.

Cowie, James. "The Affect of the Gold Rushes on Agriculture." Available online. URL: http://www.sbs.com.au/gold/story.php?storyid=129#. Accessed June 3, 2009.

Crooks, Mary. "Foreword." In *Woman Suffrage in Australia*, by Vida Goldstein, 1908, 1–2. Reprint, Melbourne: Victorian Women's Trust, 2008.

Cross, Roger. *Fallout: Hedley Marston and the British Bomb Tests in Australia*. Kent Town, S.A.: Wakefield Press, 2001.

Curl, David. "Uluru." *Australian Geographic* 80 (2005): 58–66.

Daily Telegraph, The. "Kraft Backflips on Vegemite Name iSnack 2.0." September 30, 2009. Available Online. URL: http://www.daily telegraph.com.au/news/kraft-backflips-on-vegemite-name-isnack20/ story-e6fre uy9-1225781188006. Accessed October 25, 2009.

Dalrymple, Rawdon. *Continental Drift: Australia's Search for a Regional Identity*. Fainham, UK: Ashgate, 2003.

Dampier, William. *A New Voyage around the World*. London: Argonaut Press, 1927.

David, Bruno. *Landscapes, Rock-art, and the Dreaming: An Archaeology of Preunderstanding*. New York: Leicester University Press, 2002.

Davidson, Bruce R. *European Farming in Australia: An Economic History of Australian Farming*. Amsterdam: Elsevier Scientific, 1981.

Davies, Anne, and Stephanie Peatling. "Australians Racist? No Way, Says Howard." *Sydney Morning Herald*, December 13, 2005. Available online. URL: http://www.smh.com.au/news/national/australians-racist-no-way-says-howard/2005/12/12/1134 236005950.html. Accessed May 6, 2009.

Dawkins, Kezia. "1967 Referendum." 2004. Available online. URL: http://www.abc.net.au/messageclub/duknow/stories/s888141.htm. Accessed February 9, 2009.

Dempster, Quentin. "Sir Johannes Bjelke-Petersen: Corrupt Populist." ABC NewsOnline, April 23, 2005. Available online. URL: http://www. abc.net.au/news/indepth/featureitems/s1348134.htm. Accessed April 16, 2009.

Dennett, Harley. "Equal Rights at Last." *Sydney Star Observer* online, November 27, 2008. Available online. URL: http://www.starobserver.

com.au/news/2008/11/27/equal-rights-at-last/2902. Accessed May 15, 2009.

Department of Defence. "The Kokoda Campaign, July 1942." Copyright 2004a. Available online. URL: http://www.defence.gov.au/ARMY/ahu/HISTORY/Battles/Kokoda.htm. Accessed May 29, 2009.

———. "The War in Korea, 1950–53." Copyright 2004b. Available online. URL: http://www.army.gov.au/ahu/HISTORY/korea.htm. Accessed January 29, 2009.

Department of Families, Community Services. "Policy Research Paper No. 1." 2000. Available online. URL: http://www.fahcsia.gov.au/about/publicationsarticles/research/socialpolicy/Documents/prp01/sec1.htm. Accessed June 5, 2009.

———. "Policy Research Paper No. 13, 2004." Available online. URL: http://www.facsia.gov.au/about/publicationsarticles/research/socialpolicy/Documents/prp13/sec 10.htm. Accessed October 23, 2009.

Department of Sustainability and Environment. "Ash Wednesday 1983." 2009. Available online. URL: http://www.dse.vic.gov.au/DSE/nrenfoe.nsf/LinkView/FAAF080E6756F7904A25679300155 B2B7157D5E68 CDC2002CA256DAB0027ECA3. Accessed February 19, 2009.

Department of Veterans' Affairs. "Australia's War 1939–45." Australian Government, 2007. Available online. URL: http://www.ww2australia.gov.au. Accessed May 29, 2009.

Detroit Free Press. "Boy Meets Girl," January 24, 1944. Available online. URL: http://www.geocities.com/us_warbrides/newsarticles/440124.html. Accessed May 26, 2009.

DeVries, Susanna. *The Complete Book of Great Australian Women.* New York: HarperCollins, 2003.

Diamond, Jared. *Collapse: How Societies Choose to Fail or Succeed.* New York: Viking, 2005.

———. *Guns, Germs, and Steel.* New York: W. W. Norton, 1999.

Douglas, Evan J., and Lawrence J. Cunningham. "Competitive Strategies in Australia's Airline Deregulation Experience." School of Business Discussion Papers, Bond University, 1992. Available online. URL: http://epublications.bond.edu.au/cgi/viewcontent.cgi?article=1030&context=discussion_papers. Accessed April 6, 2009.

Dow, Coral. "Background Note: 'Sorry': The Unfinished Business of the Bringing Them Home Report." Parliament of Australia, February 4, 2008. Available online. URL: http://www.aph.gov.au/Library/pubs/BN/2007-08/BringingThemHomeReport.htm. Accessed April 24, 2009.

Duckworth, Arthur. "The Australian Strike, 1890." *Economic Journal* 2, no. 7 (1892): 425–441.

Dutton, Geoffrey. "Eyre, Edward John (1815–1901)." In *Australian Dictionary of Biography*. Vol. 1. Melbourne: Melbourne University Press, 1966.

Dwyer, Jacinta. "Tasmanian Dams Case—25 Years On." *Law Review Journal* 2008. Available online. URL: http://www.shanehoward. com.au/news/Franklin25thAnniversary.html. Accessed February 17, 2009.

Dye, Alan, and Sumner J. LaCroix. "The Political Economy of Land Privatization in Argentina and Australia, 1810–1856." August 24, 2000. Available online. URL: http://www.isnie.org/ISNIE00/Papers/ Dye-LaCroix.pdf. Accessed September 15, 2008.

Dyer, Colin. *The French Explorers and the Aboriginal Australians, 1772– 1839*. St Lucia: University of Queensland Press, 2005.

The Economist. "Australia's Populist Bites Back." 358, no. 8210 (February 24, 2001): 14.

Economist Intelligence Unit. "Urban Idylls." *Economist* online, April 28, 2008. Available online. URL: http://www.economist.com/markets/ rankings/displaystory.cfm?story_id=11116839. Accessed January 8, 2009.

Einspruch, Andrew. *Australia's Government*. Port Melbourne, Vic.: Heinemann Library, 2006.

"Elder Scientific Exploring Expedition." Government of South Australia, 2007. Available online. URL: http://www.samemory.sa.gov.au/site/ page.cfm?u=497. Accessed October 30, 2008.

Electoral Council of Australia. "Preferential Voting Systems." 2000. Available online. URL: http://www.eca.gov.au/systems/single/by_ category/preferential.htm. Accessed December 3, 2008.

"Enrolment, Voting and Informality Statistics." Australianpolitics. com, 2008. Available online. URL: http://www.australianpolitics.com/ elections/enrolment/enrolment-statistics-since-1901.shtml. Accessed May 19, 2009.

Equus Marketing. "The Phar Lap Story." 2006. Available online. URL: http://www.pharlap.com.au/thestory. Accessed May 21, 2009.

Eureka Centre, The. *The Eureka Centre at the Eureka Stockade Ballarat Visitor Guide*. Ballarat: Eureka Centre, 2008.

European Network for Indigenous Australian Rights. "In the Path of Progress." 2008. Available online. URL: http://www.eniar.org/news/ creaghe.html. Accessed October 23, 2008.

Evans, Nicholas, ed. *The Non-Pama-Nyungan Languages of Northern Australia: Comparative Studies of the Continent's Most Linguistically Complex Region*. Canberra: Pacific Linguistics, 2003.

Evans, Raymond. "'. . . To Try to Ruin': Rock 'n' Roll, Youth Culture and Law 'n' Order." In *The Forgotten Fifties: Aspects of Australian Society and Culture in the 1950s,* edited by John Murphy and Judith Smart, 106–119. Melbourne: Melbourne University Press, 1997.

Fairfax Online. "Children of the Revolution." *Sydney Morning Herald,* December 26, 2003. Available online. URL: http://www.smh.com.au/articles/2003/12/25/1072308628745.html. Accessed April 8, 2009.

Farmer, Pat. "A History of Australian Road and Rail." February 2007. Available online. URL: http://www.patfarmer.com/news/downloades/HISTORYOFAUSTRALIANROADANDRAIL.pdf. Accessed October 23, 2009.

Farnsworth, Malcolm. "An Overview of the Whitlam Dismissal." 2001. Available online. URL: http://whitlamdismissal.com/overview. Accessed February 11, 2009.

"Feral Camel, The *(Camelus dromedarius).*" Australian Government Department of Environment, Water, Heritage and the Arts, 2004. Available online. URL: http://www.environment.gov.au/biodiversity/invasive/publications/camel/pubs/camel.pdf. Accessed October 22, 2008.

Finch-Hatton, Harold. *Advance Australia! An Account of Eight Years Work, Wandering, and Amusement, in Queensland, New South Wales, and Victoria.* London: W.H. Allen and Co., 1885.

Fisher, Irene. "How the NT Intervention Is Harming Children." *Crikey,* March 23, 2009. Available online. URL: http://www.crikey.com.au/Politics/20090323-How-the-NT-intervention-is-harming-children-.html. Accessed April 27, 2009.

Flannery, Tim. *Country.* Melbourne: Text, 2004.

———. *The Future Eaters: An Ecological History of the Australasian Lands and People.* PoA Melbourne, VIC: ReedBooks, 1994.

Fleiner-Gerster, Thomas. "Federalism in Australia and in Other Nations." In *Australian Federation: Towards the Second Century,* edited by Gregory Craven, 14–32. Melbourne: Melbourne University Press, 1992.

Flinders Ranges Research (1). "The Overland Telegraph," 2008. Available online. URL: http://www.southaustralianhistory.com.au/overland.htm. Accessed October 31, 2008.

Flinders Ranges Research (3). "Daisy Bates." 2008. Available online. URL: http://www.southaustralianhistory.com.au/bates.htm. Accessed December 11, 2008.

Florek, Stan. "Megafauna Extinction: Patterns of Extinction." Australian Museum Online, 2003. Available online. URL: http://www.austmus.gov.au/factSheets/megafauna.htm. Accessed September 3, 2008.

Foley, Gary. "The Road to Native Title: The Aboriginal Rights Movement and the Australian Labor Party 1973–1996." Koori History Web site, June 2001. Available online. URL: http://www.kooriweb.org/foley/essays/essay_26.html. Accessed April 9, 2009.

Franklin, Mark. "Sanctuary Australia?" *Australian Jewish News*, May 27, 2005. Available online. URL: http://www.ajn.com.au/news/news.asp?pgID=148. Accessed June 4, 2009.

Franklin, Matthew. "Fraser Was Warned on Lebanese Migrants." *Australian,* January 1, 2007. Available online. URL: http://www.theaustralian.news.com.au/story/0,25197,20996448-5018551,00.html. Accessed February 16, 2009.

Fraser, Malcolm. "Migrant Services and Programs—Statement by the Prime Minister." 1978. Available online. URL: http://www.multiculturalaustralia.edu.au/doc/fraser_2.pdf. Accessed February 16, 2009.

Freudenberg, Graham. "Calwell, Arthur Augustus (1896–1973)." In *Australian Dictionary of Biography.* Vol. 13. Melbourne: Melbourne University Press, 1993.

Friends of Catherine Freeman. "Biography." Catherine Freeman Foundation, 2007. Available online. URL: http://www.catherinefreemanfoundation.com/catherinefreeman. Accessed May 8, 2009.

Gale, S. J. "The Snowy Water Inquiry: Food, Power, Politics and the Environment." *Australian Geographical Studies* 37(3) (1999): 301–313.

Galligan, Brian, and Winsome Roberts. "Australian Multiculturalism: Its Rise and Demise." Refereed paper presented to the Australasian Political Studies Association Conference University of Tasmania, Hobart 29 September–1 October 2003. Available online. URL: http://www.utas.edu.au/government/APSA/GalliganRoberts.pdf. Accessed April 16, 2009.

Garnaut, John. "Gun Laws Credited as Lifesavers." *Sydney Morning Herald,* April 23, 2007. Available online. URL: http://www.smh.com.au/news/national/gun-laws-credited-as-lifesavers/2007/04/22/1177180487704.html. Accessed April 27, 2009.

Gascoigne, John. *Joseph Banks and the English Enlightenment: Useful Knowledge and Polite Culture.* New York: Cambridge University Press, 2003.

Gawenda, Michael. "How John Howard Shored Up Private Education, by God." *Sydney Morning Herald,* June 26, 2008. Available online. URL: http://www.smh.com.au/news/opinion/how-john-howard-shored-up-private-education-by-god/2008/06/25/1214073338065.html. Accessed October 21, 2008.

Gee, David, and Matthew Gee. "Coffee the Australian Way." *Tea & Coffee Asia,* 4th quarter, 2005. Available online. URL: http://www.barista basics.com.au/article.asp?AID=49. Accessed January 27, 2009.

Geoscience Australia. "Gold: Rock File." Australian Atlas of Minerals Resources, Mines and Processing Centres, 2008. Available online. URL: http://www.australianminesatlas.gov.au/education/rock_files/gold.jsp. Accessed October 6, 2008.

Geoscience Australia. "Australia through Time." 2007. Available online. URL: http://www.ga.gov.au/image_cache/GA10096.pdf. Accessed January 21, 2009.

———. "Climatic Extremes." 2010. Available online. URL: http://www.ga.gov.au/education/geoscience-basics/dimensions/climatic-extremes.jsp. Accessed January 21, 2009.

———. "Deserts." 2008b. Available online. URL: http://www.ga.gov.au/education/geoscience-basics/landforms/deserts.jsp. Accessed January 21, 2009.

———. "Largest Waterbodies." 2009. Available online. URL: http://www.ga.gov.au/education/geoscience-basics/landforms/largest-waterbodies.jsp. Accessed January 21, 2009.

———. "Minerals Factsheets and Education Links." 2009a. Available online. URL: http://www.ga.gov.au/minerals/education/minerals_index.jsp. Accessed October 24, 2008.

Gibbney, H. J. "Favenc, Ernest (1845–1908)." In *Australian Dictionary of Biography.* Vol. 4. Melbourne: Melbourne University Press, 1972.

———. "Sturt, Charles (1795–1869)." In *Australian Dictionary of Biography.* Vol. 2. Melbourne: Melbourne University Press, 1967.

Gibbs, Sir Harry. "Launching Address: Re-Writing the Constitution." *Proceedings of the Inaugural Conference of the Samuel Griffith Society.* Land Cove, N.S.W.: Samuel Griffith Society, 1992. Available online. URL: http://www.samuelgriffith.org.au/papers/html/volume%201/contents.htm. Accessed December 2, 2008.

Gibson, Paddy. "Rudd's 'Report Card' Based on Deceit and Hypocrisy." Press release for Stop the Intervention Collective in Sydney, February 27, 2009. Available online. URL: http://stoptheintervention.org/facts/press-releases/mr-on-rudd-s-report-card-27-2-09. Accessed May 13, 2009.

Giles, Alfred. *Exploring in the 'Seventies and the Construction of the Overland Telegraph Line.* 1926. Reprint, Adelaide: Friends of the State Library of South Australia, 1995.

Gillard, Julia. "Gillard Explains Fair Work Bill." *Australian,* November 25, 2008. Available online. URL: http://www.theaustralian.news.

com.au/story/0,25197,24704778-5013871,00.html. Accessed May 12, 2009.

Gillison, Joan. "Bon, Ann Fraser (1838–1936)." In *Australian Dictionary of Biography*. Vol. 7. Melbourne: Melbourne University Press, 1979.

Goodman, David. "Eureka Stockade." Electronic Encyclopedia of Gold in Australia. Available online. URL: http://www.egold.net.au/biogs/EG00134b.htm. Accessed October 9, 2008.

———. *Gold Seeking: Victoria and California in the 1850s*. St. Leonards, N.S.W.: Allen and Unwin, 1994.

Government of Victoria. "A Golden Heritage—Colonial Education and Wandiligong Primary School." Heritage Victoria, 2008. Available online. URL: http://www.heritage.vic.gov.au/Learning-education/Victorian-Goldfields/A-Golden-Heritage/Colonial-education.aspx#paragraph_176. Accessed June 3, 2009.

Groube, L. "The Taming of the Rain Forests: A Model for Late Pleistocene Forest Exploitation in New Guinea. In *Foraging and Farming: The Evolution of Plant Exploitation*, edited by D. R. Harris and G. C. Hillman, 292–304. London: Unwin Hyman, 1989.

Gunson, Niel. "Threlkeld, Lancelot Edward (1788–1859)." In *Australian Dictionary of Biography*. Vol. 2. Melbourne: Melbourne University Press, 1967.

Hagen, Rod. "Native Title." 1999. Available online. URL: http://rodhagen.customer.netspace.net.au/nativetitle.html. Accessed April 15, 2009.

Harcourt, Tim. "Celebration of a Trading Nation." Australian Government: Austrade. January 26, 2008. Available online. URL: http://www.austrade.gov.au/Celebration-of-a-trading-nation/default.aspx. Accessed October 6, 2008.

Harding, Ann. "Equity, Redistribution and the Tax-Transfer System." In *Equity and Citizenship under Keating*, edited by Michael Hogan and Kathy Dempsey, 11–37. Sydney: Public Affairs Research Centre, University of Sydney, 1995.

Harry M. Miller Management Group. "Lindy Chamberlain-Creighton, Rumours and Facts." Available online. URL: http://www.lindychamberlain.com/content/rumours_and_facts. Accessed June 4, 2009.

Hawker, Geoffrey. "Ministerial Consultants and Privatisation: Australian Federal Government 1985–88." *Australian Journal of Politics and History*, 52, no. 2 (2006): 244–260.

Henry, Adam. "Australian Nationalism and the Lost Lessons of the Boer War." *Journal of the Australian War Memorial*, no. 34, June 2001. Available online. URL: http://www.awm.gov.au/journal/j34/boer.asp. Accessed December 10, 2008.

Herd, Andrew. "Amplifying Outrage over Children Overboard." *Social Alternatives* 25(2) (Second Quarter 2006): 59–63. Available online. URL: http://www.uow.edu.au/arts/sts/bmartin/pubs/bf/06saHerd. html. Accessed April 24, 2009.

Hetherington, R. "Gawler, George (1795–1869)." In *Australian Dictionary of Biography.* Vol. 1. Melbourne: Melbourne University Press, 1966.

Hirst, John. *Australia's Democracy: A Short History.* Crows Nest, N.S.W.: Allen and Unwin, 2002.

————. "The Distinctiveness of Australian Democracy." In *The Distinctive Foundations of Australian Democracy: Lectures in the Senate Occasional Lecture Series 2003–2004,* edited by Kay Walsh, 113–128. Canberra: Department of the Senate, Papers on Parliament number 42, 2004.

————. *Sense and Nonsense in Australian History.* Melbourne: Black Inc. Agenda, 2005.

Hiscock, Peter. *Archaeology of Ancient Australia.* London: Routledge, 2008.

The History of Australian Television. "The 1950s." 2008. Available online. URL: http://www.televisionau.com/fifties.htm. Accessed January 30, 2009.

Hogan, Michael. "Conclusion." In *Equity and Citizenship under Keating,* edited by Michael Hogan and Kathy Dempsey, 182–190. Sydney: Public Affairs Research Centre, University of Sydney, 1995.

Hogg, Russell. "Chamberlain Case 1984." ANU High Court Project. Available online. URL: http://law.anu.edu.au/HighCourt_Project/ Chamberlain%20Case%20rtf.rtf. Accessed February 19, 2009.

Horin, Adele. "Gen Y Still Faces Gender Gap in Wages—Report." *Sydney Morning Herald,* August 8, 2007. Available online. URL: http:// www.smh.com.au/news/national/gen-y-still-faces-gender-gap-in-wages-report/2007/08/0 7/1186252708362.html. Accessed February 18, 2009.

Horne, Donald. *The Lucky Country.* Ringwood, Vic.: Penguin Books, 1971.

Horne, Gerald. *Race War: White Supremacy and the Japanese Attack on the British Empire.* New York: NYU Press, 2003.

Horton, David, ed. *Encyclopaedia of Aboriginal Australia.* Canberra: Aboriginal Studies Press, 1994.

Howard-Wagner, Deirdre. "Reconciliation as a Moral Injunction." Presented at *Re-Imagining Sociology: The Australian Sociological Association Conference,* December 2–5, 2008. Available online. URL:

http://www.tasa.org.au/conferencepapers08/Indigenous/Howard-%20 Wagner,%20Deirdre,%20Session%208%20PDF.pdf. Accessed May 13, 2009.

Hudjashova, Georgi et al. "Revealing the Prehistoric Settlement of Australia by Y Chromosome and mtDNA Analysis." *Proceedings of the National Academy of Sciences,* 104, no. 21 (May 22, 2007): 8,726–8,730.

Human Rights and Equal Opportunity Commission (HREOC). "The History: South Australia." 2007. Available online. URL: http://www. hreoc.gov.au/education/bth/download/laws/bth_lawshist_SA_12r. pdf. Accessed October 24, 2008.

Hunt, Erling M. *American Precedents in Australian Federation.* 1930. Reprint, New York: AMS Press, 1968.

Hunter, Boyd. "Conspicuous Compassion and Wicked Problem: The Howard Government's National Emergency in Indigenous Affairs." *Agenda,* 14, no. 3 (2007). Available online. URL: http://epress.anu. edu.au/agenda/014/03/mobile_devices/ch07.html. Accessed April 27, 2009.

Hunter, Thomas. "Little Children v. the PM: Same but Different?" *Crikey,* June 22, 2007. Available online. URL: http://www.crikey.com. au/Politics/20070622-gov-vs-report.html. Accessed April 27, 2009.

Inglis, Ken. "Men, Women, and War Memorials: Anzac Australia." In *Learning about Women: Gender, Politics, and Power,* edited by Jill Conway, Susan C. Bourque, and Joan W. Scott, 35–60. Ann Arbor: University of Michigan Press, 1989.

Innes, Bob. "Uluru Handover." *Desert Star,* April 7, 2008. Available online. URL: http://www.desertdreams.com.au/iblog/C1643607642/ E20060921161842/index.html. Accessed April 9, 2009.

INTERFET. "What Is INTERFET?" 2000. Available online. URL: http:// pandora.nla.gov.au/parchive/2000/S2000-Nov-7/easttimor.defence. gov.au/index.html. Accessed April 30, 2009.

Irvine, Helen. "Sweet and Sour: Accounting for South Sea Islander Labour at a North Queensland Sugar Mill in the Late 1800s." In *Proceedings 10th World Congress of Accounting Historians,* pp. 1–37. St. Louis, Missouri and Oxford, Mississippi, 2004. Available online. URL: http://eprints.qut.edu.au/archive/00013044/01/13044. pdf. Accessed October 17, 2008.

Isaac, Joe, and Stuart MacIntyre. *The New Province for Law and Order: 100 Years of Australian Industrial Conciliation and Arbitration.* Melbourne: Cambridge University Press, 2004. Available online. URL: http://www.austlii.edu.au/au/journals/UNSWLJ/2005/61.html. Accessed December 12, 2008.

Islamic College of South Australia. Available online. URL: http://www.icosa.sa.edu.au/community_societies.php. Accessed January 7, 2009.

Jakubowicz, Andrew. "Commentary on: The End of White Australia." Making Multicultural Australia. Available online. URL: http://www.multiculturalaus tralia.edu.au/library/media/Timeline-Commentary/id/13.The-end-of -White-Australia. Accessed February 4, 2009.

James, Sarah. "Constructing the Climb: Visitor Decision-Making at Uluru." *Geographic Research* 45, no. 4 (2007): 398–407.

"Janszoon, Willem." *The Columbia Encyclopedia.* 6th ed. 2008. Available online. URL: http://www.encyclopedia.com/doc/1E1-JanszoonW.html. Accessed September 30, 2008.

Johnson, Murray. *Trials and Tribulations: A Social History of Europeans in Australia, 1788–1960.* South Launceston, Tas.: Myola House of Publishing, 2007.

Jones, Evan. "On First Looking into Edwards' Keating." *Australian Review of Public Affairs,* May 17, 2004. Available online. URL: http://www.australianreview.net/digest/2004/05/jones.html. Accessed April 23, 2009.

Jones, Philip, and Anna Kenny. *Australia's Muslim Cameleers: Pioneers of the Inland, 1860s–1930s.* Kent Town, S.A.: Wakefield Press, 2007.

Jupp, James. *From White Australia to Woomera: The Story of Australian Immigration.* New York: Cambridge University Press, 2002.

———. *From White Australia to Woomera: The Story of Australian Immigration.* 2nd ed. New York: Cambridge University Press, 2007.

———. "Immigration and Multiculturalism." In *Howard's Second and Third Governments,* edited by Chris Aulich and Roger Wettenhall, 173–188. Sydney: University of New South Wales Press, 2005.

Kabir, Nahid. "The Cronulla Riot: How One Newspaper Represented the Event." Australian Sociological Association annual conference, Auckland, N.Z., December 4–7, 2007. Available online. URL: http://www.tasa.org.au/conferencepapers07/papers/268.pdf. Accessed May 6, 2009.

Kaji-O'Grady, Sandra. "Art and Life." *Architecture Australia,* September–October 2000. Available online. URL: http://www.archmedia.com.au/aa/aaissue.php?issueid=200009&article=13&ty peon=2. Accessed January 29, 2009.

Keating, Paul. "Australian Launch of the International Year for the World's Indigenous People." Paul Keating's Redfern Speech, December 10, 1992. Australianpolitics.com. Available online. URL: http://

australianpolitics.com/executive/keating/92-12-10redfern-speech. shtml. Accessed April 10, 2009.

———. "An Australian Republic—the Way Forward." June 7, 1995. Australianpolitics.com. Available online. URL: http://www.australian politics.com/executive/keating/950607republic-speech.shtml. Accessed April 15, 2009.

Kelly, Fran. "*Tampa* Issue Improves Coalition Election Prospects." Australian Broadcasting Corporation, 7:30 Report transcript, broadcast September 4, 2001. Available online. URL: http://www.abc.net. au/7.30/content/2001/s357998.htm. Accessed April 24, 2009.

Kenny, John. *Before the First Fleet: Europeans in Australia 1606–1777.* Kenthurst, N.S.W.: Kangaroo Press, 1995.

Keon-Cohen, B. A. "The Mabo Litigation: A Personal and Procedural Account." *Melbourne University Law Review,* 2000. Available online. URL: http://www.austlii.edu.au/au/journals/MULR/2000/35. html#Heading382. Accessed April 10, 2009.

Kiernan, Ben. "Why Cambodia Hasn't Found Peace." *Green Left Online,* September 7, 1994. Available online. URL: http://www.greenleft.org. au/1994/158/8928. Accessed April 8, 2009.

Kitson, Arthur. *The Life of Captain James Cook.* 1907. Reprint, Charleston, S.C.: BiblioBazaar, 2007.

Kohn, Peter. "10 Years after Pauline Hanson's Maiden Speech, Still Lessons to Be Learned." *Australian Jewish News,* September 13, 2006. Available online. URL: http://www.ajn.com.au/news/news. asp?pgID=1590. Accessed April 23, 2009.

Koorie Heritage Trust. "Coranderrk." 2004. Available online. URL: http://www.abc.net.au/missionvoices/coranderrk/default.htm. Accessed October 22, 2008.

Kraft Foods Australia. "Vegemite Discovery." 2009. Available online. URL: http://www.vegemite.com.au/vegemite/page?siteid=vegemite-prd&locale=auen1&PagecRef=670. Accessed May 21, 2009.

Kunz, Egon F. *Displaced Persons: Calwell's New Australians.* Canberra: Australian National University Press, 1988.

LaCroix, Sumner. "Property Rights and Institutional Change during Australia's Gold Rush." *Explorations in Economic History* 29, no. 2 (1992): 206–227.

Lake, Marilyn. *Getting Equal: The History of Feminism in Australia.* Sydney: Allen and Unwin, 1999.

Lake, Marilyn, and Henry Reynolds. *Drawing the Global Colour Line: White Men's Countries and the International Challenge of Racial Equality.* New York: Cambridge University Press, 2008.

Lane, Max. "EAST TIMOR: The Indonesian-Australian Invasion." *Green Left Online*, #421, September 20, 2000. Available online. URL: http://www.greenleft.org.au/2000/421/22753. Accessed April 30, 2009.

Lane, William. *The Workingman's Paradise*. 1892. Reprint, Sydney: Cosme, 1948.

Larkin, Steve. "No More Australian Troops in Afghanistan." *WA Today*, October 15, 2009. Available Online. URL: http://www.watoday.com.au/world/no-more-australian-troops-in-afghanistan-20091015-gyg8.html. Accessed on October 24, 2009.

Le Feuvre, Juliet. "The Snowy: Some Light at the End of the Tunnel?" Environment Victoria, 2008. Available online. URL: http://envict.org.au/inform.php?menu=7&submenu=206&item=1752. Accessed February 9, 2009.

Lenskyj, Helen Jefferson. "International Olympic Resistance: Thinking Globally, Acting Locally." Global Nexus Engaged Sixth International Symposium for Olympic Research, 2002, pp. 205–8. Available online. URL: http://www.la84foundation.org/SportsLibrary/ISOR/ISOR2002z.pdf. Accessed April 30, 2009.

Liebreich, Michael. "Sydney 2000—Auditor Slams Costs." Leibreich.com, April 22, 2003. Available online. URL: http://www.liebreich.com/LDC/HTM.L/Olympics/London/Sydney.html#_ftn1. Accessed April 30, 2009.

Long, Stephen. "Survey Finds Protections Lost under New IR Laws." ABC radio. May 30, 2006. Available online. URL: http://www.abc.net.au/pm/content/2006/s1651308.htm. Accessed May 6, 2009.

Lothian, Kath. "Seizing the Time: Australian Aborigines and the Influence of the Black Panther Party, 1969–1972." *Journal of Black Studies* 35 (2005): 179–200.

Lovell, Melissa. "Settler Colonialism, Multiculturalism and the Politics of Postcolonial Identity." Paper presented at the Australasian Political Studies Association meetings, Monash University, Melbourne, September 2007. Available online. URL: http://arts.monash.edu.au/psi/news-and-events/apsa/refereed-papers/au-nz-politics/lovell.pdf. Accessed April 8, 2009.

Lunney, H. W. M. "Economic Justification of the Snowy Scheme." *Energy Policy* 29 (2001): 927–937.

Macintyre, Stuart. *A Concise History of Australia*. New York: Cambridge University Press, 2004.

Macintyre, Stuart, and Anna Clark. *The History Wars*. 2d. rev. ed. Melbourne: Melbourne University Publishing, 2004.

Mackenzie, Kirsten. "Dennis Foley Eora and Wiradjari Wars, The Lecture." University of Sydney, 2004. Available online. URL: http://teaching.arts.usyd.edu.au/history/hsty2055/Eora%20and%20Wiradj uri%20Wars.doc. Accessed October 10, 2008.

Macknight, Campbell C. "Harvesting the Memory: Open Beaches in Makassar and Arnhem Land." In *Strangers on the Shore: Early Coastal Contacts in Australia,* edited by Peter Veth, Peter Sutton, and Margo Neal, 133–147. Canberra: National Museum of Australia, 2008.

Manela, Erez. *The Wilsonian Moment: Self-Determination and the International Origins of Anticolonial Nationalism.* New York: Oxford University Press, 2007.

Marchant, Leslie R. "La Pérouse, Jean-François de Galaup [Comte de La Pérouse] (1741–1788)." In *Australian Dictionary of Biography.* Vol. 2. Melbourne: Melbourne University Press, 1967.

Marchant, Leslie R., and J. H. Reynolds, "Baudin, Nicolas Thomas (1754–1803)." In *Australian Dictionary of Biography.* Vol. 1. Melbourne: Melbourne University Press, 1966.

Markham, Colin. "Myall Creek Massacre." Parliament of New South Wales, June 8, 2000. Available online. URL: http://www.parliament.nsw.gov.au/prod/parlment/hansart.nsf/V3Key/LA20000608005. Accessed October 10, 2008.

Marr, David. "Alan Jones: I'm the Person That's Led This Charge." *Age,* December 13, 2005. Available online. URL: http://www.theage.com.au/news/national/alan-jones-i-led-this-charge/2005/12/12/11342360 031 53.html. Accessed May 6, 2009.

Marriner, Cosima, and Richard Macey. "Two Days' Rain and Queensland Drought Is Over." *Age,* May 22, 2009. Available online. URL: http://www.theage.com.au/environment/two-days-rain-and-queensland-drought-is-over-200905 21-bh6y.html. Accessed May 22, 2009.

Marris, Sid. "Work Choices Ads Cost $121m." *Australian,* October 16, 2007. Available online. URL: http://www.theaustralian.news.com.au/story/0,25197,22593751-11949,00.html. Accessed May 6, 2009.

Marsh, Ian, and Larry Galbraith. "The Political Impact of the Sydney Gay and Lesbian Mardi Gras." *Australian Journal of Political Science* 30, no. 2 (July 1995): 300–320.

Masson, Mick. *Surviving the Dole Years.* Kensington: New South Wales University Press, 1993.

Maynard, John. "Fred Maynard and the Australian Aboriginal Progressive Association (AAPA): One God, One Aim, One Destiny." *Aboriginal History,* 21 (1997): 1–13.

McIntosh, Ian. "A Treaty with the Macassans? Burrumarra and the Dholtji Ideal." *Asia Pacific Journal of Anthropology* 7, no. 2 (2006): 153–172.

McLean, Ian W. "Recovery from Depression: Australia in an Argentine Mirror, 1895–1913." School of Economics, University of Adelaide, Working Paper 2005:19. Available online. URL: http://economics. adelaide.edu.au/research/papers/doc/econwp05-19.pdf. Accessed November 13, 2008.

Megalogenis, George. *The Longest Decade*. Melbourne: Scribe, 2006.

Mickelburough, Peter. "Phar Lap Death Mystery Solved." *Daily Telegraph*, October 23, 2006. Available online. URL: http://www. news.com.au/dailytelegraph/story/0,22049,20626829-5006070,00. html. Accessed May 21, 2009.

Miller, G. H., J. Mangan, D. Pollard, S. L. Thompson, B. S. Felzer, and J. W. Magee. "Sensitivity of the Australian Monsoon to Insolation and Vegetation: Implications for Human Impact on Continental Moisture Balance." *Geology* 33 (2005): 65–68.

Mills, Stephen. *The Hawke Years: The Story from the Inside*. Ringwood, Vic.: Viking, 1993.

Mitchell, Bruce. "Hargraves, Edward Hammond (1816–1891)." In *Australian Dictionary of Biography*. Vol. 4. Melbourne: Melbourne University Press, 1972.

Molloy, Fran. "Ancient Australia Not Written in Stone." ABC Science, 2008. Available online. URL: http://www.abc.net.au/science/articles/ 2008/06/19/2279784.htm.?site=science&topic=ancient. Accessed 21 August 2008.

Molony, John. *Australia, Our Heritage: The History of a Nation*. Melbourne: Australian Scholarly Publishing, 2005.

Morgan, George. "Aboriginal Protest and the Sydney Olympic Games." *Olympika: The International Journal of Olympic Studies* 12 (2003): 23–38.

Morgan, Gwenda, and Peter Rushton. *Eighteenth-Century Criminal Transportation: The Formation of the Criminal Atlantic*. Basingstoke: Palgrave Macmillan, 2004.

Mortensen, Reid. "Slaving in Australian Courts: Blackbirding Cases, 1869–1871." *Journal of South Pacific Law*, Vol. 4, 2000. Available online. URL: http://www.paclii.org/journals/fJSPL/vol04/7.shtml. Accessed October 17, 2008.

Mottram, Linda. "Coronial Inquiry Launched into the Death of Alan Bond's Daughter." ABC Radio transcript, July 7, 2000. Available online. URL: http://www.abc.net.au/am/stories/s149401.htm. Accessed April 20, 2009.

Moyal, Ann. *Platypus*. Crows Nest, N.S.W.: Allen and Unwin, 2002.

MS 8822. "Papers of Edward Koiki Mabo (1936–1992)." Available online. URL: http://www.nla.gov.au/ms/findaids/8822.html. Accessed April 20, 2009.

Mulvaney, John, and Johan Kamminga. *Prehistory of Australia*. Crows Nest, N.S.W.: Allen and Unwin, 1999.

Murphy, Sean. "Pauline Pulls the Plug as One Nation President." Transcript from *The 7:30 Report*, ABC Television, originally aired January 14, 2002. Available online. URL: http://www.abc.net.au/7.30/content/2002/s458299.htm. Accessed April 23, 2009.

Murray, R. A. "Introduction." In *Surviving the Dole Years*, by Mick Masson, xi–xxxii. Kensington: New South Wales University Press, 1993.

Murray, Tim. *Archaeology of Aboriginal Australia: A Reader.* Crows Nest, N.S.W.: Allan and Unwin, 1998.

"Myall Creek Massacre Recognized 170 Years On," Media Release, 2008. Department of Environment, Water, Heritage and the Arts, Commonwealth Government of Australia. Available online. URL: http://www.environment.gov.au/heritage/places/national/myall-creek/index.html. Accessed October 10, 2008.

National Archives of Australia. Documenting Democracy, 2005. "Immigration Restriction Act 1901 (Cth)." Available online. URL: http://www.foundingdocs.gov.au/item.asp?dID=16. Accessed December 12, 2008.

National Communications Branch Department of Immigration and Citizenship. "Fact Sheet 8: Abolition of the 'White Australia' Policy." Canberra: Australian Government, 2007. Available online. URL: http://www.immi.gov.au/media/fact-sheets/08abolition.htm. Accessed December 12, 2008.

National Council for the Centenary of Federation. "Secession." 2008. Available online. URL: http://www.slwa.wa.gov.au/federation/sec/063_sece.htm. Accessed May 20, 2009.

National Foundation for Australian Women. "Tangney, Dorothy Margaret (1911–1985)." Australian Women Biographical Entry, 2009. Available online. URL: http://www.womenaustralia.info/biogs/AWE0243b.htm. Accessed May 28, 2009.

National Heritage Trust. "The Cane Toad: *Bufo marinus*." 2004. Available online. URL: http://www.environment.gov.au/biodiversity/invasive/publications/cane-toad/pubs/cane-toad.pdf. Accessed May 18, 2009.

National Indigenous Times. "Rudd Finally Delivers Indigenous Progress Report." February 27, 2009. Available online. URL: http://www.nit.com.au/story.aspx?id=17195. Accessed May 13, 2009.

National Museum of Australia. "Charles Perkins." 2007–2008. Available online. URL: http://indigenousrights.net.au/person.asp?pID=983. Accessed February 9 and 12, 2009.

National Railway Museum. "A History of Rail in South Australia." 2001. Available online. URL: http://www.natrailmuseum.org.au/common/nrm_a01_index.html. Accessed January 5, 2009.

Nautilus Institute. "Australia in Afghanistan: Quick Guide." Updated April 30, 2009. Available online. URL: http://www.globalcollab.org/Nautilus/australia/afghanistan/australia-in-afghanistan-q-and-a. Accessed May 1, 2009.

Neighbour, Sally. "The Convert." Transcript, Four Corners, originally broadcast on ABC Television on February 27, 2006. Available online. URL: http://www.abc.net.au/4corners/content/2006/s1580223.htm. Accessed April 28, 2009.

Newbury, Paul. *Aboriginal Heroes of the Resistance: From Pemulway to Mabo.* Surry Hills, N.S.W.: Action for World Development, 1999.

News.com.au "Republic Not a Top Priority: Rudd." March 29, 2009. Available online. URL: http://www.news.com.au/story/0,27574,25261584-421,00.html. Accessed May 14, 2009.

———. "Rudd Plans Republic Referendum." July 25, 2007. Available online. URL: http://www.news.com.au/story/0,23599,22132062-2,00.html. Accessed May 14, 2009.

News Corporation. "Newspapers and Information Services." 2009. Available online. URL: http://www.newscorp.com/operations/newspapers.html. Accessed June 3, 2009.

New South Wales Aboriginal Land Council. "Dispossession and Land Rights—the Story So Far." 2007. Available online. URL: http://www.alc.org.au/resources/History/history.htm. Accessed October 22, 2008.

Nguyen, Terese. "Tasmanian Devils to Be Listed as Endangered Species." *Age,* May 22, 2009. Available online. URL: http://www.theage.com.au/environment/tasmanian-devils-to-be-listed-as-endangered-species-20090522-bht3.html. Accessed May 22, 2009.

Nicholson, Margaret. *The Little Aussie Fact Book.* New ed. New York: Penguin Books, 1998.

Northern Land Council. "An Overview: Land Councils and the Top End." 2003. Available online. URL: http://www.nlc.org.au/htm.l/over_nt.html. Accessed October 29, 2008.

———. "1998—the Native Title Amendment Bill." 2003b. Available online. URL: http://www.nlc.org.au/htm.l/land_native_amend.html. Accessed April 24, 2009.

————. "1996—the Wik Case." 2003a. Available online. URL: http://www.nlc.org.au/htm.l/land_native_wik.html. Accessed April 24, 2009.

O'Brien, Natalie. "Voyage to the Darkest Side for Mamdouh Habib." *Australian,* October 25, 2008. Available online. URL: http://www.theaustralian.news.com.au/story/0,25197,24547702-5001561,00.html. Accessed May 8, 2009.

O'Connell, J. F., and J. Allen. "Dating the Colonization of Sahul (Pleistocene Australia–New Guinea): A Review of Recent Research." *Journal of Archaeological Science* 31 (2004): 835–853.

————. "Pre-LGM Sahul (Australia–New Guinea) and the Archaeology of Early Modern Humans." JOC-FJA Cambridge 06 d.3a:1. Available online. URL: http://www.anthro.utah.edu/PDFs/Papers/oconnell_allen06.pdf. Accessed August 21, 2008.

OECD. "Current Query: Australia." 2009. Available online. URL: http://stats.oecd.org/wbos/viewhtml.aspx?queryname=18144&querytype=view&lang=en. Accessed May 14, 2009.

O'Farrell, Patrick. *The Irish in Australia: 1788 to the Present.* 3d ed. Sydney: University of New South Wales Press, 2000.

Office of Legislative Drafting. "Australian Antarctic Territory Acceptance Act 1933." Attorney-General's Department, Canberra, 2000. Available online. URL: http://fedlaw.gov.au/ComLaw/Legislation/Act Compilation1.nsf/0/A5C48A5B89BD4251CA25 709900234730/$file/AustAntarcTerrAccept1933_WD02.pdf. Accessed May 29, 2009.

O'Grady, Geoff, and Ken Hale. "The Coherence and Distinctiveness of Pama-Nyungan." In *Australian Languages: Classification and the Comparative Method,* edited by Claire Bowern and Harold Koch, 69–92. Amsterdam: John Benjamins, 2004.

"Pacific Islands Labourers Act 1901." National Archives of Australia. Available online. URL: http://www.foundingdocs.gov.au/item.asp?dID=15. Accessed October 17, 2008.

Painter, Martin. *Collaborative Federalism: Economic Reform in Australia in the 1990s.* New York: Cambridge University Press, 1998.

Palm, Carl Magnus. *Bright Lights Dark Shadows: The Real Story of Abba.* New York: Omnibus Press, 2002.

Palmer, Mick. "Inquiry into the Circumstances of the Immigration Detention of Cornelia Rau: Report." Commonwealth of Australia, 2005. Available online. URL: http://www.immi.gov.au/media/publications/pdf/palmer-report.pdf. Accessed May 7, 2009.

"Papers of Charles Perkins (1936–2000)." National Library of Australia. Available online. URL: http://nla.gov.au/nla.ms-ms8047. Accessed February 12, 2009.

Paterson, Heather. "Peacekeepers Claim Success as They Prepare to Leave East Timor." *Independent,* February 22, 2000. Available online. URL: http://www.etan.org/et2000a/february/20-29/23aust.htm. Accessed April 30, 2009.

Penny, Barbara R. "Australia's Reactions to the Boer War: A Study in Colonial Imperialism." *Journal of British Studies* 7, no. 1 (1967): 97–130.

Perkins, Rachel. First Australians, episode 1. Broadcast first on SBS Television, Australia, October 12, 2008. Available online. URL: http://www.sbs.com.au/firstaustralians/index/index/epid/1. Accessed October 15, 2008.

———. First Australians, episode 2. Broadcast first on SBS Television, Australia, October 14, 2008. Available online. URL: http://www.sbs.com.au/firstaustralians/index/index/epid/2. Accessed October 15, 2008.

———. First Australians, episode 7. Broadcast first on SBS Television, Australia, November 2, 2008. Available online. URL: http://www.sbs.com.au/firstaustralians/index/index/epid/7. Accessed April 10, 2009.

Petridis, Alex. "Things Must Really Be Bad—AC/DC Are No. 1 Again." *Guardian,* October 27, 2008. Available online. URL: http://www.guardian.co.uk/music/2008/oct/27/acdc-music-recession. Accessed February 20, 2009.

Pettinger, T. "Gold Standard Explained." Economics Help, 2009. Available online. URL: http://www.economicshelp.org/2009/02/gold-standard-explained.html. Accessed May 8, 2009.

Phillips, Janet, and Adrienne Millbank. "Protecting Australia's Borders." Research Note no. 22 2003-04, Parliament of Australia. 2003. Available online. URL: http://www.aph.gov.au/library/pubs/rn/2003-04/04rn22.htm. Accessed April 24, 2009.

Phillips, Tony. "James Cook and the Transit of Venus." Available online. URL: http://science.nasa.gov/headlines/y2004/28may_cook.htm. Accessed August 28, 2008.

Phoenix, Dave. "Burke and Wills Web." 2008. Available online. URL: http://www.burkeandwills.net.au/index.htm. Accessed October 22, 2008.

Pilger, John. "Charles Perkins: A Tribute." Johnpilger.com, October 19, 2000. Available online. URL: http://www.johnpilger.com/page.asp?partid=166. Accessed February 12, 2009.

———. *A Secret Country.* New York: Vintage, 1992.

"Pinjarra massacre." Available online. URL: http://www.westaustralianvista.com/pinjarra-massacre.html. Accessed August 24, 2008.

Potts, E. Daniel, and Annette Potts. *Young America and Australian Gold: Americans and the Gold Rush of the 1850s.* St. Lucia: University of Queensland, 1974.

Pratt, Angela, and Scott Bennett. "The End of ATSIC and the Future Administration of Indigenous Affairs." Parliament of Australia, 2004. Available online. URL: http://www.aph.gov.au/library/pubs/CIB/2004-05/05cib04.htm.#establish. Accessed April 10, 2009.

Priestley, Michael. "Australia's Free Trade Agreements." Parliament of Australia, December 2, 2008. Available online. URL: http://www.aph.gov.au/LIBRARY/pubs/bn/2008-09/AustFreeTradeAgreements.htm. Accessed May 4, 2009.

Public Record Office Victoria. "Eureka on Trial." Updated May 2003. Available online. URL: http://eureka.imagineering.com.au/focus.htm. Accessed October 9, 2008.

Queensland Government. "A Brief History of Government Administration of Aboriginal and Torres Strait Islander Peoples in Queensland." Available online. URL: http://www.slq.qld.gov.au/__data/assets/pdf_file/0008/93734/Admin_history_guide-CPH.pdf. Accessed October 24, 2008.

Racism, No Way! "Key Dates in Australian History." Available online. URL: http://www.racismnoway.com.au/library/history/keydates/index-1800s.html. Accessed August 24, 2008.

Ranald, Patricia, and Louise Southalan. "Ten Devils in the Detail: Patricia Ranald and Louise Southalan Explain the Finer Points of the Text of the Australia US Free Trade Agreement." Evatt Foundation, November 15, 2005. Available online. URL: http://evatt.labor.net.au/publications/papers/123.html. Accessed May 4, 2009.

Reconciliation Australia. "Reconciliation Timeline." Copyright 2007. Available online. URL: http://www.reconcile.org.au/getsmart/pages/get-the-basics/reconciliation-timeline.php. Accessed April 10, 2009.

Reporting Diversity. "Journalism in Multicultural Australia." 2007. Available online. URL: http://reportingdiversity.murdoch.edu.au/cs_four.pdf. Accessed May 6, 2009.

Ricci, Colleen. "Between a Rock and a Sacred Place." The Age, July 20, 2009. Available Online. URL: http://www.theage.com.au/national/education/between-a-rock-and-a-sacred-place-20090716-dmoa.html. Accessed on October 24, 2009.

Ridgeway, Aden. "We Must All Act to Build on the Legacy of Senator Neville Bonner." *On Line Opinion: Australia's e-Journal of Social and Political Debate,* October 7, 2003. Available online. URL: http://

www.onlineopinion.com.au/view.asp?article=769&page=1. Accessed February 18, 2009.

Riemer, Andrew. *Inside Outside: Life between Two Worlds.* Pymble, N.S.W.: Angus and Robertson, 1992.

Robins, Jane. "Renaissance Down Under." *Economist* 311, no. 7601 (May 6, 1989): S5–S8.

Robson, Peter. "Rudd: Apology but No Compensation." *Green Left,* #738, February 1, 2008. Available online. URL: http://www.greenleft. org.au/2008/738/38203. Accessed May 12, 2009.

Romsey Australia. "Bush Fires in Victoria 1851 Black Thursday." 2008. Available online. URL: http://home.iprimus.com.au/foo7/fire1851. html. Accessed September 30, 2008.

Ross, Liz. "It Was a Riot! 30 Years since Australia's First Mardi Gras." *Socialist Alternative,* 125, February 2008. Available online. URL: http://www.sa.org.au/index.php?option=com_content&task=view&i d=1600&Itemid=106. Accessed February 18, 2009.

Rowse, Tim. "'Out of Hand': The Battles of Neville Bonner." *Journal of Australian Studies* 54–55 (1997): 96–107.

Sanders, Will. "Never Even Adequate: Reconciliation and Indigenous Affairs." In *Howard's Second and Third Governments,* edited by Chris Aulich and Roger Wettenhall, 152–172. Sydney: University of New South Wales Press, 2005.

Senate Finance and Public Administration Legislation Committee. *Plebiscite for an Australian Republic Bill 2008.* Canberra: Parliament of Australia, June 2009. Available online. URL: http://www.aph. gov.au/SENATE/committee/fapa_ctte/republic_bill/report/index.htm. Accessed July 27, 2009.

Serle, Geoffrey. "Curtin, John (1885–1945)." In *Australian Dictionary of Biography.* Vol. 13. Melbourne: Melbourne University Press, 1993.

———. "Murdoch, Sir Keith Arthur (1885–1952)." In *Australian Dictionary of Biography.* Vol. 10. Melbourne: Melbourne University Press, 1986.

Shark Bay World Heritage Area. "1772 François de Saint-Alouarn." 2007. Available online. URL: http://www.sharkbay.org/default. aspx?WebPageID=179. Accessed August 29, 2008.

Sheehan, Colin. "Strangers and Servants of the Company: The United East India Company and the Dutch Voyages to Australia." In *Strangers on the Shore: Early Coastal Contacts in Australia,* edited by Peter Veth et al., 6–34. Canberra: National Museum of Australia Press, 2008.

"Ships Associated with James Cook in Newfoundland." Available online. URL: http://pages.quicksilver.net.nz/jcr/ships. Accessed October 1, 2008.

Silvester, John. "Push Begins to Win 'Breaker' a Pardon." The Age, October 19, 2009. Available online. URL: http://www.theage.com. au/national/push-begins-to-win-breaker-a-pardon-20091018-h2x7. html. Accessed October 23, 2009.

Singleton, Gwynneth. "Issues and Agendas: Howard in Control." In Howard's Second and Third Governments, edited by Chris Aulich and Roger Wettenhall, 3–18. Sydney: University of New South Wales Press, 2005.

Smeeding, Timothy M. "Globalisation, Inequality and the Rich Countries of the G–20: Evidence from the Luxembourg Income Study (LIS)." Syracuse, N.Y.: Maxwell School of Citizenship and Public Affairs, Syracuse University, 2002.

Snow, Dianne. "Family Policy and Orphan Schools in Early Colonial Australia." Journal of Interdisciplinary History 22, no. 2 (1991): 255–284.

Snowy Hydro. "Engineering Facts." 2007. Available online. URL: http:// www.snowyhydro.com.au/LevelThree.asp?pageID=266&parentID=6 6&grandParentID=4. Accessed February 9, 2009.

———. "The History." 2007. Available online. URL: http://www.snowy hydro.com.au/LevelThree.asp?pageID=67&parentID=66&grandParent ID=4. Accessed February 9, 2009.

"The Snowy Mountains Scheme." Australian Government Culture and Recreation Portal. 2008. Available online. URL: http://www.cultureand recreation.gov.au/articles/snowyscheme. Accessed February 9, 2009.

Socialistworld.net. "Refugees, Racism and Capitalism in Australia." August 5, 2003. Available online. URL: http://72.14.235.132/ search?q=cache:vllqHzRkoRIJ:socialistworld.net/eng/2003/08/ 05australia e.html+Hawke+AND+Cambodia&cd=9&hl=en&ct=clnk &gl =au&client=firefox-a. Accessed April 8, 2009.

"Sorry Day and the Stolen Generations." Australian Government Culture Portal, 2007. Available online. URL: http://www.acn.net.au/ articles/indigenous/sorry. Accessed May 11, 2009.

Souter, Gavin. Lion and Kangaroo: Australia: 1901–1919: The Rise of a Nation. Sydney: Fontana Books, 1976.

Sport Business International. "Sydney Olympics Budget Blows Out to A$2.6 Bln." September 28, 2001. Available online. URL: http://www. sportbusiness.com/news/129559/sydney-olympics-budget-blows-out-to-a-2-6-bln. Accessed April 30, 2009.

Sports Card World. "Tribute to Cathy Freeman." 2006. Available online. URL: http://users.chariot.net.au/çbyoung/freeman.htm. Accessed May 8, 2009.

St. Kilda Historical Society. "Tolarno Boutique Hotel, Bar and Bistro, 42 Fitzroy Street, St Kilda." A Place of Sensuous Resort: The Buildings of St. Kilda and Their People, 2005. Available online. URL: http://www.skhs.org.au/SKHSbuildings/17.htm. Accessed January 27, 2009.

Stephenson, Peta. "Reaffirming Aboriginality through Allah: Indigenous Muslims in Australia." Paper presented at the conference: Challenges and Opportunities for Islam and the West—the Case of Australia, Griffith University, Brisbane, Australia. March 3–5, 2008. Available online. URL: http://www.griffith.edu.au/__data/assets/pdf_file/0005/58316/Stephenson.pdf. Accessed January 15, 2009.

Stitt, Ingrid, and Michele O'Neil. "Untold Damage: Why Women Need New IR Laws." Available online. URL: http://www.asuvic.org/index.php?option=com_docman&task=doc_view&gid=636. Accessed May 6, 2009.

Stone, John. "The Dismal Beginning to the Fraser Years." *Quadrant* 51, nos. 7–8 (2007): 12–19.

Strom, Marcus. "Rattling Multicultural Myths: The 2005 Cronulla Riots Expose Official Multicultarism (sic) as a Broken Edifice." Labor Tribune, 2006. Available online. URL: http://www.labortribune.net/ArticleHolder/CronullaandtheleftPt1/tabid/55/Default.aspx. Accessed May 6, 2009.

Summers, Anne. *Damned Whores and God's Police*. 2d rev. ed. Camberwell, Vic.: Penguin Books, 2002.

Sun, ed. "Australia Boosts Afghanistan Troop Commitment to 1,550." *China View*, April 29, 2009. Available online. URL: http://news.xinhuanet.com/english/2009-04/29/content_11280146.htm. Accessed May 1, 2009.

"Sydney Harbour Bridge." Australian Government Culture Portal, 2008. Available online. URL: http://www.cultureandrecreation.gov.au/articles/harbourbridge. Accessed May 19, 2009.

Sydney Morning Herald. "Behind the Madness of Martin Bryant." April 24, 2009. Available online. URL: http://www.smh.com.au/national/behind-the-madness-of-martin-bryant-20090423-agtv.html. Accessed April 27, 2009.

———. "The David Hicks Affidavit." December 10, 2004. Available online. URL: http://www.smh.com.au/news/World/David-Hicks-affidavit/2004/12/10/1102625527396.html. Accessed April 28, 2009.

———. "Mob Violence Envelops Cronulla." December 11, 2005a. Available online. URL: http://www.smh.com.au/news/national/mob-violence-envelops-cronulla/2005/12/11/1134235936223.htm.l?page=fullpage#contentSwap2. Accessed May 6, 2009.

————. "Parliament in Uproar as IR Bill Tabled." November 2, 2005b. Available online. URL: http://www.smh.com.au/news/national/parliament-in-uproar-as-ir-bill-tabled/2005/11/02/11308 23257420. html. Accessed May 6, 2009.

————. "Prostitute Used in Habib Torture: Lawyer." January 27, 2005c. Available online. URL: http://www.smh.com.au/articles/2005/01/26/1106415668003.html. Accessed May 7, 2009.

————. "Rudd Still Preferred PM—Poll." April 7, 2009a. Available online. URL: http://news.smh.com.au/breaking-news-national/rudd-still-preferred-pm--poll-20090407-9v2h. html. Accessed May 12, 2009.

Sydney Olympic Park Authority. "Sport History." 2008. Available online. URL: http://www.sydneyolympicpark.com.au/Home_of_sport/sport_history. Accessed April 30, 2009.

Symons, Michael. *One Continuous Picnic: A History of Eating in Australia.* Adelaide: Duck Press, 1982.

Tasker, Belinda. "Britain Blasted over Maralinga Tests." Sydney Morning Herald Online, January 23, 2009. Available online. URL: http://www.smh.com.au/news/world/britain-blasted-over-maralinga-tests/2009/01/22/12324714 96243.html. Accessed February 6, 2009.

Tasmania Parks and Wildlife Service. "Thylacine, or Tasmanian Tiger, *Thylacinus cynocephalus*," 2008. Available online. URL: http://www.parks.tas.gov.au/index.aspx?base=4765. Accessed May 18, 2009.

Taylor, Peter. *An End to Silence: The Building of the Overland Telegraph Line from Adelaide to Darwin.* Sydney: Methuen, 1980.

Taylor, Stephen. "Transcript of Interview with Ex-Guantanamo Bay Detainee Mamdouh Habib." Broadcast on February 13, 2005, Channel 9, 60 minutes. Available online. URL: http://freedetainees.org/924. Accessed May 8, 2009.

Taylor, Tracy. "Netball in Australia: A Social History." Sydney: University of Technology, Sydney School of Leisure, Sport and Tourism, Working Paper No. 2, 2001.

Thinee, Kristy, and Tracy Bradford. *Connecting Kin—Guide to Records: A Guide to Help People Separated from Their Family Search for Their Records.* Sydney: New South Wales Department of Community Services, 1998.

Thompson, Elaine. *Fair Enough: Egalitarianism in Australia.* Sydney: University of New South Wales Press, 1994.

Thornton, Kristen. "'The Last Man': George Witton and *Scapegoats of the Empire.*" Deakin University Library, 2008. Available online. URL: http://www.deakin.edu.au/library/spc/exhibitions/wittonscapegoats. php. Accessed December 11, 2008.

Todd, R. K. "Morant, Harry Harbord (Breaker) (1864–1902)." In *Australian Dictionary of Biography*. Vol. 10. Melbourne: Melbourne University Press, 1986.

Totten, Samuel, William S. Parsons, and Israel W. Charny. *Century of Genocide: Critical Essays and Eyewitness Accounts*. 2d ed. New York: Routledge, 2004.

Tull, Malcolm. "French Maritime History in WA—Wait, There's More—and It's Sensational!" *Quarterly Newsletter—The Australian Association for Maritime History*, no. 79, June 2000. Available online. URL: http://www.aamh.asn.au/news/0079.pdf. Accessed August 29, 2008.

UNDP. "Human Development Reports 2009: Australia." Available online. URL: http://hdrstats.undp.org/en/countries/country_fact_sheets/cty_fs_AUS.html. Accessed October 20, 2009.

UNDP 2. "Human Development Report 2009: United States." Available online. URL: http://hdrstats.undp.org/en/countries/country_fact_sheets/cty_fs_USA.html. Accessed January 8, 2009.

United Nations Development Program. *Human Development Indices: A Statistical Update 2008*. Available online. URL: http://hdr.undp.org/en/media/HDI_2008_EN_Content.pdf. Accessed January 8, 2009.

United Nations General Assembly. "Resolution Adopted by the General Assembly, International Year of Reconciliation, 2009." November 20, 2006. Available online. URL: http://daccessdds.un.org/doc/UNDOC/GEN/N06/495/45/PDF/N0649545.pdf?OpenElement. Accessed May 13, 2009.

Uniting Church of Australia. Available online. URL: http://www.uca.org.au. Accessed February 18, 2009.

"University of Sydney Teaching Notes." Available online. URL: http://teaching.arts.usyd.edu.au/history/hsty2055/Pacific%20Islander%20Labour%20notes.doc. Accessed October 17, 2008.

Vanderzee, Michael, and Graeme Turner. "The Snowy Flows Again: Intergovernmental Co-Operation on Water Reform." Paper presented to the Fourth Water Law and Policy Conference in Sydney on October 24–25, 2002. Available online. URL: http://www.ourwater.vic.gov.au/_data/assets/pdf_file/0004/9976/TheSnowyFlowsAgain.pdf. Accessed February 9, 2009.

Veth, Peter Marius, Peter Veth, Mike Smith, and Peter Hiscock. *Desert Peoples: Archaeological Perspectives*. Melbourne: Blackwell, 2005.

Victorian Women's Trust. *Annual Report, 2006–07*. Melbourne, Vic.: Victorian Women's Trust, 2008.

Wainwright, Robert, and Paola Totaro. *Born or Bred? Martin Bryant: The Making of a Mass Murderer,* excerpted in *Good Weekend,* April 25, 2009. Pymont, N.S.W.: Fairfax Media, 2009.

Watson, Ian, and Peter Browne. "The 2007 Federal Election: Exit Poll Analysis." Australian Policy Online, September 2008. Available online. URL: http://www.sisr.net/apo/2007election.pdf. Accessed May 7, 2009.

Welsh, Frank. *Great Southern Land: A New History of Australia.* New York: Allen Lane, 2004.

Wharton, Geoff. "The Day They Burned Mapoon: A Study of the Closure of a Queensland Presbyterian Mission." Honor's Thesis, University of Queensland, 1996.

Whittaker, Elvi. "Public Discourse on Sacredness: The Transfer of Ayers Rock to Aboriginal Ownership." *American Ethnologist* 21, no. 2 (1994): 310–334.

"Who Do You Think You Are? Catherine Freeman." Aired originally on SBS Television, Sydney, February 3, 2008. Review. Available online. URL: http://www.smh.com.au/news/tv-reviews/who-do-you-think-you-are/2008/02/01/1201801011287.html. Accessed October 28, 2008.

Who's Who in Australian Military History. "Lieutenant Henry Harboard (Harry) 'The Breaker' Morant." Australian War Memorial, 2008. Available online. URL: http://www.awm.gov.au/people/267.asp. Accessed December 11, 2008.

Wild, Rex, and Patricia Anderson. "Ampe Akelyernemane Meke Mekarle—Little Children Are Sacred: Report of the Northern Territory Board of Inquiry into the Protection of Aboriginal Children from Sexual Abuse." 2007. Available online. URL: http://www.inquirysaac.nt.gov.au/pdf/bipacsa_final_report.pdf. Accessed April 27, 2009.

"Wild Rivers National Park—Highlights." Parks and Wildlife Service Tasmania, 2008. Available online. URL: http://www.parks.tas.gov.au/index.aspx?base=3949#all. Accessed October 24, 2008.

Wilderness Society, The. "History of the Franklin River Campaign 1976–83." The Wilderness Society Archive, 2008. Available online. URL: http://www.franklin25th.com/history.htm. Accessed February 17, 2009.

Willett, Graham. "The Darkest Decade: Homophobia in 1950s Australia." In *The Forgotten Fifties: Aspects of Australian Society and Culture in the 1950s,* edited by John Murphy and Judith Smart, 120–132. Melbourne: Melbourne University Press, 1997.

Wilson, Bill, and O'Brien, Justin. "'To Infuse an Universal Terror:' A Reappraisal of the Coniston Killings." *Aboriginal History* 27 (2003): 59–78.

Women for an Australian Republic. "News Update," May 4, 2009. Available online. URL: http://www.womenrep.netspeed.com.au/news. htm. Accessed May 14, 2009.

Wong, Penny. "A New Target for Reducing Australia's Carbon Pollution." Media Release, Parliament of Australia, May 4, 2009. Available online. URL: http://www.environment.gov.au/minister/wong/2009/ mr20090504c.html. Accessed May 15, 2009.

Wood, G. Arnold. *The Discovery of Australia,* revised by J. C. Beaglehole. South Melbourne: Macmillan, 1969.

Wright, R. V. S. "Bates, Daisy May (1863–1951)." In *Australian Dictionary of Biography.* Vol. 7. Melbourne: Melbourne University Press, 1979.

APPENDIX 6

SUGGESTED READING

Diversity—Land and People

Higgins, Geoff, and Neil Hermes. *Australia: The Land Time Forgot.* Frenchs Forest, N.S.W.: Child and Associates, 1988.

Jupp, James. *The Australian People: An Encyclopedia of the Nation, Its People and Their Origins.* 2d ed. Cambridge: Cambridge University Press, 2002.

Lawrence, Michel. *All of Us.* Carlton North, Vic.: Scribe, 2008.

Moore, Bruce. *Speaking Our Language: The Story of Australian English.* South Melbourne, Vic.: Oxford University Press, 2008.

Naumann, Ruth. *Australian Basics 1: My Country, My People.* South Melbourne, Vic.: Thomson Learning, 2008.

Nicholson, Margaret. *The Little Aussie Fact Book.* New ed. New York: Penguin, 1998.

Aboriginal History (60,000 BP–1605 C.E.)

Diamond, Jared. *Guns, Germs, and Steel.* New York: W. W. Norton, 1999.

Ellis, Jean A. *Aboriginal Australia: The Dreaming, Traditional Lifestyle, Traditional Art, Language Groups.* Penrith, N.S.W.: Kaliarna, 2001.

Flannery, Tim. *Country.* Melbourne: Text, 2004.

Flood, Josephine. *Archaeology of the Dreamtime: The Story of Prehistoric Australia and Its People.* Rev. ed. Sydney: Angus and Robertson, 1995.

Keen, Ian. *Aboriginal Economy and Society: Australia at the Threshold of Colonisation.* Oxford: Oxford University Press, 2004.

Murray, Tim, ed. *Archaeology of Aboriginal Australia: A Reader.* St. Leonards, N.S.W.: Allen and Unwin, 1998.

Narogin, Mudrooro. *Aboriginal Mythology: An A–Z Spanning the History of the Australian Aboriginal People from the Earliest Legends to the Present Day.* London: Aquarian, 1994.

European Exploration and Early Settlement (1606–1850)

Drummond, Allen, and Sally Bradley. *Elizabeth Macarthur.* Mentone, Vic.: Green Barrow, 2003.

Frost, Alan. *Arthur Phillip: His Voyaging, 1738–1814.* New York: Oxford University Press, 1987.

Gerritsen, Rupert. *And Their Ghosts May Be Heard.* Fremantle: Fremantle Arts Centre Press, 2002.

Grassby, Al, and Marji Hill. *Six Australian Battlefields.* Melbourne: Angus and Robertson, 1988.

Horwitz, Tony. *Blue Latitudes: Boldly Going Where Captain Cook Has Gone Before.* New York: Henry Holt, 2002.

Kitson, Arthur. *The Life of Captain James Cook.* Whitefish, Mont.: Kessinger, 2004

Lowenstein, Wendy, Kathleen Dunlop Kane, and Marjorie de Saint-Ferjeux. *Gondwana to Gold: A Chronological History of Australia.* Melbourne: Informit Publishing and Training, 1996.

Macknight, Campbell C. *The Voyage to Marege: Macassan Trepangers in Northern Australia.* Melbourne: Melbourne University Press, 1976.

McHugh, Evan. *1606: An Epic Adventure.* Sydney: University of New South Wales Press, 2006.

Moyal, Ann. *Platypus.* Crows Nest, N.S.W.: Allen and Unwin, 2002.

Willmot, Eric. *Pemulwuy: Rainbow Warrior.* Sydney: Weldon's, 1987.

Gold Rush and Governments (1851–1890)

Carey, Peter. *True History of the Kelly Gang.* New York: Vintage Books, 2001.

Crotty, Martin, and Erik Eklund, eds. *Australia to 1901: Selected Readings in the Making of a Nation.* Croydon, Vic.: Tertiary Press, 2003.

Jones, Philip, and Anna Kenny. *Australia's Muslim Cameleers: Pioneers of the Inland, 1860s–1930s.* Kent Town, S.A.: Wakefield Press, 2007.

Macinnis, Peter. *Australia's Pioneers, Heroes and Fools: The Trials, Tribulations and Tricks of the Trade of Australia's Colonial Explorers.* Millers Point, N.S.W.: Pier 9, 2007.

Monteath, Peter, ed. *The Diary of Emily Caroline Creaghe, Explorer.* Adelaide, S.A.: Gould Genealogy, 2004.

Potts, E. Daniel, and Annette Potts. *Young America and Australian Gold: Americans and the Gold Rush of the 1850s.* St. Lucia: University of Queensland Press, 1974.

McCalman, Iain, Alexander Cook, and Andrew Reeves, eds. *Gold: Forgotten Histories and Lost Objects of Australia.* New York: Cambridge University Press, 2001.

Newbury, Paul. *Aboriginal Heroes of the Resistance: From Pemulwuy to Mabo.* Surry Hills, N.S.W.: Action for World Development, 1999.

Thomson, Alice. *The Singing Line.* New York: Vintage, 2000.

Wawn, William T. *The South Sea Islanders and the Queensland Labour Trade,* edited by Peter Corris. Canberra: Australian National University Press, 1973.

Federation and Identity Formation (1890–1919)

Brasch, Nicolas. *Birth of a Nation: Eyewitness to Federation, 1850 to 1901.* Port Melbourne, Vic.: Heinemann Library, 2007.

Crotty, Martin, and Erik Eklund, eds. *Australia to 1901: Selected Readings in the Making of a Nation.* Croydon, Vic.: Tertiary Press, 2003.

Haebich, Anna. *For Their Own Good: Aborigines and Government in the Southwest of Western Australia, 1900–40.* Perth: University of Western Australia, 1988.

Hunt, Erling M. *American Precedents in Australian Federation.* 1930. Reprint, New York: AMS Press, 1968.

Irving, Helen. *To Constitute a Nation: A Cultural History of Australia's Constitution.* New York: Cambridge University Press, 1997.

Travers, Robert. *The Grand Old Man of Australian Politics: The Life and Times of Sir Henry Parkes.* Sydney: Kangaroo Press, 2000.

Realignment (1920–1946)

Armstrong, Geoff, and Peter Thompson. *Phar Lap.* St. Leonards, N.S.W.: Allen and Unwin, 2003.

Edwards, Penny, and Shen Yuan Fang, eds. *Lost in the Whitewash: Aboriginal-Asian Encounters in Australia, 1901–2001.* Canberra: Humanities Research Centre, Australian National University, 2003.

Gregory, R. G., and N. G. Butlin, eds. *Recovery from the Depression: Australia and the World Economy in the 1930s.* Cambridge: Cambridge University Press, 1988.

Grose, Peter. *An Awkward Truth: The Bombing of Darwin, February 1942.* Crows Nest, N.S.W.: Allen and Unwin, 2009.

Macdougall, A. K. *Anzacs, Australians at War: A Narrative History Illustrated by Photographs from the Nation's Archives.* Balgowlah, N.S.W.: Reed Books, 1991.

Macinnis, Peter. *Kokoda Track: 101 Days.* Fitzroy, Vic.: Black Dog Books, 2007.

McKernan, Michael. *All In! Fighting the War at Home.* St. Leonards, N.S.W.: Allen and Unwin, 1995.

Scott, Jean. *Girls with Grit: Memories of the Australian Women's Land Army.* St. Leonards, N.S.W.: Allen and Unwin, 1995.

Populate or Perish (1947–1974)

Attwood, Bain, and Andrew Markus. *The Struggle for Aboriginal Rights: A Documentary History.* Crows Nest, N.S.W.: Allen and Unwin, 1999.

Cockington, James. *Mondo Weirdo: Australia in the Sixties.* Port Melbourne, Vic.: Octopus Publishing Group, 1992.

Joske, Percy Ernest. *Sir Robert Menzies, 1894–1978: A New, Informal Memoir.* Pymble, N.S.W.: Angus and Robertson, 1978.

Jupp, James. *From White Australia to Woomera: The Story of Australian Immigration.* 2d ed. New York: Cambridge University Press, 2007.

Mora, Mirka. *Wicked but Virtuous: My Life.* Ringwood, Vic.: Viking, 2000.

Murphy, John, and Judith Smart, eds. *The Forgotten Fifties: Aspects of Australian Society and Culture in the 1950s.* Melbourne: Melbourne University Press, 1997.

Riemer, Andrew. *Inside Outside: Life between Two Worlds.* Pymble, N.S.W.: Angus and Robertson, 1992.

Street, Jessie. *Truth or Repose.* Sydney: Australasian Book Society, 1966.

Zable, Arnold. *Cafe Scheherazade.* Melbourne: Text, 2001.

Constitutional Crisis (1975–1983)

Ayres, Philip. *Malcolm Fraser: A Biography.* Richmond, Vic.: William Heinemann Australia, 1987.

Chamberlain-Creighton, Lindy. *Through My Eyes.* Port Melbourne, Vic.: Mandarin, 1990.

Kelly, Paul. *The Unmaking of Gough.* Sydney: Angus and Robertson, 1976.

McQueen, James. *The Franklin: Not Just a River,* with an introduction by David Bellamy. Ringwood, Vic.: Penguin, 1983.

Tasmanian Wilderness Society. *Franklin River Wilderness: World Heritage Threatened*. Hobart, Tas.: Tasmanian Wilderness Society, 1983.

Wherrett, Richard, ed. *Mardi Gras! True Stories*. Ringwood, Vic.: Penguin Books Australia, 1999.

Whitlam, Gough. *The Truth of the Matter: His Powerful Account of the Dismissal*. Melbourne: Melbourne University Press, 2005.

Willett, Graham. *Living Out Loud: A History of Gay and Lesbian Activism in Australia*. St. Leonards, N.S.W.: Allen and Unwin, 2000.

Contradiction and Change (1983–1996)

Edwards, John. *Keating: The Inside Story*. Ringwood, Vic.: Viking, 1996.

Hage, Ghassan. *White Nation: Fantasies of White Supremacy in a Multicultural Society*. Sydney: Pluto Press, 1998.

Hawke, Bob. *The Hawke Memoirs*. Melbourne: Heinemann, 1994.

Loos, Noel, and Koiki Mabo. *Edward Koiki Mabo: His Life and Struggle for Land Rights*. St. Lucia: University of Queensland Press, 1996.

Russell, Peter H. *Recognizing Aboriginal Title: The Mabo Case and Indigenous Resistance to English-Settler Colonialism*. Toronto: University of Toronto Press, 2005.

Sharp, Nonie. *No Ordinary Judgement: Mabo, The Murray Islanders' Land Case*. Canberra: Aboriginal Studies Press, 1996.

Whitton, Evan. *The Hillbilly Dictator: Australia's Police State*. Sydney: ABC Books for the Australian Broadcasting Corporation, 1993.

The Howard Years (1996–2007)

Errington, Wayne, and Peter van Onselen. *John Winston Howard*. Melbourne: Melbourne University Press, 2007.

Habib, Mamdouh, with Julia Collingwood. *My Story: The Tale of a Terrorist Who Wasn't*. Carlton North, Vic.: Scribe, 2008.

Kingston, Margo. *Not Happy, John! Defending Our Democracy*. Camberwell, Vic.: Penguin, 2004.

Reconciliation and Republicanism? Australia since 2007

Jackman, Christine. *Inside Kevin07: The People, the Plan, the Prize*. Carlton, Vic.: Melbourne University, 2008.

Manne, Robert, ed. *Dear Mr Rudd: Ideas for a Better Australia*. Melbourne: Black Inc. Agenda, 2008.

INDEX

Note: **Boldface** page numbers indicate primary discussion of a topic. Page numbers in *italic* indicate illustrations. The letters *c* and *m* indicate chronology and maps, respectively.